The Montana Heritage

An Anthology of Historical Essays

The Montana Heritage

An Anthology of Historical Essays

Edited by
Robert R. Swartout, Jr.,
and
Harry W. Fritz

Montana Historical Society Press, Helena
1992

Except for those noted below, the essays in this anthology are from:

Montana The Magazine of Western History
Montana Historical Society
225 N. Roberts St.
Helena, Montana 59620

Grateful acknowledgement is made to the authors and publishers who granted permission to use the following essays:

"Who Murdered Tom Manning? In a Company Town, Company Justice"
by Dave Walter (copyright Dave Walter)
Montana Magazine
3020 Bozeman
Helena, Montana 59601

"The Orange and the Green in Montana: A Reconsideration of the Clark-Daly Feud"
by David M. Emmons
Arizona and the West (now *Journal of the Southwest*)
1052 N. Highland
University of Arizona
Tucson, Arizona 85721

"One River, One Problem: James Murray and the Missouri Valley Authority"
by Donald E. Spritzer (copyright Donald E. Spritzer)
Montana and the West: Essays in Honor of K. Ross Toole (1984)
Pruett Publishing Co.
2928 Pearl St.
Boulder, Colorado 80301

"One Cow, One Vote — A Strenuous Session in the Montana Legislature"
by Margaret Scherf
© 1966, *Harper's Magazine*
666 Broadway
New York, New York 10012

The Montana Historical Society Press

Cover art, *The Story Teller*, by Charles M. Russell (Courtesy of The Thomas Gilcrease Institute of American History and Art, Tulsa, Oklahoma)
Cover design by Finstad Visual Design, Helena, Montana
Typeset in Baskerville by Arrow Graphics & Typography, Missoula, Montana
Printed by BookCrafters in Chelsey, Michigan

Library of Congress Cataloging-in-Publication Data
The Montana heritage : an anthology of historical essays / edited by
    Robert R. Swartout, Jr., and Harry W. Fritz.
        p.   cm.
    Includes bibliographical references and index.
    ISBN 0-917298-25-X : $11.95
    1. Montana—History.   I. Swartout, Robert R., 1946–
II. Fritz, Harry W., 1937–
    F731.5.M654   1992   91-44516
    978.6—dc20   CIP

Contents

Illustrations

Preface

"In the American West, we are struggling to revise our dominant mythology, a story called The Western, hoping to see through to the so-called Real West." So writes William Kittredge in the introductory essay to this volume. Kittredge thinks artists help us recognize ourselves. We, the editors of this volume, stand for historians. In the end, they are the same: Historians are artists who paint pictures of the past.

Every ten years or so, it seems, we need a new anthology of historical articles to tell us who we are. Michael P. Malone and Richard B. Roeder offered such an anthology in 1969 (revised, 1973).[1] Robert Swartout assembled a new collection of essays on Montana history in 1981.[2] The essays these editors deemed important were pivotal pieces, interpretive landmarks of Montana historiography, valuable then and now, and readable still. But their arguments were so good, so meaningful, that they have passed into the historical record and become part of the conventional wisdom. Classroom lectures incorporate their insights, while textbooks reduce their once-startling conclusions to commonplace facts.

The present anthology contains a few old favorites never before reprinted, but the essays included here represent the efforts of recent historians "to revise our dominant mythology." In recent years the scope of historical inquiry has widened considerably. Scholars now investigate people and conditions that have received little consideration previously—in particular, women, Native Americans, immigrant groups, the environment, and the twentieth century. This anthology compensates for what has not before been emphasized by including recent essays on these topics while also offering articles on more traditional subjects like Lewis and Clark, labor strife, Montana politics, and even Custer's Last Stand.

The late K. Ross Toole once remarked that "The historical literature is so heavily freighted with published works on the territorial period

1. Michael P. Malone and Richard B. Roeder, eds., *The Montana Past: An Anthology* (Missoula: University of Montana Press, 1969), revised as *Montana's Past: Selected Essays* (Missoula: University of Montana Press, 1973).

2. Robert R. Swartout, Jr., ed., *Montana Vistas: Selected Historical Essays* (Washington, D.C.: University Press of America, 1981).

and the 'War of the Copper Kings' that a basic unbalance exists." [3]
We seek to right the balance by shifting the primary focus of this
anthology from the pioneer period and nineteenth century to the
turn-of-the-century Progressive era and to contemporary topics in
the twentieth century.

In addition we would like to introduce students and other readers
to historians who thus far may have escaped their notice. Younger
scholars, and those writing on hitherto esoteric subjects, are presented here in samples of their work.

We claim timeliness, not timelessness. Other historians in the year
2000 will find this collection dated and commonplace. The frontiers
of history are continually pushing forward, capturing new subjects
and experimenting with new methodologies. We eagerly await the
new findings. But for now, we offer these articles in the spirit of Bill
Kittredge, who sees history "as a kind of storytelling that triggers our
imaginations into the vital act of seeing freshly into the patterns of
our lives."

---

3. Quoted in Harry W. Fritz, "An Uncommon Man: K. Ross Toole, 1920–1981,
in Rex C. Myers and Harry W. Fritz, eds., *Montana and the West: Essays in Honor of K.
Ross Toole* (Boulder: Pruett Publishing Co., 1984), 11.

Robert R. Swartout, Jr.
Carroll College
Helena, Montana

Harry W. Fritz
University of Montana
Missoula, Montana

November 1991

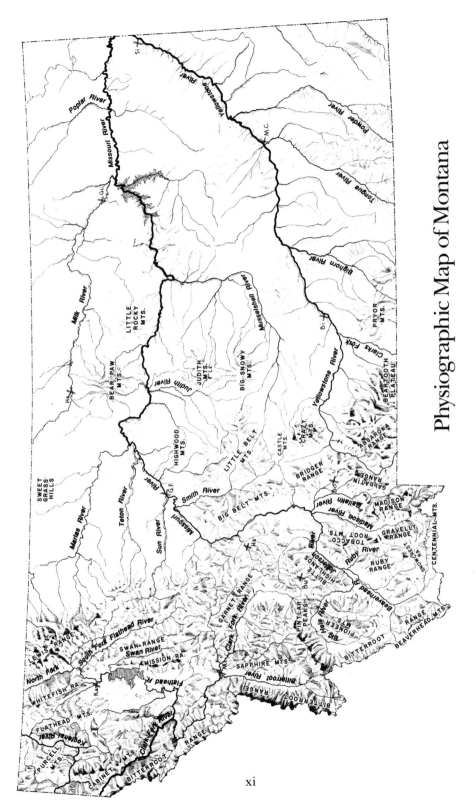

Physiographic Map of Montana

(E. S. Smyrl, cartographer, from *Montana Maps, 1974*, by Robert L. Taylor, et. al., Montana State University Foundation)

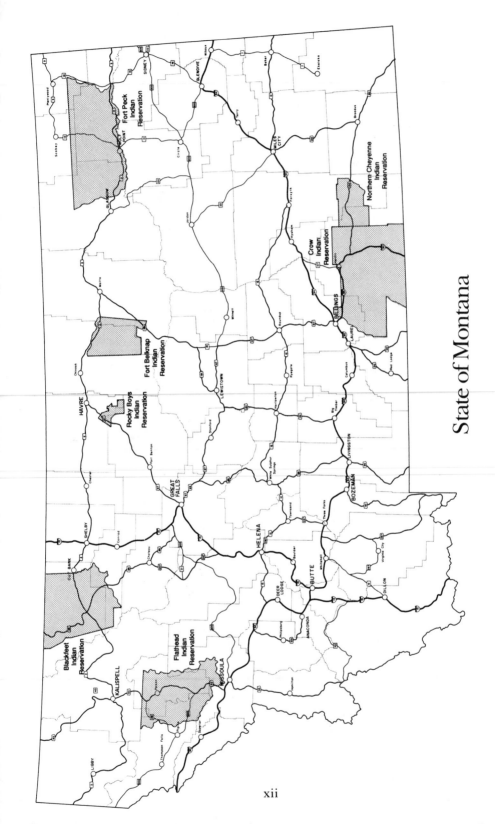

State of Montana

(from *Montana Maps, 1974*, by Robert L. Taylor, et. al., Montana State University Foundation)

Pictographs near Rock Creek, Montana. (Montana Historical Society Photograph Archives)

INTRODUCTION

New to the Country

William Kittredge

Someone once said that out West you need wide-angle lenses in your eyes. Bill Kittredge provides those lenses in this introductory essay, "New to the Country," by expanding our perspectives of what western history, Montana history, is all about. Kittredge, professor of English in the University of Montana, is not a professional historian, but is a writer, an artist, and he knows from experience where we have been and what we have done. He is not happy.

Throughout his personal journey we encounter a theme of declension — the notion that once, perhaps when Indians silently contemplated the land, things were much better. "Instead of creating a great good place," he writes, "we were destroying our natural oasis." Certainly the themes of "progress" and "development" have dominated both the Montana past and the writing of Montana history. But progress had a price. Writers like Kittredge and historians whose works are represented here are beginning to tote up the costs. One might ask, however, how much of Kittredge's artistic imagery is grounded in the past and whether his mythological history is truly a metaphor for Montana.

In July of 1969 I came to Montana to stay, bearing a new Master of Fine Arts degree from the flooding heartland of Iowa. I had just finished up as a thirty-five-year-old, in-off-the-ranch graduate student in the Writer's Workshop, and I had lucked into a teaching job at the University of Montana. I was running to native cover in

*William Kittredge, "New to the Country," *Montana The Magazine of Western History*, 36 (Winter 1986), 2–11.

the West; I was a certified writer, and this was the beginning of my real life at last.

During that summer in Iowa City—drinking too much, in love with theories about heedlessness and possibility—I was trying to figure out how to inhabit my daydream. We lived in an old stone-walled house with flooded basement out by the Coralville reservoir, listening to cockroaches run on the night-time linoleum and imagining Montana, where we would find a home.

Every morning the corn in the fields across the road looked to have grown six inches, every afternoon the skies turned green with tornado-warning storms, and every night lightning ran magnificent and terrible from the horizons. My wife said they ought to build a dike around the whole damned state of Iowa and turn it into a catfish preserve. The U-Haul trailer was loaded. After a last party we were history in the Midwest, gone to Montana, where we were going to glow in the dark.

The real West started at the long symbolic interstate bridge over that mainline to so many ultimately heartbreaking American versions of heaven, the Missouri River. Out in the middle of South Dakota I felt myself released into significance. It was clear I was aiming my life in the correct direction. We were headed for a town studded with abandoned tipi burners.

But moreso—as we drove I imagined Lewis and Clark and Catlin and Bodmer and even Audubon up to Fort Union on the last voyage of his life in 1843, along with every wagon train, oxcart, cattle drive, and trainload of honyockers, all in pursuit of that absolute good luck which is some breathing time in a commodious place where the best that can be is right now. In the picture book of my imagination I was seeing a Montana composed of major postcards. The great river sliding by under the bridge was rich with water from the Sun River drainage, where elk and grizzly were rumored to be on the increase.

Engrossed in fantasies of traveling upriver into untouched territory, I was trying to see the world fresh, as others had seen it. On April 22, 1805, near what is now the little city of Williston in North Dakota, Meriwether Lewis wrote:

> . . . immence herds of Buffaloe, Elk, deer, & Antelopes feeding in one common and boundless pasture. we saw a number of bever feeding on the bark of the trees alonge the verge of the river, several of which we shot, found them large and fat. [1]

By 1832, at the confluence of the Missouri and the Yellowstone, the painter George Catlin was already tasting ashes while trying

---

1. Bernard DeVoto, ed., *The Journals of Lewis and Clark* (Boston: Houghton Mifflin Company, 1953), 98.

to envision a future—just as I was trying to imagine what had been. Catlin wrote:

> ... the native Indian in his classic attire, galloping his wild horse, with sinewy bow, and shield and lance, amid the fleeting herds of elks and buffaloes. What a beautiful and thrilling specimen for America to preserve and hold up to the view of her refined citizens and the world, in future ages! A *nation's park*, containing man and beast, in all the wild and freshness of their nature's beauty! [2]

Think of Audubon responding eleven years later, on May 17, 1843, in that same upriver country around Fort Union:

> Ah! Mr. Catlin, I am now sorry to see and to read your accounts of the Indians *you* saw—how very different they must have been from any that I have seen! [3]

On July 21, Audubon wrote:

> What a terrible destruction of life, as it were for nothing, or next to it, as the tongues only were brought in, and the flesh of these fine animals was left to beasts and birds of prey, or to rot on the spots where they fell. The prairies are literally *covered* with the skulls of the victims. . . . [4]

On August 5, Audubon finished the thought:

> But this cannot last; even now there is a perceptible difference in the size of the herds, and before many years the Buffalo, like the Great Auk, will have disappeared; surely this should not be permitted. [5]

In our summer of 1969 we poked along the edge where the Badlands break so suddenly from the sunbaked prairies, imagining the far-away drumming of hooves, Catlin's warriors on their decorated horses coming after us from somewhere out of dream. Not so far south lay Wounded Knee.

We studied the stone faces of our forefathers at Mount Rushmore and didn't see a damned thing because by that time in the afternoon we were blinded by so much irony on a single day. We retired for the night to a motel somewhere south of the Devil's Post Pile in

---

2. Quoted in Frank Bergon, ed., *The Wilderness Reader* (New York: New American Library, 1980), 70.

3. John James Audubon, *Audubon and His Journals*, ed. Maria R. Audubon, (2 vols., New York: Dover, 1960 [1897]), 1:497.

4. Audubon, *Audubon and His Journals*, 2:107.

5. Ibid., 131.

Wyoming. I was seeing freshly but not always what I hoped to see. The distances were terrifying.

By the time we reached Missoula, I had disassociated my sensibilities with whiskey, which gave me the courage to march up the concrete steps to Richard Hugo's house, only a block from the Clark Fork River, where the Village Inn Motel sits these days. I rapped on his door. He studied me a moment after I introduced myself. "You're very drunk," he said.

Well hell, I thought, now you've done it.

"Wait a minute," Hugo said. "I'll join you."

Home, I thought, childlike with relief. This was the new country I had been yearning for, inhabited by this man who smiled and seemed to think I should be whatever I could manage.

That particular pilgrimage started years before. Like so many of the students at the University of Montana, those who have grown up rural and so seemingly isolated from anything our national media culture defines as significant, I felt myself cut off from the so-called Great World in irrevocable ways. So many of us in the West feel deprived and driven to the contrary idea that the things we know are worthless, or at least of no interest to anybody else, because they are so private. Dick Hugo helped us disabuse ourselves of such notions.

In the far outback of high desert basin and range country where I was a young man, a land-locked peat-ground valley just north of the Nevada state line in southeastern Oregon, we lived a long way from bookstores. And I believed myself ruined for this isolation by my dumbfounded discovery of books and ideas, nodding my head in dimwitted agreement with Camus, terrified by *The Magic Mountain*, subscribing to *The New York Times Book Review*, the *Kenyon Review*, the *Sewanee Review*, the *Hudson Review*, and the *Virginia Quarterly Review*, ordering eight or ten deeply serious books a month long distance from San Francisco— occasionally a good one—hungering at the meager collections shelved in stationery stores when I got to town, twenty-six years old, home from some years in Strategic Air Command intelligence on Guam, a grown man with family, ill-educated and close to paralyzed by my inability to want any life I could imagine as possibly mine. My yearnings seemed almost perverse. Why couldn't the immediacy of family and work and property be enough?

How right and ironic it seemed that afternoon in Shaw's Stationery in Klamath Falls, as I leafed through a recent reissue of *Oregon Place Names* and found the name Lonely. It turned out to be the former name of Adel in Warner Valley, the place where I had been raised and was living right at the moment. Not one thing about such a sappish discovery loomed comic at that time in my life.

Eventually I made other finds in Shaw's Stationery—Theodore Roethke's *Collected Poems*, for one—and I read, in "The Far Field":

Among the tin cans, tires, rusted pipes, broken machinery,—
One learned of the eternal [6]

The poem goes on to talk about dead rats and tomcats and ground beetles amid named, specific flowers and birds, referring to Roethke's childhood wanderings amid his father's greenhouses in Michigan, but I was transfixed right there in Klamath Falls. Roethke's experience in some back corner was valuable if only because he cherished it in such accurate language, and mine might be, someday, maybe. In any event, I recognized chances I had to take but could not name in Roethke, and about then began another version of my life, a story to tell myself and live by. So to hell with lonely, I'll just be whatever it is I can't quit. Another romance with myself, as if they all weren't.

By early October of those years in the early 1960s our four old John Deere 36 combines had been dragged into a row out behind the Caterpillar shop. The light over the harvested barley fields would come up golden and clean for a couple of dozen perfect days.

The great fault-block of Warner Rim lifted three thousand feet just at our backs, marked in long terraces by the remnants of rocky shoreline left behind as some ancient sea dried up. A few miles north, along a thin curve of peninsula reaching out into a shallow flood-water lake, we had found chipped obsidian arrow-points by the bucketful when I was a child. The native peoples must have camped there on these same kinds of limitless fall days, awaiting the calling, undulating rafts of waterbirds and the good hunting. In my imagination those people were absolutely quiet and at peace with their intentions. For them, things had always been like this.

Archaeologists know of a quarter-million points picked up along the shores of Crump Lake, and kids in the country, like me, had a hundred or two stored in a shoebox somewhere. In seasons when the water was low we would wander amid the shredding expanses of dry tule and find the points in clusters of a dozen or more. At the end, people were out there with shovels and screens, like miners, determined to reap their share of whatever bounty they imagined this was. I knew a man who had a half dozen horseshoe nail kegs filled with arrowheads in his garage.

---

6. Theodore Roethke, "The Far Field," *The Collected Poems of Theodore Roethke* (Garden City, New York: Anchor Press, 1975), 193. Reprinted by permission, from The Far Field, © 1962, by Beatrice Roethke, Administratrix of the Estate of Theodore Roethke. From The Collected Poems of Theodore Roethke. Published by Doubleday and Co., Inc.

By the early 1960s, the shore of Crump Lake felt too lonesome
for anybody in my spiritual condition. The afternoons there didn't
seem inhabited any more. But south along the thread of gravel road
there were huge smooth-sided boulders etched with lichen growing
along the traces of dim pictograph drawings, snakes and sunrises,
figures of animals and men, perhaps drawn there in acts of celebration or supplication. Who could know? In any event, the boulders
were a truckload each, and nobody had carried them away to a garage.
On those fine October days I would study those drawings and wonder
what it could have been like to be native in that place where I felt
so distant from any hint of proper purpose.

Several hundred feet up the scree slopes, along the terraced rocky
lines that marked the shores of that ancient sea, there were caves
at the foot of the occasional layered lava-rock outcroppings. Nobody
I knew had ever climbed up to them, likely because our energies
in that valley went mostly to work, and sweating up some scree
slope toward those unimpressive thin line of shadow looked to be
such a thunderingly pointless thing to do. But anybody could see
that those old hunting-gathering people who painted their designs
on the boulders along the road might have sheltered themselves
up there, and I was looking for somebody to be. Maybe I could
be an intellectual rancher who did bookish things like archaeology
on the side.

Such are the stories we tell ourselves. I didn't know anybody like
that, but I entertained thoughts of buying the weekly newspaper over
in the county seat and being the rancher/newspaper guy who wrote
a fascinating column every week with cowshit on his boots. As I say,
I was twenty-six and ruined for the country generosities of the life
I had inherited. A good crop of barley was in the bin that fall, and
it wasn't enough. So I climbed up to the caves, packing a No. 2
irrigating shovel.

From that elevation, through the stillness of October, I gazed out
across the valley we mostly owned. It was so clearly demarcated by
what I think of as our own etchings, our ways of making the world
captured and sensible: the green geometric patternings of the high
irrigation ditches and dragline drainage canals leading to the pumps,
the yellow fields of stubble we had so recently harvested, the fence-
lines where I could have been stalking ring-necked pheasant that
afternoon. But I didn't spend much time contemplating the vista.
If there was anything I knew by heart, it was the configuration of
that property.

The rough, sloping roof over the mouth of the shallow cave was
black and encrusted, and I had read enough to guess what that
meant—soot and animal fats, a long history of cook fires, maybe over
centuries. My theories were right; people had sheltered themselves

here. I was truly and immediately excited, my hands trembling as I envisioned some great simple goldfield find, trying to put aside my fantastical notions of who I would be now that such impossible bonanza luck had come my way.

What I remember next is the shoveling, there in the mounded rubble at the mouth of the cave, where I had room to stand and work while fighting back the feeling that this was make-believe and not part of my actual life at all. Since the end of harvest I had been searching, unconsciously or not, seeking signs and omens to kick me forward into the process of creating a story of who I should be. Those that I acknowledged had brought me to this hillside above the place where I had always lived, digging for buried secrets. It was a scenario my cattle rancher friends might understand as quite literally indicative of craziness. And more than anything I was terrified that they might be right about someone so unmoored from the routines of normal life as it was supposed to be lived in our valley.

But before long my shoveling turned up a reward that at first I could not make sense of—a fragment of fine matting woven from rushes. It seemed impossible that the people who drew those slapstick marks on the boulders below could have known how to work so intricately with materials so commonplace in the valley. But connections started forming.

A few miles away, on the flat-topped lava outcroppings along the eastern side of the valley, there were smooth cylindrical holes worn maybe ten or fifteen inches into the fundamental stone by Modoc or Shoshoni or Klamath natives grinding the native grains. The holes are like bowls, and once worked into the outcropping they could not be destroyed by enemies. Whatever tribe it was and how many thousands of hours at the grinding it took to wear those holes no one knows; but for me, like the crumbling woven mat, that stone worn to the shape of the work came to exist as metaphor.

There in the mouth of my shallow cave I realized my connection to the unimagined continuities of life in the place where I lived. It was an instant that cannot help but sound soft-headed in the recounting—you cannot describe the ineffable, you have to trigger readers into imagining it for themselves—but I now think of it as a quite classical instant of recognition, in which I began to sense in the most inarticulate of ways the legitimacy of my urge to tell stories.

Over the next weeks and months, what had been a slowly accumulating intention began to become resolve. On the day after Thanksgiving in 1965, when I was thirty-three years old, I started writing stories that I have learned to understand as useful, if they are ever useful, precisely as that broken bit of woven matting and those bowls worn in the fundamental stone were useful to me, as gestures passing from one person to another.

A mythology can be understood as a story that contains a set of implicit instructions from a society to its members, telling them what is valuable and how to conduct themselves if they are to preserve the things they value. In the American West, we are struggling to revise our dominant mythology, a story called The Western, hoping to see through to the so-called Real West. In essence, we are trying to find a new story to inhabit.

The struggle is of extraordinary importance. Our laws control our lives, and they are designed to preserve a model of society based on values learned from our mythology. Only after re-imagining our myths can we remodel our laws and hope to keep our society in a realistic relationship to what is actual.

It is important to understand that the mythology of the American West is the most central mythology of our nation and that it is part of a much older world myth, the myth of law-bringing. Which means it is a mythology of conquest.

The story begins with a vast innocent continent, natural and almost magically alive, capable of inspiring us to reverence and awe, and yet savage — a wilderness. The story goes on to a pastoral people who come from the East, bringing law and civilization. But the law does not command much respect from the original inhabitants of the land, who after all had laws of their own to respect. The law does not always command much respect even from those who bring it. People seeking frontiers are often people seeking escape from law, bringing terrible demons with them — lust and greed for property and power and that ultimate abstraction, which is money.

Our good pastoral people are often, because they are law-abiding, too weak to enforce their laws and need help, which comes in the form of a magical hero — the good warrior from the sacred and inno- cent wilds who possesses wilderness skills and the existential knowl- edge that it is sometimes necessary to kill, to be essentially lawless in the service of law and order. This hero saves our people from the savage forces of lust and greed. He alone has the magical wilderness speed of hand and the willingness to kill. And he has the sad knowl- edge of his responsibilities. His knowledge is sad because he has to go away after he is finished with the killing, back to the mythological wilderness. His willingness to embrace violence, even in the service of law, is a disruptive force in society. He is a killer in a society that cannot endorse violence. He does our dirty work, then carries our guilt away with him, leaving us to go about the business of our days with clean hands and souls.

This is our great paradoxical, problematic American teaching story. It is also the plot of *Shane*. It is a story as ancient as the prob- lem of law and law-bringing.

The holy and innocent hero comes from the wilderness and slays the dragon that is threatening society, then rides away like a movie star. An obvious societal good has been served by the violence of an outsider. The story is as old as settlements and invading armies and deeply problematic because it is at the heart of a racist, sexist, imperialist mythology of conquest. It is a rationale for violence, against other people and against nature. It is The Western, a morality play that was never much acted out anywhere in the "Real West." Or anywhere.

The actual West was no doubt violent at times, but never so obsessed with killing as our story would have us imagine. Nobody would have been left alive. More people have been killed in Missoula in the last few weeks than in Dodge City in its heyday. Certainly the West was not much traveled by holy gunfighters engaged in the business of setting things right.

At the same time, that mythology is a lens through which we continue to see ourselves. Many of us like to imagine ourselves as honest, pastoral yeomen who sweat and work in the woods or the mines or the fields for a living. And many of us are. We live in a real family, a work-centered society, and we like to see ourselves as people with the good luck and sense to live in a place where some remnant of the natural world still exists in working order. Many of us hold that natural world to be sacred in some degree, just as it is in our myth. Lately, more and more of us are coming to understand our society in the American West as an exploited colony, threatened by greedy outsiders who want to take our sacred place away from us, or at least strip and degrade it beyond sacredness.

In short, we see ourselves as a working society of mostly decent people who live in some connection to a holy wilderness, threatened by those who lust for power and property. We look for Shane to come riding out of the Tetons, and we see Exxon and the Sierra Club. One looks about as alien as the other.

Our mythology tells us we own the West, absolutely and morally; we own it because of our history. Our people brought law to this difficult place; they suffered and they shed blood and they survived, and they earned this land for us. The myth tells us this place is ours, and will always be ours, to do with as we see fit.

That's a most troubling and enduring message, because we want to believe it—and we do believe it, so many of us, despite the ironies and wrongheadedness involved, despite the fact that we took this place from someone else. We try to ignore a genocidal history of violence against the Native Americans.

The truth is, we never owned all the land and water, and we don't even own very much of it, privately. And we don't own anything absolutely or forever. As our society grows more and more complex and interwoven, our title is less and less absolute, more and more likely to be diminished legally. Our rights to property will never take precedence over the needs of society. Nor should they, we all must agree in our grudging heart of hearts. Ownership of property has always been a privilege, granted by society and revokable.

So we find that our mythology, the story by which our society is ordered, has been telling us an enormous lie, and we are mortally angered by the deception. My father grew up on a homestead place on the sagebrush flats outside Silver Lake, Oregon. He tells of hiding under the bed with his sisters when strangers came to the gate. He grew up believing that the one sure defense against the world was property, as we all did in that country and era.

By the time he was thirty-five, my grandfather had bought the cattle ranch in Warner Valley, where I grew up. We summered our cattle on Taylor Grazing Land, where we owned most of the water there was, and it was ours. The government was as distant as news on the radio.

Outside work was done mostly by men and horses and mules, and our ranch valley was filled with life. But we went to tractors and drained the swamps and plowed the tule marshes and draglined the sloughs and bought more machinery and made our way around the corner into agribusiness. The valley went deader and deader as the years passed and our fields were scaled to work, and the work scaled to machinery.

By the time I was old enough to run the farming we had miles of canals and hundreds of redwood headgates, eighteen-inch electric pumps—the works. The most intricate part of my job was called "balancing water," a night-and-day process of opening and closing pipes and running pumps. That system was the finest and most intricate plaything I ever had.

Despite the mud and endless hours, the work remained play for a long time, the perfecting of that irrigation system a kind of artistry, the making of a thing both functional and elegant. That's how we thought of it; we were bringing order to the world, doing God's work and creating a good place on earth, living the pastoral yeoman dream. Our work surely earned us the right to absolute control over the thing we had created.

So you can imagine our surprise and despair, our sense of having been profoundly cheated, when things began to go wrong. We wanted to build a reservoir and litigation started. Our laws were being used against us by people who wanted a share of what we thought of as our water. As the fieldwork became more and more mechanical, we couldn't hire anyone who cared enough to do it right. The peat ground we had drained began to go saline. The waterbirds stopped coming in the great rafts we had so loved to hunt. Instead of creating a great good place, we were destroying our natural oasis. We had lived the right lives, according to mythology, and the mythology had lied. Or the world had proven too complex, the myth too simple-minded.

The myth had told us to bring order to nature, and our order had proven deadly; nature would not fit our industrial model, and we could not endure the boredom of our mechanical work. We killed off the coyotes, and rodents destroyed our alfalfa. We sprayed Parathion for clover mite and shortened our own lives. We started with a sanctuary and ended with a landscape organized like a machine for growing crops and fattening cattle, a machine that creaked a little louder each year, a dreamland gone wrong. We had shaped our piece of the West according to the model provided by our mythology, we had brought it to order, and such order had given us enormous power over nature — a blank perfection of fields — and nature had died.

All over the West, as in all of America, the old story is dying. We find ourselves weathering a rough winter of discontent, snared in the uncertainties of a transitional time and urgently yearning to inhabit a story that might bring sensible order to our lives, even as we know such a story can only evolve through an almost literally infinite series of recognitions of what we hold sacred, individual by individual. If we're lucky, it might be a story that teaches us to abhor our old romance with conquest and progress so that we might revere the particular, where, as Roethke said, "One learned of the eternal."

What I am working toward is an idea of history as a kind of storytelling that triggers our imaginations into the vital act of seeing freshly into the patterns of our lives, both private and public.

Artists help us recognize ourselves. It's their job. We are lucky in Montana, because we have a tradition of vivid and useful storytelling — *The Journals of Lewis and Clark* and *The Big Sky, Wolf Willow, Wind from an Enemy Sky, A River Runs Through It, Winter in the Blood, This House of Sky* — make your own list.

Making Sure It Goes On, the Collected Poems of Richard Hugo heads mine. Dick loved to drive Montana, his trips imaginative explorations into other lives as a way toward focusing on his own complexities. He made the game of seeing into art, and his poetry and life form a story that lies rock bottom in my understanding of what art is for.

Once we drove over to fish the Jefferson River on a summer day when we were both hung-over to the point of insipid visionary craziness. We didn't catch any fish, and I came home numb, simply spooked; but Dick saw some things and wrote a poem called "Silver Star."

Each time I read "Silver Star" I rediscover an implied story about homes, and the courage to acknowledge such a need, a story about

Dick and his continual refinding of his own life, an instruction about storytelling as the art of constructing road maps, ways home to that ultimate shelter that is the coherent self. It's a gift. Montana is a landscape reeking with such conjunction and resonance. They fill the silence.

Not long ago, on a bright spring morning, I stood on the cliffs of the Ulm Pishkun where the Blackfeet drove dusty hundreds of bison to fall and die. Gazing east I could dimly see the great Anaconda Company smokestack there on the banks of the Missouri like a finger pointing to heaven above the old saloon-town city of Great Falls where Charlie Russell painted and traded his pictures for whiskey, only a little upstream from the place where Meriwether Lewis wrote, having just finished an attempt at describing his first sight of the falls:

> after writing this imperfect discription I again viewed the falls and was so much disgusted with the imperfect idea which it conveyed of the scene that I determined to draw my pen across it and begin agin, but then reflected that I could not perhaps succeed better. . . . [7]

After so many months of precise notation, all in the service of Thomas Jefferson's notion of the West as useful, in one of the most revealing passages written about the American West, Lewis seems to be saying:

> But this, this otherness is beyond the capture of my words, this cannot be useful, this is dream.

The dam builders, of course, did see it his way.

Behind me loomed the fortress of the rock-sided butte Charlie Russell painted as backdrop to so much history, with the Rockies off beyond on the western horizon, snowy and gleaming in the morning sun. This listing could go on, but I was alone and almost frightened by so many conjunctions visible at once, and so many others right down the road: the Gates of the Mountains and Last Chance Gulch and even make-believe—Boone Caudill and Teal Eye and Dick Summers over west on the banks of the Teton River, where it cuts through the landscapes of *The Big Sky*—history evident all around and the imaginings of artists and storytellers intertwined. Charlie Russell and Bud Guthrie and Dick Hugo and Meriwether Lewis created metaphoric territory as real as any other Montana in the eye of my imagination.

We all play at imagining ourselves into history, new to the country, seeing freshly, reorienting ourselves and our schemes within the complexities of the world. It is a powerful connection to history, and the grand use we make of storytelling as we incessantly attempt to recognize that which is sacred and the point of things.

---

7. DeVoto, *Journals of Lewis and Clark*, 138.

Ulm Pishkun (buffalo jump), southwest of Great Falls, with Square Butte in the background.
(John Smart, photographer, Montana Historical Society Photograph Archives)

In his entry on February 25, 1806, Clark described a small fish, the Eulachon, with which he was not familiar, then noted, "on the next page I have drawn the likeness of them as large as life." (from Gary E. Moulton, *Journals of Lewis and Clark Expedition*, vol. 6)

PART I

Pioneer Montana

The history of Montana prior to statehood in 1889 is marked by several important themes, one of which is the way natural resources drew people to the Upper Missouri region and the Northern Rockies. Native and non-native peoples alike came in search of buffalo, the natural grasslands, beaver pelts, and gold and silver. The arrival of non-Native people into what would become Montana eventually gave rise to permanent communities. These communities—places such as Virginia City and Helena—would produce new economic opportunities of their own. A by-product of this development was the formal establishment of Montana Territory in 1864.

A heterogeneous society constitutes another important theme of nineteenth-century Montana. In addition to the great variety of Indian tribes and bands that occupied much of the territory, an unusually broad mix of people began arriving from other states and territories and from abroad. Chinese immigrants were but one example of an ethnic pluralism that characterized much of the post–Civil War West.

With the influx of new people, pressures on Native Americans grew correspondingly. Confronted by white economic demands and political expansion, and, worst of all, by the introduction of new diseases for which they had few immunities, Montana Indians struggled to maintain control over their lands and their way of life. By the 1880s, an oppressive reservation system had supplanted traditional Native American autonomy and self-reliance.

Frederic Remington portrayed Meriwether Lewis and William Clark with other members of the Lewis and Clark expedition for the May 12, 1906, Collier's *magazine. The illustration was one of ten in Remington's series, "The Great Explorers."*

'A Knowledge of Distant Parts'
The Shaping of the Lewis and Clark Expedition

James P. Ronda

The famed Lewis and Clark expedition of 1804–1806 — officially known as the Corps of Discovery — had a profound impact on the region that would become known as Montana. Historian K. Ross Toole noted in his most influential book, *Montana: An Uncommon Land*, that the expedition "traveled farther into Montana and spent more time there than in any other area. Its most important discoveries and its greatest crises occurred in Montana." Toole summarized his description of Lewis and Clark by declaring that "although they left only the ashes of their campfires behind, Montana would never be the same again." The expedition solidified America's claims to the upper Missouri region and the Northern Rockies, it helped to usher in the heyday of the American fur trade, and it brought with it the potential for growing conflicts in Indian-white relations.

Yet as important as the expedition was to the development of Montana history, historians have not always understood or appreciated the complex nature of its origins. As Professor James P. Ronda of the University of Tulsa makes clear in the following essay, the expedition was not simply the result of such immediate factors as the Louisiana Purchase or the search for a northwest passage — important though they may have been. In a broader historical sense, the expedition was a product of the European Enlightenment and its emphasis upon scientific inquiry, direct observation, and practical use. The Enlightenment provided the philosophical backdrop for the expedition, and the discoveries of the British explorer Captain James Cook

*James P. Ronda, " 'A Knowledge of Distant Parts,' The Shaping of the Lewis and Clark Expedition," *Montana The Magazine of Western History*, 41 (Autumn 1991), 4–19.

provided the more precise model upon which President Thomas Jefferson based his bold plan for discovery. The Lewis and Clark expedition turned out to be a grand adventure for the United States, but it also epitomized major characteristics of a global Age of Discovery.

———

M ore than a century and a half ago an obscure employee of the powerful North West Company, Canada's boldest fur enterprise, acknowledged the Lewis and Clark Expedition's primacy in the exploration of western North America. "By the journey of Captains Lewis and Clark," wrote Peter Corney, "the whole of that western region is now laid open." [1]

In the years since, the results of the expedition have come into sharper focus. Decades of Lewis and Clark scholarship have revealed an expedition rich in science, geography, ethnography, and imperial history. Few would now challenge Bernard DeVoto's declaration that the expedition was a turning point in American and perhaps even global history. [2] While the meanings and consequences of the expedition have become clearer over the years, much confusion remains about its origins. Eager to launch the Corps of Discovery on its epic journey, scholars and expedition fellow travelers have paid scant attention to the compelling world of discovery and exploration that inspired Thomas Jefferson and gave shape to his several exploratory ventures.

Traditional answers to the question "where did the Lewis and Clark Expedition come from" fall into several predictable categories. Textbook wisdom instructs young students that the expedition was the product of Jefferson's lifelong fascination with the West and Native Americans. Commentators with a less romantic bent emphasize the Corps of Discovery as Jefferson's political response to the growing British presence in the Northwest. More recently the expedition has been linked to a search for the fabled Passage to India, a dream that reached back to the Age of Columbus. One student of the enterprise has connected it to Jefferson's political philosophy and the need to preserve the nation's rural values. [3]

———

1.   Peter Corney, *Voyages in the North Pacific, 1813–1818* (1821; reprint, Fairfield, Wash.: Ye Galleon Press, 1965), 91.

2.   Bernard DeVoto to Garrett Mattingly, December 2, 1948, Wallace Stegner, ed., *The Letters of Bernard DeVoto* (Garden City, New York: Doubleday, 1975), 305.

3.   For a review of expedition historiography see James P. Ronda, " 'The Writingest Explorers': The Lewis and Clark Expedition in American Historical Literature," *Pennsylvania Magazine of History and Biography*, 112 (October 1988), 607–30.

Each of those answers catches a bit of the expedition's complex origins. Jefferson had a genuine interest in all things western, although it came late in his life. The expedition did not spring from long years of careful planning. Instead, it grew quickly after the president read Alexander Mackenzie's *Voyages from Montreal*. That important expedition narrative contained British strategy for economic and political dominion in the West, a strategy that forced Jefferson to begin planning the American response. A considerable part of the intellectual energy behind Jefferson's commitment to exploration and expansion was generated by his republican ideology. Jefferson believed that the future of the American republic depended on an unending supply of good agricultural land. Without the promise of land, Americans were sure to slip into the moral decay and political tyranny that had corrupted urban Europe. Each of these answers, however, neglects the wider context. Some twenty-five years ago William Goetzmann wrote that "the exploration of the American West was never an isolated event. It belongs to world rather than national history." [4] To begin to grasp the origins of the Lewis and Clark expedition we need to look to the broader age of global discovery.

The master detective Sherlock Holmes once observed that "from a drop of water a logician could infer the possibility of an Atlantic or a Niagara without having seen or heard of one or the other." [5] One small event, even a passing comment, can reveal worlds of meaning. So it was with Meriwether Lewis's journal entry for April 7, 1805. Surveying the Corps of Discovery as it prepared to leave Fort Mandan for the final push west, Lewis compared his expedition to those of Columbus and James Cook. "Altho not quite so rispectable" as the ships and crews of his predecessors, Lewis insisted his "little fleet" was "still viewed by us with as much pleasure as those deservedly famed adventurers ever beheld theirs." [6] Perhaps Lewis imagined his perogues following in the wake of Columbus's caravels and Cook's sloops.

Nearly a year later, as the expedition made its way home on the Columbia, William Clark forged his link to James Cook. At the Kathlamet Indian village near present-day Knappa, Oregon, Clark saw two "very large elegant canoes inlaid with shells." A quick look seemed to suggest that the shells were human teeth, an impression seconded when several Indians said those were the teeth of vanquished enemies. But on closer inspection it was plain that the "teeth"

---

4. William H. Goetzmann, *Exploration and Empire: The Explorer and the Scientist in the Winning of the American West* (New York: Alfred A. Knopf, 1966), 3.

5. Arthur Conan Doyle, *The Complete Sherlock Holmes* (Garden City, New York: Doubleday and Co., 1960), 23.

6. Gary E. Moulton, ed., *The Journals of the Lewis and Clark Expedition* (7 vols., Lincoln: University of Nebraska Press, 1983–1991), 4:9.

were indeed shells. Then in a remarkable postscript Clark noted: "Capt. Cook may have mistaken those shells very well for human teeth without a close examination." [7] This was more than one explorer quietly correcting another. Like Lewis, Clark knew that Cook was the premier explorer of the era. Evidently Clark had read an account of Cook's third voyage, an ill-starred search for the Northwest Passage. Recognizing Cook's vast influence, both Lewis and Clark took pains to associate themselves with his great achievements. In so doing they point us toward the tradition that shaped American exploration in the Age of Jefferson.

Thomas Jefferson's explorers — Meriwether Lewis, William Clark, Zebulon Montgomery Pike, Thomas Freeman, William Dunbar, and Peter Custis — lived during a time of discovery. Not since the sixteenth century had there been such a rush to voyage the seas and march the continents. The eighteenth-century age of discovery was an epoch of mutual encounter as the peoples of the world confronted each other face to face. Captain George Vancouver caught the spirit of the era when he exclaimed that "the ardour of the present age is to discover and delineate the true geography of the earth." [8] Eighteenth-century explorers ranged the continents and ploughed the seas, charting what had once seemed trackless and unknown. For those wayfarers with a mission, the motto of the age might have been a phrase taken from the instructions issued for Cook's first (1768–1771) Pacific voyage. The great navigator was directed to search out "a Knowledge of distant parts." [9]

The remarkable burst of scientific exploration that began in the 1760s was guided by key ideas in the European Enlightenment. Exploration history, so often portrayed in the language of romance and adventure, gains deeper meaning when we connect it to the larger world of thought. And it was thinking — a special brand of thinking about knowledge and its uses — that guided the journeys of James Cook, George Vancouver, and Alexander Mackenzie. Although some of its ablest practitioners were English, the approach to exploration during the Enlightenment knew no national boundaries. Vancouver once declared that he was "a servant of the world," thus keeping company with explorers like the Frenchman Jean François de Lapérouse and the Spaniard Alejandro Malaspina. [10] Those voyagers

---

7. *Reuben G. Thwaites, ed., Original Journals of the Lewis and Clark Expedition* (8 vols., New York: Dodd, Mead, and Co., 1904–1905), 4:199.

8. W. Kaye Lamb, ed., *The Voyage of George Vancouver, 1791–1795* (4 vols., London: Hakluyt Society, 1984), 1:275.

9. J. C. Beaglehole, ed., *The Journals of Captain James Cook on His Voyages of Discovery, 1728–1779* (4 vols., Cambridge: The Hakluyt Society, 1955–1969), 1:pt. 1, p. cclxxxii.

10. Lamb, *Vancouver,* 4:1591.

embodied what one naturalist called "the thirst for knowledge," a quest that eventually would take hold on the life of the third president of the United States.[11]

Three fundamental questions dominated the Age of Enlightenment. The first addressed the subject of inquiry. What should thoughtful people study? For centuries Europeans asserted that God and the supernatural were the only appropriate objects for investigation. By the end of the seventeenth century that theocentric view of knowledge was under sharp attack. As the English poet Alexander Pope wrote, "the proper study of mankind is man." Students of natural history would have added that man was but part of a larger natural world worthy of careful scrutiny. The influential French naturalist Comte de Buffon described just how broadly the Enlightenment defined the study of nature. "Natural history," he declared, "is an immense history, it embraces all the objects that the universe presents."[12]

Eighteenth-century explorers and their patrons agreed. The new Enlightenment agenda quickly transformed the goals of exploration. Voyages of discovery that once had been solely for profit or imperial advantage now became scientific enterprises as well. When British officials drafted comprehensive instructions for James Cook's second voyage (1772–1775) to the Pacific, they put the Enlightenment's sweeping definition of nature at the heart of the document. Cook and his corps of scientists were to study "the nature of the soil and the produce thereof; the Animals and Fowls that inhabit or frequent it; the Fishes that are to be found in the Rivers or upon the Coasts." Nothing was to escape Cook's scientific gaze. The explorers were to keep eyes open for "Mines, Minerals, or valuable stones . . . seeds of Trees, Shrubs, Plants, Fruits, and Grains peculiar to the country."

Eighteenth-century explorers also expected to find populated worlds of wonder. Those "new" peoples were to be studied both for possible economic advantage and for clues about what the Enlightenment was confident were universal laws of cultural development. The planners of Cook's voyage directed him to "observe the Genius, Temper, Disposition, and Number of the natives."[13] Jefferson's guidelines for his explorers reflected the same broad conception of the natural world. Writing to Thomas Freeman, the president ordered him to see "the soil and face of the country."[14] For Jefferson the

11. Michael E. Hoare, ed., *The Resolution Journal of Johann Reinhold Forster, 1772–1775* (4 vols., London: Hakluyt Society, 1982), 3:438.

12. Barbara Maria Stafford, *Voyage into Substance: Art, Science, Nature, and the Illustrated Travel Account, 1760–1840* (Cambridge, Mass.: MIT Press, 1984), 55.

13. Beaglehole, *Cook Journals,* 2:pt. 1, p. clxviii.

14. Thomas Jefferson to Thomas Freeman, April 14, 1804, Dan L. Flores, ed., *Jefferson and Southwestern Exploration: The Freeman and Custis Accounts of the Red River Expedition of 1806* (Norman: University of Oklahoma Press, 1984), 321.

country's "face" meant plants, animals, terrain, and native peoples. Nature was a book to be read, its pages opened and turned by travelers with a wide vision of what Jefferson once called "an extensive, rich and unexplored field." [15]

If the first Enlightenment question expanded exploration goals, the second defined, for voyages of discovery, a fresh approach to gathering knowledge. How should nature be studied? The Enlightenment stressed direct observation. As Vancouver wrote, "the whole of our time should be usefully occupied in acquiring every knowledge of the distant regions we are to visit." [16] Earlier ages had honored ancient wisdom, sacred tradition, and secluded meditation as appropriate ways to gather information. The Enlightenment challenged the notion of thought isolated from direct experience. Captain William Bligh, master of Cook's ship *Resolution* and an explorer in his own right, insisted that mapping errors "arose only from sheer ignorance not knowing how to investigate the fact and it is a disgrace to us Navigators to lay down what does not exist." [17]

The Enlightenment also emphasized close observation and immediate participation, an approach surely congenial to exploration. Mungo Park, who explored West Africa at the end of the eighteenth century, made all this intensely personal. "I had a passionate desire to examine into the productions of a country so little known, and to become experimentally acquainted with the modes of life and the character of the natives." [18] The Cook voyages elevated to a guiding principle for scientific exploration what naturalist Georg Forster called "the rage of hunting after facts." Cook's scientists were to observe, measure, describe, and classify everything from prominent terrain features to plants and animals new to European scholars. Seeing the face of the country firsthand became fundamental to exploration. Cook's instructions repeated again and again one key phrase — "carefully observe." [19] The message was unmistakable. Explorers were not merely tourists seeking the picturesque. Rather, they were agents of science busy expanding the empire of the mind.

Not only were explorers to study nature at close quarters, they also were commanded to make painstaking records of all they saw. The Enlightenment taught that observation unrecorded was knowledge

---

15. Henry Steele Commager, "Jefferson and the Enlightenment," in Lally Weymouth, ed., *Thomas Jefferson; The Man, His World, His Influence* (New York: G. P. Putnam, 1973), 40.

16. Lamb, *Vancouver*, 4:1566.

17. Beaglehole, *Cook Journals*, 3:pt. 4, p. 1565.

18. Mungo Park, *Travels into the Interior of Africa* (London: J. Rennell, 1799), 1.

19. Beaglehole, *Cook Journals*, 3:pt. 1, p. ccxxiii; Georg Forster, *A Voyage round the World* (2 vols., London: J. Rennell, 1799), 1:xi.

lost. Travelers and adventurers in earlier times had kept fragmentary diaries and logs. The scientific spirit of the Enlightenment went further, demanding precise record-keeping. As Jefferson explained to one would-be explorer, science now required "very exact descriptions of what they see." [20]

As before, the Cook voyages set the pattern with three distinct kinds of records. Written accounts were in ships' logs, personal journals, and scientific and topographic descriptions. Many of these eventually were published in revised form, and at least six found places in Jefferson's extensive library. In an age before photography, painting and drawing were essential tools for scientific inquiry, and all the Cook voyages employed artists like John Webber, William Ellis, Alexander Buchan, and the incomparable Sydney Parkinson to document native life, topographic features, and important expedition events. Their illustrations comprise the first flowering of expedition art. In many ways George Catlin, Karl Bodmer, Richard Kern, and the artists of the Pacific Railroad Surveys followed paths already marked by those who sketched and painted for Cook. Maps and charts were a third category of records. Cook, his officers, and expedition draftsmen all worked on what were called "coastal profiles." These "views" and highly detailed hydrographic surveys remained an important part of Pacific navigation well into the twentieth century.

The Cook voyages also set an important precedent for the ownership and publication of expedition documents. At the end of each voyage, Cook was ordered to collect all records and specimens—except those held by civilian scientists—and deliver them to the admiralty. The royal government argued that because the voyages were a public enterprise backed by the national treasury, the records belonged to the state. Publication for personal profit might come later but the crown had first claim on the harvest of discovery. Jefferson agreed and in 1816 insisted that the Lewis and Clark journals were indeed public property. [21]

The Enlightenment gave explorers fresh missions, prepared them with the latest scientific methods, and then defined the purposes explorers' knowledge should serve. Here, then, was the third question that guided Enlightenment explorers. What should be done with so much data often collected at great risk? Information laboriously gathered from the close study of nature was not valued for its own sake. Enlightenment explorers and their patrons believed that knowl-

---

20. Jefferson to Charles Thompson, Paris, September 20, 1787, Jefferson Papers, Library of Congress, Washington, D.C. (hereafter Jefferson Papers).

21. Beaglehole, *Cook Journals*, 1:pt. 1, pp. cclxxxiii–iv, 2:pt. 1, pp. clxix–xlxx, 3:pt. 1, pp. ccxxiii–iv; Jefferson to Jose Correa da Serra, Monticello, January 1, 1816, Jefferson Papers.

Captain James Cook   (Public Archives of Canada, Ottawa)

edge found its true value in useful application. When Sir Joseph Banks and a small group of fellow scientists established the Royal Institution in 1799, they made clear this commitment to practical science. The Institution was dedicated to "the application of science to the common purposes of life." [22]

22.   David Mackay, "A Presiding Genius of Exploration: Banks, Cook, and Empire, 1767–1805," in Robin Fisher and Hugh Johnston, eds., *Captain James Cook and His Times* (Seattle: University of Washington Press, 1979), 26.

The word "useful" was everywhere in this age of discovery. Its spirit was expressed by Benjamin Franklin when he declared that "the knowledge of nature if well preserved seldom fails producing something useful to Man." [23] Franklin first suggested what later became the American Philosophical Society in a broadside aptly titled "A Proposal for Promoting Useful Knowledge Among the British Plantations in America." The American Philosophical Society itself put the phrase "useful knowledge" in its corporate title. Utility was the yardstick by which to measure everything—from a newly discovered plant to a national revolution.

For explorers "useful knowledge" meant many things. The phrase certainly had territorial dimensions. Reporting on the successful conclusion of the first Cook voyage, London's *Public Advertiser* confidently announced that "the territories of Great Britain will be widely extended in consequence of those Discoveries." [24] Exploration science was expected to expand the boundaries of empire. Banks, like Jefferson, had an enduring interest in economic botany. A clearer understanding of new plants, animals, and mineral resources might spark and sustain a growing empire.

"Useful knowledge" also played a key role in the increased pace of privately funded, corporate-sponsored exploration. Nowhere was this clearer than in the connection between the fur trade and North American exploration. Journeys of discovery sponsored by the North West Company and John Jacob Astor's Pacific Fur Company sought useful geographic knowledge, knowledge that would show itself in the warehouse and on the ledger. Alexander Ross, a notable Astorian and chronicler of fur trade exploration, made all the connections between knowledge, empire, and business in the following lines: "The progress of discovery contributes not a little to the enlightenment of mankind; for mercantile interest stimulates curiosity and adventure, and combines with them to enlarge the circle of knowledge. To the spirit of enterprise developed in the service of commercial speculation, civilized nations owe not only wealth and territorial acquisitions, but also their acquaintance with the earth and its productions." [25]

No single exploratory venture more fully represented these Enlightenment ideas than the three Pacific voyages led by Captain James Cook. The Cook journeys did more than merely symbolize the union of empire, science, and discovery. They set a standard of pro-

---

23. J. A. Leo Lemay, ed., *Benjamin Franklin Writings* (New York: Library of America, 1987), 357.

24. Beaglehole, *Cook Journals*, 1:pt. 2, p. 652.

25. Alexander Ross, *Adventures of the First Settlers on the Oregon or Columbia River, 1810–1813* with an introduction by James P. Ronda (1849; reprint, Lincoln: University of Nebraska Press, 1986), 34.

fessionalism and a model of organization that Jefferson sought to match. The Cook model was built on the notion of exploration as a carefully planned, large-scale enterprise. In each of the Cook voyages, British government officials joined forces with members of the Royal Society and the Royal Institution. That collaboration produced detailed institutions, a program of discovery that led Cook's expeditions to probe every aspect of the natural world. Unlike earlier explorations that went in search of a single objective, the Cook voyages were directed by a highly flexible, multifaceted concept of exploration. Professional scientific observers such as Banks, Johann Reinhold and Georg Forster, and David Nelson accompanied each Cook journey. Their presence represented the alliance between science and exploration, a connection that Jefferson put at the heart of his exploration design. The Cook expeditions were a national enterprise, using public funds, ships, and men. In size, scale, and scope, exploration had entered the modern age. Naturalist Johann R. Forster characterized the vision behind the Cook voyages as "so extensive and noble a plan." [26]

It was the notion of a plan that most appealed to Jefferson. Like so many others in the Enlightenment, he believed that any inquiry needed to follow a logical step-by-step program. He fully accepted the Enlightenment scheme of questions and answers, a format that would move an investigator forward to reach universal generalizations. Jefferson's only published book, *Notes on Virginia*, followed that comprehensive approach. The possibilities for such studies in North America seemed boundless. "The Botany of America is far from being exhausted, its Mineralogy is untouched, and its Natural History, or Zoology, totally mistaken and misrepresented." [27] In an age of plans, projects, and schemes, Jefferson knew that American exploration could advance only if it followed a carefully charted course.

Jefferson became aware of the Cook approach in two ways. His ever-growing library was filled with volumes on travel and exploration. By the end of the 1780s Jefferson had six of the Cook accounts on his shelves. [28] Perhaps the most important was John Rickman's *Journal of Captain Cook's Last Voyage to the Pacific*, published in 1781. A lieutenant on board the *Discovery*, Rickman had an intimate knowledge of exploration in the Cook style. His detailed account of Cook's reconnaissance along the Northwest coast in the spring and summer of 1778 undoubtedly interested Jefferson. Reading the Cook

26. Hoare, *Forster*, 3:439.

27. Jefferson to Joseph Willard, Paris, March 24, 1789, Jefferson Papers.

28. E. Millicent Sowerby, comp., *The Catalogue of the Library of Thomas Jefferson* (5 vols., Washington, D. C: Library of Congress, 1952–1959), 4:146–49.

narratives taught him important lessons about expedition planning and organization. How well those lessons were learned became clear in the winter of 1802 when the Lewis and Clark Expedition began to take shape.

Jefferson knew about the Cook enterprises through the world of print, but he had personal knowledge as well. In Paris, as American ambassador to the French court, the Virginian grew closer to the intellectual and official centers of Enlightenment exploration. Goaded into action by Cook's great achievements in the Pacific, the French government mounted its own probe of the South Seas. Jean François de Lapérouse, an experienced naval officer, was to the French what James Cook was to the British. The Lapérouse expedition was a full-fledged scientific venture, something Banks recognized when he lent the French explorer some of Cook's instruments. Jefferson eventually heard of the voyage, feared that it might signal the renewal of French imperial designs on North America, and detailed John Paul Jones to scout Lapérouse's intentions. His report allayed Jefferson's fears since French officials seemed more interested in the South Pacific than the Northwest coast. At the same time, he received a detailed account of how French planners put Cook's scientific emphasis at the heart of their enterprise. It was a lesson not lost on the American diplomat. [29]

Jefferson became even more familiar with the Cook tradition through John Ledyard. Born in Connecticut in 1751, Ledyard served as corporal of marines on Cook's third voyage. The Yankee adventurer took part in the beginnings of the lucrative sea otter trade between the Northwest coast and China and by the mid-1780s was deeply involved in several schemes to exploit that trade. One of Ledyard's proposals was a west-to-east expedition across Siberia and through North America. Both Jefferson and Banks got letters from the eager adventurer asking for money and personal support. Through both the Lapérouse and Ledyard ventures Jefferson grew closer to the world of the great navigator Cook. [30]

President Thomas Jefferson always summered at Monticello. It was a time to escape Washington's oppressive heat and the press of national business. Those summer days offered a chance to read and reflect away from the clatter of provincial politics and local gossip. Sometime during the summer of 1802 Jefferson began to read Alexander Mackenzie's recently published *Voyages from Montreal*. Most of that volume was a dreary, ghost-written account of Mackenzie's

29. Donald Jackson, *Thomas Jefferson and the Stony Mountains: Exploring the West from Monticello* (Urbana: University of Illinois Press, 1981), 48–56.

30. Ibid., 45–48.

voyages to the Arctic and Pacific oceans. But a brief section at the end of the book pushed Jefferson into action.

Like Cook, Banks, and Vancouver, Mackenzie grasped the connection between exploration and the course of empire. What he proposed was a daring expansion of the British colonial domain through the West and on to the Pacific. One sentence alone must have caught the president's eye. "By opening this intercourse between the Atlantic and Pacific Oceans, and forming regular establishments through the interior, and at both extremes, as well as along the coasts and islands, the entire command of the fur trade of North America might be obtained." [31]

Jefferson immediately understood what the "entire command of the fur trade" really meant. Mackenzie was not advocating a simple business venture. Generations of empire builders had used the fur trade to secure Indian allies, forestall potential imperial rivals, and expand territorial domain. The fur trade was always more than stacks of pelts and the whims of male fashion. The course of empire hung on the trade and Jefferson knew it.

But the Canadian explorer had more in mind than a fur trade empire. Mackenzie envisioned permanent colonies in the Northwest. These were the same lands that Jefferson believed would secure the agrarian future of the American republic. Mackenzie's bold plan was a challenge that could not be ignored. The president's response was to fashion an expedition in the Cook mold, a voyage of discovery inspired not so much by the American West as by the far reaches of the Pacific Ocean.

By the end of 1802 Jefferson was busy creating his own Cook expedition. At the center of the English voyages lay the premise that discovery was a national undertaking. Jefferson never doubted that his reply to the Mackenzie challenge should be a federally funded project using experienced military officers. The president's private secretary, Captain Meriwether Lewis, was selected to lead the expedition early in the planning process. [32] There is no evidence that Jefferson ever considered employing private traders or independent agents for the journey. He assumed that once government agents made initial reconnaissances, other explorers would follow in their tracks.

Jefferson knew that he could not precisely duplicate the size and scope of the Cook voyages. Maritime exploration required larger numbers of men and greater stores of supplies than an overland

---

31. W. Kaye Lamb, ed., *The Journals and Letters of Sir Alexander Mackenzie* (Cambridge: Hakluyt Society, 1970), 417.

32. "Lewis's Estimate of Expenses," late December 1802, Donald Jackson, ed., *Letters of the Lewis and Clark Expedition with Related Documents, 1783–1854*, 2nd ed. (2 vols., Urbana: University of Illinois Press, 1978), 1:8–9.

journey. Budget concerns alone made such large-scale enterprises unlikely. The Cook expeditions took along professional observers and trained artists. While Jefferson was committed to scientific exploration, he recognized the limitations imposed by a small and barely professional American scientific community. Banks and other European exploration planners could draw on a large pool of trained scholars and artists. Jefferson had far fewer choices. As he later explained, "these expeditions are so laborious and hazardous, that men of science, used to the temperature and inactivity of their closet, cannot be induced to undertake them." [33] Jefferson readily acknowledged Lewis's scientific limitations but was also confident that later expeditions would include professionally trained observers. What seemed important now was an initial survey. Scientific exploration following the Cook tradition had to become a matter of federal policy. Subsequent ventures might more fully match the ambitious English, Spanish, and French efforts.

The Cook voyages emphasized not only national financing but the central role of comprehensive instructions for each voyage. Since the Enlightenment advanced a sweeping definition of nature, explorers' guidelines were equally wide-ranging. While directions for specific Cook expeditions were never published, even a casual reading of printed narratives reveals the broad outlines of those documents. Jefferson's first experiment in instruction writing came when he drafted directions for André Michaux's abortive 1793 journey to the Pacific. Those who planned Cook's expeditions consistently gave him one key goal — to find the southern continent or the Northwest Passage — and then many secondary missions. Jefferson followed that pattern. Michaux was directed to locate the best passage across the continent to the Pacific. On the way he was to observe and record everything from Indian life and cultures to new plants and animals. In that western land of wonders Jefferson hoped the intrepid Frenchman would encounter packs of llamas, traces of the great mammoth, and exotic things "useful or very curious." [34]

Although the Michaux expedition failed when the explorer abruptly changed his loyalties, the effort did give Jefferson important practical experience in expedition planning. When he came to draft instructions for Lewis during the spring of 1803 the Cook tradition was the guiding force. Jefferson drew up a preliminary document and then circulated it among scientifically inclined friends and political advisers both in and out of official Washington. Working from suggestions made by those experts, he moved to prepare what

33. Jefferson to C. F. de C. Volney, Washington, February 11, 1806, Jefferson Papers.
34. Jackson, *Letters*, 2:670.

became the charter for federal exploration in the West. Like Cook, Lewis and Clark were given one central mission. Using words now familiar to every student of western exploration, Jefferson told his captains to "explore the Missouri river, and such principal stream of it, as, by it's course and communication with the waters of the Pacific ocean, whether the Columbia, Oregan, Colorado or any other river may offer the most direct and practicable water communication across this continent for the purposes of commerce." [35]

Just as Cook's journeys had many missions, however, Jefferson gave Lewis and Clark generous marching orders. England's Royal Society had once instructed sailors bound across the seas to "study Nature rather than Books." [36] Jefferson wanted his explorers to "study Nature" in the largest sense. A careful reading of his instructions reveals seven areas of scientific investigation. Geographic observation in the Cook tradition was of major importance. Jefferson ordered his captains to take careful note of landforms, waterways, and portages. The American Garden — Jefferson's hopeful image of the West — had to be plotted, marked, and measured just as Cook had charted the vast Pacific. The Enlightenment had a special passion for studying non-European, supposedly "primitive" peoples. Most European scholars, including Jefferson, believed that all cultures went through an evolutionary process that began with hunting societies and ended with "civilized" farmers. To study Indians was to study "civilized" man at the earliest stages of cultural development.

There was a certain touchy nationalism in Jefferson's injunction to study native cultures. Some European scholars had argued that the American environment had a degenerative effect on all living things. Since native people were the most representative part of the American landscape, patriotism demanded that science vindicate Indian physical and mental accomplishments. Lewis and Clark were to examine every aspect of native life, from daily routines and "ordinary occupations" to diplomacy and political leadership. Jefferson hoped his expedition ethnographers might gather a virtual compendium of Native American life. In this he was not disappointed.

Along with geographic description and ethnography were what Jefferson termed "other objects worthy of notice." Those "other objects" amounted to an ambitious scientific program. Geology, botany, and zoology led the list followed by archaeology and climatology. Cook's instructions contained similar lists, but for the American explorers the full burden of scientific inquiry fell on a few

---

35. Ibid., 1:61.
36. Bernard Smith, *European Vision and the South Pacific, 1768–1850*, rev. ed. (New Haven: Yale University Press, 1985), 8.

shoulders. Despite other pressing responsibilities, Lewis and Clark managed to observe, describe, and collect in most of the categories Jefferson prescribed. And it needs to be remembered that the instructions drafted for Lewis and Clark were not just for one expedition but would serve as the master agenda for all subsequent federal enterprises.

The eighteenth century was equally an age of exploration and an age of rival empires. In the struggle for political and economic dominion, explorers were the vanguard of empire. Cook's voyages were a British imperial thrust into the Pacific. Instructions for each of his voyages emphasized both economic expansion and the direct acquisition of territory. The phrase "commerce and navigation," so common in the writings of Cook, Banks, and Vancouver, always carried the implications of empire. Jefferson fully embraced the relationship between exploration and territorial expansion. Lewis and Clark were to find a passage through the American garden "for the purposes of commerce." The president believed that unlimited western lands might secure future generations the blessings of rural life and republican virtue. But without an adequate transportation system to foreign markets, American farmers and settlers would never march beyond the Mississippi. Jefferson expected the American nation to eventually stretch from Atlantic to Pacific. Although he sometimes talked about separate eastern and western republics, all of Jefferson's presidential actions pointed toward a single continental nation. Like Cook and Vancouver, Lewis and Clark aimed at being soldiers of empire.

Moving through all of this was Jefferson's conception of his own role in exploration. After the first Cook voyage, Sir Joseph Banks emerged as Britain's most powerful advocate of scientific exploration. As president of the Royal Society and informal advisor to several branches of government, Banks was perfectly placed to encourage voyages of discovery. One young English explorer called Banks "the common Center of we discoverers." [37] J. C. Beaglehole, Cook's great twentieth-century biographer, has aptly characterized Banks as a "presiding genius of exploration." [38] In many ways Jefferson became an American Banks. The two men corresponded on matters of common scientific concern, and both shared an interest in botany. Both served as president of their respective scientific institutions, recognizing the need for organization in modern scholarly inquiry. Most important, Jefferson borrowed Banks's strategy of coordinated explor-

---

37. James King to Joseph Banks, October 1780, quoted in Mackay, "A Presiding Genius of Exploration," 29.

38. J. C. Beaglehole, *The Life of Captain James Cook* (London: Hakluyt Society, 1974), 291.

ation. Banks believed that successful exploration involved the systematic efforts of several ships or parties. Cook was an early convert to this approach and used it on his second and third voyages. As a patron of exploration Jefferson pursued the same design. By late 1803 he had developed a complex strategy for western exploration.

Jefferson's ambitious plan envisioned four distinct expeditions. Lewis and Clark would pursue the most ambitious assignment, the search for the Pacific passage. A second party would push up the Mississippi and then explore overland toward the Missouri. A third expedition would conduct a reconnaissance of the Red and Arkansas rivers, while the fourth group would probe present-day Minnesota. Journeys by Zebulon Montgomery Pike, William Dunbar, and the Freeman-Custis party fulfilled at least some of these complex objectives. Both Jefferson and Banks understood that the voyages of discovery had meaning beyond the drama and excitement of travel and adventure. As advocates of a new kind of exploration, both men expected voyages of discovery to yield empires of power and intellect. The Lewis and Clark Expedition was sometimes called the Corps of Discovery. Actually, Jefferson's real Corps of Discovery was more than a single expedition. He made it so by becoming the American Banks and joining himself to the Cook tradition.

Early in March 1803, Secretary of the Treasury Albert Gallatin wrote Jefferson telling the president that he was busy marking the routes of Cook and Vancouver on a large blank map. [39] Soon enough that map would have the lines of American explorers as well. Those American expeditions were shaped by a larger tradition, the voyages of the ships *Endeavor, Resolution, Adventure,* and *Discovery.* Lewis and Clark knew as much when they made places for themselves in what one of Cook's lieutenants called "the old trade of exploring." [40]

THE GREATER CORPS OF DISCOVERY

Thomas Jefferson once called the Lewis and Clark expedition his Corps of Discovery. By the time the president ordered his captains west to the Pacific the ranks of that company were already filled with enterprising adventurers from many countries. Exploration had become a global endeavor well before Lewis and Clark made their overland journey. The senior members of the larger Corps of

---

39. Albert Gallatin to Jefferson, Washington, March 14, 1803, Jefferson Papers.
40. Charles Clerke to Banks, Cape of Good Hope, November 23, 1776, Beaglehole, *Cook Journals,* 3:pt. 4, p. 1519.

Discovery were the English maritime explorers James Cook and George Vancouver. They represented a professionalism, skill, and experience that others could only hope to match.

No single explorer more fully dominated his era than James Cook. Born in humble beginnings on a Yorkshire farm, Cook seemed destined to spend a life of landlocked labor. Opportunity came when Cook's father sent him to apprentice with a grocer in the English fishing port of Staithes. It was the sea, not shopkeeping, that attracted Cook, and in 1746 he joined the merchant firm of John and Henry Walker. The Walkers were shipowners at the port of Whitby and active in the coastal coal trade. Cook learned seamanship aboard the coal colliers. Here the lessons were of wind, weather, tide, and current. Ashore he studied mathematics. In 1755 Cook was offered command of a coal collier but instead joined the Royal Navy as a common seaman. His extraordinary abilities advanced him quickly, and by 1759 he was master of a naval vessel. During the 1760s the Admiralty ordered Cook to conduct detailed surveys of the waters off Labrador, Nova Scotia, and Newfoundland. His outstanding work on those complex surveys made Cook the prime candidate to lead what would eventually be three epic voyages of discovery to the Pacific. Cook died in 1779, the victim of a tragic encounter with Hawaiian natives.

Cook's voyages provided a school for many future explorers. No one was a better pupil than George Vancouver. In 1772, at fourteen, Vancouver joined the crew of Cook's ship, *Resolution*. A journey of three years taught him the fundamentals of seamanship and an appreciation for the scientific reconnaissance Cook exemplified. Vancouver served aboard the *Discovery* on Cook's third Pacific venture. In 1791 Vancouver was given command of a major expedition ordered to chart large portions of the north Pacific. That voyage, lasting until 1795, put Vancouver in the highest ranks of Enlightenment explorers.

For the great European powers of the late eighteenth-century, exploration of the Pacific was a growing priority. Both French and Spanish expeditions followed in the wake of Cook. French efforts were led by Jean François de Lapérouse. An experienced naval officer, Lapérouse had been deeply influenced by the Cook tradition. What Cook had done was not lost on a French government eager to expand national power and glory. King Louis XVI and Minister of Marine Charles Claret designed a Pacific expedition much like Cook's final journey. With two ships and considerable scientific gear, Lapérouse sailed the Pacific in the years 1786–1788. Sometime during 1788 his fleet came to grief north of the New Hebrides with the loss of all hands.

Spain's response to Cook and Lapérouse came with the Malaspina expedition of 1791–1792. Like so many others in the greater Corps of Discovery, Alejandro Malaspina was a well-traveled naval officer. He was profoundly influenced by earlier English and French voyages and in the late 1780s offered Spanish authorities a plan for a similar enterprise. With two ships and an impressive group of artists and scientists, the Malaspina expedition conducted a comprehensive survey of the Pacific coast from California to Alaska.

The American branch of the Enlightenment Corps of Discovery could not compare with the European company in scientific education, formal organization, and official funding. The United States would not mount anything as complex as the Cook voyages until the Wilkes expedition of 1838–1842. Nevertheless, Jefferson's explorers did share much with their fellow adventurers. Attracted to the Pacific as the last great imperial frontier, the European nations employed naval officers as explorers. In North America the exploration frontier was not the space of sea but the space of land. Army officers were Jefferson's logical choices. Meriwether Lewis, William Clark, and Zebulon Montgomery Pike all came to western exploration by way of the profession of arms. Lewis joined the Virginia militia during the 1794 Whiskey Rebellion and entered the regular army the following year. In 1796 he was assigned to the First Infantry Regiment and served at paymaster and recruiting duties. Although other young officers saw much action during the Ohio Indian wars of the 1790s, Lewis gained no combat experience. What would have been a routine career took a dramatic turn in 1801 when Jefferson selected Lewis his private secretary. Far too much has been made of Lewis's scientific abilities. Largely self-taught, he was a keen amateur naturalist but surely no match for his European contemporaries. Nor is there compelling evidence that Lewis spent time studying scientific subjects at Jefferson's Monticello library.

William Clark's military career far better suited him for exploration than did Lewis's limited experience. Son of a distinguished military family, the young Clark followed in the footsteps of his older brother George Rogers Clark. William Clark's Ohio Indian wars service included covert diplomatic missions and several engagements under hostile fire. As a soldier, he learned the value of planning and careful organization. More important, Clark became a skilled cartographer and adept diplomat. Those abilities would be put to good use on the way to the Pacific.

Lewis and Clark came as close as any Americans to full membership in the greater Corps of Discovery. Zebulon Montgomery Pike aspired to join the ranks but like so many other things in his short life, doing so was a dream unfulfilled. Son of a respected army officer, Pike was an ambitious young lieutenant burdened by an inadequate education and an inflated sense of his own importance. While others who sought admission to the global Corps of Discovery read national history and studied mathematics, Pike pored over volumes on strategy and tactics. What promised to be a lackluster career was suddenly changed in 1805 when General James Wilkinson selected Pike to lead two western expeditions, one up the Mississippi (1805–1806) and the second into the Southwest (1806–1807). Pike hoped those journeys would bring him a measure of the acclaim being showered on Lewis and Clark. But unfortunate circumstances—the loss of his papers, his own weak education, and an accidental link to the Wilkinson-Burr plot—conspired to make such praise elusive. Pike was killed in 1813 during the War of 1812.

Faced with a shallow pool of talent for his Corps of Discovery, Jefferson was forced to use civilians for his important explorations of the Red River country. Questions of diplomacy and defense required accurate information about the Red River and the boundaries between Louisiana and Spanish territories. Jefferson entrusted much of the planning to William Dunbar, a successful Natchez planter. Dunbar had wide-ranging interests, including medicine, botany, and astronomy. Others associated with the ultimately unsuccessful Red River efforts included surveyor Thomas Freeman and naturalist Peter Custis. While these voyages did not produce what Jefferson had in mind, they did represent one more effort to pattern American exploration on European Enlightenment models.

JPR

Bibliographic Essay

Few periods in exploration history have produced so rich a harvest of personal accounts, narratives, diaries, letters, maps, and graphic records as the years between the 1760s and the 1820s. That era saw the passion of the scientist for precise detail blend with the romantic curiosity of the traveler to see and describe what seemed strange, remote, and exotic. The result is a literature of discovery that is both scientifically accurate and deeply personal. In those documents of discovery modern readers can relive the encounters of peoples and cultures, encounters that continue to shape our world.

There is no better way to participate in the Age of Cook than to read the day-by-day journals kept by Cook and others during the three great Pacific expeditions. J. C. Beaglehole, ed., *The Journals of Captain James Cook on His Voyages of Discovery* (4 vols., Cambridge: Hakluyt

Society, 1955-1969) is the keystone collection for the whole era. Cook's ablest successor was Captain George Vancouver. The documents for Vancouver's ambitious maritime exploring journey are in W. Kaye Lamb, ed., *The Voyage of George Vancouver 1791-1795* (4 vols., Cambridge: Hakluyt Society, 1984). Land explorers soon followed the Cook tradition. The two Mackenzie expeditions (1789 and 1792-93) are recounted in W. Kaye Lamb, ed., *The Journals and Letters of Sir Alexander Mackenzie* (Cambridge: Hakluyt Society, 1970). Among the Canadian fur traders who advanced the Cook tradition none was more important than David Thompson. Richard Glover, ed., *David Thompson's Narrative, 1784-1812* (Toronto: Champlain Society, 1962), prepared by the explorer late in life, is the best edition of recollections. Most of Thompson's original journals remain unpublished.

The journals and diaries of Jefferson's explorers are readily available in superbly edited volumes. The new *Journals of the Lewis and Clark Expedition*, ably edited by Gary E. Moulton and published by the University of Nebraska Press, supersedes all previous editions. Donald Jackson once wrote that it is no longer useful to think of the Lewis and Clark expedition as the efforts of two men. Jackson's indispensable *Letters of the Lewis and Clark Expedition and Related Documents, 1783-1854*, 2nd ed., (2 vols., Urbana: University of Illinois Press, 1978) illustrates how deeply the Cook tradition dominated Jefferson's thinking about western exploration. The American explorations of the Red and Arkansas river country are documented in Dan Flores, *Jefferson and Southwestern Exploration: The Freeman and Custis Accounts of the Red River Expedition of 1806* (Norman: University of Oklahoma Press, 1984). Zebulon Montgomery Pike aspired to the Cook tradition, with a dash of the great Alexander von Humboldt. The definitive edition of Pike's writings is Donald Jackson, ed., *The Journals of Zebulon Montgomery Pike with Letters and Related Documents* (2 vols., Norman: University of Oklahoma Press, 1966). The last of the Jeffersonian expeditions is traced in Maxine Benson, *From Pittsburgh to the Rocky Mountains: Major Stephen Long's Expedition, 1819-1820* (Golden, Colorado: Fulcrum Press, 1988).

The scholarly literature analyzing exploration in the Age of Cook is vast and varied. The following works provide good introductions to the period: William Goetzmann, *New Lands, New Men: America and the Second Great Age of Discovery* (New York: Viking, 1986), 1-60; Richard A. Van Orman, *The Explorers: Nineteenth Century Expeditions in Africa and the American West* (Albuquerque: University of New Mexico Press, 1984); P. J. Marshall and Glyndwr Williams, *The Great Map of Mankind: Perceptions of New Worlds in the Age of Enlightenment* (Cambridge: Harvard University Press, 1982). Several important books on the Cook voyages enhance our appreciation of those expeditions and their

American counterparts. Among the best recent studies are: Hugh Cobbe, *Cook and the Peoples of the Pacific* (London: British Museum, 1979); Robin Fisher and Hugh Johnston, eds., *Captain James Cook and His Times: Some New Perspectives* (Seattle: University of Washington Press, 1979); David Mackay, *In the Wake of Cook: Exploration, Science, and Empire, 1780–1801* (New York: St. Martin's Press, 1985); Bernard Smith, *European Vision and the South Pacific, 1768–1850,* rev. ed. (New Haven: Yale University Press, 1985); Lynne Withey, *Voyages of Discovery: Captain Cook and the Exploration of the Pacific* (Berkeley: University of California Press, 1989). An important Spanish dimension to all these expeditions can be found in Iris W. Engstrand, *Spanish Scientists in the New World: The Eighteenth-Century Expeditions* (Seattle: University of Washington Press, 1981).

A Crow camp on the Little Bighorn River near Crow Agency in November 1887 during the Sword Bearer incident. (Montana Historical Society Photograph Archives)

Sword Bearer and the 'Crow Outbreak,' 1887

Colin G. Calloway

The United States government's creation of tribal reservations in the nineteenth century, and the ofttimes forced movement of Native Americans onto those reservations, had a profound impact on the history of Montana. Numerous Indian tribes, of course, lost access to and control over much of their traditional lands. In addition, specific government actions, such as the 1887 Dawes Act, frequently stripped tribes of what little political power they retained, while also attacking key cultural institutions and beliefs.

The harshness of life on the reservations was not limited to those tribes that had traditionally been antagonistic toward white encroachment on their lands—such as the Sioux and the Blackfeet. Conditions for the Crow Indians, a tribe that historically had cooperated with the United States government, were equally grim. As professor of history in the University of Wyoming, Colin G. Calloway, remarks, "during the late 1880s, the Crow were a people in crisis, living amid the ruins of their former world." The government's political, economic, and cultural assaults upon the Crow lifestyle not only created rising tensions between government agents and the tribe, but even more tragically, governmental policies and actions served as catalysts for factional fighting between different tribal groups. The following essay recounts one such episode that has been overlooked all too frequently in the history of Indian-white relations.

In the sweep of western history, the "Sword Bearer incident" has received little more than passing mention. Sandwiched in time and dwarfed in magnitude by dramatic and bloody encounters at

*Colin G. Calloway, "Sword Bearer and the 'Crow Outbreak,' 1887," *Montana The Magazine of Western History*, 36 (Autumn 1986), 38–51.

Little Bighorn and Wounded Knee, the actions of Sword Bearer, an obscure Crow medicine man, and the suppression of his brief rebellion might easily be overlooked. An uprising of members of a tribe with a record of peaceful relations with whites a full decade after the suppression of hostilities on the northern plains, however, demands some explanation.

To some observers, Sword Bearer was merely an imposter and a troublemaker who played on the superstitions of his people, with the U.S. Army applying some well-timed military force to put an end to the disturbance. Others saw Sword Bearer as a visionary who touched deep discontents among the Indians of the northern plains; contemporaries identified the Sword Bearer affair as a test case of the old and the new. Young warriors responded to Sword Bearer's vision. In a brief but dramatic demonstration of support, they directly challenged the authority of government agents who sought to eradicate traditional ways and of older chiefs who advocated compromise and accommodation.

On August 31, 1887, just a month before Sword Bearer threw the Crow Indian Reservation into upheaval, Crow Agent Henry E. Williamson submitted his annual report to the Commissioner of Indian Affairs. Progress was "slow, very slow indeed," he reported, but he was confident that with capable and conscientious agents great strides could be made toward "civilizing" the Crow. Williamson predicted that the agency would

> at no very distant day . . . be dotted by farms with comfortable buildings and exhibiting all the improvements necessary to enable the Indians to maintain themselves in comfort whenever the Government shall withdraw its fostering hand.

The Billings *Daily Gazette* shared the agent's optimistic views. People accustomed to seeing the "thieving Indians" loafing around Billings, the newspaper claimed, would be pleasantly surprised by a visit to the agency, about sixty-five miles to the east of the Little Bighorn River, where the "traditional blanket is discarded . . . and the youthful farmers appear in civilized garb with clipped hair." [1] But Williamson and the *Daily Gazette* were neglecting some deep-seated problems on the Crow Indian Reservations.

---

1. Report of Henry E. Williamson, August 31, 1887, in Commissioner of Indian Affairs, *Annual Report*, 50th Cong., 1st sess., 1887, H. Ex. Doc. 1, pt. 5 (Serial 2542), 215–18; Billings *Daily Gazette*, October 11, 1887. See also Billings *Daily Gazette*, October 3, 13, 1887. The author is grateful to Frederick E. Hoxie, director of the D'Arcy McNickle Center for the History of the American Indian, for his comments on a preliminary version of this paper.

During the late 1880s, the Crow were a people in crisis, living amid the ruins of their former world. For over a century, Crow warriors had battled to hold their rich tribal heartland against numerous and powerful enemies. The end of intertribal conflicts and the military subjugation of the Sioux in the late 1870s had brought a measure of security to the Crow, but life on the reservation had imposed even greater strains on their culture and further tested their resilience. Crow warriors lacked outlets for traditional ambitions, such as attaining prowess in battle and in hunting, and found little meaning in reservation life. The last bison herd had disappeared in 1884, and formerly mobile and prosperous Crow were reduced to depending on the federal government, while influenza, tuberculosis, and bronchitis thinned their numbers.

Crow society came under increasingly strenuous attack from government agents, missionaries, schoolteachers, farmers, and "friends of the Indian." Impatient reformers shared the opinion expressed in 1884 by Crow Agent Henry J. Armstrong that attempts "to *coax* or *persuade* the Indians to forsake their heathenish life" were futile and should give way to imposed change and compulsion. During 1883–1884, Armstrong oversaw the relocation of the Crow agency over one hundred and twenty miles east to the valleys of the Little Bighorn and Bighorn rivers, "that portion of their reservation most favorable for agriculture, so that they might settle down and do something for themselves." [2]

The campaign to transform Indians into self-supporting U.S. citizens who could "do something for themselves" culminated in passage of the Dawes General Allotment Act in February 1887. The act's primary purpose was to terminate tribal ownership of lands, distribute plots to individual families, and open "surplus" lands to white settlers. Several Sioux leaders, including Sitting Bull, protested the Dawes Act and visited tribes in the northern Rockies and the Great Plains to urge resistance to the allotment plan. Agent James H. Howard's allotment committee made little headway among the Crow during the summer of 1887, and there were disturbances that fall at the Yankton, Crow Creek, and Lower Brulé agencies. Many Crow feared that the government intended to dispossess them of their remaining lands. [3]

2. Francis Paul Prucha, ed., *Americanizing the American Indians: Writings by the "Friends of the Indian," 1880–1890* (Lincoln: University of Nebraska Press, 1978); Report of H. S. Armstrong, August 31, 1884, in Commissioner of Indian Affairs, *Annual Report*, 48th Cong., 2d sess., 1884, H. Ex. Doc. 1, pt. 5 (Serial 2287), 152–55.

3. Report of Brigadier General Thomas Howard Ruger, September 15, 1888, in Secretary of War, *Annual Report*, 50th Cong., 2d sess., 1888, H. Ex. Doc. 1, pt. 2 (Serial 2628), 151; Billings *Daily Gazette*, October 11, 15, 3, 1887.

Tensions grew at the Crow agency when the Indians accused Agent Williamson of peculation, heavy drinking, and violent and threatening behavior. Controversy over allocation of grazing privileges and trespass by white hunters added to the friction on the reservation; and, as often happened at times of unrest, "squaw men" came under attack as troublemakers who were opposed to dividing up the land.[4] On September 30, thirty days after Agent Williamson had submitted his reassuring report, a young warrior named Cheez-tah-paezh gave the lie to the agent's claim that all was well in the Crow agency.

Cheez-tah-paezh, or Wraps-Up-His-Tail, was about twenty-four years old in 1887. He was probably half-Bannock and seems to have enjoyed no special status among the Crow before that summer.[5] Although the reason for his sudden prominence is not clear, like other Indian visionaries Cheez-tah-paezh underwent some kind of spiritual experience that induced him to see himself as a prophet and savior of his people.

During the summer of 1887, several young Crow warriors participated in a sun dance held by the Cheyenne, and Cheez-tah-paezh apparently displayed such courage that the Cheyenne presented him with a red medicine saber. Other accounts report that he performed the sun dance at one of the Sioux agencies. Cheez-tah-paezh himself claimed that he received the sword from the Great Spirit during a vision in which he saw the Son of the Morning Star fell trees with a sweep of his saber. Interpreting this to mean that U.S. soldiers would fall before his sword, Cheez-tah-paezh maintained that he and his followers were immune from injury as long as he carried the weapon.[6]

---

4.   Billings *Daily Gazette*, October 3, 1887; St. Paul *Pioneer Press*, quoted in Billings *Daily Gazette*, October 10, 1887; Ruger to Assistant Adjutant General, November 30, 1887, *Letters Received by the Office of the Adjutant General, 1881–1889*, AGO 1887, M–689, Roll 557 (hereafter AGO), National Archives, Washington, D.C.; Billings *Daily Gazette*, October 19, 20, 1887. See also William T. Hagan, "Squaw Men on the Kiowa, Comanche and Apache Reservation: Advance Agents of Civilization or Disturbers of the Peace?" in *The Frontier Challenge: Responses to the Trans-Mississippi West*, ed. John G. Clark (Lawrence: University Press of Kansas, 1971), 171–202.

5.   Richard Upton, ed., *Fort Custer on the Big Horn, 1877–1898: Its History and Personalities as Told and Pictured by Its Contemporaries* (Glendale, Calif.: Arthur H. Clark Company, 1973),131; Glendolin Damon Wagner and William A. Allen, *Blankets and Moccasins: Plenty Coups and His People, the Crows* (Caldwell, Idaho: Caxton Printers, 1936), 236.

6.   Special Agent James R. Howard to Commissioner of Indian Affairs, October 8, 1887, AGO; *Harpers Weekly*, November 5, 1887, p. 803; Billings *Daily Gazette*, October 8, 1887; Upton, *Fort Custer*, 155; Mark H. Brown, *Plainsmen of the Yellowstone* (Lincoln: University of Nebraska Press, 1969), 441. Contrary to legend, the sword was not a relic of the Battle of the Little Bighorn. See Wagner and Allen, *Blankets and Moccasins*, 238; Upton, *Fort Custer*, 155.

Cheez-tah-paezh took the name of "Sword Bearer" and began to cultivate a reputation as a medicine man and prophet. He impressed his followers with demonstrations of his supernatural power, which had been endowed on him by the Great Spirit and enabled him to predict storms and foretell unusual occurrences. Even Sword Bearer's enemies did not deny the accuracy of his predictions, choosing instead to formulate some logical explanation or to dismiss them as coincidence and good fortune.[7] Whites discounted Sword Bearer's claims as the fabrications of a charlatan; but in the Crow cosmos, where no gulf separated "natural" and "supernatural," his story was entirely credible. Visions played a crucial role in Crow life; and in every generation there were medicine men, or *batse maxpe*, who possessed outstanding powers.[8]

Sword Bearer soon attracted a following of discontented warriors seeking an escape from the despair of reservation life. The principal chief, Pretty Eagle, admitted that his people were in awe of Sword Bearer's medicine, and reports of his prowess and special powers even spread to the Cheyenne.[9]

Sword Bearer and his friends had given the troops some trouble in June 1887 when the military had escorted Sioux visitors from the Rosebud off the Crow agency, and Agent Williamson had warned them against future "misconduct." Their discontent came to a head in September after Sword Bearer led twenty-two Crow warriors on a horse raid against the Piegan on the Blackfeet Indian Reservation in north-central Montana. Generations of conflict had entrenched horse stealing as an integral element of the warrior cult, and the practice was not easily set aside just because of the government's insistence that the tribes stick to their reservations and take up the plough. Only the year before, Crow raiders had driven off some two hundred horses from the Piegan, producing a Piegan counterraid into Crow country. Whites in Montana feared that the raiding would escalate and maintained that white ranchers inevitably lost stock whenever Indians went horse stealing.[10]

---

7. Wagner and Allen, *Blankets and Moccasins*, 238–39; Billings *Daily Gazette*, October 31, November 3, 4, 1887; Upton, *Fort Custer*, 162; Theodore Roosevelt, "In Cowboy Land," *Century Magazine*, 46 (June 1893), 283.

8. Robert H. Lowie, *The Crow Indians* (1935; reprint, New York: Holt, Rinehart and Winston, 1956), 170, 238.

9. Billings *Daily Gazette*, October 31, November 7, 1887; John Stands in Timber and Margot Liberty, *Cheyenne Memories* (Lincoln: University of Nebraska Press, 1972), 249–50.

10. Ruger to Assistant Adjutant General, November 30, 1887, AGO; Commissioner of Indian Affairs, *Annual Report*, 1887, p. 216; Billings *Daily Gazette*, September 30, October 5, 1887.

On September 30, Sword Bearer's band returned from their raid in triumph with some sixty Piegan horses. Their celebrations were particularly boisterous, and their behavior became threatening when they heard that Agent Williamson intended to arrest them. According to one version, Williamson's overreaction "fanned into quick flame the vindictive hatred toward himself which had for long been smoldering in the hearts of all of them." That evening, as preparations were in progress for issuing rations the next day, Sword Bearer and fifteen or sixteen warriors rode through the agency in full war paint and feathers. One group shot up the agency buildings and threatened Williamson and other agency employees; a warrior pointed his gun at the interpreter's chest and then fired directly over his head. [11]

The next day, October 1, Williamson sent for troops from Fort Custer and telegraphed the Commissioner of Indian Affairs urging the immediate arrest of the Indians. [12] Colonel Nathan A. M. Dudley, commanding officer at Fort Custer, dispatched Captain Max Wessendorf and 100 men of the 1st Cavalry to the agency. An advance squad of nine men arrived to find the Indians in a threatening mood, with the defiant raiders on a hill just west of the agency, ready for action. Young Crow warriors began to crowd the soldiers, evidently trying to force a fight. In this volatile situation, Major C. H. Barstow apparently strode calmly across the lawn and spoke with Crow chiefs Bull Nose, Medicine Crow, Fringe, Bull Chief, and Bull-Goes-Hunting. The chiefs, "forcing themselves between the two lines and raising their quirts beat such a tatoo upon the foreheads of the ponies that for the space of half a minute the proceedings were suggestive of a hailstorm." The Indians fell back and moved their old people, women, and children across the river. The immediate danger passed when Wessendorf and the main body of the troops arrived; but the warriors remained defiant, and Bull Nose had to exert his influence again that evening to avoid blood shed. [13]

---

11. Billings *Daily Gazette*, October 15, 1887; Report of the Lieutenant General of the Army, November 1, 1887, in Secretary of War, *Annual Report*, 50th Cong., 1st sess., H. Ex. Doc. 1, 1887 (Serial 2533), 73; Howard to Commissioner of Indian Affairs, October 8, 1887, AGO; Wagner and Allen, *Blankets and Moccasins*, 228, 242.

12. Telegram, Henry E. Williamson to Colonel Nathan A. M. Dudley, October 1, 1887, Crow Indian Agency Records, 1877–1894 Letterpress Book, September 30, 1887–February 9, 1888, Archives, Montana Historical Society, Helena (hereafter Crow Agency Records); Williamson to Commissioner John D. Atkins, October 1, 1887, AGO.

13. Report of General Ruger, 146, 151; Billings *Daily Gazette*, October 3, 15, 1887; Howard to Commissioner of Indian Affairs, October 8, 1887, AGO; Alexander Upshaw to Secretary of the Interior, October 14, 1887, ibid. Barstow's daughter, Elizabeth, gave her account of the incident in the Billings *Daily Gazette*, September 18, 1903; cited in Upton, *Fort Custer*, 159–66.

As tensions relaxed, the military force at the agency was reduced. The officers were under orders to protect agency employees and property and to make no arrests without further instructions. On October 3, Williamson instructed storekeepers at Fort Custer to sell no ammunition to Crow Indians. Colonel Dudley awaited orders from Washington, D. C., and assured Yellowstone citizens there was no danger. [14]

General Alfred E. Terry, Commander of the Division of the Missouri, and others distant from the scene recognized that the affair required sober consideration. Terry suspected that there were deeper causes to the trouble, especially since the Crow had been "loyal" to the United States throughout the Sioux wars. With conflicting reports coming out of the area, the government sent Special Agent Frank E. Armstrong to investigate. [15]

In Montana Territory, rumor and fear spread growing alarm at the prospect of an Indian uprising. Montanans believed that the government was slow in reacting to the confrontation, and the local press seized on the incident as a test case and a challenge to the authority of the Indian Department. The *Daily Gazette* declared that the authorities in Washington underestimated the gravity of the situation at the agency, where "a wide-spread and deep-seated dissatisfaction is prevalent among the Crows." The newspaper advocated swift punishment to teach the tribe a lesson they would not forget:

> The time for mawkish sentiment in these matters has gone by, and the stern hand of the law should never relax its hold on these Indians until the whole Crow tribe have a wholesome respect for its mandates inculcated into their rebellious hearts.

In the *Gazette's* opinion, the affair constituted another strong argument for throwing open the reservation to white settlement. [16]

By mid-October, the *Daily Gazette* reported, the trouble seemed to be spreading, with the allotment issue as a pretext for continuing the disorder. With total disregard for long-standing animosities between the Crow and the Sioux, the *Gazette* warned its readers that

14. Report of General Ruger, 146, 151; Williamson to Dudley, October 5, 1887, Crow Indian Agency Records; Billings *Daily Gazette*, October 5, 11, 1887; Williamson to Messrs. Borup and Co., October 3, [1887], Crow Indian Agency Records; Billings *Daily Gazette*, October 5, 1887.

15. General Alfred E. Terry to Adjutant General, October 1, 1887 AGO; Acting Secretary of War to Secretary of the Interior, October 4, 1887, ibid; Henry J. Armstrong to Secretary of the Interior, October 17, 1887, ibid. Two years before, Armstrong had warned that there would be trouble unless the government took steps to protect the Crow from Piegan marauders.

16. Billings *Daily Gazette*, October 3, 8, 1887.

a general outbreak embracing the several agencies in eastern Montana and western Dakota could be very serious:

> Over 12,000 Sioux bucks can be brought together at short notice, and it is claimed that Sitting Bull's influence over the Crows is such that he could cause them to rise at any time. . . .

To the north, Canadian Indian agents noted "a decidedly hostile spirit," which they were unable to control, among the Blood and Blackfeet Indians. The *Daily Gazette* interpreted these "signs of the times" as indications of the failure of U.S. Indian policy and hoped that the War Department would "use more vigorous measures to subdue this longing for paint and feathers." Nevertheless, the *Gazette* declared that some disturbances were inevitable before the Indians settled down for good:

> . . . like clearing up showers after a heavy storm, they will come and go, leaving a clearer understanding on the part of the Indian that to become a white man is the only alternative to extinction. [17]

The situation at the Crow agency remained tense. There were rumors of Piegan war parties, and the Crow began to set up their lodges around the agency for protection. Sword Bearer was reported to be in the mountains making medicine, while his followers held war dances and new recruits swelled their ranks daily. The rest of the tribe showed no sign of supporting the insurgents, and some said that many of the older Indians wanted Sword Bearer punished. The troops stood ready for trouble on ration day, but the day passed without incident. On October 8, Agent Howard submitted his report to the Commissioner of Indian Affairs, concluding that Sword Bearer "is a very bad Indian, and if he and his followers are not arrested, all the progress the Indians have made will be lost for years to come, and the whole Crow Nation completely demoralized." [18]

In mid-October, Sword Bearer came down from the mountains, where he had been talking with the spirits of his grandfathers, and camped with his followers about six miles south of Fort Custer. His band was reported to be "full of courage," but Colonel Dudley was confident that his soldiers could round up the malcontents in a few hours, once the authorities granted him permission. [19]

On October 18, the *Daily Gazette* reported that prompt and decisive action in arresting the ringleaders had stifled the incipient rebellion

---

17. Ibid., October 17, 1887.

18. Ibid., October 7, 8, 1887; Howard to Commissioner of Indian Affairs, October 8, 1887, AGO.

19. Billings *Daily Gazette*, October 18, 1887.

at the Brulé agency, where Indians were incensed at the surveying being carried out in preparation for allotment there. Here was a lesson for the slow-moving authorities near Billings:

> Nothing discourages the Indians more than a judicious display of force and the deprivation of such a band, of its leaders. These leaders are generally medicine men who have wrought themselves by torture and fasting into a state of reckless daring, but the main body do not partake of this suppositious invincibility, and when they see their prophet, their bullet proof leader, either dead or deprived of his liberty it cools their ardor for battle with the whites to such a degree that they want peace at any price.

Force was the only way to deal with Indians, claimed the newspaper: ". . . inculcate fear and obedience first and civilization afterwards." The *Gazette* headlines approval of prompt action taken by Special Agent Armstrong in expelling ten visiting Assiniboine from the reservation as the first step toward restoring order. [20]

On the evening of October 19, Agent Williamson penned a report of the day's news to Colonel Dudley. Interpreter Tom Stewart had interrogated the Crow chief of police, Boy That Grabs, and other members of the police force and had learned that Sword Bearer and about thirty "Bucks, Women & Children" had gone to the Cheyenne agency on Tongue River. Rumor in the Crow camp claimed that Sword Bearer had singled out four men at the agency who must die if any attempt was made to arrest him. The four were Boy That Grabs, interpreter Stewart, and Bull Nose and Old Dog because they had spoken for the whites when the trouble broke out. The Indians who had instigated the disturbance were at different places on the reservation, on the Little Bighorn and Bighorn rivers and on Pryor Creek. [21]

By the time news of the visit to Tongue River had reached the press, Sword Bearer's entourage was reputed to have grown considerably; he was soon reported to be leading as many as one hundred warriors in full war trappings. Apparently, Sword Bearer asked permission to hold a dance with the Cheyenne as a sign of friendship; but Two Moons, the Cheyenne chief, was eager to keep his people clear of the trouble and refused. The Crow may have hoped to secure a pledge of neutrality, if not outright assistance, from the Cheyenne in case they made a break; but the Cheyenne were unlikely to make common cause with their longtime Crow enemies. Even so, Brigadier General Thomas Howard Ruger, commanding the Department of the Dakota, was taking no chances and dispatched troops to the Tongue

---

20. Ibid.
21. Williamson to Dudley, October 19, 1887, Crow Agency Records.

River agency as soon as he heard that the disaffected Crow were making overtures to the Cheyenne. [22]

When the first reports of the disturbance at the Crow agency had reached Washington, Lieutenant General of the Army Phil Sheridan had traveled to St. Paul, intending to continue to Fort Custer if the crisis warranted. Once he received a full report from General Ruger, however, Sheridan decided that his personal intervention was unnecessary. He ordered Ruger to go to the trouble spot and assemble a force that would overawe the malcontents and render resistance impossible. Ruger was also to enlist about thirty Crow warriors as scouts "to further quiet the restless young men among them." Meanwhile, Special Agent Armstrong telegraphed his report to Secretary of the Interior L. Q. C. Lamar, confirming the substance of Howard's report and urging the arrest of Sword Bearer and his seventeen immediate followers. Lamar requested the War Department to take prompt action. [23]

On October 21, General Ruger left Fort Custer with orders to arrest the defiant Indians. It seemed unlikely that the Crow as a tribe would break into open hostility, but Ruger could not be certain of their sentiments and had no idea how many might try to resist the arrest of the insurgents. He decided to call in reinforcements before taking further action. A powerful concentration of troops was soon assembled at Fort Custer. Meanwhile, the forty soldiers stationed at the Crow agency had been digging trenches and throwing up earthworks in anticipation of an attack. [24]

As troops continued to arrive, it became clear that a showdown was imminent. One hundred and one families were missing on issue day, although their absence was attributed to fear rather than belligerence. The majority of the tribe had left their farms and houses and were gathered in large camps on the Bighorn and the Little Bighorn rivers. Scouts reported that Sword Bearer had about two hundred warriors with him and was camped on the Little Bighorn near the Custer battlefield. [25]

---

22. Billings *Daily Gazette*, October 24, 25, 1887; Miles City *Yellowstone Journal*, October 26, 1887, cited in Billings *Daily Gazette*, October 28, 1887; Report of General Ruger, 147, 152. First reports indicated that some thirty Indians had gone to Tongue River; the number then grew to fifty. Secretary of the Interior L. Q. C. Lamar to Secretary of War, October 20, 1887; Upshaw to Commissioner of Indian Affairs, October 20, 1887; Upshaw to Secretary of the Interior, October 22, 1887; Acting Secretary of the Interior to Secretary of War, October 22, 1887, AGO.

23. Secretary of War, *Annual Report*, 1887, p. 73; Billings *Daily Gazette*, October 24, 1887; Armstrong to Secretary of the Interior, October 17, 1887, AGO; Lamar to Secretary of War, October 18, 1887, ibid.

24. Report of General Ruger, 146-47, 152; Report of Brigadier General John R. Brooke, August 30, 1888, in Secretary of War, *Annual Report*, 50th Cong., 2d sess., 1888, H. Ex. Doc. 1 (Serial 2628), 173; Billings *Daily Gazette*, October 27, 1887.

25. Billings *Daily Gazette*, October 28, 29, 1887.

The troops at Fort Custer were preparing to take the field in a few days, weather permitting. Officers at the fort knew that "this is no boys' play"; no such preparations for war had been seen since 1876. From the first the *Daily Gazette* had identified the disturbance as "a vital question between the Indians and the government" and was happy to see vigorous measures adopted now. Displaying incredible ignorance of the Crow Indians' role during the 1876 campaigns, the *Gazette* thrilled at the prospect of inflicting on them a crushing defeat "on the scene of their former triumphs—the Custer Battleground." The arrest and humiliation of the rebellious Crow, the newspaper believed, would settle the horse-raiding question and convince the Indians once and for all that the old days were over. [26]

The army anticipated little resistance, but no one knew for certain how the rest of the tribe would react. Armstrong reckoned that only about forty warriors would actually fight, and General Terry thought no more than one hundred; but some of the principal chiefs said they would support the medicine man, and Pretty Eagle warned that a large number of the tribe would rally to Sword Bearer's aid if the soldiers tried to arrest him. The authorities acted promptly to keep the Crow isolated, and twenty Gros Ventre who crossed the Yellowstone in late October were arrested and detained as a precaution until the trouble was over. [27]

After the disturbance on September 30, about three-quarters of the Crow tribe banded together on the Bighorn River some miles south of the agency. With the exception of a few young men who joined the camps on the Bighorn, most of the other members of the tribe, who belonged to Plenty Coups's band of Mountain Crow, remained on the western part of the reservation. Plenty Coups, whom Agent Williamson had described as "a very progressive, self-reliant Indian," made clear his opposition to the malcontents. The chief came to play a pivotal role in this transitional era; whites regarded him as a "good Indian" and a moderating influence, and Pretty Eagle turned to him increasingly for advice. When the trouble broke out at the agency, Plenty Coups was sent for. Colonel Dudley may have hoped to delay taking action until the chief arrived; but Plenty Coups could not be found and did not arrive in time to stop the fight. [28]

Urged on by the old chief Deaf Bull and the war chief Crazy Head, both of whom opposed Plenty Coups's accommodationist policies, Sword Bearer was being driven into a corner. He could not defy the

---

26. Billings *Daily Gazette*, October 27, 29, 1887.
27. Terry to Adjutant General, October 25, 1887; Lamar to Secretary of War, October 26, 1887, AGO; Billings *Daily Gazette*, October 28, 29, 1887.
28. Report of General Ruger, 147–48; Commissioner of Indian Affairs, *Annual Report*, 1887, p. 215; Wagner and Allen, *Blankets and Moccasins*, 233, 237, 248; Billings *Daily Gazette*, November 5, 1887.

army indefinitely, but to submit now would expose him to ridicule, show his medicine to be weak, and hand an unearned victory to Plenty Coups and his supporters. Soldiers continued their regular duties at Fort Custer, but they were ready to march at thirty minutes' notice and the cavalry's saddles were loaded with enough supplies for a ten-day expedition. The officers were eager to take the field, and there was a strong feeling that Sword Bearer should be killed. The majority of the Crow waited expectantly to see what would happen.[29]

General Ruger feared that piecemeal arrests might scatter the tribe; in consultation with Armstrong and Agent Williamson, he decided to assemble the tribe at the agency "and there determine the matter with lasting effect." Orders were issued to all the Crow to assemble at the agency by November 4. There were rumors that Indians were refusing to come in and that white men had been killed, and the citizens of Billings were making plans to organize a militia company. But by November 4, all of the Crow except Plenty Coups's band and a few stragglers had arrived at the agency.[30]

By this time, the military force at the agency comprised nine troops of cavalry, six companies of infantry, and two Hotchkiss gun detachments. Although the Indian camp was quiet, the Crow expected trouble, and many dug holes near the tipis for protection. Sword Bearer continued to come and go freely and boasted that he would ride through the agency and the soldiers' camp and prove that no one could harm him. A cordon of police under the command of Boy That Grabs was thrown around the agency buildings with orders to let Sword Bearer ride inside the lines and then to close in and arrest him. If he resisted, the police were authorized to shoot and kill him.[31]

On November 4, frontiersman William Hamilton, who had lived among the Crow, walked into the office of the *Daily Gazette* and announced that he had come from talking with the "hostiles." He reported that the Indians had said they would fight only if forced. They were poorly armed, and more were leaving Sword Bearer than were joining him. That same day, the Hunkpapa Sioux at the Standing Rock agency held a council to discuss the situation. It was believed that Sitting Bull would counsel war if he could get enough warriors to follow him; but he sat quietly during the council while his rival, Gall, proclaimed that in the event of hostilities he would help the soldiers against his old Crow enemies.[32]

---

29. Wagner and Allen, *Blankets and Moccasins*, 247–48; Billings *Daily Gazette*, November 3, October 31, 1887.

30. Billings *Daily Gazette*, November 3, 4, 1887; Report of General Ruger, 148, AGO; Terry to Adjutant General, November 3, 1887, ibid.

31. Billings *Daily Gazette*, November 5, 1887; Report of General Ruger, 148, p. 152–53.

32. Billings *Daily Gazette*, November 4, 1887.

Matters were clearly coming to a head. The army wanted to find and arrest nineteen Indians: Sword Bearer, Deaf Bull (who was said to be the instigator of the whole affair), and seventeen of the original horse raiders. The group was unlikely to submit without a fight, and everything depended on how the arrests were handled. There were two thousand Indians at the agency: "If they are stampeded now come morning will show a lot of tepees missing and it will be next to an impossibility to get them in again." [33] The authorities consistently downplayed Sword Bearer's influence and asserted that there was no fear of a general outbreak, but they did not really know how deep his influence ran in the tribe. Armstrong apparently revised his opinion after speaking with several of the leading chiefs, acknowledging that the medicine man's power was "simply wonderful." Most of the Indians were unusually sullen and reluctant to talk, but Pretty Eagle told the inspector that the Crow were afraid of Sword Bearer:

He is a great man, all things bend before him and the very ground is now shaking before he does his great deeds. He says that he will destroy the white soldiers, and that when he does he will destroy those Indians that resist him.

General Ruger proceeded with caution. If violence erupted, the uncommitted Indians might rally to the defense of their prophet, which, according to the *Daily Gazette*, "would result in the almost total annihilation of the Crow tribe." [34]

The showdown came the next day, November 5. At around ten o'clock in the morning, General Ruger dispatched chief of scouts James Campbell and an interpreter named Tobacco Juice or Tobacco Jake to the Crow camp to tell the chiefs and the principal men to come in for a council. After a brief parley, about a dozen Indians— including Pretty Eagle, Crazy Head, and Old Kearney—rode up to Ruger's quarters. Armstrong told them he had been sent by the Great Father in Washington to settle the trouble but that since they refused to hand over the troublemakers he had turned everything over to the soldier chief. Armstrong demanded that Crazy Head bring in his son, Knows His Coups, who was one of the insurgents. Ruger said that his orders were to arrest those responsible for the disturbance, and he gave the chiefs an hour and a half in which to deliver the offenders before he was compelled to take them. The chiefs departed to hold council. [35]

---

33. Ibid., November 5, 1887.

34. Secretary of War, *Annual Report*, 1887, p. 73; Billings *Daily Gazette*, November 7, 1887.

35. Billings *Daily Gazette*, November 6, 7, 1887; *Harpers Weekly*, December 3, 1887, p. 878.

While the conference was taking place, some of the Indians had been dismantling tipis and moving closer to the agency. The main camp stretched for a mile along the west bank of the Little Bighorn below and to the north of the agency buildings. Pretty Eagle had moved his camp a mile farther down the valley to put some distance between his followers and the trouble. He evidently counseled moderation and urged the wanted men to give themselves up, but to no avail. Young warriors could be seen hurrying to the council where the chiefs were assembled. When the Indians made no move to return, Colonel Dudley's 1st Cavalry and Major Snyder's 5th Infantry battalion prepared for action, and two Hotchkiss guns were positioned on the hill commanding the village. The soldiers then waited to see what the Indians would do. [36]

During the ninety minutes that Ruger had allotted, many young warriors congregated around their camp farthest from the agency. Sword Bearer could be seen riding up and down haranguing them. According to one eyewitness, the medicine man galloped headlong toward the troops with his war bonnet trailing behind him. The troops stood uncertainly as he rode around them, throwing his sword in the air and catching it by the hilt before riding back into the Crow ranks. [37]

As time ran out, Sword Bearer rode out from the camp with between one hundred and one hundred fifty Indians behind him. Interpreting their move as an attempt to escape into the hills, General Ruger sent Colonel Dudley with two troops of cavalry to intercept them. The Indians suddenly began to yell, fired their guns in the air to announce their intention of fighting, scattered, and rode furiously down the Bighorn Valley. Troops E and K of the 1st Cavalry charged down the valley to head them off, but the warriors whirled their ponies and rode back and forth at a distance of about half a mile, shouting and firing their guns. The Hotchkiss guns opened fire from the hill, killing one Crow outright. As the cavalry reached the bottomland near the river, they were met by a volley of shots that killed one soldier and wounded two others. The soldiers deployed in a skirmish line, and for a few moments the exchange of fire was "fast and furious." The Indians then pulled back to the brush and a group of warriors emerged carrying a flag of truce, asking that those who did not want to fight be given a chance to join the peaceful camp at the agency.

During the ensuing brief lull in the hostilities, a number of Crow sought refuge in the village near the agency buildings. En route, they passed within range of the infantry companies stationed between the

36. Report of General Ruger, 148–49; Wagner and Allen, *Blankets and Moccasins*, 245–46; Billings *Daily Gazette*, November 7, 1887.

37. Billings *Daily Gazette*, November 7, 1887; Roosevelt, "In Cowboy Land," 284.

agency and the village, but commanding officer Captain D. W. Benham saw that they offered no resistance and held his fire. Other Indians seized the opportunity to retreat across the river and into the brush, where they recommenced shooting; but the soldiers gradually drove them out of the river bottom. At some point, Sword Bearer was killed, and after a brisk skirmish, the Indians broke and ran for the hills. The action was over by three o'clock that afternoon.

Major J. M. Hamilton and two troops of cavalry pursued those who had fled to the southeast. Captain E. D. Dimmick and Captain Miles Moylan went up the Little Bighorn Valley to search the area eighteen miles to the south near the Sand Hills, where Crazy Head and Deaf Bull had been camped.[38] Armstrong fired off a telegram to Secretary Lamar:

> Troops were fired upon by Indians in attempting to arrest medicine man & others. Had sharp skirmish and killed medicine man & others. All quiet except few renegades out which troops will get.

The *Daily Gazette* stopped the presses on its November 5 edition to bring its readers the news that Sword Bearer had been killed and was now "a Good Indian." On Sunday, November 6, the newspaper printed an extra edition, detailing the skirmish and the events leading to it. Monday's *Gazette* carried the same story but with additional accounts.[39] At first, only three Indians were thought to have been killed, but the final tally listed Sword Bearer and seven others as dead and a number wounded. One Indian had shot himself rather than surrender. The only casualties suffered by the army were those sustained during the charge in the valley: one dead, two wounded.[40]

Accounts of Sword Bearer's death differ. Historian Richard Upton was unable to find a reliable contemporary record of his killing and obtained what he believed to be an accurate version in 1970 from Mike Reynolds, son of former Crow agency superintendent Major S. G. Reynolds. Reynolds's report is complemented by accounts given by Elizabeth Barstow and Allie Stevenson. All of these accounts agree that Sword Bearer was not killed in the exchange of fire with the 1st Cavalry, although it does appear that he was wounded. Sword Bearer was killed on the bank of the Little Bighorn River by an Indian policeman named Fire Bear.

---

38. Report of General Ruger, 149; Secretary of War, *Annual Report*, 1888, p. 173; Terry to Adjutant General, November 6, 1887 AGO; Report of Lieutenant Dimmick, November 20, 1887, ibid.; Billings *Daily Gazette*, November 7, 1887.

39. Telegram, Armstrong to Secretary of the Interior, November 5, [1887], Crow Agency Records; Billings *Daily Gazette*, November 5, 6, 7, 1887.

40. Billings *Daily Gazette*, November 1, 1887; Report of General Ruger, 149–50.

After the Indians scattered, a number of warriors, including Sword Bearer, stopped at the river to wash off their paint. While Sword Bearer was thus engaged, Fire Bear rode up to him, saying, according to one account, "You have been the cause of all this trouble, and I am going to kill you." He then shot Sword Bearer in the head with his service revolver, threw the body over his saddle, rode back to the agency, and dumped it at Agent Williamson's feet. Fire Bear's act lost him respect in the tribe, and many Crow believed the government gave the policeman lifelong employment simply to protect him from vengeance by Sword Bearer's kinsmen. [41]

Sword Bearer's corpse was laid out on the prairie in full view of the Indians "to show them their bullet proof prophet," and the Crow dispersed almost as soon as they saw that his medicine was broken. But even the *Daily Gazette* acknowledged the inspirational effect of Sword Bearer's vision:

> It was one of the most remarkable incidents in the history of the northwestern Indians that nearly 200 of them should stand before 15 companies of soldiers and a battery of Hotchkiss rifles on the strength of such a belief. [42]

Equally remarkable, when contrasted with the carnage that occurred at Wounded Knee just three years later, was the restraint shown by the army, which was "determined that there should be no Crow war." General Ruger commended the 1st Cavalry for their steadiness in action and noted that others not actually engaged in the fighting deserved equal commendation for their forbearance "from humane motives under circumstances of provocation." The Crow remembered this restraint and said they would always be friends of the soldiers "who had spared them when they might have killed them all." [43]

For a while after the fight, it seemed the trouble might not be over. Deaf Bull was still at large, and from forty to one hundred and fifty warriors remained defiant. Army officers dreaded the prospect of a winter campaign, but it quickly became clear that the "rebellion" had collapsed with Sword Bearer's death. Crazy Head gave up and brought his son to the agency on November 5. The troops who had gone in pursuit of Deaf Bull returned empty-handed on the night of November 6, only to find that Deaf Bull, Looks With His Ears, Rock, Bank, and Big Hail had given themselves up at General Ruger's headquarters earlier that day. Most of the other wanted Indians came in

41. Upton, *Fort Custer*, 151, 156–59, 165; Lowie, *Crow Indians*, 11.

42. Billings *Daily Gazette*, November 7, 1887; *Harpers Weekly*, December 3, 1887, p. 878.

43. Terry to Adjutant General, November 6, 1887, AGO; Report of General Ruger, 150; Billings *Daily Gazette*, November 7, 1887.

In November 1887 at Crow Agency, soldiers posed with captured and manacled followers of Sword Bearer before sending them to Fort Snelling, Minnesota. Some of the Crow prisoners were sent on to Carlisle Indian School in Pennsylvania and others were allowed back on the reservation within a few months, but it was two years before all of the prisoners returned to Crow Agency. (Montana Historical Society Photograph Archives)

around daybreak on the next day. A chief named Carries His Food remained at large, and a few young warriors and a chief named Black Hawk and his family were still out, but they were expected to return within a few days. [44]

Plenty Coups and his band arrived the day after the fight. Scout James Campbell had finally located the chief in the mountains

---

44. Billings *Daily Gazette*, November 7, 8, 1887; Terry to Adjutant General, November 7, 1887, AGO.

mourning the death of his wife. Whether Plenty Coups's presence would have affected the outcome of the affair is impossible to say, but it is unlikely that he could have made much headway with the young insurgents where Pretty Eagle had failed. By the time Plenty Coups reached the agency, the rebels had been subdued and "the authority of those well-disposed was restored." Armstrong met with the Crow leaders and reported that everything was permanently settled. [45]

Armstrong and Ruger suggested that the ringleaders be sent to Fort Snelling, Minnesota. President Cleveland concurred, adding that final determination of their case should be hastened: "I feel like treating them with as much moderation as is consistent with safety." [46] Carries His Food, Looks With His Ears, Rock, Bank, He Knows His Coups, Big Hail, Deaf Bull, and Crazy Head went to Fort Snelling in chains. Except for Deaf Bull and Crazy Head, all were young men. The first four had participated in the raid on the Peigan and had fired on the agency buildings. He Knows His Coups and Big Hail were not on the raid but had taken part in the disturbance. All of the young men had fought with Sword Bearer on November 5. Deaf Bull and Crazy Head were known to have urged the warriors to resist arrest, and a sergeant of the 1st Cavalry had seen Crazy Head fire on the troops. General Ruger advocated keeping the prisoners away from the reservation for at least a year, preferably two; he recommended that they be made to work at practical employments and earn their release by good behavior. Describing Deaf Bull as sullen and intractable, Ruger suggested that the longer he was kept away the better. Crazy Head was "relatively intelligent," he continued, but was "crafty and inimical to authority" and should be kept away for at least two years. [47]

The *Daily Gazette* opined that the prisoners fully deserved their punishment. Deaf Bull was "one of the worst Indians of the tribe," the newspaper reported, and Crazy Head "one of the most independent." Having deceived both the young warriors and the whites, they were the real cause of the trouble. The rest of the Crow had been taught a lesson they would never forget and were

> . . . either in camp eating their rations with a humble heart or else in the guard house meditating on the strength and power of the whites,

45. Wagner and Allen, *Blankets and Moccasins*, 251–52; Billings *Daily Gazette*, November 5, 1887; Report of General Ruger, 151; Terry to Adjutant General, November 7, 1887; Armstrong to Secretary of the Interior, November 7, 1887, AGO.

46. President Cleveland to Secretary Lamar, November 7, 1887, AGO.

47. Report of General Ruger, 151; Ruger to Assistant Adjutant General, November 30, 1887, AGO.

and the weakness of the medicine by which young Sword Bearer was going to clean the whites from the face of the earth.

Seeing their prophet dead and their leaders in shackles, wrote the *Gazette*, the Crow now wanted peace at any price.[48]

In August 1888, Williamson's successor, Agent E. P. Briscoe, reported that all was quiet at the Crow agency and that nothing worthy of note had occurred since he had assumed his post.[49] Things were not as quiet elsewhere, however. On the night of February 15, 1888, "a hell of a row" broke out among the row prisoners at Fort Snelling. Just after midnight, when the others were asleep, Deaf Bull got up and with a small pocketknife "began cutting and slashing in the most desperate manner, as though bent upon killing as many of his companions as possible and then himself." He then applied the knife to his own throat. In the struggle to restrain him, Deaf Bull received a broken arm and a musket blow to the head. When the confusion subsided, the old chief had "a fearful wound" over the right carotid and jugular, a scalp wound, a fractured left arm, and numerous scratches and bruises. Crazy Head had a laceration on his forehead and stab wounds in his right breast and side. Carries His Food had an eight-inch wound in his right arm and shoulder and wounds on the back of his head and right ear. A bad cut on the left side of the throat had exposed Bank's carotid artery, and Crazy Head's son had been stabbed in the foot. When W. H. Forwood, who reported the chaos, asked Deaf Bull why he had done it, the chief replied that the others had been abusing him and lying about him until he could stand it no longer. Forwood thought Deaf Bull was crazy.[50]

That spring, on the recommendation of Agent Howard and General Dudley and with Plenty Coups pledging himself responsible for their future good behavior, the president directed that Bank and Looks With His Ears be released and sent home. With the exception of Deaf Bull, the remaining prisoners were transferred to Carlisle Industrial School in Pennsylvania. After some confusion among the authorities as to just which Indians had been sent to Carlisle, all but Big Hail and Rock were returned to the Crow Indian Reservation. Bank and Looks With His Ears returned home in about June 1888;

---

48. Billings *Daily Gazette*, November 8, October 29, November 7, 9, 1887.

49. E. P. Briscoe to Commissioner of Indian Affairs, August 15, 1888, in Commissioner of Indian Affairs, *Annual Report*, 50th Cong., 2d sess., 1888, H. Ex. Doc. 1, pt. 5 (Serial 2637), 153.

50. W. H. Forwood to Campbell, February 16, 1888, AGO.

both died soon after. Crazy Head, his son, and Carries His Food returned in about November 1888. [51]

Back in Fort Snelling, Deaf Bull had apparently undergone a reformation during his two-year confinement and was reported to be working harder than the average white prisoner, gardening and growing vegetables. The chief was rheumatic and anxious to get home to his family. Plenty Coups and Pretty Eagle vouched for his future good conduct, and the consensus among the white authorities was that it would be good policy to release him. On August 1, 1889, the Commissioner of Indian Affairs gave orders for Deaf Bull's release. [52] More detailed knowledge of the changes and tensions in Crow society is essential for a fuller understanding of the Sword Bearer outbreak, but some conclusions and tentative explanations can be offered. Sword Bearer was not simply a troublemaker with a few hot-headed followers. Native American societies regularly produced prophets and messiahs at times of extreme crisis; and, like other Indian visionaries, Sword Bearer generated mixed emotions, attracting those who saw power in his vision and alarming those who feared that his promise of a return to better days threatened to overturn the established order. [53] Many Crow saw him as a messiah; even his enemies grudgingly acknowledged his charisma, "shrewd intellect," and rare gift for leadership. But most members of the tribe were reluctant to commit themselves to an unproved medicine man and waited expectantly to see what the outcome of Sword Bearer's actions would be. Even those Indians who did not want war might have reacted differently "if this wonderful power proved to be on their side." [54]

---

51. Howard to Commissioner of Indian Affairs, February 28, 1888; Dudley to Howard, February 22, 1888; Atkins to Secretary of the Interior, April 11, 1888; Secretary of War William Endicott to Secretary of the Interior, April 11, 1888; Secretary of War William Endicott to Secretary of the Interior, April 18, 1888; Adjutant General to Commanding General, Division of the Missouri, [May 10?], 1888; Acting Secretary of the Interior to Secretary of War, June 30, 1888; J. F. B. Marshall to Endicott, January 16, 1888; Endicott to Marshall, May 11, 1888; Lieutenant Colonel Arnold to Assistant Adjutant General, July 9, 1889; unheaded, July 5, 1889; Memorandum: Defraying traveling expenses of the Crow Indians from Carlisle Indian school to Crow Agency Montana, [1890], AGO.

52. Ruger to Assistant Adjutant General, July 15, 1889; Arnold to Assistant Adjutant General, July 6, July 9, 1889; Colonel Mason to Adjutant General, July 3, 1889; Commissioner of Indian Affairs Thomas J. Morgan to Secretary of the Interior, August 1, 1889, AGO.

53. James Mooney, *The Ghost Dance Religion and Wounded Knee* (New York: Dover Publications, 1973), chaps. 1–10; L. G. Moses and Margaret Connell Szasz, " 'My Father, have pity on me!' Indian Revitalization Movements of the Late Nineteenth Century," *Journal of the West*, 23 (January 1984), 5–15.

54. Wagner and Allen, *Blankets and Moccasins*, 236–37, 243; Billings *Daily Gazette*, November 9, 1887.

The events of November 5 dashed any such hopes, but some Crow never lost faith in Sword Bearer's vision. They attributed his failure to phenomena consistent with their view of the world: Sword Bearer's dreams were true and his power real; the medicine man must in some way have misinterpreted his vision or misapplied his power. The man had failed, but the force that motivated him remained unquestioned. In this way, Crow warriors had retained their faith in the protective powers of their spiritual guardians even as their losses in battle escalated. [55] Young Crow warriors had responded to new crises during the 1880s as their ancestors had in the past. They did not turn in blind desperation to a wild-eyed agitator but placed their faith in an individual who had received supernatural support as a result of a sacred vision.

Nevertheless, the Sword Bearer affair revealed deep divisions within Crow society. While Plenty Coups seemed ready to replace Pretty Eagle as spokesman for the older generation, which remembered how the U.S. government had helped them in wars against the Sioux, Sword Bearer won the support of younger warriors who had grown up since the end of intertribal wars. The medicine man's vision and actions appealed to these restless young men, "writhing under the pressure of the white man's foot upon their necks." Delayed action by the authorities had lent substance to Sword Bearer's claim that whites were afraid of him, increasing his prestige among the young warriors. The decentralized nature of Crow society made it impossible for one or two chiefs to exert control and for "older and wiser heads" to prevail. Moreover, according to General Ruger, Sword Bearer had reduced the older and well-disposed Indians to passive compliance with his schemes "by intimidation and working upon their superstitious fears." [56]

It is not surprising that admirers of Plenty Coups regarded Sword Bearer as an ambitious agitator who was jealous of Plenty Coups's growing influence. Wagner and Allen asserted that, "like most agitators, this modern Achilles bungled at the high pinnacle of success and brought disaster down upon himself and his followers." Others believed that Deaf Bull and Crazy Head had used Sword Bearer as a "cat's paw" for their own purposes. [57] In 1883, Armstrong had declared:

> . . . there is no Crow, not even the best and most progressive, who does not prefer his wild life to that of the white people, but there is a con-

---

55. Lowie, *Crow Indians*, 238.

56. Wagner and Allen, *Blankets and Moccasins*, 237; Ruger to Assistant Adjutant General, November 30, 1887, AGO; Report of General Ruger, 148.

57. Wagner and Allen, *Blankets and Moccasins*, 237; Billings *Daily Gazette*, November 3, 1887.

siderable number who are sensible enough to see that the old times are past and can never return. we can reason with such men. . . . [58]

Sword Bearer not only reasserted old ways that the government was determined to eradicate, he also challenged the standing of progressive chiefs like Plenty Coups, whom the government had identified as "reasonable men" who would lead their people along the path of assimilation.

Sword Bearer's vision was not unique. Other Native American prophets preached similar messages with wider appeal and great effect. Nevertheless, the young medicine man's vision and his defiance of the assembled might of the U. S. Army inspired hope in his people at a time of crisis. Chafing under the imposed authority of government agents and the accommodationist stance of older chiefs, young warriors seized the opportunity to demonstrate the enduring vitality of traditional values in the face of coercion and change.

---

58.   Henry J. Armstrong to Commissioner of Indian Affairs, August 15, 1883, in Commissioner of Indian Affairs, *Annual Report*, 48th Cong., 1st sess., 1883, H. Ex. Doc. 1, pt. 5 (Serial 2191), 157.

From Kwangtung to the Big Sky:

The Chinese Experience in Frontier Montana

Robert R. Swartout, Jr.

The discovery of major gold deposits in the northern Rockies in the early 1860s dramatically altered the landscape that became known as Montana. It seemed as though almost overnight rough-hewed urban communities sprang up in the high mountain valleys — Bannack along Grasshopper Creek on the upper reaches of the Jefferson River in 1862, Virginia City in Alder Gulch in 1863, and Helena in a place called Last Chance Gulch in 1864. Almost as quickly, such new transportation routes as the Mullan Road, the Bozeman Trail, and James Liberty Fisk's Northern Overland Route began tying the region to outside national and international forces. The sudden explosion of the non-Indian population also led directly to territorial status for Montana in 1864.

As mining activities, and other related economic enterprises, spread throughout the region, an unusually broad mix of peoples were drawn to Montana from across the country and, indeed, from around the world. Among these groups were Chinese pioneers, many of whom had come to Montana by way of California. The following essay by Robert R. Swartout, Jr., professor of history at Carroll College, shows how these Chinese played a vital role in the development of nineteenth-century Montana. Too often, popular accounts of western history have either ignored the contributions of Asian-Americans or have used them as a backdrop for "Chinatown" adven-

*Robert R. Swartout, Jr., "From Kwangtung to the Big Sky: The Chinese Experience in Frontier Montana," *Montana The Magazine of Western History*, 38 (Winter 1988), 42–53.

The labor of Chinese workers, such as those in this section gang photographed on the Clark Fork River, was essential to completion of the Northern Pacific Railroad through Montana. (F. Jay Haynes, photographer, Haynes Foundation Collection, Montana Historical Society Photograph Archives)

tures. Only in the past few years have historians begun to appreciate the richness and importance of the Asian experience in America.

Into the early twentieth century, Montana contained a remarkably heterogeneous society, with significant numbers of native Americans, Irish, black Americans, Scandinavians, Jews, and Slavs — to name only a few of the many groups living and working in the region. Among the racial and ethnic minorities that contributed to this fascinating mix, the Chinese were certainly one of the most important. Yet, for far too long many of the historical studies about Chinese immigration to the American West have tended to use these Chinese pioneers simply as a backdrop for analyzing the thinking and behavior of non-Chinese groups.[1] It is time that we begin to focus more of our attention on the Chinese themselves.[2]

---

1. See Elmer Clarence Sandmeyer, *The Anti-Chinese Movement in California* (Urbana: University of Illinois Press, 1939); Alexander Saxton, *The Indispensable Enemy: Labor and the Anti-Chinese Movement in California* (Berkeley and Los Angeles: University of

By focusing more directly on the Chinese experience, we may better appreciate the valuable economic and cultural contributions that these Asian pioneers made to the development of early Montana society. To understand the extent of the Chinese involvement in Montana's history, we must move beyond the retelling of "colorful and humorous" accounts. The Chinese struggle — and it was a struggle — to achieve social and economic security in Montana was demanding, and it deserves serious historical attention. [3]

The Chinese immigrants arriving in America in the mid-nineteenth century overwhelmingly came from the delta region surrounding Canton in Kwangtung Province. The general reasons behind the desire of certain Chinese to emigrate during the nineteenth century are not too difficult to identify. The great population explosion in China between roughly 1700 and 1850 had placed tremendous pressures on China's traditional agrarian production, and in many parts of China the population had outstripped the land's ability to produce adequate foodstuffs. Another factor contributing to emigration was the gradual decline of the Ch'ing dynasty. The dynasty's inability to rule effectively had resulted in a series of rebellions, the largest and most famous of which was the Taiping Rebellion of 1850–1864. In a broader sense, the decline of the dynasty also led to a rise in both government corruption and banditry, problems that created special burdens for the peasantry. [4] Finally, there was the American factor itself. Between the 1840s and the 1890s, the resource-rich, labor-poor American West offered opportunities to foreign workers searching for financial and material security. In many important respects,

---

California Press, 1971); Stuart Creighton Miller, *The Unwelcome Immigrant: The American Image of the Chinese, 1785–1882* (Berkeley and Los Angeles: University of California Press, 1969); Robert Edward Wynne, *Reaction to the Chinese in the Pacific Northwest and British Columbia, 1850–1910* (New York: Arno Press, 1979). In calling for greater attention to the Chinese experience itself, it is not my intention to dismiss the valuable contributions that works such as these have made to our understanding of U.S. history. The American response to Chinese migration is clearly an important historical issue and will be dealt with later in this essay.

2. An excellent example is the recent book by Sucheng Chan, *This Bittersweet Soil: The Chinese in California Agriculture, 1860–1910* (Berkeley and Los Angeles: University of California Press, 1986).

3. To see how the Montana experience fits into a broader, international context, see Michael H. Hunt, *The Making of a Special Relationship: The United States and China to 1914* (New York: Columbia University Press, 1983), especially chapters 2, 3, 7; Shih-shan Henry Tsai, *China and the Overseas Chinese in the United States, 1868–1911* (Fayetteville: University of Arkansas Press, 1983).

4. Hunt, *The Making of a Special Relationship*, 63–64; Jack Chen, *The Chinese of America: From the Beginnings to the Present* (San Francisco: Harper & Row, 1981), 6–9; Frederic Wakeman, Jr., *Strangers at the Gate: Social Disorder in South China, 1839–1861* (Berkeley and Los Angeles: University of California Press, 1966).

Montana was a perfect microcosm of these forces at work within the developing American West. [5]

Why the Chinese immigrants would come almost exclusively from Kwangtung Province—in fact, from just three major regions within the province—is more difficult to pinpoint. [6] One factor might have been the influence of the West on and around Canton during the first half of the nineteenth century. The penetration of imperialist powers during this era certainly led to considerable social and economic dislocation for the Chinese. [7] Another factor might have been the maritime traditions of the southeastern China coast. The story of Chinese emigration to America during the nineteenth century is just part of a much larger movement. For decades, people of this area had traveled abroad in search of wealth and adventure. Between 1850 and 1900, roughly five million Chinese from the southern coast area would leave the country, only a half-million of whom would go to the United States. [8] Perhaps one of the most critical local forces leading to emigration was that many of these people were "have-nots," with only limited ties to the traditonal Chinese order. Some were members of an ethnic minority known as the Hakka, while many others were locally oriented rural poor who viewed emigration simply as a "means of survival" for themselves and their families. [9]

Large-scale Chinese immigration to America began in the late 1840s and early 1850s. Spurred on initially by the great gold discoveries in California, first hundreds and then thousands of Chinese headed east across the Pacific Ocean. [10] With the gradual decline in the placer fields, Chinese workers entered other lines of employment and moved on to other regions of the western United States and Canada. By the 1860s and 1870s, important Chinese communities had been established all along the West Coast—in Oregon, Washington, British Columbia, and California—and within the interior

---

5. Chen, *The Chinese of America*, 35–124; Gunther Barth, *Bitter Strength: A History of the Chinese in the United States, 1850–1870* (Cambridge, Mass.: Harvard University Press, 1964), 32–49; Kil Young Zo, *Chinese Emigration into the United States, 1850–1880* (New York: Arno Press, 1978), 81–92.

6. The three regions were San-i (Sam Yup in Cantonese), Ssu-i (Sze Yup in Cantonese), and Hsiang-shan (Hueng-shan in Cantonese; later renamed Chung-shan). See Hunt, *The Making of a Special Relationship*, 61–62.

7. See June Mei, "Socioeconomic Origins of Emigration: Guangdong to California, 1850–1882," in *Labor Immigration under Capitalism: Asian Workers in the United States before World War II*, ed. Lucie Cheng and Edna Bonacich (Berkeley and Los Angeles: University of California Press, 1984), 219–47.

8. Hunt, *The Making of a Special Relationship*, 61; Chen, *The Chinese of America*, 10–13.

9. Hunt, *The Making of a Special Relationship*, 63.

10. Chen, *The Chinese of America*, 15–29; Barth, *Bitter Strength*, 50–76; Zo, *Chinese Emigration into the United States*, 114–45.

West—in places like Nevada, Idaho, Colorado, Wyoming, and Montana. [11] Of all these Chinese, few have received less attention from historians than those found in the isolated Rocky Mountain state of Montana. [12]

By 1870, census surveyors counted 1,949 Chinese in the first official census taken for the territory of Montana. This may not appear to be an impressive figure, but those 1,949 Chinese represented approximately 10 percent of Montana's official population in 1870. Moreover, because census records were often notorious for underestimating the Chinese population in any given community, the actual Chinese population may have been much higher—by perhaps 50 percent or more. In 1880, the official figure for the Chinese population in Montana dipped to 1,765; but by 1890 it was back up to 2,532. From that point on, the number of Chinese in the state, and in the United States as a whole, steadily declined. This decline was due partly to local factors as well as to the passage of various Chinese exclusion acts passed by the U.S. Congress during the 1880s and 1890s. By 1920, there were fewer than 900 Chinese residents left in Montana out of a total state population of 548,889. [13] It is clear, then, that the major period for Chinese influence in Montana was roughly the last third of the nineteenth century. This period not only represented the largest number of Chinese immigrants within the region, but it was also a time when those Chinese made up a large percentage of Montana's total population.

---

11. See Ping Chiu, *Chinese Labor in California, 1850–1880: An Economic Study* (Madison: University of Wisconsin Press, 1963); Saxton, *The Indispensable Enemy*; Chan, *This Bittersweet Soil*; Wynne, *Reaction to the Chinese in the Pacific Northwest and British Columbia*; James Morton, *In the Sea of Sterile Mountains: The Chinese in British Columbia* (Vancouver: J. J. Douglas Ltd., 1974); Jeffrey Barlow and Christine Richardson, *China Doctor of John Day* (Portland: Binford & Mort, 1979); John R. Wunder, "Chinese in Trouble: Criminal Law and Race on the Trans-Mississippi West Frontier," *Western Historical Quarterly*, 17 (January 1986), 25–41.

12. To date, only three scholarly articles have been published on the Chinese historical presence in Montana: Larry D. Quinn, " 'Chink Chink Chinaman': The Beginnings of Nativism in Montana," *Pacific Northwest Quarterly*, 58 (April 1967), 82–89; John R. Wunder, "Law and Chinese in Frontier Montana," *Montana The Magazine of Western History*, 30 (Summer 1980), 18–30; Stacy A. Flaherty, "Boycott in Butte: Organized Labor and the Chinese Community, 1896–1897," *Montana The Magazine of Western History*, 37 (Winter 1987), 34–47. Moreover, these articles deal primarily with the reaction of white Montanans to Chinese rather than with the experiences of the Chinese themselves.

13. U.S., Department of the Interior, Census Office, *Eleventh Census of the United States, 1890: Population, Part I* (Washington, D.C.: Government Printing Office, 1895), 29, 439; U.S., Department of Commerce, Bureau of the Census, *Fourteenth Census of the United States, 1920: Population, Volume III* (Washington, D.C.: Goverment Printing Office, 1922), 574, 577.

As was true in so many other regions of the West, the discovery of major gold deposits during the early 1860s had a profound effect on the history of Montana. The great gold-mining boom in the high mountain valleys of the Northern Rockies would attract thousands of American miners and would-be miners almost overnight and would lead directly to the creation of the Territory of Montana in 1864. [14] And as was the pattern in many other western states and territories, the development of the goldfields also resulted in the arrival of the first Chinese pioneers in Montana.

As placer camps like Bannack, Virginia City, and Last Chance Gulch built up across western Montana, word went out to the older mining districts of the new opportunities in Montana Territory. Chinese miners—many with extensive mining experience in California, Oregon, Idaho, or elsewhere—began moving into Montana. An 1870 federal government study on mining in the American West reported that "some 2,000 to 3,000 Chinese are domiciled in the Territory of Montana. . . . It is reasonable to expect that their numbers will rapidly increase." The same report commented on the techniques of Chinese miners:

> The Chinese work their own placer claims, either taking up abandoned ground or purchasing claims too low in yield to be worked profitably by white labor. The ground thus obtained sometimes turns out to be very valuable, but usually they work or rework only what would otherwise remain untouched. . . . They are frugal, skillful, and extremely industrious. Frequently maltreated by evil-disposed whites, they rarely, if ever, retaliate.

The author of this valuable report had the insight to note that, contrary to much popular opinion, the Chinese miners working in Montana "are not coolies or living in a state of slavery. . . . They seem to be their own masters, only associating together for mutual assistance." [15]

By the early 1870s there were dozens of Chinese mining operations in western Montana. The 1880 census listed 149 Chinese in Missoula County, 710 in Deer Lodge County (which included Butte), 265 in Madison County (Alder Gulch), and 359 in Lewis and Clark County (Helena). Many mining camps that are almost forgotten today, such as the small community of Pioneer located southwest of present-

---

14.   Michael P. Malone and Richard B. Roeder, *Montana: A History of Two Centuries* (Seattle: University of Washington Press, 1976), 50–55.

15.   Rossiter W. Raymond, "Statistics of Mines and Mining in the States and Territories West of the Rocky Mountains," 41st Cong., 2d sess., 1870, H. Ex. Doc. 207 (Serial 1424), 260.

day Garrison, were the site of widespread Chinese activities. Unfortunately, the very success of these Chinese miners helped create a backlash among many members of Montana's white population. For example, in 1872 the territorial legislature passed a bill prohibiting aliens (that is, Chinese) from holding titles to any placer mine or claim. Even though this law was later struck down by the territorial supreme court, it was typical of much of the popular sentiment of the day. [16]

Because the passage of such laws was, at least in part, racially motivated, supporters of the legislation consistently overlooked the contributions that Chinese miners made to the development of Montana. As one outsider commented at the time, the law concerning Chinese mining titles

> is certainly destructive of the interests of the community, as may be shown in numerous instances where the Chinese have purchased, for cash, claims which white men could no longer afford to work, and have proceeded to make them productive, at a smaller profit to themselves than to the Territory. Besides being bad policy, this course toward the Chinese is rank dishonesty. [17]

The notion that Chinese miners competed directly against white miners and thus "stole" badly needed work from them is largely untrue. In fact, Chinese miners generally complemented the work being done by white miners and played a vital role in helping to develop the mineral and commercial resources of the territory. [18]

As placer mining began to fade from the scene during the late 1870s and 1880s, the role of the Chinese immigrants in Montana also began to change. [19] Chinese railroad workers in America had first

---

16. Montana Territory, Legislative Assembly, *Laws, Memorials, and Resolutions of the Territory of Montana, Seventh Session* (Deer Lodge: James H. Mills, Public Printer, 1872), 593–96; Montana Territory, Legislative Assembly, *Laws, Memorials, and Resolutions of the Territory of Montana, Eighth Session* (Helena: Robert E. Fisk, Public Printer, 1874), 97; Wunder, "Law and Chinese in Frontier Montana," 24–25. The original law stated: "No aliens shall be allowed to acquire any title, interest, or possessory or other right to any placer mine or claim, or to the profits or proceeds thereof, in this territory."

17. Rossister W. Raymond, "Statistics of Mines and Mining in the States and Territories West of the Rocky Mountains," 42d Cong., 2d sess., 1872, H. Ex. Doc. 211 (Serial 1513), 292.

18. See Randall E. Rohe, "After the Gold Rush: Chinese Mining in the Far West, 1850–1890," *Montana The Magazine of Western History*, 32 (Autumn 1982), 18.

19. Most Chinese miners in Montana worked small placer claims, either individually or with various partners. Generally speaking, the Chinese did not play an important role in the development of industrial mining in Montana, partly because employers were reluctant to hire them and partly because there were fewer Chinese left in the state by the time industrial mining came into its own around the turn of the century.

been used on a large scale in the construction of the Central Pacific Railroad during the 1860s. In fact, roughly four-fifths of all the grading done from Sacramento, California, to Ogden, Utah, was completed by Chinese laborers. Of the 13,500 workers on the Central Pacific payroll at the time of construction, 12,000 were Chinese. [20]

It is not too surprising, then, that Chinese railroad workers found their way to Montana. During the early 1880s, the first transcontinental railroad to pass through Montana—the Northern Pacific—was being constructed at a frantic pace under the leadership of Henry Villard. Because of the critical shortage of skilled labor at the western end of the project and the reputation of the Chinese as experienced and dependable workers, Villard and his associates hired 15,000 Chinese to work on the Northern Pacific line through Washington, Idaho, and Montana. [21]

The press often referred to these Chinese workers, especially those constructing the Northern Pacific along the Clark Fork River in northern Idaho and western Montana, as "Hallett's Army" after construction manager J. L. Hallett. This region of the Clark Fork contained some of the most rugged terrain found anywhere along the Northern Pacific line. One newspaper reported on October 28, 1882:

> One must ride over the completed track, or watch the thousands of men at work in these rock-ribbed hills, see the deep cuttings, the immense fillings, count the bridges and miles of trestle-work that carry the trains safely over streams and arms of lakes and inlets, to fairly realize the expenditure of muscle . . . necessary for such a work as building a great railway route through this mountainous country. At places, for instance, a point near Cabinet Landing, to the men who do the labor, and even to subordinate leaders, the passage seemed closed against them. The mountain towers like a prop to the sky, and from the water's edge it rises like a wall, presenting no break or crevice for a foothold. [22]

The special skills, dedication, and perseverance of the Chinese workers were critical in overcoming these tremendous obstacles. The same reporter took note of this Chinese contribution, although in somewhat condescending terms. To conquer nature's

---

20.   Chen, *The Chinese of America*, 65–77; Tzu Kuei Yen, "Chinese Workers and the First Transcontinental Railroad of the United States of America," (PH.D. diss., St. John's University, New York, 1977).

21.   "First Across the Northwest—The Northern Pacific," MS, 5, box 515, President's Subject files, Northern Pacific Railway Company Records, Minnesota Historical Society Archives, St. Paul (hereafter NP Records).

22.   Newspaper clipping, October 28, 1882, Secretary Scrapbooks, 1866–1896, box 4, vol. 25, NP Records.

insurmountable barrier . . . cable ropes holding a plank staging go down the precipitous sides of the mountain. Down rope ladders, to this staging clamber Chinamen armed with drills, and soon the rock sides are filled with Giant powder. Then they clamber up, the blast is fired, and the foothold made by the explosives soon swarms with Celestials; the "can't be done" has been done . . . . [23]

Chinese workmen not only had to overcome great physical obstructions, but they also had to contend with bitter winter weather: "It was terrible work last winter," one source noted, "with deep snow to clear away at every step, the thermometer registering on an average ten and twelve degrees below zero [fahrenheit], abetted by razor-like winds." [24]

The Chinese also played a crucial role in constructing the Mullan Tunnel, which enabled the Northern Pacific to cross over the Continental Divide not far from Helena, Montana. Chinese workers built the critical stretch of line leading to Stampede Pass in Washington Territory's North Cascade Mountains, which allowed the Northern Pacific to reach Puget Sound. For all of these remarkable efforts, the average Chinese worker was paid about one dollar per day, approximately half of what white workers received. [25] This disparity was but another indication of the racial attitudes that permitted white employers to exploit Chinese laborers because of their "inferiority."

Once the Northern Pacific Railroad reached Puget Sound in 1887, the railroad dismissed most of its Chinese workers, retaining only a few Chinese as section hands. The Great Northern Railroad, which also built a transcontinental line across Montana (it was completed in 1893), employed very few Chinese workers. Both railroads turned increasingly to an even cheaper source of labor, the Japanese workers.

The contributions of Chinese railroad workers to the development of Montana are of significant historical importance. Their expertise in grading, drilling, masonry, and demolition was vital to the construction of the Northern Pacific, which opened Montana to settlement, particularly during the homestead era of the early twentieth century. Thousands of pioneer homesteaders would move into the state and transport their bountiful farm products to market outside the state along tracks laid by the forgotten pioneers of another sort— the Chinese.

---

23. Ibid.
24. Ibid.
25. Anderson to Harris, August 7, 31, 1886, Letters Received, Registered: President and Vice President (1882–1893), President's Department, box 19, NP Records; *Weekly Missoulian*, February 16, 1883.

The arrival of Chinese miners and railroad workers during the 1860s, 1870s, and 1880s helped to create other economic opportunities for Chinese pioneers. Local Chinese communities began to develop through much of western Montana. For example, the 1890 census listed 602 Chinese living in Lewis and Clark County (Helena) and another 584 living in Silver Bow County (Butte). [26] Throughout the late nineteenth and early twentieth centuries, the state's largest "Chinatowns" were in Helena and Butte.

These urban residents came from a variety of backgrounds. Some were former miners and railroad workers who had been in Montana for some time, while others were recent arrivals from the West Coast who brought with them particular skills and trades. A few came directly from China, enticed to Montana by relatives and friends already living in the state.

Once the Chinese settled in Montana communities, they pursued a variety of occupations. They owned and operated restaurants, grocery stores, tailor shops, mercantile stores, vegetable gardens, and laundries. In 1890, Helena alone had twenty-six Chinese-owned laundries. [27] Laundry businesses were common because some Chinese had experience in this area, but also because it took little capital to start up such a business and, at least for a while, Chinese laundries posed little threat to established white businesses. [28] In addition to commercial activities, many Chinese provided important social and professional services. In 1900, Butte had at least seven Chinese physicians, some of them serving white as well as Chinese patrons. [29] Chinese skills and diligence were such that their movement into new fields of work was limited only by the willingness of the larger white community to accept the Chinese as equal members of society.

Despite intermittent white hostility, Chinese entrepreneurs were valuable to the general community. For instance, they operated pharmacies, laundries, restaurants, mercantile stores, and vegetable gardens that might have otherwise been absent in Montana's early frontier towns. Less well known is the contribution that Chinese businessmen made to the community by paying local taxes, which helped to support community growth not commonly associated with the Chinese. The 1870 tax lists for Lewis and Clark County, for instance, reveal a total assessment of Chinese taxpayers of $38,900. By 1890, the figure had climbed to $80,905. Similar statistics can be

---

26. *Eleventh Census of the United States, 1890: Population, Part I*, 439.

27. *Helena City Directory, 1890* (Helena: R. L. Polk & Company, 1890), 465–66.

28. See Paul Ong, "An Ethnic Trade: The Chinese Laundries in Early California," *The Journal of Ethnic Studies*, 8 (Winter 1981), 95–113. Although laundries were labor-intensive businesses, they did require some capital. In California, "investments ranged from $400 to $1,600, with the average being about $800" (p. 101).

29. *Butte City Directory, 1900* (Butte: R. L. Polk & Company, 1900), 689–90.

found for other Montana communities that had significant Chinese populations. [30] At the pre-inflation prices of nineteenth-century America, these figures represented a sizable amount of taxable property.

These figures also indicate that many Chinese were not "day laborers" simply passing through the state. Nor were they all sojourners planning to return immediately to China. Although large numbers did return to their homeland, still others decided to remain in the United States to establish what they hoped would be permanent livelihoods for themselves and their families. Perhaps most impressive of all, these self-reliant entrepreneurs were often forced to struggle against significant odds in their efforts to create businesses that would become an integral part of their local communities.

The Chinese pioneers in Montana created a vibrant and complex social network. As was true for many other immigrant groups in nineteenth-century America, the recent arrivals from China organized The Panic of 1893, second only to the Great Depression of the 1930s in its economic severity, had significant repercussions for Montana. Montana was one of the nation's largest producers of silver by the early 1890s; the importance of silver mining, and of quartz mining in general, helped to transform the economic structure of Montana society. By 1893 much of Montana, especially the western part of the state, was rapidly becoming both industrialized China, Chinese immigrants were often able to maintain or to create new social organizations based along traditional clan or district lines. This was especially important because local districts in China, even at the village level, had their own distinct lineages and dialects. Place of origin thus played a critical role in the development of Chinese social relationships in America. [31]

Another important feature of Chinese society in America was the general absence of women. The 1870 census listed only 123 females out of a total Chinese population of 1,949. In 1880, the figures were 80 women out of 1,765; in 1890, 59 out of 2,532; and in 1900, 39 out of 1,739. Chinese women made up no more than 7 percent, and sometimes as little as 2 percent, of the total Chinese population in Montana during the nineteenth century. [32]

30.　Lewis and Clark County Tax Lists, 1870, 1890, Archives, Montana Historical Society, Helena (hereafter MHS); Rose Hum Lee, *The Growth and Decline of Chinese Communities in the Rocky Mountain Region* (New York: Arno Press, 1978), 155–65.

31.　Hunt, *The Making of a Special Relationship*, 65–73; Zo, *Chinese Emigration into the United States*, 131–39.

32.　U.S., Department of the Interior, Census Office, *Ninth Census of the United States, 1870: Population, Volume I* (Washington, D.C.: Government Printing Office, 1872), 609; *Tenth Census of the United States, 1880: Population* (Washington, D.C.: Government Printing Office, 1883), 545; *Eleventh Census of the United States, 1890: Population, Part I*, 488; *Twelfth Census of the United States, 1900: Population, Part I* (Washington, D.C.: Government Printing Office, 1901), 492.

The absence of women in the Chinese community had a clear effect on the nature of Chinese society in America. To begin with, it helps explain the difficulty the Chinese had in producing future generations in America after the passage of the Chinese exclusion acts. Moreover, Chinese men could not depend on a traditional family dwelling to provide all their social and cultural needs. Consequently, Chinese communities in this country worked to establish institutions that would help to bind people together as they attempted to adjust to the difficulties of living in a new and sometimes hostile country. [33]

One of the most important institutions within Montana's Chinese communities was the local temple, or joss house. Sometimes this institution was contained within a store or private dwelling; other times, particularly in Butte, it was a separate structure entirely. The joss house was a focal point for both social and religious activities within the Chinese community. "The great Chinese Joss," a November 1882 Butte newspaper reported,

> arrived last night by express from California, and is being feasted to-day with all the delicacies of the season. . . . The room in which he has taken up his quarters is gaily decorated with flags, roast hogs, chickens, drums, and a thousand and one articles which defy description. [The Chinese] will wind up with a grand free lunch to-night, at which at least three hundred will be present. [34]

Butte's Chinatown had two separate temples, one of which was not torn down until 1945. [35]

Another institution that sometimes played an important role in the lives of early Montana settlers was the Chinese masonic temple. In addition to providing its members with an opportunity for relaxation and entertainment, this institution, with its emphasis on brotherhood, also reinforced Chinese social and cultural values.

In an effort to maintain a sense of order and group identification, members of the Chinese Masonic Temple in Virginia City compiled a list of twenty-one regulations. Some were designed to protect the group from outside interference and threats. For example, members were required to defend the secrecy of the lodge, and if a member were arrested, he "may not compromise any other brother"

---

33. Normal male-female relations were skewed even further because an unusually large percentage of the Chinese women in the American West in the nineteenth century were employed as prostitutes. See Lucie Cheng, "Free, Indentured, Enslaved: Chinese Prostitutes in Nineteenth-Century America," in *Labor Immigration Under Capitalism*, ed., Cheng and Bonacich, 402–34.

34. Butte *Weekly Inter Mountain*, November 23, 1882.

35. Lee, *The Growth and Decline of Chinese Communities*, 263.

Longtime resident and physician Dr. Huie Pock sold merchandise and goods to the Chinese community. His shop at 227 S. Main Street established a respected Chinese presence in Butte's business community. (Paul Eno Collection, Montana Historical Society Photograph Archives)

of the lodge. [36] Members were also prohibited from assisting Chinese who might belong to rival organizations.

Other regulations were guidelines for ethical social behavior. For instance, members were not to "covet the wife or sisters of brethren because of their beauty." They were warned: "do not occupy by force the property of your brethren" nor "deceive your brethren through fast talking." Members were prohibited from quarreling or feuding in public for fear of damaging the reputation of the brotherhood. More powerful members of the lodge were reminded not to "bully your brethren because of your might." Finally, the regulations established rules for the proper handling of such im-

---

36. Chinese masonic temple banner, March 3, 1876, Virginia City, Montana Historical Society Museum, Helena. Regulations translated by Fr. John Wang of Missoula.

portant social occasions as weddings and funerals.[37] To ensure obedience, specific punishments—such as 306 strokes with a cane—were enumerated.

Taken as a whole, these regulations indicate that Chinese pioneers were often concerned about maintaining order within their communities. Moreover, the masonic temple, like other Chinese institutions, provided its members with a sense of belonging and a feeling of comradery in an apparently harsh and frequently intimidating world.

In the case of Butte, a council of elders representing the four-clan associations eventually formed to provide valuable leadership for the Chinese community. The council, generally made up of leading businessmen, also attempted to resolve conflicts that might flair up among the Chinese.[38] One early Chinese resident in Butte recalled:

> When I first came to Butte about fifty years ago [1890s], there were about thirty-two laundries in the city. About twenty belonged to our clan cousins, while the others belonged to the members of the opposite four-clan association. There were then two large four-clan associations, but the members were not friendly toward each other. Many disputes arose between associations.
>
> In case of a dispute within our own association, it would be settled here. The elders—businessmen and those men who have lived in Butte longest—would hear the facts from the parties in dispute. The council of elders would decide who was right and who was wrong.[39]

When a dispute could not be resolved locally, the case was sent to association headquarters in San Francisco for final settlement. The Chinese communities in Montana, although geographically isolated, were still able to maintain important social, economic, and cultural ties with the outside world.

The celebration of traditional festivals was also an important feature of Chinese social life. Celebrations included the Ching Ming, Dragon Boat, Moon, and Winter Solstice festivals, but most important of all was the New Year festival.[40] The February 15, 1872, Helena *Weekly Herald* began its story on the Chinese New Year by declaring: "One of the most interesting days we have ever spent in the Territory was on yesterday, during a visit which we made to Chinatown. When we went there, we put ourselves under the care of Tong Hing, and Tong, with his usual urbanity and courtesy, put us through the more prominent of the Celestials." The reporter described in detailed, if

37. Ibid.
38. Lee, *Growth and Decline of Chinese Communites*, 226–32.
39. Quoted in ibid., 229.
40. See ibid., 273–80.

rather patronizing, terms the local arrangements made to celebrate this most famous of Chinese festivals. [41]

Ancestor worship, a product of China's strong Confucian heritage, was reinforced through funeral rites and special days of commemoration. [42] The *Herald* reported on April 8, 1869, that

> to-day is the [Chinese] annual Josh Day, on which occasion their custom is to visit the burial places — as our China men and women have done, closing their ceremonies about 2 p.m. — burn incense and innumerable small wax candles about the head stones or boards of the graves, deposit a liberal lunch of choice eatables and drinkables, designed for the spirits of the departed; recite propitiatory prayers to their savior (Josh), and otherwise show themselves sacredly mindful of the welfare of their dead. [43]

While reflecting certain religious duties, these activities served another important purpose. They enabled Chinese pioneers in Montana to maintain a cultural and spiritual link with family and clan members in China. It was unfortunate that various Sinophobic groups in the country would use the very strength of these enduring Chinese customs as a weapon against the immigrants. All too often Americans viewed Chinese social and cultural practices as "proof" that these immigrants could never be assimilated into American society. Some critics even claimed that because of their different ways and values, Chinese immigrants posed a direct threat to the traditional social order in America.

White Montana's response to Chinese immigration largely reflected contemporary regional and national attitudes. Although Chinese settlers in Montana were never the victims of the kind of mass violence that erupted in Rock Springs, Wyoming, in 1885 and along the Snake River in 1887, they were physically and mentally abused and politically exploited well into the early twentieth century. [44] It was not unusual to hear about individual Chinese being harassed or beaten in many nineteenth-century Montana communities. [45] Moreover, even before

---

41. Helena *Weekly Herald*, February 15, 1872.

42. See *Weekly Missoulian*, June 17, 1881.

43. Helena *Weekly Herald*, April 8, 1869.

44. See Robert R. Swartout, Jr., "In Defense of the West's Chinese," *Oregon Historical Quarterly*, 83 (Spring 1982), 25–36; David H. Stratton, "The Snake River Massacre of Chinese Miners, 1887," in *A Taste of the West: Essays in Honor of Robert G. Athearn*, ed. Duane E. Smith (Boulder, Colo.: Pruett Publishing Company, 1983), 109–29.

45. See Helena *Weekly Herald*, May 31, 1883, September 24, 1885; Helena *Daily Herald*, January 26, 1870; Butte *Tribune Review*, August 4, 1906; Great Falls *Daily Tribune*, December 20, 1903; Livingston *Post*, December 6, 1906; Miles City *Yellowstone Journal*, April 5, 1884; Quigley *Rock Creek Record*, June 13, 1896; Deer Lodge *New North-West*, December 23, 1881; Butte *Weekly Miner*, December 27, 1881, August 7, 1891; Butte *Semi-Weekly Miner*, October 3, 1885; Butte *Daily Miner*, October 2, 3, 1893; Butte *Daily Inter Mountain*, August 24, 1901; Anaconda *Standard*, January 21, March 8, 1892, January 8, 1893, September 5, 1899.

Montana became a state in 1889, lawmakers in the territory passed and attempted to pass laws discriminating against Chinese residents, including one aimed at ownership of mining properties.

A typical example of these anti-Chinese sentiments was expressed in an 1872 law that established a special tax, or "license," on Chinese laundries. In one form or another, this law remained on the books well into the twentieth century. [46] Discrimination against the Chinese became even more pronounced once Montana achieved statehood. In the decade or so after 1889, Montana judicial decisions systematically upheld a number of anti-Chinese laws. "By 1902," writes historian John R. Wunder, "the doors to economic opportunity and cultural equality for Chinese Montanans had been closed with appropriate legal fanfare." On March 3, 1909, the final insult was added when the state legislature passed an anti-miscegenation law prohibiting interracial marriage — a law directed against black Americans and Japanese immigrants as well as against the Chinese. [47]

Why was such animosity directed toward the Chinese, especially when they represented one of the most peaceful and diligent groups in Montana? Nineteenth-century critics of Chinese immigration often emphasized that the Chinese introduced tremendous social evils into Montana. Yet, as a group the Chinese were much more law-abiding than many whites were. Between 1900 and 1918, only six Chinese residents of Montana were sent to the state peniteniary, four of them for the same crime. This does not necessarily indicate that Montana's Chinese communities were crime-free, but the evidence does argue against the stereotypical view of Chinese communities as places "teeming" with "tong wars" and "hatchetmen." [48] Some Chinese did have an opium habit (partly because of the Western world's role in expanding the opium trade during the early nineteenth century), but "authorities generally agree that the Chinese were able to exercise better control over opium than most white miners

---

46. Montana Territory, Legislative Assembly, *Laws, Memorials, and Resolutions of the Territory of Montana, Seventh Session*, 589; State of Montana, *The Codes and Statutes of Montana, 1895, Vol.I* (Butte: Inter Mountain Publishing Company, 1895), 562; State of Montana, *The Revised Codes of Montana, 1907, Vol.I* (Helena: State Publishing Company, 1908), 807. Although Chinese were not specifically named in the law, female-operated laundries and, later, steam-type laundries were exempt from paying the tax. These descriptions were synonymous with white-operated laundries. The intent of the law was obviously discriminatory.

47. Wunder, "Law and Chinese in Frontier Montana," 30; William L. Lang, "The Nearly Forgotten Blacks on Last Chance Gulch, 1900–1912," *Pacific Northwest Quarterly*, 70 (April 1979), 57.

48. Records of the Montana State Board of Prison Commissioners, 1887–1962, RS 197, MHS.

could over whiskey and that they seemed no better or worse for the habit."[49]

Opponents of Chinese immigration also cited the "economic" threat posed by Chinese workers. During the city-wide boycott against against Chinese merchants and laborers in Butte in 1897 to 1899, union leaders in the mining city frequently referred to unfair labor competition. Such notions, however, were largely fictitious.[50] To begin with, the Chinese often did the kind of work that many white workers refused to do. Moreover, when the two groups did compete for the same job, the Chinese, who were ususally excluded from most white-controlled labor unions, were often forced to accept lower wages. The few times when Chinese workers did attempt to strike for higher wages, they found themselves caught between a hostile management and an indifferent general public.[51]

Ultimately, the overriding reason behind the anti-Chinese sentiment in Montana and the rest of the American West was racism—a racism based on cultural stereotypes as well as skin color. It was unfortunate for these Chinese pioneers that their migration to America occurred at a time when racism was especially fashionable in the United States. In fact, the animosity directed toward the Chinese coincided with similar attitudes and acts of violence against black Americans. As the country became increasingly industrialized and urbanized, minorities often became convenient scapegoats for other groups who felt "victimized" by rapid economic and social changes.[52]

An 1893 editorial published in a Butte newspaper gave voice to this racism: "The Chinaman is no more a citizen than a coyote is a citizen, and never can be." After making obligatory references to cheap labor and opium, the scathing editorial continued:

---

49. W. Eugene Hollon, *Frontier Violence: Another Look* (New York: Oxford University Press, 1974), 89.

50. Members of the Butte Chinese community eventually took the boycott leaders to court. See *Hum Fay et al. vs. Frank Baldwin et al.* Records, MC 43, MHS. Local newspapers gave the case extensive coverage, especially the Anaconda *Standard*, the *Inter Mountain*, and the Butte *Miner*. The Chinese won the case in the federal courts in May 1900, but they received no damages to cover their financial losses. See Butte *Miner*, April 4, 1899; *Daily Inter Mountain*, May 19, 1900; United States District Courts (U.S. Circuit Court—Montana), Final Record, Case #40, RG 21, National Archives—Seattle Branch. For an outstanding study of the entire affair, see Flaherty, "Boycott in Butte," 34–47.

51. See Yen, "Chinese Workers and the First Transcontinental Railroad," 129–31; Chen, *The Chinese of America*, 74–75.

52. See especially Saxton, *The Indispensable Enemy*, and Luther W. Spoehr, "Sambo and the Heathern Chinee: Californians' Racial Stereotypes in the Late 1870s," *Pacific Historical Review*, 42 (May 1973), 185–204.

The Chinaman's life is not our life, his religion is not our religion. His habits, superstitions, and modes of life are disgusting. He is a parasite, floating across the Pacific and thence penetrating into the interior towns and cities, there to settle down for a brief space and absorb the substance of those with whom he comes into competition. His one object in life is to make all the money he can and return again to his native land, dead or alive. His very existence in our midst is an insult to our intelligence. Pestilence and disease follow in his wake, no matter what sentimentalists say to the contrary. Let him go hence. He belongs not in Butte. [53]

These racist and stereotypical attitudes were not confined to Butte, but were prevalent in many Montana communities during the late nineteenth century. [54] The power and popularity of such racial sentiments help to explain the ease with which the Montana legislature and the federal government could pass so many discriminatory laws aimed at the Chinese. These laws not only limited economic opportunities and cultural equality for Chinese pioneers, but they also effectively shut off the flow of new arrivals from China. Without new, especially female, emigrants, the once-vibrant Chinese communities of the intermountain states were bound to disappear.

Several important observations can be made from this rather brief description of the Chinese experience in nineteenth-century Montana. First of all, one is struck by the great diversity of occupations that the Chinese pioneers pursued in Montana. They did not limit themselves to placer mining or railroad building, but were willing to try almost any occupation that might allow them to achieve financial security and independence. Ultimately, the ability of the Chinese to branch out into new lines of work was limited not so much by their own prejudices and cultural habits as by the prejudices of the larger white community.

One of the most important aspects of the Chinese experience was their contribution to the economic development of nineteenth-century Montana. Chinese pioneers were an integral part of the infant mining industry in the territory helping to pump thousands of dollars into the local economy while exploiting resources that other miners often ignored. The Chinese role in building the Northern Pacific Railroad was of tremendous value to the future development of the

---

53. Butte *Bystander*, February 11, 1893.

54. As early as 1871, a Missoula reporter declared: "The Chinaman lands upon our shores a serf, and remains so. He clings to his idolatry and heathenism with the tenacity of life; lives upon less than the refuse from the table of a civilized man, and devotes his sister to the basest lusts of humanity . . . ." Missoula *Pioneer*, June 22, 1871. For similar comments, see, for example, *Yellowstone Journal*, April 5, 1884; Livingston *Post*, December 6, 1906; Anaconda *Standard*, January 4, 1903.

state, as the railroad made possible the greatest growth in the state's history, from 1890 to 1920. In Montana's budding urban communities, Chinese entrepreneurs provided valuable services to non-Chinese as well as Chinese patrons. Taken as a whole, these contributions played a crucial part in transforming Montana from a primitive, isolated patchwork of localities into an increasingly sophisticated, urbanized and economically prosperous society.

As these Chinese pioneers contributed to Montana's economic development, they also built a complex and semi-permanent subcommunity of their own. This subcommunity often stressed traditional ties of clan and region, which were reinforced through participation in various cultural and religious acitivities. Unfortunately, the same customs that gave Chinese pioneers a sense of identity and purpose were used by critics to "prove" that Chinese immigrants were "polluting" America's cultural values and social order. Such attacks made it difficult for non-Chinese Americans to comprehend the richness and subtleties of Chinese customs and traditions.

This inability or unwillingness to appreciate the value of Chinese contributions was a direct result of the racial attitudes of the day. In that sense, the reaction of many white Montanans to the presence of Chinese settlers was all too typical of broader national and regional patterns. Montanans generally supported the passage of federal laws prohibiting Chinese immigration to America. At the local level, Montanans passed a series of state laws, which were upheld by the state supreme court, that intentionally discriminated against Chinese Montanans. These prejudices were so pervasive that recognition of the Chinese role in the development of modern Montana would come only after most of the Chinese pioneers and their descendants had left the state.

Elizabeth Chester Fisk in traveling costume   (Montana Historical Society Photograph Archives)

Mothers and Daughters of Eldorado

The Fisk Family of Helena, Montana, 1867–1902

Paula Petrik

For many middle-class American women in the nineteenth century, the Victorian values of piety, purity, submissiveness, and domesticity— collectively known as "True Womanhood"—largely defined their status and self-image in American society. Indeed, these "feminine" traits were often cited as justifications for denying women access to politics, education, vocational training, and professional employment.

As significant numbers of Americans began moving into Montana Territory in the 1860s and 1870s, they brought these values with them. But could such values and ideals remain intact in a new and constantly changing environment? Paula Petrik, associate professor of history in the University of Maine, argues that conditions on the frontier—such as the scarcity of domestic help, the frequent absence of husbands due to the isolated nature of early Montana communities, and the lack of traditional female social institutions—forced these middle-class women to reevaluate the "Cult of True Womanhood." Over time, they often became more self-reliant, more independent, and more politically active. These changes in attitude, however, were more evolutionary than revolutionary in nature. For all their new-found independence, Montana women continued to focus their energies on what might be termed traditional women's issues, particularly that of temperance. This emphasis on social reform would

*Paula Petrik, "Mothers and Daughters of Eldorado: The Fisk Family of Helena, Mt., 1867–1902," *Montana The Magazine of Western History*, 32 (Summer 1982), 50–63.

last well into the twentieth century and would serve as a basis for the participation of women in the Progressive movement.

————————

Helena, Montana, like so many other mining towns along the Rocky Mountain cordillera represented a kind of Eldorado for its settlers whether they came prospecting for gold or intended to profit from supplying the miners. In both cases, mining camp dwellers anticipated "bettering their condition in life"—to use a popular nineteenth-century phrase. The settlement of these Eldorados, however, was not solely a process wherein the camp citizens raised cities out of the wilderness; the frontier also worked its changes upon its inhabitants. For Helena's Elizabeth Chester Fisk, and for other Eldorado women who were married and of the middling sort, the frontier proved to be a transforming experience. In a number of ways, both the nature of the community and its special demographic circumstances affected women and brought them to new perceptions of themselves.

First, the frontier eroded women's informal networks— structures that underpinned nineteenth-century women's lives—and cast women back into the home and domesticity. Second, the peculiar demography of the frontier, especially the disproportionate number of men to women, created a scarcity of domestic help that increased the burdens of managing a household for middling women. Third, the isolation of these mining towns necessitated that these women's husbands be absent for long periods; during these times women were left to manage on their own. And fourth, the frontier environment undermined the social institutions in which nineteenth-century women normally anchored their power and countenanced community activities that were frankly antithetical to women's traditional familial concerns. Elizabeth Chester Fisk was one of countless women who experienced these frontier changes.

A particularly reliable witness, Elizabeth Fisk very nearly corresponded to what might be termed the statistically average, middle-class woman living in Helena between 1867 and 1900. In 1870, if the census enumerator had been inclined to generalize about Helena's female population, he would have described a typical example as twenty-two years old, married, "keeping house," born in the Northeast, and living in a nuclear-family household composed of four persons— husband, wife, child, and either a boarder or a servant. This average woman's husband would have been approximately nine years her senior. [1] In that census year, Elizabeth Fisk, a native of Connecticut, was twenty-four and her husband, Robert Emmett Fisk, a former New Yorker and the editor of the Helena *Herald*, was eight years older than she. As editor of one of the town's newspapers, Robert Fisk occupied a secure middle position, neither in the same social or economic class as Helena's capitalists nor among the city's mechanics and artisans. [2] The Fisk household on Rodney Street consisted of Elizabeth and Robert, their young daughter, Grace, and May Bromley, Elizabeth's present boarder and future sister-in-law. [3]

Spanning over three decades, Elizabeth Fisk's correspondence breathes life into an otherwise bland demographic description and illuminates the relationship between women's lives and the frontier. Because Elizabeth Fisk had a daughter, it is also possible to gauge the effect of the frontier on two generations of women.

Born in February of 1846 in Vernon, Connecticut, to Azubah and Isaac Chester, a Congregational minister, Elizabeth grew up in an atmosphere of New England piety and gentility. Except for the Chesters' ardent abolitionism, the family was generally conservative, and supported the Union's cause during the Civil War. As part of her contribution to this effort, Elizabeth, like many other northern women, helped manufacture blankets for the Union Army. In one of these bundles of blankets, she pinned a patriotic and encouraging note. Captain Robert Fisk, who received Elizabeth's blanket and note, was so taken with the sentiments expressed in her message that he commenced a correspondence with Elizabeth and continued it for the remainder of his military service. After the war ended, Robert determined to thank his correspondent and benefactor in person and traveled to Connecticut to meet her. [4] Well-pleased with each other, Robert and Elizabeth decided to marry after she finished teaching in the spring of 1867. Elizabeth's matrimonial decision betokened greater changes in her life than leaving the classroom; her husband planned to settle on the western frontier.

One of six brothers, Robert Fisk came from an equally genteel, upstate New York family. The elder Fisk brothers had early appreciated the promise of the West and had established themselves in

---

1. Derived from statistical analysis of the *U.S. Manuscript Census, 1870.* It should be noted, however, that this statistical paradigm holds only for 1870. As the age structure of the community shifts, Elizabeth Chester Fisk becomes a representative of her age cohort.

2. Stephan Thernstrom, *The Other Bostonians: Poverty and Progress in the American Metropolis, 1880–1970* (Cambridge: Harvard University, 1973), 289–92.

3. *U.S. Manuscript Census, 1870.*

4. Helena *Independent*, April 22, 1927.

St. Paul with an eye to leading expeditions across the Dakota plains into Montana. In the early 1860s, James Liberty Fisk had done precisely that and had persuaded the Fisk brothers to stake their fortunes on a small but rich gold camp in the Prickly Pear Valley, now grown into the town of Helena. With the demise of the town's first journal, the *Montana Radiator*, the community lacked a newspaper, and the Fisks stepped in, buying the defunct paper's presses and inventory. Because Robert had had experience as a journalist in Indiana, the brothers Fisk pressed him into service as editor and general manager of the undertaking. In the winter of 1867, Robert traveled east to solicit advertising, to purchase printing supplies, and to claim his bride. That spring Elizabeth and Robert married and by the end of May they were aboard the steamer *Little Rock* headed up the Missouri River to Fort Benton and Helena, Montana Territory. [5]

Elizabeth's transition from New England to the trans-Mississippi frontier was much swifter and less arduous than the same journey was for the immigrants on the overland trail. None of the physical strain or the conflicts between husbands and wives that had characterized the immigrants bound for Oregon and California touched the river-route travellers. [6] Passage by steamboat into the Rocky Mountains was normally a fairly relaxed and comfortable experience. When Elizabeth arrived in Fort Benton in late July 1867, both her household and ideological baggage arrived intact. Her allegiance to the "cult of true womanhood" — the nineteenth-century prescription that directed women to be pure, submissive, and self-sacrificing — remained unshaken, and it had been safely transported to the mining frontier.

Once in Helena, Elizabeth immediately entered into the life and work of the household she and Robert shared with his elder brother, James, and his family. Like many nineteenth-century women, Elizabeth conceived her role as more than a housekeeper for an individual home. For Elizabeth, the task of housekeeping extended to the community and beyond. "My first impressions of Helena," she wrote to her sister, Fannie,

> have been generally confirmed. I like the place much; it is not like home, but there is a wide field for usefulness here, and entering upon the work earnestly and prayerfully we need never be lonely or

---

5. Guide to Fisk Family Papers (hereafter Fisk Family Papers), MC 31, Montana Historical Society Archives, Helena (hereafter MHS); Elizabeth Chester Fisk to Frances Chester, May 8, 1867; Elizabeth Chester Fisk to the Fisk Family, May 17, 1867, Fisk Family Papers.

6. John Mack Faragher, *Women and Men on the Overland Trail* (New Haven: Yale University Press, 1979), chaps. 3–5.

disheartened. There is *room* here for every one to win a name and an influence that shall be widespread and shall ever be for good on all those around. [7]

Similarly, Elizabeth agreed with traditional nineteenth-century definitions of the proper roles of men and women. On the one hand, Elizabeth applauded restrained, lady-like behavior, but on the other hand, she abhorred its excess—"ladyism." [8] She was also impatient with and accordingly critical of overblown masculinity. Elizabeth conceived of gender roles as characterized by restraint, purpose, usefulness, and suitability as a marriage partner. Like most women of her century, Elizabeth held that women were more naturally moral and more amenable to marriage than men. Women's better nature she set against male corruptness and sensuality. [9]

Ideologically undamaged as she was, Elizabeth immediately encountered problems that forced her to make certain alterations in her thinking. The first involved her living arrangements. Initially, Robert and Elizabeth joined Robert's brother and his family. Sharing a household with her indifferent sister-in-law and fractious niece did not suit Elizabeth, and the necessity for the Robert Fisks to acquire their own home became a *leitmotif* in Elizabeth's letters. [10] Besides undermining Elizabeth's sense of domestic purpose and usefulness, May Fisk's social diffidence obstructed Elizabeth's entree into Helena's society. Had her sister-in-law not been occupied, she would have provided Elizabeth with an introduction into the town's social circles. Putting aside nineteenth-century etiquette, Elizabeth began venturing out on her own in September 1867, card case in hand, to make friends. [11] To her pleasure, Lizzie succeeded and entered Helena's miniature world of female networks.

Nineteenth-century, informal female networks functioned in a variety of ways. They were instrumental in establishing cultural institutions and assisted women in their attempts to regulate society. Additionally, the bonds between women acted as a means by which women shared information on a number of topics ranging from health and child care to fashion. These female friendships consoled women in

---

7. Elizabeth Chester Fisk to Frances Chester, July 31, 1867, Fisk Family Papers.

8. Elizabeth Chester Fisk to Frances Chester, June 1, 1867, Fisk Family Papers.

9. Ibid.; Elizabeth Chester Fisk to Frances Chester, April 27, 1867, Fisk Family Papers.

10. Elizabeth Chester Fisk to Azubah Clarke Chester, August 8, 22, 1867, October 1867, November 6, 1867; Elizabeth Chester Fisk to Frances Chester, October 15, 1867, Fisk Family Papers.

11. Elizabeth Chester Fisk to Frances Chester, September 2, 1867, Fisk Family Papers.

their times of trouble, defined norms for the group, and relieved the tedium, loneliness, and drudgery of women's domestic work. In the nineteenth century, women derived more of their emotional sustenance from each other than from the men in their lives. [12]

Having already confronted the problems of housing on the frontier, Elizabeth faced the ambiguity of making friendships there. In Helena there were few women, and those few were markedly different from women she had known in the East. In religious, ethnic, and class terms, Helena's female population was heterogeneous. [13] In the process of making friends, Lizzie came into contact with Jews, Catholics, non-believers, and women who were uneducated or socially unrefined. To alleviate her isolation and to reenter the female world, which was central to a nineteenth-century woman's well-being, Lizzie had to learn a measure of tolerance. Her friendships cut across the social boundaries so dear to the nineteenth century. [14] In Mrs. Ashley, no paragon of the domestic order Elizabeth respected, she found much to admire. And, although Mrs. Scribner was a devout Catholic, Elizabeth thought highly of her. Anti-Semitism had no place in Elizabeth's world; Helena's Jewish merchants had been generous to her and to Dr. Bullard, her friend. [15]

Yet even as the frontier broadened Elizabeth's experience of other women, the transiency of its population undermined her efforts to form stable, sustaining relationships with women. In May of 1868 Elizabeth noted that ". . . every day parties are leaving . . . still, as the boats bring us greater numbers than they carry away, we do not despair or complain." [16] Nonetheless, this constant turnover began to blunt Elizabeth's attempts to form friendships. Her two friends, Mrs. Smith and Mrs. Norris, moved away. Speaking of Mrs. Smith, Elizabeth wrote, "When I think how much I shall lose in losing her kind friendship and society, I am almost determined never to make

---

12.   Women's networks and their importance and function have been discussed by several historians: Julie Roy Jeffrey, *Frontier Women, The Trans-Mississippi Frontier, 1840–1880* (New York: Hill and Wang, 1979), chap. 4; Nancy Cott, *The Bonds of Womanhood, "Women's Sphere" in New England, 1780–1835* (New Haven: Yale University Press, 1977); Carroll Smith-Rosenberg, "The Female World of Love and Ritual: Relations Between Women in Nineteenth Century America," in Michael Gordon, ed., *The American Family in Social-Historical Perspective* ([1973]; reprint, New York: St. Martin's Press, 1978), 334–58.

13.   Derived from statistical analysis of the *U.S. Manuscript Census, 1870.*

14.   Elizabeth Chester Fisk to Azubah Clarke Chester, November 6, 1867, Fisk Family Papers.

15.   Elizabeth Chester Fisk to Azubah Clarke Chester, August 22, 1867, Fisk Family Papers.

16.   Elizabeth Chester Fisk to Azubah Clarke Chester, May 17, 1868, Fisk Family Papers.

a warm friend, a mere passing acquaintance will do. . . ." [17] In consequence of these experiences, Elizabeth pondered a solution:

> . . . I often ask myself what shall be my course of conduct, how shall
> I live in such a community. *The temptation is often great to make my home,
> when I shall gain it, my world, to seek no other companionship outside* its *little
> circle.* . . . Nothing is permanent. One's best friends leave them in a
> day and pleasant acquaintances prove mere gossips. I have only one
> lady friend that I could depend on should misfortune or sorrow should
> come. . . . *One needs to learn to stand alone, to find within one's self the highest
> delight.* [18] (Italics mine)

In this Elizabeth alluded to both the fragility of frontier female networks and the necessity of learning to live apart from a web of relationships. A condition shared by Elizabeth and her peers—frequent
and long periods apart from their husbands—reinforced her need
"to learn to stand alone."

Owing to Helena's geographic isolation, many of Helena's wives,
and especially those married to businessmen, found themselves alone
for months at a time. The nature of their husband's businesses demanded that these entrepreneurs leave the city periodically to nego-
tiate credit or to buy merchandise. [19] For Elizabeth the winter of 1868
was one of those periods of separation. Shortly after Christmas,
Robert determined that it was necessary for the survival of the *Herald*
that he return east to solicit advertising and to purchase printing
supplies. [20] The first five months of 1868 marked a crucial point in
Elizabeth's frontier career.

Bereft of Robert and with her role in the household ill-defined,
Elizabeth experienced personal freedom. Immediately, she set about
finding some useful occupation for herself and took up tutoring. [21]
In a month's time her little school had grown, and she added an additional source of income—dressmaking. "I prefer," she wrote, "to work
for money rather than sew for Mrs. Fisk. There is no necessity for

---

17. Ibid.
18. Elizabeth Chester Fisk to Azubah Clarke Chester, May 24, 1868, Fisk Family
Papers.
19. Harriet P. Sanders, Diaries, 1868, 1888, Wilbur F. Sanders Collection, MC 53,
MHS. Both the Helena *Herald* and the Helena *Independent* note the arrival and departure of various Helena entrepreneurs on a regular basis. While some of these journeys
were short trips to nearby towns, many of them, especially in the early period, were
longer and to more distant places.
20. Elizabeth Chester Fisk to Azubah Clarke Chester, December 28, 1867, Fisk
Family Papers.
21. Elizabeth Chester Fisk to Azubah Clarke Chester, January 19, 1868, Fisk Family
Papers.

my doing either. I only followed my inclination in the matter." [22] While
Elizabeth's work provided a pleasant alternative to loneliness, her attitude toward her employment reflected a growing realization of her
own autonomy and capabilities. "I am," wrote Elizabeth soon after
her husband's departure, "at liberty to go out whenever and wherever
I wish, and I have the time to manufacture all sorts of pretty things." [23]
Although reluctant to do so in her first months in Helena, Lizzie
now took advantage of the opportunities the mining town's prosperity
afforded its citizens. Money could buy sufficient domestic service to
free women from domestic drudgery, and Robert had thoughtfully
provided her with a Chinese manservant.

Released from the bonds of her domestic responsibilities, Elizabeth
went out. She went for late-night walks and attended the theater by
herself. [24] Part of this new freedom extended to her relationships with
men in the community, and Elizabeth tested these social boundaries
with her brother-in-law, Van Fisk, and with an attractive bachelor,
Dr. Bullard. The time she spent with the good doctor became a
matter of public concern, and Lizzie confessed in a letter to her
husband: "They tell me I'm flirting with the Dr. Do you fear to trust
me, Rob?" [25] A month later, commenting on a ride to a nearby mining camp with Dr. Bullard, she revealed something of the ambiguity
of her position: "Was there any harm in doing so? This town is
so different from my old home that I need one to advise me often.
I have often depended on my mother's judgment in matters of
this kind." [26]

Besides experimenting with the social definitions of her female
role, Elizabeth also tried the intellectual ones. With her gentlemen
callers, she felt free to discuss a variety of scientific and philosophical
topics and, with Mr. Stuart, she discussed the business side of publishing a newspaper. [27] Within a month of Robert's departure, Elizabeth had developed a sense of herself apart from her husband
and marriage:

---

22. Elizabeth Chester Fisk to Azubah Clarke Chester, January 24, 1868, Fisk
Family Papers.
23. Elizabeth Chester Fisk to Robert Emmett Fisk, January 8, 1868, Fisk
Family Papers.
24. Elizabeth Chester Fisk to Azubah Clarke Chester, February 15, 1868, Fisk
Family Papers.
25. Elizabeth Chester Fisk to Robert Emmett Fisk, January 12, 1868, Fisk Family
Papers.
26. Elizabeth Chester Fisk to Robert Emmett Fisk, February 1, 1868, Fisk Family
Papers.
27. Elizabeth Chester Fisk to Frances Chester, January 26, February 22, 1868;
Elizabeth Chester Fisk to Azubah Clarke Chester, February 29, 1868, Fisk Family
Papers.

I did not think it possible when Rob left me that I could be so happy without him, and especially in this place. I do not call it home. But I have learned, if I knew it not before, that one can be happy independent of externals. I sometimes wonder at the self-contained life I lead. I am dependent on no one for my comfort and serenity of mind, although my friends are kind and serve me in every possible way. [28]

For some women, the freedom to come and go as they pleased, the ubiquity of male companionship, and Helena's booming prosperity resulted in something more than tame flirtations. In February of 1868, Elizabeth observed: "Divorces are fashionable here, and it is a common remark that a man in the mountains cannot keep his wife." [29] In Elizabeth's harmless dalliances, she had skated close to the dangers besetting frontier marriages and revealed the opportunities — both legitimate and illegitimate — available to frontier women. Unfortunately for Elizabeth, circumstances involving the Fisk paper and the legion Fisk family members cut short Elizabeth's new-found independence, and Robert was recalled from the East to take command of the situation. [30]

Now that help was on the way, Elizabeth reflected upon her experiences. In doing so, she revealed the central tension that would vex her for the remainder of her years in Helena. On the one hand, she viewed her winter interlude as a reaffirmation of the "cult of true womanhood." Elizabeth wrote that she had gained some measure of personal strength,

. . . .and I trust laid the foundations of a glorious, would I might a *perfect* womanhood. I never yet fully realized what and how much it is to be a true-whole-souled woman. Such capacities for doing, being, and suffering, such striving for the good and the pure, not only or chiefly for ourselves, but for those we love. [31]

While Elizabeth acknowledged the nineteenth-century role of self-sacrifice and selflessness, she had also experienced its alternative. A few weeks before her husband's return, she had:

---

28. Elizabeth Chester Fisk to Frances Chester, January 25, 1868, Fisk Family Papers.

29. Elizabeth Chester Fisk to Azubah Clarke Chester, February 1, 1868, Fisk Family Papers; Paula Petrik, "Occasions of Unhappy Differences: Divorce on the Rocky Mountain Mining Frontier, Lewis and Clark County, Montana, 1865–1900," unpublished paper.

30. Elizabeth Chester Fisk to Frances Chester, March 22, 1868; Elizabeth Chester Fisk to Azubah Clarke Chester, March 29, 1868, March 10, 1868, Fisk Family Papers.

31. Elizabeth Chester Fisk to Azubah Clarke Chester, April 4, 1868, Fisk Family Papers.

come to the determination to be independent of any and every one, to seek my own enjoyment where I can best find it, independent of all who would *selfishly* seek to oppose my plans. This listening to and heeding the advice of *all* my friends has caused me much vexation and sorrow during all the winter, and independence is the only comfortable plan. [32]

Despite Elizabeth's flirtation with independence and in the face of her disappointment with women friends, she quickly determined her new course of action. Referring to Robert's brief trip to Fort Benton, just after his return from the East, Elizabeth wrote, ". . . having given up all my friends for him, I cannot well lose him also, even for a day." [33] Elizabeth was about to begin a long detour into the home, but before she closed the door on Rodney Street she still maintained contact with the community through the church.

Because she was a Protestant and because there was no Congregational church, Elizabeth presented her letter of good standing to the Methodist minister and shortly afterward started a Sabbath school for young boys. But as the months passed, Elizabeth gradually became disenchanted with the poor church attendance and with the even more wretched sermons. [34] The quality of preaching notwithstanding, Elizabeth joined the Methodist women's organization and served as its secretary. [35] Unfortunately, her involvement proved disheartening. [36] The congregation, attempting to maintain its footing on the frontier, made concessions to mining-town realities and sanctioned gaming and dancing. The congregation's stand on these two issues, and the poor preaching, frustrated Elizabeth's effective participation.

Not only did the frontier undermine the traditional sources of women's influence, but it also created an environment inimical to Elizabeth's sense of community spirit and morality. At the same time the church alienated Elizabeth, she became increasingly estranged from the community. The result: Elizabeth made a conscious decision to forsake any involvement in either the church or community and busied herself exclusively with her new home. [37] But even in her

---

32.   Elizabeth Chester Fisk to Azubah Clarke Chester, April 1868, Fisk Family Papers.

33.   Ibid.

34.   Elizabeth Chester Fisk to Azubah Clarke Chester, December 15, 1867, Fisk Family Papers.

35.   Elizabeth Chester Fisk to Azubah Clarke Chester, June 21, 1868, Fisk Family Papers.

36.   Elizabeth Chester Fisk to Azubah Clarke Chester, July 5, 1868, Fisk Family Papers.

37.   Elizabeth Chester Fisk to Azubah Clarke Chester, June 21, 1868, July 13, 1868, Fisk Family Papers.

self-imposed isolation, Elizabeth did not entirely forget the lessons of the past winter. When her mother asked what would become of Elizabeth should she be deprived of her natural protector, Elizabeth replied: ". . . I have come to the conclusion that I am abundantly able to take care of myself. Every kind of labor with head or hand, is well remunerated." [38] She could do a variety of things: open a school, take in boarders, or open a wash house. Elizabeth observed that the last option would be the most lucrative—the Chinese would do most of the work. [39] More important, wrote Elizabeth, ". . . I have no little ones to prevent my labors of either kind and I might add, do not intend to have until we can better afford it." [40] In the fall of 1868, however, two events occurred which pushed Elizabeth further into a domestic existence.

Another fracas at the *Herald*, which briefly split Helena into two warring camps, resulted in Elizabeth's social ostracism. If Elizabeth had chosen isolation before, she now found it forced upon her from without. [41] Concomitant with this episode and despite Elizabeth's recent vow to postpone childbearing until a financially auspicious time, she found herself pregnant. On May 21, 1869, she gave birth to her first child, a daughter, whom she named Grace Chester. By the end of November of 1869, Elizabeth had come to accept the vagaries of the various Fisk personalities and had made her family her primary circle. What had begun as a temporary decision to isolate herself had been transformed into a firm resolution. The birth of her child only served to rationalize further her separation from the community, the church, and the company of other women. Elizabeth summed up her situation when she wrote to her sister:

> On the whole, I am pleased with the state of things and feel sufficiently independent of all outsiders to put up with the inevitable. *We are numerous enough a family to form a community by ourselves.* [42] (Italics mines)

Elizabeth's response to Helena's frontier society was withdrawal into the family and the conceptualization of women's role in an even narrower fashion. She had commenced in earnest her long circuit into domesticity.

---

38. Elizabeth Chester Fisk to Azubah Clarke Chester, August 30, 1868, Fisk Family Papers.

39. Ibid.

40. Ibid.

41. Elizabeth Chester Fisk to Azubah Clarke Chester, September 21, 27, 1868, October 25, 1868; Elizabeth Chester Fisk to Frances Chester, November 29, 1868, Fisk Family Papers.

42. Elizabeth Chester Fisk to Frances Chester, November 14, 1868, Fisk Family Papers.

The Fisks and their house at 305 N. Rodney. Left to right, they are Robbie, Robert E., Elizabeth holding Jamie, Grace holding Florence, and Asa. (Montana Historical Society Photograph Archives)

The decade of the 1870s marked Elizabeth's increasing involvement with the minutiae of domesticity and child care to the exclusion of all else. The advent of three additional children intensified her child rearing responsibilities. By 1877, Elizabeth oversaw four children under the age of eight. And the lack of household help further aggravated the restrictions of the domestic circle. Nineteenth-century women normally anticipated employing one or more domestics to assist them in the tasks of household drudgery, but in this hope Elizabeth met only disappointment. In one six-month period, she saw fourteen servants come and go from Rodney Street. [43] Her last pregnancy had highlighted the vague unease she had begun to sense. Referring to her last confinement, Elizabeth vented her frustration:

> I did *not* want any more children, and there have been times in the last few months when I have felt *utterly unreconciled* to the state of affairs, and even now I sometimes think I *cannot* care for any more little ones. [44]

---

43. Elizabeth Chester Fisk to Azubah Clarke Chester, May 20, 1873, August 10, 1873, Fisk Family Papers.

44. Elizabeth Chester Fisk to Azubah Clarke Chester, October 28, 1877, Fisk Family Papers.

Concomitant with Elizabeth's impatience with her position, she began to adopt a quasi-adversary position with respect to men. [45] This was best illustrated in her tart comments regarding the famous Beecher-Tilton adultery trial. "I believe," wrote Elizabeth, "that no one exercises the least charity toward women, and let her err *even in thought* while all are ready to invent excuses for the 'Lords of Creation.'" [46] Elizabeth had departed from her earlier view of women's unrelieved self-sacrifice and service. What she had conceived of previously as separate-but-equal duties had been translated into a vague sense of the inequity of the social relations between the sexes. But Elizabeth's criticism, as reflected in her attitude toward politics and woman suffrage, remained ill-defined.

Having forsaken what she conceived as her public responsibilities, Elizabeth expressed impatience with women who espoused a political position, especially that of women's rights. When Mrs. Ashley, the territorial governor's wife, came to dinner, Elizabeth observed, "Everything passed off nicely except that Mrs. Ashley *would* introduce her favorite topic of women's rights and argufy on the subject until everyone was weary." [47] Yet, there was the sense that Lizzie was vaguely disturbed by her own abdication, and she noted with relief when Mrs. Ashley moderated her support of women's rights.

While Elizabeth willingly participated in local government, she still viewed state and national politics as potentially damaging to women's moral superiority. [48] Nonetheless, Elizabeth allowed herself to become a legislative spectator in 1876. In company with some acquaintances, she visited the statehouse. "It was a novel experience," she noted, "but we came home congratulating ourselves that female suffrage had never been extended to Montana and that nothing compelled us to undergo forty days of law-making." [49] More important than politics to Elizabeth was her growing realization of the disparity between what her children learned at home and what they learned elsewhere.

To insulate her sons and daughters from Helena's secular and pernicious influence, Elizabeth determined to make her home a bastion

---

45. Elizabeth Chester Fisk to Azubah Clarke Chester, February 8, 1874, Fisk Family Papers.
46. Elizabeth Chester Fisk to Azubah Clarke Chester, August 2, 1874, Fisk Family Papers.
47. Elizabeth Chester Fisk to Frances Chester, November 21, 1869, Fisk Family Papers.
48. Elizabeth Chester Fisk to Azubah Clarke Chester, March 15, 1876, Fisk Family Papers.
49. Ibid.; Elizabeth Chester Fisk to Azubah Clarke Chester, February 14, 1876, Fisk Family Papers.

of Christian values and conduct. [50] But combating the town's worldliness demanded constant vigilance and the perpetual supervision
of her children. Her husband, too, encouraged Elizabeth's unrelieved
attendance upon the young Fisks. Robert's expectations especially
exasperated Elizabeth when he deserted his familial obligations for
recreational excursions. As a result, Elizabeth felt stifled. "I think
some days," she wrote, "that I will either go crazy or run away." [51]
Neither did Elizabeth embrace madness nor did she run away, but
she did increase her activities outside the home and set aside time
for herself. [52]

By 1880 Elizabeth's dissatisfaction with her situation reached a
critical point. She felt, by this time, taken for granted and desired
time apart from Rodney Street. Elizabeth proposed that she and
Robert take a trip to White Sulphur Springs, a local mineral spa.
Robert demurred, saying she should wait until the entire family could
make the trip. That, replied Elizabeth, was not the idea and pointed
out that she had not been away from the children for *eight* years.
Despite Robert's domestic wheedling, Elizabeth departed for a two
week vacation to White Sulphur Springs. [53]

Elizabeth's sojourn prompted further forays outside the home, and
she increased her community activities and took up painting. Her
displeasure at men's ability to come and go at will crystallized into
frank resentment. "It does not seem right," she opined, "for them
to have all the pleasure while we mothers stay home and take care
of the children." [54] For the remainder of 1881, Elizabeth pleased
herself. Once again, Elizabeth's independence was shortlived. In 1882,
she found herself an unwilling mother-to-be and, reflecting on her
condition and surveying the past fifteen years, she wrote bitterly:

> If I felt really well and like myself, I could say many lovely and pleasant
> things of these fifteen years of my life.
>
> But just now it is a good deal of a burden to live at all and while
> I know all the "lovely and pleasant things" have been, are still with
> me, I do not fully appreciate them or feel prepared to say much in
> their praise. [55]

---

50. Elizabeth Chester Fisk to Azubah Clarke Chester, October 28, 1878, November
19, 1879, Fisk Family Papers.
51. Elizabeth Chester Fisk to Azubah Clarke Chester, August 6, 1879, Fisk Family
Papers.
52. Elizabeth Chester Fisk to Azubah Clarke Chester, July 14, 1879, Fisk Family
Papers.
53. Elizabeth Chester Fisk to Azubah Clarke Chester, July 27, 1880, Fisk Family
Papers.
54. Elizabeth Chester Fisk to Azubah Clarke Chester, July 7, 12, 1880, Fisk Family
Papers.
55. Elizabeth Chester Fisk to Azubah Clarke Chester, March 28, 1882, Fisk Family
Papers.

On April 24, 1882, Elizabeth gave birth prematurely to twins, her second daughter and fourth son. If Elizabeth had despaired of the cares of motherhood before, her depression now became all the greater. But at long last, her parents made their long-postponed trip west, and their visit acted as a tonic for Elizabeth. Their assistance with the babies and the household chores helped Elizabeth regain her health and her enthusiasm. Once more she turned her thoughts to matters outside her domestic circle. "My responsibility, my accountability," she wrote, "are great in my own household. How far my duty extends outside I have not decided." [56] For the next two decades, Elizabeth would define the limits of her duty outside her family.

The first indication of which direction she would take occurred a few days before the end of 1883. In her years in Helena, Elizabeth's stand on temperance was a personal one, confined to her home and to church temperance activities for children. She determined to carry her private conviction into the public sphere and attended a reception given under the auspices of the Women's Christian Temperance Union. [57]

Among Elizabeth's myriad community organization memberships—Poor Committee, Home for Working Women, Women's Helena for the Capital Club, Women's Relief Corps—her association with the Women's Christian Temperance Union (WCTU) proved the most important to Elizabeth's ideological development. On the social level, the Helena chapter mobilized women's influence in the home by sponsoring a number of colloquia centered on women's work in the Bible. [58] Generally well-received, these gatherings were not quite so successful in persuading Helena's womenfolk to sign the pledge. [59] Undaunted, the local WCTU and Elizabeth became more overtly political. In addition to circulating petitions for a local option liquor law, WCTU members collected signatures for raising the female age of consent. [60] In the later instance Elizabeth assumed the role of lobbyist and pressed her cause with the territorial legislators. In 1887 she testified before a legislative committee in support of stricter rape

---

56. Elizabeth Chester Fisk to Azubah Clarke Chester, October 14, 1883, Fisk Family Papers.

57. Elizabeth Fisk's benevolent and community activities were numerous, and her reportage of such activities consumed much of her correspondence and time. For examples see: Elizabeth Chester Fisk to Azubah Clarke Chester, February 11, April 24, May 8, 1887, March 11, December 18, 1888, May 28, June 23, 1889, Fisk Family Papers. See also: Miscellany, Helena Women's Helena for the Capital Club Collection, MC 48, MHS.

58. Elizabeth Chester Fisk to Azubah Clarke Chester, November 14, December 12, 1886, Fisk Family Papers.

59. Elizabeth Chester Fisk to Azubah Clarke Chester, October 20, 1886, Fisk Family Papers.

60. Elizabeth Chester Fisk to Azubah Clarke Chester, January 9, 1887, Fisk Family Papers.

statutes. Never forthcoming in sexual matters, Elizabeth overcame her repugnance in the interests of this women's cause. "I cannot tell you," she commented, "how hard it was to go before this committee of whom one was a *cranky bachelor* and talk about these things." [61]

Elizabeth's temperance work was not limited to local affairs. Beginning in 1886 and for several succeeding years, she attended the territorial WCTU conventions. In the report of the Helena Union for 1886, the chapter reported that the female membership had used their ballot to elect temperance advocates to the school board. Among other resolutions passed at this and other conventions was one supporting the enfranchisement of women, and Elizabeth, along with other Montana WCTU members, unanimously endorsed the woman suffrage proposition. [62] Elizabeth had traveled a long way from the days when she had criticized Mrs. Ashley for her women's rights position.

Under the temperance banner, Elizabeth had moved from informal political activity to formal political activism, from a single issue to a broad-based program of women's social reform, and from a political spectator to political activist. Yet, Elizabeth, whose politics grew out of her experience of motherhood, remained essentially conservative and drew the line at women in politics as candidates. When she heard Ella Knowles, the female Populist candidate, speak in 1892, she pronounced the occasion "simply disgusting." [63]

As Elizabeth's political outlook shifted so did her views of child rearing. As her eldest child, Grace, approached adolescence, Elizabeth noted the differences between herself and her daughter. Of Grace she observed:

> She is a fine scholar and spurs the rest on, and as the "big boys" all admire her and listen to what she says, she has a good influence over them. I often wonder at her, she is so fearless and independent and says most unmerciful things to the careless and lazy ones. [64]

While Elizabeth still attempted to carry out her mother's uncompromising child-rearing precepts, she remarked that Grace's boldness forced her to make concessions. She, moreover, admitted that fron-

61. Elizabeth Chester Fisk to Azubah Clarke Chester, February 23, 1887, Fisk Family Papers.

62. Minutes of the Montana Woman's Christian Temperance Union, 1886. See also: Minutes of Montana Woman's Christian Temperance Union, 1887, 1888, 1890, Montana Women's Christian Temperance Union Collection, MC 160, MHS.

63. Elizabeth Chester Fisk to Azubah Clarke Chester, November 8, 1892, Fisk Family Papers.

64. Elizabeth Chester Fisk to Azubah Clarke Chester, May 17, 1881, Fisk Family Papers.

tier society forced some accommodation, else a girl felt "badly used." [65] Elizabeth brushed aside her mother's fears by pointing out that Grace was "more mature than many girls . . . and has been thrown so often on her own resources in the last two years that she has become very womanly and self-reliant." [66]

In her description of Grace, Elizabeth betrayed yet another shift in perception. Although she had toyed with autonomy in her first years in Helena, Elizabeth identified womanhood with self-sacrifice and with service to others. As Grace neared adulthood, Elizabeth saw it in terms of self-reliance, a quality she wished for her daughter. To that end, Elizabeth insisted that Grace enter college at Carleton College in Northfield, Minnesota.

Grace, however, spurned the opportunity for advanced scholarship and chose to remain in Helena among her friends. [67] Although Grace disappointed her mother in this, she showed signs of increasing independence and ability. Along with some friends, she explored the possibilities of homesteading but was frustrated because she was still a minor. [68] She turned instead to painting and sold several of her works. [69] Elizabeth preferred that her daughter learn to set type, a useful skill. In fact, Elizabeth believed that in addition to domestic skills every young woman should acquire some useful trade. [70] On the subject of female moral education Elizabeth remained silent. In this area she reserved her energies for her sons. ". . . [A] boy or young man," she wrote, "is constantly exposed to many temptations in a town like this, and without Christian principles one is never safe." [71]

In 1890 Grace commemorated her majority by having herself listed separately in the city directory as an artist. [72] The act, which was more gesture than anything because Grace's craft did not support her, demonstrated her desire to identify herself separately with some gainful employment. In June of that same year, Robert and Elizabeth, in a mood of self-congratulation, presented Grace with a piano,

---

65. Elizabeth Chester Fisk to Azubah Clarke Chester, January 24, 1886, Fisk Family Papers.

66. Ibid.

67. Elizabeth Chester Fisk to Azubah Clarke Chester, January 15, 1888, Fisk Family Papers.

68. Elizabeth Chester Fisk to Azubah Clarke Chester, November 27, 1887, April 11, 1888, Fisk Family Papers.

69. Elizabeth Chester Fisk to Azubah Clarke Chester, February 20, April 11, 1888, Fisk Family Papers.

70. Elizabeth Chester Fisk to Azubah Clarke Chester, October 21, 1888, Fisk Family Papers.

71. Elizabeth Chester Fisk to Azubah Clarke Chester, April 25, 1892, Fisk Family Papers.

72. *Helena City Directory, 1890* (Helena: R. L. Polk and Company, 1890).

rewarding her postponement of marriage. [73] The gift was premature. In August Grace announced her intention of marrying Hardy Bryan, a bookkeeper at the Broadwater Hotel. [74]

Elizabeth was dismayed by Grace's choice but did not take the announcement seriously. After all, Mr. Bryan was only one of an endless parade of young men who had courted Grace. Elizabeth had hopes Grace would emulate Agnes McLean, a friend of Grace's who had made a home and career for herself before she chose a husband. [75] But Grace determined to do otherwise and succeeded in obtaining her father's conditional consent. Robert Fisk passed the final responsibility to Elizabeth; he would give his consent if she would give hers. Elizabeth adamantly refused, and the Fisk clan divided over the issue. [76]

Shortly Elizabeth found herself in the minority and in the role of familial monster. She was profoundly hurt. Although Elizabeth had some hint that women harbored wickedness, she was disconcerted to find it in her own daughter. [77] She had endeavored to protect her sons from the town's corrupt influences, counting on her daughter's innate moral sense as adequate protection for her. To win adherents to her suit, Grace roundly condemned her mother's present and past maternal conduct. [78]

In the process of answering her own mother's queries, Elizabeth articulated her position and illustrated the obsolescence of "whole-souled-woman-hood." Wrote Elizabeth:

> I do not feel that I have ever neglected home or home duties for any outside work or pleasure. I cannot live wholly within that narrow circle nor do I think it any woman's duty to do so. There have been many years of my married life when the children were small that I could not get away from them and then I stayed at home. *But I think every mother should have hours of rest and relaxation, of freedom from care, and she must find it outside the home.* She has more strength and patience, is better fitted to care for her little ones, if she can sometimes get away from

73. Elizabeth Chester Fisk to Azubah Clarke Chester, June 1, 1890, Fisk Family Papers.

74. Elizabeth Chester Fisk to Azubah Clarke Chester, August 24, 1890, Fisk Family Papers.

75. Elizabeth Chester Fisk to Azubah Clarke Chester, September 7, 1890, Fisk Family Papers.

76. Ibid.

77. Elizabeth Chester Fisk to Azubah Clarke Chester, October 21, 1888, August 11, 1889, Fisk Family Papers.

78. Elizabeth Chester Fisk to Azubah Clarke Chester, September 23, 1890, Fisk Family Papers.

them. . . . In the light of recent events I am sure it is a mistake to deny oneself for the children. [79] (Italics mine)

In consequence, Elizabeth resolved to be less amenable to others' wishes and to acquire those household conveniences she had delayed. Elizabeth stood her ground, but Grace proceeded with her plans and married Hardy Bryan on October 1, 1890. [80] Elizabeth, also, made good on her decision. In short order, she had plumbing installed and, in successive years, had the Rodney Street house equipped with central heating and electricity. [81]

Elizabeth's censure of Grace exceeded the normal boundaries of disapproval; Grace was no longer welcome in her parents' home. Although Elizabeth relented somewhat after the birth of her first grandson, she remained unreconciled to the situation. She noted but kept her counsel when Grace fell in with the "latest insane fashion" of dispensing with a petticoat. [82] The gulf between mother and daughter remained unbridgeable until 1897 when Grace's marriage once again provided the cynosure for the generations of Fisks.

Bowing to financial necessity, Hardy Bryan made his way to New York City in 1897. He expected Grace and his son to join him once he was settled. Apparently, neither New York nor Bryan appealed to Grace. She simply refused, moved back to her parent's home, and took a job as a telegraph editor with the *Herald*. There she joined her mother who had been employed as a proofreader since 1896. The following year, Grace petitioned the court for a divorce, charging her husband with failure to support her during the preceding year and suing for custody of their son. [83]

Among the twenty-six divorce actions filed in 1898, *Bryan v. Bryan* was notable in that Hardy Bryan contested his wife's suit and brought a cross-bill against her, alleging desertion and misconduct. [84] Unlike modern dissolutions in which the occasion of "unhappy differences"

---

79. Ibid.

80. Elizabeth Chester Fisk to Azubah Clarke Chester, November 2, 1890, Fisk Family Papers.

81. Elizabeth Chester Fisk to Azubah Clarke Chester, September 23, 1890, September 24, 1891, September 25, 1892, Fisk Family Papers.

82. Elizabeth Chester Fisk to Azubah Clarke Chester, October 9, 1892, Fisk Family Papers.

83. *Helena City Directory, 1896* (Helena: R. L. Polk and Company, 1896); *Helena City Directory, 1897* (Helena: R. L. Polk and Company, 1897); Civil Case No. 4365, New Series, Office of the Clerk of Court, Lewis and Clark County, Old Courthouse, Helena, Mont., (hereafter OCH).

84. Petrik, "Occasions of Unhappy Differences: Divorce on the Rocky Mountain Mining Frontier," unpublished paper.

constitutes cause for divorce, nineteenth-century Montana law took pains to establish blame when the parties disagreed. In a contested proceeding a jury heard testimony and by a three-fourths vote determined the guilty party.

In September of 1898, Hardy Bryan returned to Helena to appear in court and to see his son. Grace had apparently arrived at her mother's estimation of Bryan. Not only would she not speak to Bryan herself, but she also refused Bryan permission to see his son. In the face of a threat from outside the family, the Fisks closed ranks behind Grace and conspired against Bryan with legal flim-flam. Nonetheless, the jury heard the case in October of 1898. [85]

Bryan's lawyer's arguments rested on a strict interpretation of the law concerning the duties of wives to husbands, namely, that a man's abode became his wife's and that she was legally constrained to accompany him. Grace's attorney stressed that a husband's choice of home must be a reasonable one and acceptable to his spouse. Each counsel's instructions to the jury reflected his bias. The judge, however, was at liberty to deny or sustain the lawyers' recommendations, and, in this instance, the bench chose to emphasize the liberal interpretation of a married woman's duty. Grace Fisk Bryan eked out a favorable verdict by a vote of eight to four. [86]

Both Grace and her mother found themselves in the same place in 1898–1899—the Helena *Herald*. Elizabeth discontinued full-time employment at the turn of the century but continued intermittently as a proofreader thereafter. Grace remained at the paper either as an editor or as a reporter until 1902. [87] In that year, following disputes between the corporation and the Fisk family, the Fisks disposed of their interests in the *Herald* and, except for one son, migrated *en masse* to Berkeley, California. [88]

Elizabeth finally got her wish—a house with a decent furnace and a community of suitable moral temper. Shed of Hardy Bryan, Grace remarried and settled near her parents. Six years later, in 1908, Robert Emmett Fisk died. Elizabeth outlived him by nearly twenty years, dying on April 22, 1927, at the age of eighty-two. [89]

85. Civil Case No. 4365, OCH.

86. Ibid.

87. *Helena City Directory, 1898* (Helena: R. L. Polk and Company, 1898); *Helena City Directory, 1899* (Helena: R. L. Polk and Company, 1899); *Helena City Directory, 1900* (Helena: R. L. Polk and Company, 1900); *Helena City Directory, 1901* (Helena: R. L. Polk and Company, 1901); *Helena City Directory, 1902* (Helena: R. L. Polk and Company, 1902); Elizabeth Chester Fisk to Robert Emmett Fisk, August 19, 1900, Fisk Family Papers.

88. Helena *Herald*, December 27, 1902.

89. Helena *Independent*, December 28, 1908, April 22, 1927.

In *Angle of Repose*, his novel of the mining frontier, Wallace Stegner observed of his fictional heroine, ". . . every drop, indistinguishable from every other, left a little deposit of sensation, experience, feeling. In thirty or forty years the accumulated deposits would turn my cultivated, ladylike, lively, talkative, talented, innocently snobbish grandmother into a western woman in spite of herself." [90] Stegner might well have been describing Elizabeth Chester Fisk's transformation. Elizabeth herself more mundanely said, "Truly, this is a world of change." [91] Just as Elizabeth's urban frontier had altered over three decades, so had she undergone a metamorphosis in the process of adapting to frontier society.

Elizabeth Chester Fisk's biography does not depict the events of a feminist epiphany; it is rather the story of woman's gradual conversion to the cause of woman suffrage conditioned by the special circumstances of the mining frontier. Initially, Elizabeth successfully transported the "cult of true womanhood" from New England to Montana. She arrived in Montana fully prepared to replicate Connecticut in a mountain setting and attempted to accomplish this through familiar avenues of female influence: women's networks and the church.

Her efforts to enter and to make use of female networks failed not so much because she lacked initiative or energy but because the memberships of Helena's groups were constantly dissolving and reforming. As a result, Elizabeth consciously decided, before the birth of her first child dictated it, to retreat into the group which remained the most stable and congenial in her changing world—the family. Likewise, her attempts to influence the community via the church were inhibited as that institution attempted to compromise with Helena's worldliness. In the end Elizabeth effectively walked into her kitchen and slammed the door, her domestic capitulation assured by the lack of household help.

Before Elizabeth retired into her home, the frontier environment had fostered circumstances that created an ideology in competition with the "cult of true womanhood." In her first winter alone and succeeding periods apart from her husband, Elizabeth perceived the glimmering of an autonomous existence and a definition of herself and her capabilities beyond her marital role. In addition, the venal nature of frontier society gave special meaning and substance to the idea of "civic housekeeper." As her children matured, the concept became critically important to her and brought her to the point of

---

90. Wallace Stegner, *Angle of Repose* (New York: Fawcett-Crist, 1971), 90.
91. Elizabeth Chester Fisk to Azubah Clarke Chester, December 4, 1892, Fisk Family Papers.

political spectator. All these were not the hallmarks of a suffragist; they were, however, signs of Elizabeth's re-evaluation of nineteenth-century womanhood.

Between 1883 and 1900 Elizabeth's ideas about women's nature and proper role became less ambiguous and conflicting. When a family crisis forced her to articulate her definition of suitable motherly conduct, she answered that woman's involvement beyond the home and time for herself were necessary components of sane motherhood and of domestic well-being. Bereft of steady domestic help and often of her husband's company, Elizabeth had more than enough time to meditate upon unrelieved domesticity and to examine motherhood critically. The results were a dim, half-formed sense of the inequity between the sexes, and a frank, personal discontent. Both her need for time apart from her children and a sense of duty inherited from her century sent Elizabeth into benevolent work.

Her involvement with charitable work quickly shaded into reform activity with the WCTU. As a member, Elizabeth found herself drawn into woman suffrage and other specifically women's issues. This transition also marked her progress from informal participation in local political process to formal involvement as lobbyist, witness, and petitioner. Elizabeth's benevolent work and her experiences with her own daughter and with a class of Helena's womenfolk redefined for her women's nature and women's relationship to work.

What had begun for Elizabeth as a formless concept of work providing a desirable discipline and a pleasant alternative to loneliness had turned into a necessity for all young women. A useful trade, in Elizabeth's mind, underpinned self-reliance and womanliness. With respect to women's nature, Elizabeth questioned the nineteenth-century notions of women's duty, purity, and self-sacrifice.

The place Elizabeth arrived at after thirty years on the mining frontier was the place from which her daughter started out. Elizabeth had lived out her adulthood in Helena; Grace had grown up there. Mother and daughter Fisk in crisis highlighted the changes that had overtaken Elizabeth and illuminated the differences between the generations. For Elizabeth "whole-souled-womanhood" had become an ideological relic; for Grace the ideals embodied in the concept simply had never had substance. Her self-reliance and independence cut across all her social relationships, even those of her family and marriage.

This difference between the generations was probably best illustrated in Elizabeth's and Grace's attitudes towards their husbands and marriages. Where Elizabeth endured and rationalized, Grace refused. In an era when divorce was uncommon, Grace contrived the dissolution of her own marriage. Implicit in her action was a rejection of woman's dependency upon her husband and an equal, self-confident commitment to personal and economic autonomy. When the opportunity arose in the year of separation from her husband, Grace went to work and found herself physically, if not ideologically, beside her mother. The generations of Eldorado mothers and daughters had converged.

The Immediate Demands of the I. W. W.

(Oregon Historical Society, Portland)

PART II
Progressive Montana

From roughly 1890 to the 1920s, Montana underwent tremendous changes. The population jumped from 132,159 in 1890 to 548,889 by 1920. This unprecedented population growth was driven largely by two major developments: industrialization and the homestead boom. Industrialization primarily was tied to the western half of the state, particularly to the mining and smelting of copper in Butte and Anaconda. Indeed, Butte, with its booming industrial base, had clearly become the state's largest and most dominant city by 1900. Meanwhile, the arrival of the railroads and the forced shrinkage of Indian lands in eastern and northern Montana helped usher in a massive homestead boom in those regions.

The homestead movement and industrialization had a profound impact on the politics of Montana. In the industrial parts of the state, exploitation of workers led to increasing conflicts between labor and industry. The vast personal fortunes that were made from industry—especially from copper mining—also allowed certain individuals to manipulate political institutions for their own profit. As political reformers, such as the Populists and the Progressives, attempted to combat these excesses, they frequently drew their support from the morally minded homesteaders of eastern Montana, who identified so strongly with traditional Jeffersonian values.

Coxey's Army in camp at Forsyth in 1894 (L. A. Huffman, photographer, Montana
Historical Society Photograph Archives)

Coxey's Army in Montana

Thomas A. Clinch

The Panic of 1893, second only to the Great Depression of the 1930s in its economic severity, had significant repercussions for Montana. Montana was one of the nation's largest producers of silver by the early 1890s; the importance of silver mining, and of quartz mining in general, helped to transform the economic structure of Montana society. By 1893 much of Montana, especially the western part of the state, was rapidly becoming both industrialized and urbanized. The city that most reflected transformation from a traditional frontier society to a complex urban community was, of course, Butte.

Butte, like the rest of the state and the nation, fell victim to the economic depression of 1893. When, on October 30 of that year, the administration of President Grover Cleveland forced the repeal of the 1890 Sherman Silver Purchase Act, the bottom fell out of Montana's silver mining industry, and with it, the economy of Butte. Banks closed and savings were lost as serious unemployment became a common feature in the mining city. By the spring of 1894 Butte's economic crisis spurred one of the most colorful figures in Montana's history—William Hogan—to take action. Thomas A. Clinch, an associate professor of history at Carroll College at the time he wrote this essay, shows that Hogan's attempt to lead a large number of Butte's unemployed on a protest march to Washington, D.C., ultimately failed. The essay also illustrates, however, how the size—and apparent popularity—of Hogan's "army" could graphically demonstrate the deep

*Thomas A. Clinch, "Coxey's Army in Montana," *Montana The Magazine of Western History*, 15 (Autumn 1965), 2–11.

affect of national economic ills on Montana. In subsequent years, such economic changes would help fuel growth of the state's infuential Populist movement.

The Great civil rights march on Washington, D.C., in 1963, and subsequent demonstrations there, evoke memories of similar protests at the national capital by suffragettes, bonus marchers, and General Jacob S. Coxey and his army. One national news magazine's background coverage of the civil-rights march spoke of pre-1963 protestants "with causes no grander than a skimpy wallet or no less than the salvation of mankind" and went on to observe that Coxey's army "wrote only its name in history, not its program." [1]

There was admittedly enough of the bizarre in Jacob Sechler Coxey's conduct to lead his contemporaries, as well as recent analysts, to conclude that he was a crank. Therefore we are prone to discount the impact of the man, and his visionary, advanced socioeconomic program on American history. The naming of his son, Legal Tender; his selection of Carl Browne, the colorful theosophist from California, as his principal lieutenant; and his designation of his army as "The Commonweal of Christ" are but a few cases in point. [2] However, if the historian allows the general a wide degree of freedom to indulge in nonconformity, his program and its advanced objectives deserve serious attention.

A prosperous quarry operator in Massillon, Ohio, worth approximately $200,000, Coxey was an advocate of change at a time when affluent businessmen were rare in the ranks of reformers. As a youth, Jacob Coxey had warmed to the ideology of the Greenbackers, and when their party declined, he soon joined the People's party. As a Populist and incipient reformer, Coxey developed the first stage of his startling program in 1892 with the drafting and presentation to Congress of his "Good Roads Bill," a measure calling for government issuance of $500 million in legal-tender notes to be expended in work on construction and improvement of the nation's roads. The unemployed were to be hired for the necessary physical labor at a minimum wage of $1.50 per eight-hour day. [3] Coxey felt that the bill, if adopted, would provide needed inflation of the money supply, promote public works, and solve the problem of unemployment.

---

1. *Newsweek*, 62 (September 2, 1963), 19.
2. Donald L. McMurry, *Coxey's Army, A Study of the Industrial Army Movement of 1894* (Boston: Little, Brown and Co., 1929), 24, 30, 34ff., 46.
3. Ibid., 25.

Congress did not enact the bill, but the Ohioan, undismayed, continued to publicize its objectives through the J. S. Coxey Good Roads Association of the United States. He conducted an extensive correspondence and, in the resulting interchange, became aware of the friendly criticism that the bill helped only the farmers and not the nation's cities. [4]

Meanwhile the devastating Panic of 1893 had demoralized the nation's economy. More convinced than ever of the validity of his ideas, Coxey devoted concerted effort to improving the "Good Roads Bill." On January 1, 1894, he announced the formulation of the "Noninterest-bearing Bonds Bill," a proposal which attacked the same problems as had the "Good Roads Bill," but was far more ambitious. It authorized any state, territory, county, township, or municipality to issue noninterest-bearing bonds on the basis of half of its assessed property value. The bonds would then be deposited with the Secretary of the Treasury as security for loans of legal-tender notes to finance construction of public works, including needed roads, educational facilities, and municipal structures. In this bill Coxey had answered critics of the "Good Roads Bill." He was satisfied that if Congress would enact both measures their combined effect would go far toward relieving the continued economic dislocation and high unemployment following the Panic of 1893. [5]

Early in 1894, with unemployment at over two and a half million and the Cleveland administration adamantly hostile to positive measures for economic relief, Coxey outlined his strategy. His plans called for the introduction of both the "Good Roads Bill" and the "Noninterest-bearing Bonds Bill" in Congress. To insure passage of both measures, Coxey then planned to lead a march of the unemployed, "a petition with boots on," to Washington, D.C., to confront the government with living proof of the need for action. [6]

On March 14, 1894, Senator William A. Peffer, the Kansas Populist, introduced Coxey's bills in Congress. The Senate sent both to the Committee on Education and Labor, although the "bonds bill" later went to the Committee on Finance. The "bonds bill" died in committee, and the "roads bill" returned to the Senate with an adverse report. It was indefinitely postponed. [7] The mood of Congress was unalterably hostile to such advanced reform.

In the meantime, Coxey's army departed Massillon, Ohio, on Easter Sunday, March 25, 1894. Approximately 100 of the nation's un-

---

4. Ibid., 26.
5. Ibid., 27.
6. Ibid., 33.
7. *Congressional Record*, 53d Cong., 2d Sess., 1894, 26, pt. 4:3076, 3603.

employed were in its ranks, a far cry from the 100,000 the general hoped to bring to Washington, D.C. By the time of the force's arrival at the national capital, it had grown only to about 500. [8]

Coxey's efforts to present the "petition in boots" failed. Police at the capitol arrested him and his principal lieutenants for violating an ordinance prohibiting walking on the grass. The efforts of reformists in Congress to win even a hearing for the General failed. [9] With the passage of time the "Commonweal army" gradually left Washington, D.C., as did its commanding general. However, Coxey remained an ardent champion of reform during the rest of his life. [10]

Meanwhile, in the West, the unemployed manifested a keen interest in the Coxeyite program. A number of "armies" were formed there with the objective of joining the Ohio reformer in Washington, D.C., and seconding his efforts. Among the principal Western forces were General Lewis C. Fry's in Los Angeles, Charles T. Kelly's in San Francisco, S. S. Sander's Cripple Creek Brigade in Colorado, and numerous "armies" in Oregon and Washington. General William Hogan commanded a militant following among the copper and silver miners of Butte, Montana. [11]

The programs outlined by the leaders of these groups were much broader than that of Coxey. They stressed opposition to Chinese immigration and alien land ownership, while advocating government employment of the jobless, the free coinage of silver, and government irrigation projects in the West as desirable public works programs. [12] Donald L. McMurry, in his study of the Coxeyite movement, asserts that "the western armies . . . represented the most extensive, spontaneous, and genuine movement of real workingmen" in 1894. [13]

The emergence of one of the industrial armies in Butte was not extraordinary. Men from the "richest hill on earth" had a long tradition of militant, vigorous trade unionism. Butte's miners union had first appeared in 1878. By 1893 Butte was the "Gibraltar" of a state trade union movement with approximately 10,000 members in its ranks, and in that same year the city served as the birthplace and first headquarters of the Western Federation of Miners, an organization representing 60,000 hardrock miners in Montana, Idaho, Utah, Colorado, and South Dakota. [14]

---

8. McMurry, *Coxey's Army*, 72ff., 115ff.

9. *Congressional Record*, 53d Cong., 2d Sess., 1894, 26, pt. 4:3752; pt. 5:4060, 4334, 4442, 4562.

10. McMurry, *Coxey's Army*, 117, 259.

11. Ibid., 127, 149, 206, 215.

12. Ibid., 129.

13. Ibid., 127.

14. Anaconda *Standard*, May 20, 1893; Butte *Bystander*, May 20, 1893; see also Vernon H. Jensen, *Heritage of Conflict, Labor Relations in the Nonferrous Metals Industry up to 1930* (Ithaca, N.Y.: Cornell University Press, 1950), 17.

Pay scales were high in the Treasure State with miners receiving
$3.50 per shift and other trade unionists also earning good wages. [15]
But high pay was of little avail in the wake of the Panic of 1893 and
the repeal of the Sherman Silver Purchase Act that same year. The
panic was bound to have serious effects in Montana. Heavy dependence on out-of-state investment, much of it Eastern and European,
and a high degree of speculation in the mining industry laid the state
open to the worst effects of economic dislocation. Western Montana,
heartland of the mining industry, suffered to an extreme degree.
Eastern Montana — primarily an agricultural region — suffered also,
but not with the same intensity, since the demand for beef and grain
did not drop as sharply as that for silver. [16] In the western sector of
the state, mines shut down, and in a few cases silver mining centers
completely disappeared. Banks closed in alarming numbers, and
business houses dependent on mining failed by the score. Late in
1893, a total of 20,000 workers were out of jobs in Montana, and labor
newspapers warned out-of-state jobless against coming to the state
to seek employment. Pitiful crowds of the unemployed gathered at
the gates of mines still open to beg the uneaten portion of the buckets
of miners coming off shift. [17]

Some of the mining companies in Montana attempted to alleviate
unemployment in originating the "tribute" system by which they
leased their underground workings to the miners, sold them equipment at slightly above cost, and in turn received from the men twenty-
five percent of the smelting charges for the ore produced. [18] Municipal
governments also lent a hand by hiring the unemployed on public
works such as paving and flume construction. [19] However, the continued drop in the price of silver and a sharp decline in tax revenue
defeated both efforts to mitigate the panic's effects.

The prospects of renewed prosperity were dim as 1894 dawned.
However, with the emergence of Coxey and his program, many of
the workers took heart. Large numbers of them were Populists, and
this heightened their devotion for the reformer from Ohio. [20] The
cells from which an army of unemployed might emerge were present in the "industrial legions," groups of radical Populists, chiefly

---

15. *First Annual Report of the Bureau of Agriculture, Labor and Industry of Montana
for the Year Ended November 30, 1893* (Helena, 1893), 177.

16. Anaconda *Standard*, August 6, 1893.

17. Butte *Bystander*, August 12, 1893; *Third Annual Report of the Bureau of Agriculture,
Labor and Industry of Montana for the Year Ended November 30, 1895* (Helena: State
Publishing Co., 1896), 97.

18. Anaconda *Standard*, July 4, November 6, 15, 1893.

19. Ibid., September 23, November 12, 1893.

20. Thomas A. Clinch, "Populism and Bimetallism in Montana" (Ph.D thesis,
University of Oregon, 1964), passim. Trade unionists, not agrarians, were the mainstay
of the Populist party in Montana.

laborers, formed after the election of 1892 "to propagate the principles of the Omaha Platform." Carl Browne, Coxey's aide, had been one of their promoters. [21] There were three such legions in Montana, the most important being the one at Butte. [22]

In April 1894, Industrial Legion Number Three at Butte came under the leadership of a young firebrand, William Hogan, about whom little is known, although it is likely that he was an unemployed teamster at the Moulton mine. [23] Coxey had already left Massillon for the national capital, and this inspired the unemployed at Butte to organize an army under Hogan's direction and get to Washington, D.C., as soon as possible to support the Ohio Populist's "petition in boots."

Early in April 1894, Hogan approached both the county commissioners and the mayor of Butte to enlist their support in obtaining transportation. He failed in these efforts, and by the middle of the month, as the army grew to about 500 men, including recruits from other Montana cities, he decided to act independently. On April 19, 1894, his men failed in an effort to capture a Northern Pacific freight train. On the following day the railroad officials indicated willingness to transport the Hoganites. Then just as suddenly, they withdrew the offer. At the same time, in the state capital at Helena, Northern Pacific officials obtained an injunction from Federal Judge Hiram Knowles forbidding further efforts at seizure of any trains. Federal Marshal William McDermott then left for Butte—but strangely failed to serve Hogan with the injunction. [24] Various groups of Butte businessmen, who had already contributed large quantities of foodstuffs to Hogan and his men, unsuccessfully attempted to obtain some kind of preferential rate for the transportation of the army and offered to pay it themselves. However, General Superintendent J. W. Kendrick of the Northern Pacific informed them that the issue was not one concerning revenue. He stressed the fact that the railroad could not transport the army in view of possible depredations on its part outside the state. [25]

By this time Hogan's rag-tag army had set up camp on the outskirts of Butte near the Northern Pacific yards. The general and his aides maintained strict discipline as did other commanders of similar

21.   McMurry, *Coxey's Army*, 34.

22.   Anaconda *Standard*, May 9, 1893. The locations of the other legions are unknown.

23.   Ibid., April 4, 1894. The *Standard* identifies him only as "a young man named William Hogan." See *Polk's Butte City Directory* (St. Paul: R. L. Polk and Co., 1895), 202.

24.   Anaconda *Standard*, April 20, 21, 1894. The Northern Pacific was then in receivership.

25.   Ibid., April 21, 1894.

forces. They discharged two of their troops, one for drunkenness and another for lying about funds that he had received. [26]

With the situation at an impasse, Hogan decided to act. At 2:00 A. M. on April 24, 1894, experienced railroad men in his army broke into a roundhouse, manned an engine, and to it coupled a boxcar for provisions and six coal cars for the men. Reports reaching the East indicated that while Hogan's men were getting up steam, the marshal had tried to arrest them and that they had locked him up. Such reports lacked foundation. McDermott, at an earlier date than April 24, had made plans to depart Butte and head east to intercept Hogan and his men in the event that they succeeded in capturing a train. These plans did not materialize. At the same time McDermott was experiencing great difficulty in deputizing assistants in Butte. Popular sentiment was against him. The local citizenry referred to those joining the marshal as "bloodsuckers" and "rounders." There was also a good possibility that the local militia would stack arms if called out against Hogan's army. As the situation finally developed, McDermott contented himself with directing the pursuit of the Hoganites once they had captured a Northern Pacific train. [27]

In any event, Hogan's force left Butte bound east at breakneck speeds, replying to a warning to slow down with the rejoinder, "We are running this train!" The entourage arrived in Bozeman at 5:30 A.M. to the tune of a rousing welcome from the local populace. Here the men exchanged the coal cars for boxcars and again headed east. A cave-in at the mouth of a tunnel halted the train until the men had cleared away mud and debris with commandeered railroad shovels and other equipment. At 4:45 P.M. the Hoganites reached Livingston where the citizenry again gave them a warm welcome. East of Livingston the train encountered a roadblock of rocks dynamited from a hillside onto the tracks. The troops removed the rocks, the train moved through, and the men then thoughtfully replaced the obstruction. [28]

In the meantime, the Division Superintendent of the Northern Pacific, J. Finn, wired the sheriff of Yellowstone County at Billings, ordering him to arrest Hogan's force there. Finn had previously run unsuccessfully against the Billings sheriff, and the undersheriff thought that the wire was a joke. The deputy consequently replied in a humorous vein, "County attorney and sheriff out in Bull Moun-

26. Ibid.

27. Ibid., April 23, 25, 1894. *Standard* correspondents kept a close watch on the Hoganites, and one accompanied them after their departure from Butte. I have thus used this newspaper as the most reliable source.

28. Ibid., April 25, 1894.

tains laying out additions to Billings. All of able bodied men are busy selling real estate. Stop Coxey's army at Livingston."[29]

Late on April 24 Hogan and his men reached Columbus, west of Billings, and made camp there for the night. Here about sixty-five deputies, appointed by McDermott, caught up with them, demanding that they surrender, but being outnumbered, did not press the point when Hogan refused. McDermott's men contented themselves with following the army into Billings the next day. There about 100 recruits and another large, sympathetic crowd were awaiting Hogan's arrival. For some strange reason the deputies decided to act at this point. In the ensuing battle, one Billings resident was killed and a number of Hogan's and McDermott's men wounded. The deputies then retreated, and Hogan's men again headed east and made camp for the night at Forsyth.[30]

In the meantime, Governor John E. Rickards of Montana had wired President Grover Cleveland, informing him of the situation. After consulting with Attorney General Richard Olney, Cleveland ordered federal troops at Fort Keogh near Miles City, Montana, to capture Hogan's army. The troops left the fort on the night of April 25 and proceeded rapidly west by train to Forsyth where they arrested most of Hogan's men with the exception of a few who escaped into the nearby hills.[31] Later the troops transferred Hogan and his men to Helena for trial in the federal court.

At the trial, presided over by Judge Knowles, Preston H. Leslie, United States Attorney, and Joseph K. Toole, counsel for the Northern Pacific, represented the prosecution. George Haldorn and Robert Burns Smith, both Populists lawyers, represented the Hoganites. The complaint against Hogan and his men charged seizure of property without warrant. Haldorn and Smith stressed the failure of Marshal McDermott to serve Hogan with the injunction issued on April 20, 1894, by Judge Knowles, concluding that this omission constituted implied permission to take the train. Toole replied that the proceedings placing the Northern Pacific in receivership at an earlier date than the beginning of the Hoganite movement constituted an implied injunction against interference with the railroad's property. He went on to argue that there was thus no requirement to serve the defendant with a legal document. On May 14, 1894, Judge Knowles decided against the defendants, sentencing Hogan to six months in jail for contempt of court. The engineer, the fireman, and forty of Hogan's officers received thirty-day sentences, and the rest

---

29. Ibid.
30. Ibid., April 26, 1894.
31. Ibid.

United States infantry troops captured Hogan's Army at Forsyth, Montana, on April 26, 1894.   (L. A. Huffman, photographer, Montana Historical Society Photograph Archives)

of the men gained their freedom on promising to desist from further efforts at stealing trains. [32] The citizens of Helena then provided the liberated troops with transportation to Fort Benton where they embarked on the Missouri on flatboats bound for St. Louis, Missouri, and, hopefully, Washington, D.C. By July 9 reports reached Montana that 400 Butte miners had reached St. Joseph, Missouri. Whether any of them reached the capital is not known. [33]

However, this did not mean that following Hogan's arrest and trial Montana was free from manifestations of Coxeyism. In mid-May, 1894,

---

32.   Helena *Daily Herald*, May 15, 1894.

33.   *Second Annual Report of the Bureau of Agriculture Labor and Industry of Montana for the Year Ended November 30, 1894* (Helena: State Publishing Co., 1895), 13. The Billings *Weekly Times*, August 16, 1894, quoting a St. Louis news report, stated that the army got as far as Carondelet, Missouri, where it disbanded after its treasurer and secretary allegedly absconded with $440. The St. Louis source is suspect and smacks of journalistic hostility toward the Coxeyites. It is furthermore extremely unlikely that the Montanans had $440 with them on their arrival in Missouri. See McMurry, *Coxey's Army*, 205–6.

small detachments of armies from the Pacific coast may have succeeded in getting through the state. Large groups failed, however.
One got as far as Arlee in western Montana with a captured Northern Pacific train before the authorities halted it, while a second group
captured another and got some distance into Montana before derail-
ing the conveyance. [34] In fact, a combination of effects stemming from
northwestern tendencies to highjack public carriers established
precedents for federal actions in the Pullman Strike in July 1894. [35]
By mid-June, however, the Treasure State had experienced the last
of the attempts of Coxeyites to journey to the national capital and
join the "petition in boots."

An assessment of the efforts of Hogan and his army reveals that
they did not occur in a vacuum. The violence and bloodshed charac-
terizing the Montana episode profoundly shocked General Charles
T. Kelly who was in Atlantic, Iowa, when news reached him of the
Billings affray. "I fear our cause is ruined," he commented, adding,
"We are now reduced to the level of a mob. The militia may be called
out at any moment to stop our progress. I would give my life to have
this day's work undone." [36] The Butte *Bystander*, a Populist newspaper
and official journal of the Western Federation of Miners, likewise
lamented the Billings incident, although it placed the responsibility
squarely on the shoulders of the federal authorities, notably Marshal
McDermott. [37] Most Montanans, particularly the members of its
Populist party, sympathized with Hogan and his men. [38] The *Bystander*
merely reflected majority sentiment. That the general and his followers welcomed violence is extremely doubtful. The fact that they
did react violently to attempts to stop them can best be explained
by the desperate economic conditions then prevalent. A peaceful
journey to the national capital to join Coxey and petition for a redress
of grievances was their first consideration.

In the second place, an historiographical question about the
Populist nature of the entire Coxeyite movement arises. Here the
stereotype of the typical Populist as an embattled farmer creates difficulty. Answering such a question requires the observation that
nationally, Coxeyism was a "restricted brand of Populism" with the
principal emphasis placed on public works and monetary inflation

---

34. Missoula *Evening Missoulian*, May 19, 22, 1894.
35. McMurry, *Coxey's Army*, 226.
36. Butte *Bystander*, April 28, 1894.
37. Ibid.
38. The citizens of Butte had petitioned Congress for a change of the laws
that had caused the jailing of Coxey and his aides. They did not confine their sympathies to local Coxeyites. See *Congressional Record*, 53d Cong., 2d Sess., 1894, 26,
pt. 5:4438.

as cures for current economic dislocation. But, any effort to dissociate Coxeyism and Populism completely involves ignoring the prominent place occupied in the party's official dogma by arguments favoring monetary inflation and by condemnations of interest-bearing bonds and the then current banking system. [39]

In Montana Coxeyism and Populism were inseparable. Hogan's efforts to reach Washington, D.C., were a natural outgrowth of the dominant position of laborers in Montana Populism. It was only natural that trade unionists in the Treasure State, adversely affected by the Panic of 1893 and the repeal of the Sherman Silver Purchase Act, would be attracted to Coxeyite activities. Coxeyism in Montana was definitely not a "restricted brand of Populism."

Coxey and his followers throughout the nation failed in their efforts to win the acceptance of their progressive programs in their own day. Nevertheless they had fought fearlessly for the primacy of human rights over property rights and for the acceptance by the federal government of an activist role in the nation's economic life. Empty wallets had not been their sole consideration. The tragedy of Coxey, so well described by Henry Steele Commager, was that he, "his shambling army of unemployed," and his followers throughout the nation worked for "a program of government spending during depressions that came almost half a century too early." [40]

---

39. McMurry, *Coxey's Army*, 260, 268.

40. Henry Steele Commager, *The American Mind, An Interpretation of American Thought and Character Since the 1880's* (New Haven: Yale University Press, 1950), 52, 233.

Never Sweat Mine crew, circa 1902   (Montana Historical Society Photograph Archives)

Who Murdered
Tom Manning?

In a company town, company justice

Dave Walter

By the end of the nineteenth century, heavy industry was firmly entrenched in the American West. The mining, lumber, and railroad industries in states like Montana increasingly attracted both domestic and foreign investors. With this rise in industrialization also came the growth of various labor organizations, including such union groups as the Knights of Labor, the American Federation of Labor, the Western Federation of Miners, and the American Railway Union. Perhaps the most colorful, though by no means the largest, labor organization active in the West prior to the 1920s was the Industrial Workers of the World (IWW), whose members were usually referred to as Wobblies.

The Wobblies, organized under the leadership of William D. "Big Bill" Haywood in 1905, hoped to unify all industrial workers in America under their banner. Their stated economic goal was socialism: They intended to organize society into cooperative labor groups that in turn would control the means of production, distribution, and exchange. While their rhetoric threatened American industrialists, their efforts were designed primarily to protect the basic rights of migrant workers in American mining, agricultural, and lumber industries, workers who were often unskilled and excluded from the specialized craft unions of the day.

During World War I, the organizing efforts of the IWW and other unions collided directly with the most powerful corporate force in

*Dave Walter, "Who Murdered Tom Manning? In a company town, company justice," *Montana Magazine*, September/October 1989, 54–59.

Montana—the Anaconda Copper Mining Company. The outcome of this collision is described in dramatic detail by Dave Walter in the following essay. Walter is Reference Librarian at the Montana Historical Society and one of the leading authorities on Montana's history.

———————

In the matter of the inquest held in Silver Bow County, Montana, from April 29 to May 13, 1920, we jurors find the following verdict:

That Thomas Manning died on April 25, 1920, at St. James Hospital in Butte, from the effects of a wound caused by a .32-caliber bullet fired from a pistol in the hands of some person to this jury unknown.

By 1920 labor strife had racked Butte for six years. In 1914 the Butte Miners' Union hall had been dynamited, the Montana National Guard had occupied the city, and Butte's Socialist government had collapsed. Rising copper prices during World War I (1914–1918) accelerated labor conflict, as miners fought for better working conditions underground and higher wages. Walkouts and strikes occurred with greater frequency—some triggered by such tragedies as the Speculator Mine Disaster (June 8, 1917), in which 164 miners lost their lives.

Throughout this six-year period, the radical Industrial Workers of the World (IWW) gained strength among Butte wage-earners. The "Wobblies" advocated the overthrow of the capitalistic system through the "direct action" of a working-class revolution. Their cause advanced considerably when, early on the morning of August 1, 1917, six masked men hustled IWW organizer Frank Little from his boarding house on North Wyoming Street, dragged him behind their auto to the outskirts of town, beat him severely, and hanged him from a Milwaukee Road trestle. No one ever was indicted for Little's murder, although local opinion identified the killers as men associated with Butte's primary employer, the Anaconda Copper Mining Company.

World War I also fostered rampant jingoism and the repression of both thought and action considered un-American, Bolshevik, or revolutionary. The Montana Council of Defense led a state-wide campaign against dissent, including an attempt to shut down Bill Dunne's Butte *Daily Bulletin*, the radical voice of Butte labor and the major alternative to the Anaconda Company's captive press.

To expose sedition and treason, the federal government operated a national program of political surveillance—with its U.S. Justice

Department Bureau of Investigation and its Military Intelligence agents spread throughout the Butte mining community. Other infil-trators among the miners represented the private-detective firms con-tracted by the Company. One undercover informant noted (Jerry W. Calvert, *The Gibraltar: Socialism and Labor in Butte, Montana, 1895–1920*, Helena: Montana Historical Society Press, 1988, p. 124):

> If they [the Wobblies] only knew who the stools are and how many of them there are, they would sure be a dismayed bunch. To think that so many of their supposed best men are paid agents makes me laugh every time I think of it.

Government agents in Butte routinely shared surveillance infor-mation on "radicals" with Anaconda Company officials, and gradually the Company refined its "rustling card" employment system to deter identifiable IWW members from working in the mines. U.S. Post Office authorities regularly intercepted the mail of IWW leaders and delivered it to the Bureau of Investigation office in Butte. When federal troops occupied the city, under a martial-law declaration (August 17, 1919), they demonstrably sided with the mining com-panies against the "seditious," striking workers. During the 1914–1920 period, democratic rights and civil liberties became subordinated to an enforced intolerance against dissent and to the increased production of copper ore. The slogan "Get the rock in the box!" epi-tomized the Company's policy.

Following an unsuccessful miners' strike in 1917, IWW strength in Butte grew and was channeled through the Metal Mine Workers' Industrial Union #800. The IWW organized a two-week miners' strike in September 1918, and it directed another strike that began on February 7, 1919, when the Anaconda Company declared a $1-per-day wage cut. Large groups of strikers picketed the mines and shut down operations on the Hill. Approximately 8,000 workers ultimately joined this walkout.

Governor Samuel V. Stewart requested additional federal troops; three companies of infantry reached Butte on February 9. The next day, these soldiers moved against the pickets with fixed bayonets (wounding nine strikers) and raided the IWW headquarters in Finlander Hall on North Wyoming Street (bayonetting John Kinari in the stomach). This strike was resolved on February 17, after the troops pulled back to guard mining-company property and the strikers abandoned mass picketing.

Immediately following the 1919 strike, IWW organizers began plan-ning an even more comprehensive strike. From their many operatives within the union, both the federal Bureau of Investigation and the

Anaconda Company learned of growing miner sentiment for a general strike. The Company countered by hiring more armed guards (often non-Montanans secured through national detective agencies) and by stationing them on mine property. When the IWW local voted to call a strike for April 19, 1920, the news surprised none of the parties involved. At the time of this strike, the Montana Department of Labor and Industry estimated that more than 12,000 men worked in the Butte mines, with 8,000 of them employed by the Anaconda Copper Mining Company.

IWW circulars flooded Butte and listed the strikers' demands:

1. A work day of six hours, from collar to collar.
2. A minimum daily wage scale of $7.
3. The abolition of the "rustling card" system.
4. The end of the contract- and the bonus-mining systems.
5. At least two men working on all machines.
6. At least two men working together on all mine jobs.
7. The release of all political and industrial prisoners in the United States.

Although these demands focused on shorter hours, increased wages, and better working conditions, Demand Number Seven revealed the influence of the IWW. As "Wobbly" leaders C. W. Sellars and A. S. "Sam" Embree noted, "Our attitude and ultimate aim is to secure control of the mines, to take over all properties in the interests of the workers, in the interests of humanity." But the short-term objectives of the strikers depended on closing down the mines.

Early on Monday morning, April 19, hundreds of pickets grouped on North Main Street, on the Anaconda Road, and on other thoroughfares leading to the mines. They stopped miners who were walking and riding the streetcars to work and turned them away from the mine gates.

Although claims arose that the strikers handled some recalcitrant miners roughly, Sheriff John K. O'Rourke and his deputies neither arrested any of the pickets nor moved to protect any of the nonstrikers. IWW efforts proved so successful that practically the entire labor force failed to report to work, and mining operations on the Hill ceased.

Hundreds of pickets swarmed over the Hill again on Tuesday, April 20, enforcing the strike. That morning the *Bulletin* published an editorial that purported to quote Roy Alley, an ACM Company attorney who was the personal secretary of John D. Ryan, the president of ACM. The popular belief among Butte residents was that Alley commanded the Company's private army of security guards (the IWW called them "the gunmen").

ALLEY OPENLY URGES MURDER

The Wobblies have got us tied up again. It wouldn't be so bad if they only quit themselves, but they are interfering with our own loyal men.

We need some more killings and hangings here. And, if there were any red-blooded Americans in this camp, it would be done.

— Roy Alley, in the Thornton Hotel barber shop at 9:30 yesterday morning.

The *Bulletin* quickly responded:

So Roy Alley wants to hang someone again!
He wants more killings and hangings!
We need some more killings!
Whom does Roy Alley mean by we?
What does he want by more?

After dark on Tuesday, a large group of IWW strikers, calling themselves "the dry squad," visited saloons, hotels, pool halls, and cigar stores, demanding that the prohibition and gambling laws be enforced during the miners' strike. (Interestingly, Montana had instituted prohibition on January 1, 1919, and the federal prohibition amendment had become effective on January 16, 1920.) Finally, about midnight, the city police dispersed this group, arresting six small boys for curfew violations.

On Wednesday, April 21, events in Butte turned ugly. Sheriff O'Rourke declared that he no longer could control the situation, and he commissioned all of the ACM Company's armed guards as deputy sheriffs. The Montana Department of Labor and Industry reported:

Many clashes occurred between mine guards and picketers at various properties during the day. According to all reports, the mine guards were unusually active, as many picketers were badly beaten, some of them quite seriously. In several places the fight was bitter, but in every instance the mine guards got the better of the encounter.

By 4:30 on Wednesday afternoon, a group of 300 to 400 unarmed strikers had assembled in front of the gates to the Neversweat Mine, located on the southeast side of the Anaconda Road (so-called because miners daily trudged up this road, which began near the intersection of East Copper and North Wyoming and ran up through Dublin Gulch, to reach the Anaconda Mine and such other major mines as the Neversweat, the Diamond, and the High Ore). On the uphill slope, behind the Neversweat gates, ranged a squad of 40 to 50 guards, armed with rifles, sawed-off shotguns, revolvers, clubs, and blackjacks. The pickets hurled profane jeers at the Company guards, and the squad returned them in kind. Into this explosive situation drove Sheriff O'Rourke and three of his deputies.

Once out of the auto, the sheriff confronted Sam Embree and the other strike leaders and tried to persuade them to move down the hill. The pickets argued that they were not standing on Company property, but were lawfully assembled on a public road. Several men produced road-tax receipts to demonstrate that they had paid for maintenance on this county road. When some miners identified specific guards who had attacked and beaten them earlier in the day, O'Rourke replied, "All right! You stay right here! I'll investigate this! We're here to give protection to everybody!"

According to Embree, O'Rourke then turned and walked to a small group of men that included Roy Alley and D'Gay Stivers—the latter another attorney who reputedly was Alley's boss and supervised the Anaconda Company's security and intelligence-gathering forces. By this time the squad of guards had come down the embankment and passed through the gates of the Neversweat. Suddenly the command rang out, "Go Get 'em, Boys! Give the Sons of Bitches Hell!"

Immediately a single shot was fired, reportedly by a short, stout man, wearing glasses, a dark overcoat, and a fedora. The single shot was followed by a barrage. Into the tightly packed crowd charged the Company men, pounding strikers with their rifle butts and clubs and firing their shotguns at close range. Tom Manning and the other pro-testers panicked, broke ranks, and scattered downhill, pursued by the guards, who continued shooting. Sam Embree described the melee:

> I was knocked down, with my face to the ground. I had heard a shot fired from behind me (the direction from which the gunmen were com-ing), and then I heard a fusillade of shots. I managed to rise and began running with the other fleeing pickets down the hill. But the ground was rough, and the bullets were whistling around me and striking the ground in front of me, I saw several of my companions fall, shot in the back.
>
> I ran down to Granite Street and then went west to Wyoming and back up to Industrial Hall [Finlander Hall]. Soon some of the wounded, including Tom Manning, reached the hall, so I telephoned for doctors and an ambulance.

In all, 16 pickets were wounded in the attack—every one of them shot from behind as he fled. Dozens of other men carried bruises from clubs, blackjacks, and rifle butts. Undeniably these wounds had been inflicted by the Anaconda Company's armed guards—"the gunmen"—while serving as deputy sheriffs of Silver Bow County. Reports also would surface that members of both the city police force

From One Big Union Monthly, *July 1929* (Courtesy of the Industrial Workers of the World [IWW], San Francisco)

and the sheriff's office fired into the fleeing demonstrators. The Butte *Bulletin* speculated sarcastically (April 22, 1920):

> Sheriff O'Rourke states that his deputies did no shooting. The city police state that they did no shooting. The question occurs: "Did the 16 miners shoot themselves?" The answer to this question is: The miners were shot by the gunmen of the Anaconda Mining Company.

The Butte *Miner* (a William A. Clark newspaper tied closely to the Company) countered in an editorial (April 24, 1920):

> Those supporters of the Soviet in this community never were good sports, as is shown by the abject manner in which they squealed when they had administered to them a little of their own medicine last Wednesday afternoon.

To Tom Manning, a 25-year-old Irish miner who lived at 20 West Quartz and had worked at the Badger Mine prior to the strike, support for Soviet revolution was secondary to fighting for his life. Manning had been hit in the back by a .32-caliber, steel-jacketed, soft-nosed slug that perforated his large bowel once, ripped a hole in his stomach, and put four holes in his small bowel. The bullet remained in his body. Although doctors operated on Thursday, April 24, Manning died of peritonitis shortly after midnight on April 25.

Tom Manning left a father, a young wife, and a small son in Ireland. He had worked in Butte for three years, having followed his cousin, Jack Boyle, from the Old Country to the mines. He told Boyle that he had saved enough of his wages to bring his family to Montana in the fall of 1920. Rather than reaching these modest goals, however, Manning became a martyr to the cause of organized labor in his adopted land.

For two days, Tom Manning's body lay in state at the home of IWW sympathizer Thomas Scanlon, 316 North Idaho Street, where thousands of Butte miners and their families filed past the casket. At 9:30 on the morning of April 28, requiem mass was held at St. Patrick's Catholic Church, and approximately 3,000 mourners followed the cortege to Holy Cross Cemetery, where Manning was buried. The majority of miners in the procession wore the red arm band of the IWW.

On April 22 (the day after the attack on the Anaconda Road) almost 200 federal troops reached Butte from Fort Wright and Camp Lewis, near Spokane, Washington. On April 24 another company of reinforcements arrived. The soldiers were billeted at the Florence Hotel on East Broadway, an ACM Company building known as "The Ship." With the soldiers occupying the city, the IWW called its pickets off the Butte thoroughfares, but few miners returned to work and the strike effectively continued. For several tense days, the confrontation between the Company and the strikers was fought in the pages of "the copper press" (particularly the Butte *Miner*, the Butte *Post*, and the Anaconda *Standard*) and the union paper (the Butte *Daily Bulletin*). Butte's attention then focused on the coroner's inquest into who was responsible for the death of Tom Manning, which commenced in the Silver Bow County Courthouse on April 29.

From the outset, it appeared that truth and justice would suffer severely at the hearing. Although the inquest consumed eleven days, and 101 witnesses testified, the Company orchestrated the formal presentations and manipulated the evidence. First, Silver Bow County Coroner Dan Holland claimed a sudden illness and withdrew from the case. He was replaced by Justice of the Peace John Doran, who had been elected in 1918 with Company support. Throughout the inquest, Doran's rulings on the admissibility of evidence demonstrated his allegiances.

According to the *Bulletin*, the six-member coroner's jury appeared equally suspect. Foreman George Hagerman was a city politician with campaign support from the Company; Tom Driscoll recently was involved in several mine-property transactions with the Company; Mike Dougherty was a former employee of Hennessy's, the "company store"; Tom Fletcher was the brother of a Company-endorsed city alderman; Richard Dwyer was the uncle of ex-District Judge John V. Dwyer, who appeared as an attorney for the Company at the inquest; Mark Ezekiel was a local politician whose daughter had been linked to Company attorney D'Gay Stivers. Although some of these alleged relationships probably would not bear scrutiny, the coroner's jury did not project an image of impartiality.

At one courtroom table sat Tim Nolan and Lou Donovan, the two attorneys appointed in behalf of Thomas Manning. The other table often provided inadequate seating for the legal trust assembled. Attorneys Nick Rotering and George Bourquin, Jr., represented the Silver Bow County Attorney's Office; Dan Kelly and D'Gay Stivers appeared for the Anaconda Company, employer of the Neversweat's security guards; Company lawyers Frank Walker and John V. Dwyer represented both the sheriff's office and the city police department. Hearing spectators soon realized that the full resources of the ACM Company's legal division (located on the sixth floor of the Hennessy Building) would be applied to the case. The appearance of D'Gay Stivers at the attorney's table proved perhaps the greatest surprise, since he had been a participant in the incident on the Anaconda Road and surely would be called as a witness.

For the first four days of the inquest, only law-enforcement officers and witnesses sympathetic to the Company and its security forces testified. Through cross-examination, it was revealed that many of these witnesses had attended meetings in the office of Attorney Dwyer in the Daly Building on April 24 to standardize their accounts of the events on the Anaconda Road. Their story maintained that a single shot had been fired at the armed guards from an upstairs window in Simmons Boarding House, across the Anaconda Road from the Neversweat's gates. Witnesses from the boarding house later convincingly proved this story false.

On the other hand, from the testimony of scores of IWW pickets, a scenario developed that pointed accusatory fingers at both Roy Alley and D'Gay Stivers as on-site leaders of "the gunmen." Stivers admitted that he had increased his guard force at the Neversweat after a three o'clock phone call from Sheriff O'Rourke. He also indicated the nature of the deputy-sheriff commissions conferred on his guards. Attorney Tim Nolan pursued this issue:

Nolan: "How did George V. Vivian [an ACM Company armed guard] secure his commission as a special deputy sheriff?"

Stivers: "I don't know."

Nolan: "Didn't Sheriff O'Rourke swear him in?"

Stivers: "I don't know. Although the sheriff was at my office at about 2 o'clock."

Nolan: "Wasn't the sheriff also in your office about 4 o'clock?"

Stivers: "I don't know."

Nolan: "Isn't it true that Sheriff O'Rourke leaves with the Anaconda Copper Mining Company a lot of blank commissions with the sheriff's name signed to them and a blank space for you to place in the names of whoever you should choose?"

Stivers: "I don't know."

Nolan: "Will you say that the sheriff does not furnish you blank commissions with his name signed to them?"

Stivers: "All I can say is that I don't know."

Nolan: "Will you say that he does not?"

Stivers: "No. I don't know. I cannot say whether he does nor does not."

Testimony at the coroner's inquest did identify a number of law-enforcement officers and security guards who shot at the fleeing pickets. In instances where the accusers were IWW members, Company attorneys attempted to discount their statements by showing that they were newly immigrated aliens. This rationale focused on "the proper kind of Americanism," rather than on the pickets' Constitutional rights. That attitude extended to the report of the hearing published by the Montana Department of Labor and Industry:

The mob that defied the sheriff on April 21 was in large part composed of aliens. The testimony at the inquest brought out the fact that
13 of the 16 men shot were foreign-born and that more than half of
them were not citizens of this country.

In the end, the killer of Tom Manning could not be identified
positively by the miners, since they had been rushing downhill to
save their own lives. Given the composition of the jury, the courtroom
machinations of the Company, and Justice Dolan's rulings on ad-
missable evidence, the jury's verdict was anticipated by most of the
participants. This assumption is epitomized by Mike Ostorvitch, one
of the wounded miners, during the hearing.

> . . . When asked by Attorney Nolan to look about the courtroom
> and see if he could identify any of the gunmen, [Ostorvitch] gazed long
> and earnestly *at the members of the jury*, but finally shook his head
> negatively.

The Butte *Daily Bulletin* peevishly noted that all the jury could conclude was that "Thos. Manning Is Dead." The Company's newspaper
chain smugly reported that the jury simply could not determine Manning's killer and speculated that Manning might have been shot at
some location other than on the Anaconda Road. Other newspapers
in Montana ran stories about the strike and the inquest from the
Associated Press wire. For reasons exposed by the *Bulletin* (April 27,
1920), all of these accounts shaded facts to benefit the Company:

> The Associated Press has two correspondents in Butte. One of them
> is an editor of the *Butte Miner*—the paper owned by ex-Senator [William
> A.] Clark. The other correspondent is the assistant editor of the *Butte
> Post*—owned by the Anaconda Mining Company. The Anaconda cor-
> respondent of the Associated Press is one of the editors of the *Anaconda
> Standard* [a wholly-owned Company paper].

The inconclusive verdict of the coroner's jury in the murder of
Tom Manning signaled the end of six years of labor unrest in Butte.
For it demonstrated that the Anaconda Company controlled all
facets of mining life in Butte: from miners' wages to their working
conditions; from union activity to Constitutional rights; from legal
recourse to physical violence. It would be almost fifteen years before
another significant miners' strike occurred in Butte. On May 12
(the day before the end of the Manning hearing) the Anaconda
Company had posted notices at its mines stating "NO MEMBER OF
THE I.W.W. WILL BE EMPLOYED AT THIS PROPERTY." Calling this policy
"The American Plan," it also added three questions to its "rustling
card" application:

—"Are you a member of the I.W.W.?"
—"Do you believe in and support the principles and purposes of the I.W.W.?"
—"Are you in sympathy with the aims and objectives of the I.W.W.?"

But the Company's move to ban IWW miners was really unnecessary.

The radical union lost its power once the Manning inquest demonstrated the extensive, diverse strength of the Company. Within hours of the verdict, the Metal Mine Workers' Industrial Union #800 called off the strike, exhorting its members to apply a face-saving, slow-down, "strike on the job" tactic. This alternative proved ineffective. Federal troops withdrew from the Butte district in January 1921.

Quite rapidly the influence of the IWW declined in Butte. No strong union rose to replace it. The Butte *Bulletin* ceased publication in January 1924. Tom Manning's murder remains officially unsolved—although the answers are as clear today as they were on that bloody April afternoon in 1920, on the Anaconda Road.

'You had to make every minute count'

Women's Role in
Montana Agriculture

Laurie K. Mercier

The greatest boom in Montana's history took place between 1900 and 1920 when thousands of farmers and would-be farmers moved into the state. The reasons for the tremendous growth in Montana agriculture during this period were several. Specific government acts — such as the Homestead Act of 1862 and especially the Enlarged Homestead Act of 1909, which allowed farmers to claim up to 320 acres — played key roles. So, too, did such improved farm implements as steel plows, steam-powered threshers, and barbed wire. The popularity of "dry farming," a new technique designed to retain the soil's moisture in the semiarid region beyond the 98th meridian, was particularly important. "Boosters" in numerous small communities across eastern Montana, and the railroads that served the state, often cited "dry farming" as evidence that the region could become another Garden of Eden, the future breadbasket of America and the world. The result was that between 1900 and 1920 Montana's population more than doubled, growing from 243,329 to 548,889 people.

As Laurie K. Mercier, former Oral Historian at the Montana Historical Society, aptly illustrates in the following essay, women played a crucial role in the expansion of Montana agriculture in the early twentieth century. A special aspect of this essay is its use of oral history interviews to tell the diverse stories of these Montana pioneers. By using such interviews, Mercier is able to recapture, in very human

*Laurie K. Mercier, "Women's Role in Montana Agriculture," *Montana The Magazine of Western History*, 38 (Autumn 1988), 50–61.

terms, a part of our past that is often absent in standard written documents. She concludes that these women "did not romanticize their past, nor did they dwell on self-pity; they acknowledged the economic crises of the time and their role in the struggle." Above all else, "they had a sense of pride and accomplishment in their work."

————

At the time of statehood, Montana's population was urban, with few of the state's residents tilling the soil. In 1880, a mere 12 percent of the populace was engaged in agriculture; by 1890, the state's population had more than doubled, but only 20 percent were farming or ranching. [1] By 1910, however, the Enlarged Homestead Act of 1909, new dry farming techniques, and the promotions of the state, railroads, and developers had lured tens of thousands of people to Montana's central and eastern plains. The expansion prompted Governor Edwin Norris to comment: "'Agricultural Montana' is a term of comparatively recent application, but the magificent strides the state has made in the past few years in all lines of farming have made it a term eminently fitting." [2] Two decades after statehood, the number of farms in Montana jumped from 5,600 to 26,000, pushing the state into a new agricultural frontier.

Women were an essential part of that new frontier, yet their role is invisible in census statistics and agricultural records, often because they were not considered full-time agricultural workers. [3] Montana's census report of 1920, for example, recorded only 2,248 women employed in agriculture in a total farm population of 228,000, surely a gross underestimate. And in the field of agricultural history, women are missing from discussions of technology, income, crops, and production methods. Scholars have neglected to examine the day-to-day lives of farm and ranch families and their individual decisions, innovations, struggles, and routines that marked the human side of agriculture.

In Montana lore and literature, however, farm and ranch women have earned a distinctive place. County histories, reminiscences, and biographical accounts pay special tribute to the wives, mothers, and neighbors who labored selflessly under harsh conditions to care for family and homestead. Many have underscored women's economic

————

1. U.S. Census, 1880 and 1890.
2. *Minneapolis Journal*, March 31, 1910.
3. Joan M. Jensen and Darlis A. Miller, "The Gentle Tamers Revisited: New Approaches to the History of Women in the American West," *Pacific Historical Review*, 49 (May 1980), 209.

Many women raised chickens, cows, turkeys, or pigs to sell the meat, eggs, butter, or milk for the cash needed to provide their families with clothing, furnishings, and other things their farms could not produce.   (Montana Historical Society Photograph Archives)

role in agricultural enterprises, praising their "butter and egg money," which often carried families through hard times. Despite this general appreciation of women's work on the farm, these accounts often glorify rather than document the women's experiences.

Oral history interviews with rural women give us a broader understanding of their role in Montana agriculture. [4] These women do not

---

4. Most of the interviews used in this article were produced for the Montana Historical Society oral history project, "Montanans at Work, 1910–1945." Completed during 1981–1983, the project focused on Montanans' working experiences between 1910 and 1945. It was funded with a grant from the Montana state legislature through the Cultural and Aesthetic Projects program.

ordinarily write memoirs, nor are they remembered in newspaper or local historical accounts. But in their oral reminiscences, they describe their lives and reveal details of their work in the day-to-day operations of Montana farms and ranches. These interviews provide insights into the lives of women of all classes and backgrounds. Through their personal accounts, we can discover how crucial women were in holding together Montana farms and ranches during the first half of this century.

The success of family agricultural enterprises often rested on the industriousness of the female partner. As historian Richard B. Roeder has concluded, women were the "economic linchpins" of Montana's farms and ranches. [5] Primarily, women contributed to the care of family and farm workers: producing, preserving, and preparing food; making and mending, washing and ironing clothes; caring for and training children; scrubbing, cleaning, doctoring, haircutting; and any other task required to keep together body, soul, and household. On the surface, it might appear that this work had no monetary value, but women knew that their labor considerably affected farm and ranch finances. Women economized, saved, created, innovated, and undertook various projects to maintain family self-sufficiency, so that earnings from crops and livestock could be reinvested in the farm operation. Their work was critical to the survival of the enterprise.

Survival meant more than washing and cooking. Women had to find some way to supply, purchase, or barter for the family's basic needs, so that meager farm profits could pay for land, stock, seed, or equipment. Isabella Mogstad of Geraldine attributed her family's "good life" on the farm to their chickens, pigs, and milk cows and their products she could sell. Many of her neighbors, she noted, did not have the "good money" because they diverted precious cash resources to procure food and other necessities. [6] As a Judith Basin farm woman remarked, many operators failed because "the woman didn't work outside the family . . . they wouldn't go milk the cow, they wouldn't raise no chickens, they wouldn't do anything like that." She implied that a farm's success depended on a woman's hard work and initiative. [7]

As the linchpins of agriculture, women were expected to assume a variety of roles and complete diverse tasks that often required more skill, efficiency, flexibility, and resourcefulness than men's work.

---

5. I am indebted to Richard B. Roeder for his insights and for sharing his similar conclusions about the economic role of Montana agricultural women based on his examinations of women's written reminiscences.

6. Isabella Mogstad, interview by Laurie K. Mercier, Geraldine, Montana, March 17, 1982. Unless otherwise noted, all interviews were conducted by Mercier.

7. Saima Myllymaki, interview, Stanford, Montana, March 19, 1982.

Women were partners, mothers, operators, entrepreneurs, laborers, and domestic workers. They earned income and fed and clothed their families. They managed farm finances, time, and household and barn-yard chores, while they represented their families in political and community affairs. And they tackled any kind of work that needed doing on the farm or ranch. Their descriptions elucidate these many roles and responsibilities.

Interviews with both men and women in agriculture reveal that husbands and wives viewed their economic relationship as a partnership.[8] Men and women might have had gender-specific duties, but they respected each other's responsibilities and recognized their need for mutual success. One woman bluntly described her homesteading parents' marriage of 1916 as one of convenience and necessity:

> There were darn few marriages of love out here among these early beginners. . . . A man just couldn't work out in the field all day and then come in and start the beans boiling— it didn't work. . . . You realize that washing clothes was almost a two-day operation in the wintertime. . . . Just running the household was a full-time job, so you went out looking for a woman and you went out fast. . . . I don't think I've ever heard a homestead wife tell how much she loved her husband. That wasn't part of it, it was survival.[9]

Women joined with their mates in making decisions that affected farm operations. They helped establish priorities and advised on land acquisitions, marketing of animals, and equipment purchases. Pearl Reeves of Chinook, for example, was determined not to lose her father's ranch and decided with her husband to go into the dairy business to pay the taxes on the ranch.[10] Even when husbands did

---

8. A number of western and women's historians have challenged an earlier assumption that the lives of rural women in the West were characterized by isolation, drudgery, and clearly delineated gender roles. They discovered that most agricultural women had periodic contact with other women; they did not feel deprived; and they viewed their work as essential to the farm enterprise. See Robert V. Hine, *The American West* (Boston: Little, Brown & Company, 1984), 191; Katherine Harris, "Homesteading in Northeastern Colorado, 1873–1920: Sex Roles and Women's Experience," in *The Women's West,* ed. Susan Armitage and Elizabeth Jameson (Norman: University of Oklahoma Press, 1987), 173; T. A. Larson, "Women in the American West," *Montana The Magazine of Western History,* 24 (Summer 1974), 7; Sandra L. Myres, *Westering Women and the Frontier Experience* (Albuquerque: University of New Mexico Press, 1982), 149–65, 239–59; Susan Armitage, "Western Women Beginning to Come Into Focus," *Montana The Magazine of Western History,* 32 (Summer 1982), 7; Susan Armitage, "Farm Women and Technological Change, 1920–1960," *Plainswoman,* 5 (October 1981), 11.

9. Jewell Peterson Wolk, interview by Jackie Day, Cut Bank, Montana, November 29, 1984.

10. Pearl Reser Reeves, interview, Chinook, Montana, June 10, 1982.

not heed their advice, women continued to voice their concerns. Anna Lehfeldt, for example, openly opposed switching from the sheep to the cattle business:

> I could see there was more money in the sheep than there was in the cattle. And I kept wanting to get rid of those darn cattle, [but my husband kept saying] those cattle are going to pay out. [11]

Some women persevered in spite of their husbands' objections. Lydia Keating got into the sheep business even though her husband "hated sheep" and would not assist with feeding or lambing. And Edna McCann of Trout Creek used her own money from milking cows to file mining claims nearby in the Cabinet Mountains without her husband's support. She occasionally hired a neighbor to baby-sit while she went off prospecting for the day. [12]

Many women "kept the books" for the operation and had a firmer understanding of expenses and income than their husbands. As Anna Fletcher of Glendive remembered, her mother was more of a "financier" than her father, and after taking over the operation of the ranch she retired the family's debts. But there was another side to family finances. Many women did not have direct control or participation. Verna Carlson of Circle described her difficulties gaining access to the checkbook and bank account and recalled her own mother's frustrations with men's control of finances: "That irked my mother terribly; she wanted something of her own." Facing divorce, Bernice Kingsbury of Dupuyer realized what other women surely did, that she "hadn't stashed away five cents in spite of twenty-five years of marriage." [13]

Women knew that "luxuries," such as improvements in the home, often had to wait while earnings were invested in new agricultural equipment. Only an outstanding crop year justified the purchase of goods for the household, and women often managed without conveniences in their daily work. The Fergus County Farm Home Committee, composed mostly of women, recognized the distribution of farm income and urged the Fergus County Agriculture Economic Conference in 1927 to understand that "home improvements should go hand in hand with improvement in farming practices." They recommended that every home should install water, heating, lighting,

11.   Anna Lehfeldt, interview, Lavina, Montana, April 18, 1983.

12.   Lydia Keating, interview, Utica, Montana, March 31, 1983; Edna McCann, interview by Diane Sands, Trout Creek, Montana, June 11, 1983.

13.   Anna Fletcher, interview, Glendive, Montana, October 26, 1981; Verna Carlson, interview, Circle, Montana, October 27, 1981; Bernice Kingsbury, interview, Helena, Montana, September 17, 1982.

and drainage systems, and invest in kitchen conveniences, such as a high stool, pressure cooker, and dish drainer. [14]

Women often acknowledged that their self-sacrifice helped support the farm enterprise. When Mary Zanto received a $1,300 check from the coal rights on her parents' homestead near Stockett, she gave it to her husband to purchase their first tractor. Verna Carlson also recalled her husband's down payment on a first tractor:

> I didn't object. I had to do without things right along. It was kind of a funny thing—I don't know if I could ever confess, maybe I told somebody lately—I used to think, I wish I had some money to just go to town and spend, whenever I take the notion. If I could just ever accumulate twenty-five dollars that I could just spend and get some new things for the house or just go and buy something because I want it instead of just what I had to have. I thought about it a good many times, but I didn't complain about it. [15]

Women often managed the home place while husbands worked for wages on bigger ranches, with the railroad, or in Montana's mines and smelters. Theresa Billing stayed home in northern Custer County and looked after children, bum lambs, and chickens while her husband sheared sheep. Emma Rogers managed her Windham ranch during the winters, while her husband worked in the Lehigh coal mines for extra income. [16]

Many husbands, seeing their wives' schedules as more flexible, expected them to participate in comunity and political affairs. Men encouraged them to engage in political work on agricultural economic issues. Verna Carlson, for example, became active in the Farmers Union during the late 1920s, when she and friends became interested in "the cooperative way of doing business." Impressed with the Union's emphasis on equality, where men and women were encouraged to serve as teachers, local leaders, and organizers, she served as Union secretary for seven years. Anna Dahl spent months going door-to-door in northeastern Montana for the Union because she believed that it could obtain better prices and farming conditions. During the 1940s, she helped organize a local Rural Electrification Association in northeastern Montana, explaining: "Once we got

---

14. *A Program for the Development of Agriculture in Fergus County, Montana, Based on Farmers' Experience* (Lewistown: Agricultural Interests of Fergus County, in cooperation with the Montana State Extension Service, July 1927), 43.

15. Mary Zanto, interview, Fort Benton, Montana, April 28, 1982; Carlson interview.

16. Teresa Haughian Billing, interview, Miles City, Montana, April 19, 1983; Emma Rogers, interview by Kathleen Tureck, Stanford, Montana, September 15, 1982.

started, and once we got people interested and could see that we could do this, that it could be done, that the government was behind us, then it was much easier." Although she neglected canning and other duties to make time for REA work, her husband supported her. [17]

Keeping the family clothed and fed was the chief responsibility of farm and ranch women. Preparing food for family, hired help, and guests took an enormous amount of labor, but it was the one household duty in which women took the most pride. Meals were large, and they had immediate economic importance in fueling and satisfying workers. As Anna Dahl commented: "I prided myself on the fact that I could cook. And I never had any trouble keeping help or a man or whatever because they liked my cooking." Vina Stirling described her ranch table as one with eighteen leaves that "never came down." Women had to be highly organized to cook for so many people. Katie Adams recalled her system for feeding ten or twelve:

> I'd get breakfast, and I never washed the breakfast dishes till I was ready to set the table. I'd get all my potatoes and vegetables ready, then I'd wash the breakfast dishes. As I washed them I'd set the table and get ready for dinner. That was done all at once. Between times, I'd be preparing the vegetables . . . and I'd go out and kill the chickens during that time too. I was kept busy. [18]

The Farm Home Committee at the Fergus County Agricultural Economic Conference in 1927 reported that the average Fergus County farm housewife spent nine working hours a day in the kitchen.

Putting meals on the table involved more than just cooking. Ranch and farm women had to milk cows, feed chickens and pigs, separate cream, churn butter, plant and tend the garden, hunt, butcher, and preserve meats, vegetables, and fruits. To carry families and hands through the long winters, women stocked root cellars, often bragging about the hundreds of quarts of food they canned every summer. Many women also became skilled with a rifle. Anna Juvan recalled that her mother often hunted prairie chickens: "She was good at it. Lots of times she'd shoot seven shots and get eight chickens." [19]

Very few women enjoyed washing clothes, but it was an essential task — a weekly, all-day affair, using a washboard and tub. "Because it was so hard to get water," Minnie Christensen remembered, "you didn't wash a little dab now and then, you probably had to haul it

---

17. Carlson interview; Anna Boe Dahl, interview, Plentywood, Montana, October 20, 22, 1982.

18. Dahl interview; Vina Stirling, interview, Havre, Montana, September 3, 1981; Katie Adams, interview, Havre, Montana, April 5, 1983.

19. Anna Juvan, interview, Livingston, Montana, September 28, 1982.

a long ways." In eastern Montana, women often did not have access to good water and might have to travel several miles to fill barrels with drinking and cooking water. A closer well could supply water for bathing, washing, and livestock, but nonetheless, "you learned to be conservative with water."[20]

Although many farm duties were gender-defined, some were not. Husbands often assisted their wives, for example, by taking children with them to town, which allowed women time alone to complete sewing and canning. Many wives praised their husbands for helping with domestic duties, indicating that they saw their assistance as special. Men and women often mutually agreed to share or do a designated task. Edna McCann, for example, milked cows in exchange for her husband washing the dishes.[21] Many couples began their day by milking cows together before splitting off to field, range, garden, or home.

Although men helped care for children, child rearing was primarily the rural woman's function. How many children women had and their ages greatly affected their work schedules and the kinds of work they pursued. Although farm families considered children an economic asset for their assistance with the labor-intensive farm work and most narrators referred to them in loving terms, rural women observed that child care was demanding, time-consuming, and interfered with other economic activities. Children represented additional mouths to feed, and mothers carried the responsibility to provide the food. Some remarked that other women had large families because "they didn't know of any way of protecting themselves," and others recalled that abortions were not uncommon. Mary Zanto remembered that women commonly nursed a child for two years to avoid additional pregnancies.[22]

Young children had to be under the watchful eye of mothers who were busy gardening, washing, and cooking. One woman recalled tying her son to a clothesline while she worked in the garden, and others admitted that they just could not raise as many chickens or turkeys when children were small and needed a lot of care. Routine tasks, such as sewing and mending, became more time-consuming as the household size increased. Helen Seright recalled: "I didn't have very much time to do any fancy work when they were growing up."[23]

---

20. Minnie Sampson Christensen, interview, Plentywood, Montana, October 23, 1982; Ruby Greenwell, interview, Geraldine, Montana, April 26, 1982.

21. McCann interview.

22. Helena Seright, interview, Fort Benton, Montana, April 27, 1982; Kingsbury interview; Wolk interview; Zanto interview. In "Women As Workers, Women As Civilizers: True Womanhood in the American West," *The Women's West*, 150, Betsy Jameson noted that "a woman's work multiplied as her family did."

23. Seright interview.

The Buckley sisters cut horses in an eastern Montana corral at the turn of the century.
(Evelyn J. Cameron, photographer, Montana Historical Society Photograph
Archives)

Daughters began working as soon as they could walk. They learned
to carry potatoes and gather eggs, to pick rocks off fields, to wash
dishes and clothes, to milk and herd livestock, and to weed the garden.
Children worked in the fields "just like men. We'd all go out and work.
[My mother would] take the baby out there and put it on a blanket
and she'd work, and we'd work alongside of her." And when there
were few brothers to help with farm work, daughters assisted their
fathers in the fields, driving teams, pickups, and combines. They also
shocked grain, stacked oats, plowed, and raked hay. As Dorothy
Johnson remembered, she spent most of her youth on horseback chas-
ing after livestock. Opal Maxey's daughter worked for other ranches
and earned college tuition money by driving a stacker team. [24]

Between 1910 and 1940 — a period marked by cyclical drought and
depression, few or no crops, a lack of feed for livestock, and low
prices — women's economic role was particularly critical and valued.
Women supplied the family's income by raising fowl, pigs, milk cows,
and vegetables for gain. Mary Stephenson decided that instead of
hauling a skimpy wheat crop to Glendive, she would feed it to her
chickens. She soon doubled her flock of birds and sold eggs in nearby
Richey. She recalled: "Lots of times, that was all the money we had
was the chicken money. . . . If it hadn't been for the chickens, we'd
have starved." During the 1930s, when Anna Fletcher and her mother

---

24. Juvan interview; Dorothy Cartwright Johnston, interview, White Sulphur
Springs, Montana, September 16, 1982; Opal Maxey, interview, Livingston, Montana,
September 21, 1981.

were struggling to keep their ranch going, they purchased 500 chickens to raise and sell. They butchered and dressed the chickens forty at a time and "peddled them out" to townspeople. When wheat prices were low, the Fletchers also sold melons, potatoes, beets, and onions in Glendive from their "market garden," which even at low prices paid their taxes. Pearl Reeves also earned tax money by selling tomatoes to Italian families on Havre's east end, and Mary Zanto raised navy beans, once selling 400 pounds of them in Highwood. [25]

This part of women's labor—the cream, butter, produce, chickens, and eggs—brought cash to the family for groceries and for "spending money." One Drummond-area farm woman remembered the importance of her "cream check":

> The cream check covered everything. That was the bank account right there . . . like your cows you'd sell, that would be just a once a year thing, so that's why this cream check was so wonderful, it just gave you a little cash all through the year. . . . It sure was a lifesaver in the "good ol' days."

The cream check, another woman recalled, "bought our gasoline and our kerosene and the necessities, what the eggs didn't buy." [26]

Women's success at selling farm products encouraged others to try similar enterprises. Anna Lehfeldt of Lavina recalled that she acquired 300 chickens because, "My mother had a few chickens and I knew there was money in chickens. It was a way of income, we could trade the eggs for food and provisions and different things." Impressed that her sister-in-law made enough money selling turkeys to make a down payment on a first car, Agnes Jelinek of Coffee Creek acquired 175 turkeys herself. In spite of failing to adequately fatten up the turkeys, Agnes sold her birds and bought her children's clothes "and something extra little bit for the home." She noted that "you always wanted to make a little extra because [on] your farm, there's always a place for it." [27]

Women's economic ventures were also extremely important because they gave women some control over finances and something they could call their own. They marketed their products directly to local customers or sent them to town creameries and stores. As with grain and livestock, these goods were subject to variables in the

25. Mary Stephenson, interview, Circle, Montana, October 29, 1981; Fletcher interview; Reeves interview; Zanto interview.

26. Rose Weaver Lorenson, interview, Drummond, Montana, February 8, 1983; Lehfeldt interview.

27. Lehfeldt interview; Agnes Jelinek interview, Coffee Creek, Montana, April 30, 1982.

market. Agnes Jelinek remembered when the price of cream dropped from eight to two dollars for a five-gallon can, while her income still had to purchase the same amount of groceries for the family and shoes for her children. Fluctuations in prices, Faye Hoven remarked, "kept you guessing" about what the cream check could purchase. [28]

Some ventures, such as turkey raising, were substantial undertakings. Turkeys were relatively easy to care for, but more importantly they could all be butchered at one time in the fall and sold through a cooperative. Many women formed turkey pools in their counties to cut shipping and marketing costs and to obtain more favorable prices from large buyers. Others had smaller-scale operations, raising turkeys only at holiday times, with often fewer than fifty turkeys to dress and sell. Although it was a profitable business, many disliked "peddling" and haggling over prices with town folks, so some women specialized in breeding stock and setting eggs.

Turkey raising, however, was not without its pitfalls. Price fluctuations, disease, predators, and fire made the investment in animals and equipment a gamble. Lydia Keating of Utica, for example, had to trap coyotes to protect her turkeys who fed on grasshoppers on the range. But disaster could alway strike. One night after receiving a new shipment of 400 turkey chicks from Oregon and settling them in a new brooder house, Faye Hoven stayed up to check on them. In a matter of minutes after she had laid down on her davenport, the brooder house caught fire and she lost everything. Nonetheless, she persisted and built another brooder house and purchased more turkeys for that year. [29]

Women on Montana's ranches and farms were not confined to working in the household, garden, and chicken house. Many women toiled alongside their husbands in the fields, and others periodically changed their routines to help outdoors with such critical jobs as threshing, haying, and branding. As one woman remarked:

> I was just like a hired man. I was right there. I helped harness the horses and unharness them and hitch them up, and I followed the plow more than once, and the harrow and the rake, raked the fields. I done a lot of it. [30]

Dorothy Johnston of White Sulphur Springs noted that she "could run all of the farm machines; I could run the mowers and the combines and the rakes and I knew how to irrigate, you know, all that

---

28. Jelinek interview; Faye Hoven, interview, Hobson, Montana, March 30, 1982.
29. Keating interview; Hoven interview.
30. Adams interview.

stuff that goes with it, farm, ranch, like that." [31] Women also ran errands, hauled provisions to sheep camps, and searched town bars for sheepherders, hired hands, and threshing crews.

Although most women welcomed the challenges, prestige, and fresh air associated with outdoor farm work, many could not leave home because of childcare duties. But sometimes work demands superceded children's needs. During haying, Lucile Bridges worked in the field and "then cooked for the crew." She took her children to the hayfield to play and planned ahead so that "in a half an hour I would have the dinner on the table." Lacking a babysitter, May Applegate took her children along and drove the derrick with her ranch's haying crew. [32]

Many women pursued outdoor work once their children were older. Verna Carlson, for example, wrangled the horses while her husband milked the cows. Her children managed the household chores, and after they left for school, "we'd hitch up and go to work in the field." During the 1930s depression, the Carlsons could not afford to hire a crew, so Verna tended the threshing machine, greasing the separator and belting up the tractor. In agriculture, men and women could work closely as a team, and at least in spirit there was a genuine sense of equality. As one man boasted of his wife's talents: "She was always real strong and a good horseman; she was a good teamster and a good stockman always." [33]

Most of the women interviewed emphasized the importance of managing their time. "You had to make every minute count," Bernice Kingsbury explained. "Rarely, rarely was there enough time in the day to lie down and take a nap, you know, to rest at all. It was just constant work." Their descriptions of daily schedules contradict the popular image of a relaxed pastoral farm life devoid of time management that is usually associated with industrial work. Rural women may not have punched time clocks, but they approached assembly-line precision in getting their required work done. Mary Zanto remembered:

Oh, you ought to see the work we did. We never had any spare time. We worked from the time we got up in the morning until the time we went to bed. Many a time I didn't sit down — only when I had the babies, I had to sit down and nurse the kids, it was the only time I'd sit down, all day long, to eat or anything. I was always on the go when

31. Johnston interview.

32. Lucile Webster Bridges, interview, White Sulphur Springs, Montana, July 15, 1982; May Bell Powell Applegate, interview, Deer Lodge, Montana, March 7, 1983.

33. Carlson interview; Fred Blyth, interview, Geraldine, Montana, March 16, 1982.

I was eating. I was either feeding the kids or feeding the rest of them or something. [34]

Most women had a daily, weekly, and seasonal routine for accomplishing certain tasks, but they also had to be fexible. As Lucile Bridges said: "When I'd run out of something, then I'd start to make it." Rather than abide by a strict schedule, women relied on their creativity and efficiency to meet demands. When asked to describe their routines, women typically responded:

You'd go to bed about eleven-thirty, twelve o'clock, you'd get up at four, and you go out and help harness the horses, you milked the cows, get breakfast, strain your milk and put it away. Wash up your dishes, feed your chickens and slop the pigs. If there was any time left, you could start your washing, maybe carry your water . . . heat your water in a boiler, get your washboard and your tub . . . . Wasn't many times I'd fool around.

When there was extra time during the day, women often caught up on mending or some other ever-present task. [35]

When describing their work, women emphasized the long hours and exhaustion that accompanied such physical labor. With a daylight-to-dark schedule cooking for threshing crews, as Minnie Christensen recalled: "You just went on and on . . . if there was a few minutes you lay down on that bench [and] you'd be sound asleep." After a day of milking and irrigating, Anna Juvan would "have charley horses so bad it would just hold me . . . we worked that hard." Faye Hoven remembered her schedule as a cook on a ranch:

I had to be up by five and Pete used to always get up first and I would be so tired, I would just be paralyzed. And if he didn't see that I got up and stood on my feet before he left the house, why I'd probably stayed in bed. So he used to have to make me get up before he'd leave. And I would try to get things, I know I'd always set the table at night so I didn't have to do that in the morning. [36]

Not all ranch and farm families owned land. Many women and their husbands moved in and out of the farm economy, struggling to buy a place of their own, recovering from earlier losses, or seeking wage work to hang on to farms threatened by drought, taxes, or low prices. Although many rural women downplayed their poverty

34. Kingsbury interview; Zanto interview.
35. Bridges interview; Adams interview.
36. Christensen interview; Juvan interview; Hoven interview.

by saying "we were all in the same boat," others frequently mentioned class distinctions in farming communities. One narrator who moved back and forth between ranch and town work noted: "If you was a working girl you was a working girl, and if somebody had a little money, that was different. [There was a] lot of class distinction many years ago." [37]

Daughters often had to quit school and work as domestics to contribute to the family income: "I sent money home until the day I got married," Anna Juvan said, "every bit of it." As early as age ten or thirteen, girls would work "for some rich people" and shoulder the responsibility for cooking, keeping house, and baby-sitting. "Everyone seemed to have a hired girl," so work was easy to find, even though the pay was low. At age eleven, Saima Myllymaki cooked for a haying crew and drove a stacker team, for fifty cents a day. With her earnings, she purchased her "first boughten clothes." Minnie Christensen, who earned two dollars a week as a maid, was eager to cook for threshing crews during harvest season, because "there I got $3 a day, which was a big deal." If girls wanted to attend high school, they often had to work for their board and room by baby-sitting and doing housework for a family in town. [38]

Men and women often worked as teams on ranches or in towns for several years to secure a "grubstake" before taking up a homestead or renting or buying a ranch. When Faye Hoven's husband worked for a local ranch, she insisted on applying for a position as cook for the same outfit. Saima Myllymaki followed her husband to Butte, where she got a job preparing miner's lunches while he worked in the mines. Concepcion and Tony Bengochea moved to Montana in the 1930s and worked for the Etchart ranch in the northeastern part of the state for seven years—he as a sheepherder and tender and she as a cook—until they saved enough money to purchase their own ranch. [39]

Women generally recognized that agricultural labor was strenuous and underpaid, but they accepted their wages without complaining because it "was just the way things were." But they did comment on the discrepancies in pay between men and women. One woman cooking on a ranch was paid thirty-five dollars a month, half of what some ranch hands received, even though she "was the first one to get up and the last one to go to bed." Regardless of the pay rate, many women "worked out" to earn cash for the family farm. Young women often worked as domestics, and married women cooked for threshing and

---

37. Christensen interview.
38. Juvan interview; Christensen interview; Myllymaki interview.
39. Myllymaki interview; Hoven interview; Concepcion Bengochea, interview, Nashua, Montana, October 19, 1982.

haying crews. Anna Juvan, who worked at a neighbor's dairy for three years for twenty dollars a month, recalled that the work provided more than immediate income — she received some heifer calves and eventually started her own dairy business. [40]

For women who had completed high school, teaching school was another source of outside work, although most counties prohibited married women from teaching. Hazel Klotzbuecher remembered that in some years her earnings as a teacher paid for taxes, the grazing lease, and fuel, among other necessities. Occasionally, there were other wage opportunities: taking the census or, during the 1930s, conducting WPA farm economics classes. As Agnes Jelinek remarked: "We always had to look for something else . . . once in a while I tried to do some sewing for neighbors . . . some women would want me to do some things, so that was a little extra money." [41]

There were single women who successfully operated farms and ranches without the help of a male companion. Many proved up on their own homesteads. [42] Isabella Mogstad's sister and grandmother each took up homesteads near her and helped Isabella with her children. Two years after arriving from Norway, Kristina Fallan took up a homestead near Reedpoint, held onto it for five years, and sold the land for $1,500. Gina Lippard also kept her homestead as an investment until the late 1940s, after building her own ten-by-twelve-foot shack and raising a successful flax crop. Babe Hilger, who preferred to work outdoors with the cattle, remained single and ran the family ranch near Wolf Creek with her sister and two brothers. [43]

Women who lost husbands also operated their farms and ranches on their own or sought agricultural employment. Opal Maxey cooked and kept books for a ranch after her husband died, and she saw to it that her children attended college. When Mary Stephenson's husband died in 1941, she entered the sheep business, acquiring bum lambs and working as her own sheepherder. During the 1930s and 1940s, Peggy Dobson struggled on a Missouri River ranch south of Malta without much help from her errant husband. After she divorced him in 1945, she ran cattle on shares, borrowed a mower and team, built a haysweep out of ash poles, and made enough money

---

40. Bengochea interview; Juvan interview.

41. Hazel Klotzbuecher, interview, Chinook, Montana, June 9, 1982; Jelinek interview.

42. Katherine Harris discovered from examining homestead land entries that women homesteaders in northeastern Colorado were just as successful as men in proving up their claims. See Harris, "Homesteading in Northeast Colorado, 1873–1920: Sex Roles and Women's Experience," in *The Women's West*, 165.

43. Mogstad interview; Kristina Fallan, interview, Livingston, Montana, September 22, 1981; Gina Sophia Houge Lippard, interview, Havre, Montana, April 7, 1983; Amelia M. "Babe" Hilger, interview, Helena, Montana, November 8, 1983.

to send her children to school and to rent the ranch for the next spring. When she later married a local rancher, Peggy continued to live on and operate her own ranch independently of her husband. Another ranch woman believed that she was better off after divorcing her husband and taking over their Dupuyer ranch: "I didn't work any harder than when I was a wife of him and getting no place. I proved to myself that women can do it." She improved irrigation ditches and hay lands and within two years increased the yield from 6,000 to 20,000 bales. [44]

Despite a life of hard work, few of the women interviewed expressed bitterness about their past, insisting that agricultural life had advantages. They liked working outdoors and with animals. They had the freedom to set their own schedules and priorities, a healthy environment in which to raise children, and an independence not guaranteed women in town. Rather than focus on the drudgery, women claimed that "we were busy getting it done." They remembered fondly the more pleasant aspects of rural life: picnics, fishing and berry-picking trips, visits with neighbors, dances, and Home Demonstration, community club, farm organization and church meetings. As Anna Dahl insisted, "It wasn't just drab, drab work all the time." [45]

Montana's agricultural women played a critical economic role. Regardless of the family's fortunes they had a sense of pride and accomplishment in their work. Even if the family "dried out," lost a place to a mortgage company, or failed for some other reason to remain in agriculture, women accepted their fate and reflected that they had held up their end. They did not romanticize their past, nor did they dwell on self-pity; they acknowledged the economic crises of the times and their role in the struggle. Even though their contributions have been largely ignored by others, their reminiscences remind us that farm and ranch women had a variety of experiences and that the history of Montana's agricultural frontier cannot be accurately written without them.

---

44. Stephenson interview; Thelma "Peggy" Dobson Boyce Czyzeski, interview, Glasgow, Montana, May 21, 1982; Kingsbury interview.

45. Dahl interview.

Marcus Daly
(W. H. Hoover, photographer,
Montana Historical Society
Photograph Archives)

William Andrews Clark
(Montana Historical Society
Photograph Archives)

The Orange and the Green in Montana

A Reconsideration of the Clark-Daly Feud

David M. Emmons

Until David Emmons, professor of history in the University of Montana, pointed out its significance, no one really knew or cared that William A. Clark ate barbecued beef on an October Friday in 1888. But evidence like this has enabled the author of the award-winning *The Butte Irish: Class and Ethnicity in an American Mining Town, 1875– 1925* (1990) to reinterpret one of the pivotal events in the history of Montana—the struggle between William Clark and Marcus Daly for power and political spoils. "Traditional" interpretations of the Clark-Daly feud by K. Ross Toole and Michael P. Malone emphasized economic factors. No one denies the importance of economics, but Emmons's reconstruction restores ethnic politics to the primal position it once apparently held. If the Clark-Daly feud "affected almost every aspect of the political and economic life" of early Montana, and if Emmons is right, then clearly "almost every aspect" of the fabled "War of the Copper Kings" is subject to reevaluation.

This article has more far-reaching implications than a simple revision of a specific historical circumstance. All Montana history undoubtedly would look different if considered from an ethnic

*David M. Emmons, "The Orange and the Green in Montana: A Reconsideration of the Clark-Daly Feud," *Arizona and the West*, 28 (Autumn 1986), 225–45.

perspective. One cannot help but wonder as well: Does the clash between the Orange and the Green affect contemporary politics?

In Montana's short history few events have captured as much attention as the bitter feud between Marcus Daly and William Andrews Clark. The two men, "copper kings" in the preferred phrase, fought one another from 1888 until Daly's death in 1900. There was an epic quality to their rivalry. Both men were from Silver Bow County (Butte), both were Democrats. Both were also fiercely stubborn, politically ambitious, though in different ways, and, even as their hostility to one another began, monumentally rich. Their fight consumed the better part of twelve years and it does not stretch its significance to say that it affected almost every aspect of the political and economic life of the territory and state of Montana. Gigantic corporate mergers, the location of the state capital, the election of U.S. senators and congressmen, all were influenced if not determined by the Clark–Daly feud. [1]

Of the two, Clark appeared to be far more affected by the rivalry, at least publicly. He could scarcely speak Daly's name without venom. The man was a "veritable czar," the leader of an "infamous gang," a gang so "despotic that it would not be tolerated in Russia or anywhere else in the civilized or uncivilized world." Daly was guilty of "insolent domination," and "political debauchery." He was a "perversion of wealth," an "envious . . . and diabolical" plotter who was responsible for the "financial and moral ruin of men, the misery of women and children." Only with God's help was Clark able to "break . . . this great tyrant . . . and remove the heel of the despot forever from the necks of our people." Curiously, since Clark also described him as a "victim

------

1. For the feud, its origins, history, and significance see Michael P. Malone, *The Battle for Butte: Mining and Politics on the Northern Frontier, 1864–1906* (Seattle: University of Washington Press, 1981), 80–158; K. Ross Toole, *Montana: An Uncommon Land* (Norman: University of Oklahoma Press, 1959), 161–62, 180–82; K. Ross Toole, "Marcus Daly: A Study of Business in Politics" (M.A. thesis, University of Montana, 1948), 56–113; K. Ross Toole, "The Genesis of the Clark-Daly Feud," reprinted from the *Montana Magazine of History*, 1 (April, 1951), 21–33, in Michael P. Malone and Richard B. Roeder, eds., *Montana's Past: Selected Essays* (Missoula: University of Montana, 1973), 284–99; C. B. Glasscock, *The War of the Copper Kings* (New York: Gosset and Dunlap, 1935), 64ff; C. P. Connolly, *The Devil Learns to Vote: the Story of Montana* (New York: Covici, Friede, 1938), 93–104; Joseph Kinsey Howard, *Montana: High, Wide, and Handsome* (New Haven: Yale University Press, 1943), 58–84; Forest L. Foor, "The Senatorial Aspirations of William Andrews Clark, 1898–1901: A Study in Montana Politics," (Ph.D. diss., University of California, Berkeley, 1941).

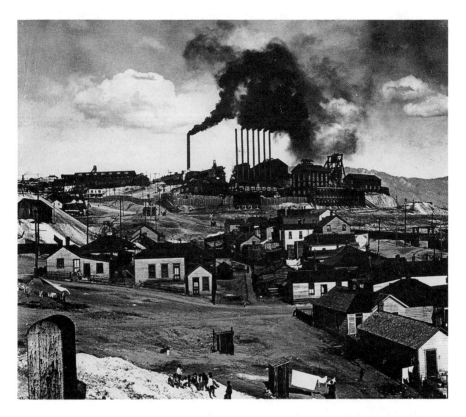

Dublin Gulch lies in the foreground of this view of the Never Sweat Mine, circa 1905.
(Mansfield Library, University of Montana, Missoula)

of his own bile . . . the most ill-tempered man I've ever known," Daly
did not reply in kind. But his hatred, if the amount of money he
spent trying to defeat Clark is any indication, was at least as deep.[2]

2.   Clark's remarks are from U.S. Congress, Senate, *Report of the Committee on
Privileges and Elections . . . Relative to the Right and Title of William A. Clark . . . as Senator
. . . from Montana*, 3 vols., Senate Report 1052, 56th Cong., 1st sess., 1900, 3:1838–41,
1849 (hereafter cited as Senate, *Report*); *Cong. Record*, 56th Cong., 1st sess., vol 33, pt.
6, May 15, 1900, 5531–36. The reference to Daly's "ill-temper" is from the New York
Herald, September 23, 1900 in Foor, "Senatorial," 223. Estimates of the amount of money
Daly spent defeating Clark are necessarily inexact. See the testimony by and about
Daly in Senate, *Report*; Malone, *Battle*, 80–110; Toole "Marcus Daly," 56–191; Paul C.
Phillips, "Marcus Daly," in Allen Johnson and Dumas Malone, eds., *Dictionary of American
Biography* (11 vols., New York: Charles Scribner's Sons, 1930), 5:45 (hereafter, DAB).

Both sides to the controversy agree that it began, or at least first manifested itself, in the fall of 1888. The issue is simply explained. Clark was the nominee of the Democratic party for the election of territorial delegate to the national Congress. The nomination, which Clark had apparently not sought, was thought tantamount to election in the overwhelmingly Democratic territory. More significantly, Montana was on the threshold of statehood and it was assumed that its last territorial delegate would be its first United States senator. Clark cannot have cared much about the office of delegate but his subsequent career indicates how very much he cared about the U.S. Senate. It was to that latter office that Montana's huge Democratic majority was, in fact, expected to send him. [3]

There were internal rifts in the territory's democracy, divisions between its two principal components: Southerners (Missourians, as they were known) and Irish Catholics, most of them employed in the mines in and around Butte City and on the railroads. But no one doubted that both groups were solidly Democratic. Careful students of ethno-cultural voting habits have asserted that 75 to a remarkable 95 percent of the Irish Catholic vote, from New York to the mines of California, went to the Democratic party. Montana's history confirmed that the young territory's significant Irish population was not likely to break the habit in 1888. For this reason, Clark's Republican challenger, the young and relatively unknown Thomas H. Carter of Helena, was accorded little chance. It was assumed, not without cause, that the Irish-born Daly and the thousands of Irishmen in his employ would support both the party and its candidate. Indeed, Daly had promised as much. There had been no open disagreements between the two men and no reason to assume that the Irish vote would be defected away from the Democratic party. [4]

---

3.   Clark said in 1900 that he had "tried to avoid" nomination in 1888. Senate, *Report*, 3:1785. See also Butte *Semi Weekly Miner*, September 11, 1888. On Montana's territorial politics see Malone, *Battle*, 11–110 and Clark C. Spence, *Territorial Politics and Government in Montana, 1864–1889* (Urbana: University of Illinois Press, 1975).

4.   On the makeup of the Democratic party see Malone, *Battle*, 84–85; Spence, *Politics*, 20–22; George Lubick, "Introduction," *Symposium on Ethnic Groups — Butte*, April 19, 1974, tape 15. For Irish Catholic support for the Democratic party see, among other sources, Lee Benson, *The Concept of Jacksonian Democracy: New York as a Test Case* (1961; reprint, New York: Atheneum, 1964), 185; Paul Kleppner, *The Cross of Culture: A Social Analysis of Midwestern Politics, 1850–1900* (New York: Free Press, 1970), 70; Richard Jensen, *The Winning of the Midwest: Social and Political Conflict, 1888–1896* (Chicago: University of Chicago Press, 1971), 60, 61, 97, 112, 297; Ronald Formisano, *The Birth of Mass Political Parties: Michigan, 1827–1861* (Princeton: Princeton University Press, 1971), 180–81, 304–6. Kevin Shannon, Butte born and long-time resident, remembers there being two political parties in Butte: Catholics and Republicans. Lubick, "Remarks," *Symposium on Ethnic Groups — Butte*. For Daly's promise of support and the absence of any pre-election disagreements between Daly and Clark, see Anaconda *Standard*, September 25, 1900; *Cong. Record*, May 15, 1900, p. 5533.

Balloting took place on November 6; Carter won by 5,126 votes, carrying Silver Bow County, Clark's home territory and consistently Democratic, by 1,537 votes. Analysis of the upset began immediately. Clark's forces noted the strong support for Carter in those parts of the territory where Daly's Anaconda Company had its greatest influence. These included parts of far western Montana, near Missoula, where Daly and/or his business associates had timber interests, those sections of the territory served by the Northern Pacific Railroad, and most particularly, those wards in Butte and Silver Bow County where Anaconda miners congregated. In every instance these were thought to be safely Democratic districts, in considerable measure because they were overwhelmingly Irish districts. It required, then, no political wizardry to figure out that the Irish, Daly included, had defected and thrown their support to Carter. Less easily determined was whether they had done so on Daly's instruction. [5]

Rumors that Daly's support for Clark's candidacy might be slipping had begun as early as October, but his final "betrayal" of Clark did not become clear until after the election. Clark, obviously, never forgave him. But historians have used language only scarcely less heated than Clark's to describe Daly's presumed disloyalty. "Behind the scenes," writes one recent historian of the feud, "Marcus Daly and his allies secretly plotted Clark's defeat." "Allies" later became "cohorts" and "henchmen," the plot became a "clandestine campaign" on which Daly "put the finishing touches." Another student of the rivalry, writing in 1941, noted that Daly employed ten men for every one employed by Clark and that he used his disproportionate influence with clumsy if telling effect, ordering his men to vote for Carter or risk their jobs. It was the kind of cynical and corrupt act expected of Robber Barons and Copper Kings. [6]

Speculation has centered around Daly's motives. The majority verdict is that Daly thought the Republican Carter would have greater leverage with what Daly and his advisors presumed would be a Republican administration in 1889, and that his leverage could and would be used to squash or at least slow the prosecution of the indictments filed by Democratic President Grover Cleveland's administra-

5. The Butte *Semi Weekly Miner* of November 14, 1888 carried county returns. The Butte *Semi Weekly Intermountain* of November 14, 1888 had a precinct-by-precinct breakdown of the vote in Silver Bow County (Butte). Clark's analysis of his defeat is from the Helena *Daily Herald*, November 22, 1888.

6. For the rumors that Daly was abandoning Clark see the Butte *Minining Journal*, October 31, 1888. The quotes are from Malone, *Battle*, 85–86; Foor, "Senatorial," 32. See also Senate, *Report* 3:1624, 1627, 2237. There is a possibility that Clark was not above such tactics. For example, in 1888, at the precinct located at Clark's Parrot Smelter, eighteen Republican candidates for various offices averaged 109 votes; the lowest had 60. Carter got 10. Butte *Semi Weekly Intermountain*, November 14, 1888.

tion against Daly and his associates' illegal timber cutting operations. It is an explanation that certainly does nothing to diminish the sinister aspect the incident has always worn. [7]

The historian most responsible for this explanation of Daly's motives was K. Ross Toole. His arguments are presented in his article, "The Genesis of the Clark-Daly Feud," written in 1951. They had, and still have, some credibility. The latest account of the feud in Michael Malone's *The Battle for Butte* is based almost entirely on Toole's account. Toole began by pointing out the obvious flaws in the earlier efforts to account for Daly's political apostasy. There were stories that Clark had treated Daly disrespectfully, that he had attempted to block Daly's acquisition of certain key water rights, or that he had insulted one of Daly's business partners. Toole convincingly disposes of each of these, choosing to accept the account of Daly's good friend, John Branagan, that the feud owed nothing to business or business-related matters. Instead Toole found evidence linking Daly and other prominent Montana Democrats in what can charitably be labeled a political sting operation, a well-conceived and carefully disguised plan to block any effort to interfere with their plunder of federal forest reserves. It could be argued that this was a "business" motive; in fact, Toole specifically states that Daly supported Carter "for economic reasons," an argument which, at the very least, confuses the issue of Branagan's explanation. But there are other and more compelling reasons for a reappraisal of Toole's interpretation. [8]

Clark, a man adjudged uncommonly shrewd by all, was strangely oblivious to what in time should have seemed a transparent case of influence peddling and graft. As late as 1900, however, though the memories of 1888 still seared, Clark did not accuse Daly of that form of corruption. Neither did he or his newspaper, the Butte *Miner*, raise the issue of timber lands to explain the election of 1888. It could be that Clark was no happier with the Cleveland administration's indictments than was Daly, and that this explains his silence on the issue. But that begs an obvious question: why would Clark not then have been an even more effective advocate of unrestricted timber cutting than Carter? The point here is not that Clark was sure of Daly's motives; only that he did not consider this one to have been among them.

---

7. This was not simply a matter of corporate greed. The jobs and safety of thousands of miners also depended on a steady supply of timber. See Butte *Mining Journal*, June 13, 1888.

8. Toole, "Marcus Daly," 73. The Branagan story also appears in John Lindsay, *Amazing Experiences of a Judge* (Philadelphia: Dorrance and Co., 1939), 72. Toole with Edward Butcher, "Timber Depredations on the Montana Public Domain, 1885–1918," *Journal of the West*, 7 (July 1968), 351–62; Malone, *Battle*, 83–87. Toole's reference to Daly's economic motives is from "Genesis," 299.

There are other problems with Toole's explanation. Perhaps the most obvious is that it simply assumes that far the greater percentage of Daly's employees would follow his lead, even if it meant supporting the representative of a party whose anti-Irish and anti-Catholic roots were deep and well known. It can be countered, indeed Toole and Malone in essence argue, that Daly's control of his men was absolute and that nothing, including nostalgia for the "old rock" and loyalty to its Butte facsimile, could get in the way of the "boss Irishman's" timber predations. The election returns from Silver Bow County as well as from those areas where Northern Pacific influence was greatest do indicate considerable Irish support for Carter. But if reasons other than Daly's command could be found to explain that vote, the charge that Daly was autocratic and corrupt and the Irish meekly submissive would at least have to be reconsidered. This is particularly the case since the *only* hard evidence that Daly coerced his employees in 1888 was provided fourteen years later by John Caplice, then as later a strong Clark supporter and the proprietor of what many believed was the "company store" for Clark's employees. [9]

There is another and related issue. Irish fidelity to the Democratic party was never entirely witless. Among Clark's many criticisms of Daly, in fact, was that the Irishman was a party "irregular," that "although claiming to be a Democrat, he really had no politics." Rather, "he elected men whom he knew would subserve his purpose . . . giving the preference often times to Republicans." Obviously, Clark intended this as further criticism of Daly and his tactics. Inadvertently, however, it absolves Daly of the charge of betrayal. The point is that Irish support for the Democratic party was always based on the party's support of the Irish. In fact, one of the times when Daly gave his preference to a Republican occurred in a Butte mayoralty campaign when he supported Lee Mantle's candidacy because Mantle had opposed anti-Irish bills during his tenure in the state legislature. [10]

---

9. For Republican nativism see David Potter, *The Impending Crisis, 1848–1861* (New York: Harper and Row, 1976), 241–65; John Higham, *Strangers in the Land: Patterns of American Nativism, 1860–1925* (1963; reprint, New York: Atheneum, 1981), 28–29, 56, 60, 79–84, 126–27; George W. Potter, *To the Golden Door: The Story of the Irish in Ireland and America* (Boston: Little Brown, 1960), 371–86; Formisano, Birth, 304–6. The "boss Irishman" quote is from Samuel J. Hauser in Senate, *Report*, 2:1402. Toole used Caplice's testimony in "Marcus Daly," 96n.17, 99. That Caplice ran a company store for Clark was charged in *The Reveille* (Butte), September 13, 1902. All other evidence of Daly's coercion was hearsay or came from Clark. For Daly's denial that he coerced anyone see Senate, *Report*, 3:2234. See also the remarks of John R. Toole, a Daly associate, ibid., 3:2147, 2167.

10. Clark's charges are from the *Cong. Record*, May 15, 1900, p. 5535. For Daly's support of Lee Mantle see Foor, "Senatorial," 15. For an example of Mantle's opposition to nativist legislation, see the Helena *Independent*, February 20, 1889.

There were other prominent Butte Irishmen during these years
who were also convinced that the Democratic party was not honor-
ing its part of the unstated agreement with Irish voters. For example,
Pat Boland and Maurice O'Connor, both Irish and both presidents
of the Butte Miners Union, joined the Republicans. So did the journalist John Kirby and, on the national level, John Devoy, head of the
militantly Irish nationalist organization, the Clan-na-Gael. This hardly
constitutes a groundswell but it does indicate that by 1888 Irish
Catholic and/or working-class support for Democrats was not auto-
matic. The national Republican platform in 1888, moreover, played
to this growing disaffection with spirited defenses of Irish Home Rule,
the remonetization of silver, and the beauties of tariff protection for
the working class. [11]

Another flaw in the Toole interpretation is that it does not account
for Daly's continuing hostility to Clark's political ambitions, except,
of course, as Daly was responding to Clark's unrelenting hatred of him.
But that leaves unanswered the question of Clark's motives. A good
case could be made that Carter's usefulness was over once the timber
suits had been derailed and that Daly, along with his dutiful Irish re-
tainers, should then have rejoined the forces of Clark. One can even
imagine Clark, described by one historian as "coldly practical in
finance and politics," understanding Daly's temporary alliance with
a Republican. After all, the stakes were high, the office was not a particularly important one except as it influenced Senate elections, and
Daly had plenty of time to return to the Democratic party before the
next senatorial election. Daly, in fact, did return to the party, but he
continued, in the absence of any substantial political or economic differences with Clark, to oppose and frustrate his senatorial hopes. As
for Daly's partners in the conspiracy, the timber and railroad barons,
their "conversion" to Republicanism was permanent—and explicable
by simple reference to the thousands of others in the United States
who made the same switch at about the same time and for the same
reasons: They were attracted to the Republican's high tariff policy. [12]

---

11. Butte *Mining Journal*, September 22, 1888, September 10, 1890; Richard
Lingenfelter, *The Hardrock Miners: A History of the Mining Labor Movement in the American
West, 1863–1893* (Berkeley: University of California Press, 1974), 190–93; John Devoy,
Devoy's Post Bag, 1871–1928, ed. William O'Brien and Desmond Ryan, (2 vols.,Dublin:
C. J. Fallon, 1948), 2:252–54. For Boland's and O'Connor's presidencies of the Butte
Miners Union see the Butte *Bystander*, June 7,1896; R. L. Polk, *City Directory . . . Butte,
1886 and 1889* (St. Paul: R. L. Polk and Co., 1886, 1889). For the Republican platform
see Donald B. Johnson and Kirk Porter, comps., *National Party Platforms, 1840–1972*
(Urbana: University of Illinois, 1973), 81–82. See also Jensen, *Winning*, 26–27, 298,
302, for a discussion of Irish Catholic Republicans.

12. The reference to Clark's "practicality" is from Paul C. Phillips, "William
Andrews Clark," DAB 4:145. On the appeal of the Republican party in 1888 to men
like Daly's associates see Jensen, *Winning*, 17–21.

Central also to Toole's explanation is the assumption that Harrison would defeat Cleveland and that a Republican delegate would be more welcome in a Republican court. Given the narrowness of Harrison's final margin and Cleveland's clear majority in the popular vote, predictions of a Republican victory border on the miraculous—or were based on a coin-flip—and elaborate political schemes to take advantage of that victory were risky at best. Put simply, what could Carter have done for Daly and his timber raiders should Cleveland win that the far better situated Clark could not have done should Harrison be elected? This is a particularly troublesome point since Harrison and the Republicans were running on a platform that promised a revision of Cleveland's land and timber cutting policies and condemned the indictments as "harassment" by "prosecutions under the false pretense of exposing frauds and vindicating the law." They hardly figured to break that promise because of the election of a Democratic delegate from Montana. [13]

Moreover, of the two parties in Montana, the Democratic platform favored "legislation to allow free use . . . of all timber on the public land." There was no mention of timber lands in the territorial Republican platform. Clark, by his own admission, was a "large consumer" of lumber and later, as senator, urged that the forests be turned over to the states in which they were located. The fact that some of the indictments were dropped or at least slowed after Carter's election, a point Toole emphasized, does not mean that the Harrison administration was following Carter's lead. Thirty-four-year-old territorial delegates did not wield that kind of power, and only because federal policy corresponded to territorial need was anyone able to claim it for him. In sum, a Harrison administration was no threat to the timber cutters, regardless of the political coloration of Montana's delegate, and the threats from a Cleveland administration might at least be parried by the election of an interested Democrat. [14]

There is one other problem with Toole's interpretation. In his M.A. thesis, on which his article on the genesis of the feud is based, Toole wrote that "Clark was a second generation [sic] Irishman, so was Carter." He does not repeat this phrase in his article, but there is no reason to think that he was not still operating on the assumption that there were no politically relevant ethnic differences between the two. This was not the case. Carter was a second generation Irish

---

13. Toole, "Genesis," 297, discusses the predictions of Harrison's victory. Johnson and Porter, *Platforms*, 81.

14. The Territorial Democrat's platform is from the Butte *Semi Weekly Miner*, September 11, 1888. The territorial Republican's platform is from the Butte *Daily Intermountain*, October 1, 1888. Toole, "Genesis," 298; Toole, "Marcus Daly," 95. For Clark's timber needs see Senate, *Report*, 3:1822. Reference to Clark's efforts to have the forests turned over the states is in Phillips, "Clark," DAB, 4:145.

Catholic, a favorite of the Montana hierarchy and the brother-in-law of Irish-born Thomas Cruse, a man whose fortune built the Helena Catholic cathedral. In other words, among the prominent Irish Catholic Republicans of Montana must be counted Thomas H. Carter. [15]

Clark, on the other hand, was quintessentially Orange, i.e., Scotch-Irish Presbyterian. Daniel J. Hennessy, admittedly a Daly friend and business associate as well as an Irish Catholic, even referred to Clark as a member of the intensely anti-Irish and anti-Catholic American Protective Association. There is no corroborating evidence of APA affiliation, but the general point does not require any. Clark's family and that of his wife were all from the Ulster County of Tyrone in the "north of Ireland"; Clark was an elder in the Presbyterian Church and a Grand Master Mason. Indeed, one of the most curious aspects of Clark's story is his affiliation with the Democratic party. The same historians who found Irish Catholics voting for the Democrats, found "Irish" Protestants voting 75 to 95 percent for the GOP. Perhaps Clark's brief stay in Missouri explains his political preference; more likely, the always politically ambitious Clark looked around him when he arrived in Montana in 1863 and did the obvious. But whether he was initially a Democrat by convenience rather than conviction is less important than the fact that more divided him from the Irish Catholic world than united him with it. Certainly, no modern reader needs to be reminded of the bitter enmity between Northern Ireland Protestants and Irish Catholics. [16]

Neither would any Butte Irishman in 1888 have needed a reminder. For example, Michael Davitt, a leader of the Irish Home Rule fight, spoke in Butte in 1886. He can only have confirmed what the large Irish-born population of the camp already knew from experience, both in Ireland and in the United States: Orange hostility to Irish Catholics and, more particularly, Irish Home Rule was intense and growing. Among his listeners that evening was Marcus Daly. Daly knew both Davitt and Charles Stewart Parnell, Davitt's partner in the fight for Home Rule. In fact, Davitt stayed at Daly's home during his visit to Butte. [17]

---

15. Toole, "Marcus Daly," 98. Clark was actually a third generation "Irishman." See *Progressive Men of the State of Montana* (Chicago: A. W. Bowen and Co., [1902]), 1104. For Carter, see Paul C. Phillips, "Thomas Henry Carter," DAB, 3:544; Butte *Mining Journal*, September 30, 1888; Joseph O'Dea, *History of the Ancient Order of Hibernians and Ladies' Auxiliary*, (4 vols., Philadelphia: Ancient Order of Hibernians, 1923), 3:1206.

16. Hennessy's remark is from *The Reveille* (Butte), September 20, 1902. Background information on Clark is from *Progressive Men of Montana*, 1106. On "Irish Protestant" voting habits see particularly Kleppner, *Cross*, 70.

17. Hugh Daly, *Biography of Marcus Daly* (Butte, Mont.: author, 1934), 10. That Davitt was Daly's guest is noted in the Robert Emmet Literary Association (hereafter, RELA), "Minute Books," October 14, 21, 1886. These "Minute Books" are a part of the Irish Collection, K. Ross Toole Archives, University of Montana (hereafter, IrC.)

Daly wore his Irish Catholicism like a badge—or a shield. Born in Ballyjamesduff, County Cavan, he was a member of the Ancient Order of Hibernians, an Irish Catholic organization whose origins went back to the often violent and always bitterly anti-British White-boys and Ribbonmen of Ireland. He was proposed for membership, which attested to his sympathy with its goals, in the Robert Emmet Literary Association (RELA), the Butte camp of the openly revolutionary Clan-na-Gael, the American equivalent of the Irish Republican Brotherhood. His good friend, John Branagan, the same who denied that the Clark-Daly feud had anything to do with business, also remembered that Daly was a regular reader of Patrick Ford's newspaper, the *Irish World and American Industrial Liberator*, a most uncommon journal for a copper king, filled as it was with advanced ideas of Irish nationalism, the rights of working classes, and the significance of a protective tariff to both. [18]

Daly's friends and closest business associates tended to be drawn from the community of Irish patriots. Branagan, for example, was conspicuous in his support of the cause of Ireland, arguing privately in 1883 that "revenge be taken for the persecution of our countrymen in the old country," and that Butte's Irish seek "retribution, an eye for an eye and a tooth for a tooth in whatever country or clime an English tyrant . . . be found." Dan Hennessy was another staunch Irish-American nationalist, as was Hugh O'Daly, Marcus Daly's "biographer." Daly's successors in the top management of the Anaconda properties, William Scallon, John Ryan, and Con Kelley, were all Irishmen and members of the AOH; two of them, Scallon and Ryan,

---

18. Ancient Order of Hibernians (hereafter, AOH), Division 1, "Membership and Dues Ledger, April 1882–March 1887," IrC; Hugh Daly, *Marcus Daly*, 2–3; Lindsay, *Experiences*, 17; Hugh O'Daly, *Autobiography*, (typescript, 1928), n.p. This is by the same Hugh Daly who wrote the short biography of Marcus Daly. He adopted the patronymic "O" only for his autobiography. I am indebted to Professor Kerby Miller of the University of Missouri for sending me a copy of the manuscript. Toole, "Marcus Daly," 1–3, 18. For the origins of the AOH, see O'Dea, *History*, vols. 2 and 3. Michael Davitt, *The Fall of Feudalism in Ireland* (1904; reprint, Dublin: Irish University Press, 1972), 42–43. For the AOH and the Clan-na-Gael see Michael Funchion, ed., *Irish American Voluntary Organizations* (Westport, Conn.: Greenwood Press, 1983), 50–61, 74–93. For Daly's nomination for membership in the RELA see "Minute Books," July 29, August 5, 1886, IrC. No one was nominated unless known to be sympathetic. H. B. C. Pollard, *The Secret Societies of Ireland: Their Rise and Progress* (London: P. Allen and Co., 1922), 307–11. On the *Irish World* see Eric Foner, "Class, Ethnicity, and Radicalism in the Gilded Age: The Land League and Irish America," in *Politics and Ideology in the Age of the Civil War* (New York: Oxford University Press, 1980), 157–62, 165–76. Daly was also a "benefactor" of the Catholic church. See, for example, Bishop John B. Brondel to Reverend Charles Brondel, January 25, 1902, Brondel Papers; Reverend James Franchi, "History of the Catholic Schools of Butte," typescript, 1910, St. Patrick's File, both in Dioceses of Helena office, Helena, Montana.

The Ancient Order of Hibernians convene outside St. Patrick's Church in Butte circa 1910. (Mansfield Library, University of Montana, Missoula)

were also affiliated with the Robert Emmets. The managers and foreman of Daly's properties included such Irish nationalists as Ed O'Bannon, Michael Moran, Michael Carroll, Patrick Kane, James Brennan, "Rimmer" O'Neill, John J. O'Farell, and James Higgins. Each was an active member of both Irish associations. [19]

There is no evidence, other than that he read Pat Ford's *Irish World*, to indicate that Daly shared Branagan's and the others' zeal. There is incontrovertible evidence, however, that he gave preferential treat-

19. Branagan's comments are from RELA, "Minute Books," December 4,7, 1883. For Hennessy, O'Daly, Scallon, Ryan, Kelley, et. al., see "Membership and Dues Ledgers" and "Minute Books" of both the AOH and the RELA, IrC. The "Irishness" of the Anaconda Company, from top to bottom, is revealed in O'Daly, *Autobiography*, n.p; Works Projects Administration, *Copper Camp: Stories of the World's Greatest Mining Town, Butte, Montana* (New York: Hasting House, 1943), viii, 173, 200–202; Lindsay, *Experiences*, 81–82; Isaac Marcosson, *Anaconda* (New York: Dodd, Mead, 1957), 22, 41, 60, 65, 100–101; Wayland Hand, "The Folklore Customs, and Traditions of the Butte Miners," *California Folklore Quarterly*, 5 (January 1946), 159, 163, 177; Hand, et. al., "Songs of the Butte Miners," *Western Folklore Quarterly*, 9 (1950), 9, 23–25, 29, 31, 33, 38, 40, 44, 46.

ment to Irishmen in hiring. From his legal department to his smelting and mining engineers, from the managing editor of his newspaper to the lowliest mucker in his mines, Marcus Daly sought out and hired Irishmen. Both his alleged company store and his avowedly company boarding house were owned and managed by Irishmen. According to one member of the territorial legislature, it was a "matter of common report that the laborers of the Anaconda were almost exclusively Irish . . . that of two men equally competent to fill a position, the Irishman invariable got it." The APA even argued that " 'NO MAN OF ENGLISH BIRTH NEED APPLY' was virtually posted on the doors of the Anaconda syndicate of mines"—a revealing variation on the conventional theme—while even the "suspicion of APA affiliation" led to immediate discharge. It was Marcus Daly, said Father Patrick Brosnan in a letter to his father in Ireland, who "made Butte an Irish town . . . he did not care for any man but an Irishman and . . . did not give a job to anyone else." [20]

The population of the place and the ethnic disposition of the Anaconda's work force reflected Daly's preference. By 1900 first and second generation Irish made up 36 percent of the town's population, making Butte, 2,500 miles from the nearest Eastern port, the most overwhelmingly Irish town in the United States. By 1887 an Irishman could get a Guiness Stout or a Dublin porter on draught and smoke a Home Rule cigar. In 1889 St. Patrick's Catholic parish numbered 7,000 members; the Mountain View Methodists had the city's second highest membership with 145. As early as 1893 the place had its first Irish Catholic mayor; it would have eight more between then and 1919. Of the first thirty-six presidents of the Butte Miners' Union, thirty-two were Irishmen. These numbers reflected Irish dominance at Daly's mines. By 1894 there were 1,251 native Irish and approximately as many second generation Irish among the Anaconda Company's 5,500 member work force; by way of striking contrast, only 365 English born worked for Daly, and this at a time when the English outnumbered the Irish in Silver Bow County. Daly's mines even closed on such exclusively Irish holidays

---

20. Glasscock, *War*, 74, 104, 133; O'Daly, *Autobiography*, n.p. Dan Hennessy, of course, owned the so-called company store and Hugh Daly and P. J. Kenny were among the Irishmen who ran the Florence Hotel, the "Big Ship," as it was known, the ACM boarding house. O'Daly, *Autobiography*, n.p.; Polk, *City Directory*, 1910. In 1900, 202 Irishmen, 180 of them miners, were staying at the Florence Hotel. U.S. Bureau of the Census, *Manuscript Census, Population Schedules*, 1900, Silver Bow County, Montana, microfilm (hereafter *MS Census*, 1900). Helena *Independent*, February 20, 1889. The APA charge was in *The Examiner* (Butte), June 15, 1895. Brosnan to his father, February 18, 1917, Brosnan letters. I am indebted, once again, to Prof. Kerby Miller for sharing these letters with me.

as St. Patrick's Day, Robert Emmet's birthday, and the day of the all Irish Societies Picnic. [21]

Few politicians, particularly Democrats, could ignore or affront this Irish constituency. One of the papers supporting Clark in 1888 reported that he was "the grandson of Irish exiles," a fluent Gaelic speaker and a direct descendent of Robert Emmet, the Protestant Irish nationalist executed by the English in 1803. The claims were untrue but that they were made is revealing. They indicate that the party, if not necessarily Clark, felt the candidate had ethnic fences to mend. It had not escaped notice, for example, that Clark gave hiring preference to Cornishmen. The work force of one of his mines, the Mountain View, was so predominantly Cornish that it was called the Saffron Bun. And when the Parrot Mine, another Clark property, was sold to the Anaconda Company a Cornishman was heard to lament, "Good bye birdie, savage [Irish] got thee; no more place for we." [22]

The problem for Clark was that Cornish Democrats were as rare as Irish Republicans — rare, but not unknown. Among Clark's most enthusiastic supporters was William J. Penrose, Cornish born and editor of the Butte *Mining Journal*. It became Penrose's self-appointed responsibility to ally Cornish and Irish miners around the banner of Clark's Democratic candidacy, a tactic that required a simultaneous courtship of both. He was almost sycophantic in the effort. Penrose "remembered the time when I was a strict Republican and the only reason I had for it was because Irishmen were Democrats." He had long since recanted. By 1887 the Catholic church was a "wondrous religious organization"; St. Patrick was described in language that would have embarrassed the most fervent Hibernian; the conquest of Ireland was "England's disgrace and shame." As for the Cornish, the Republicans had badly mistreated them in 1886 and intended to use them as "vote fodder" in 1888. Fortunately, however, "That time

---

21. MS *Census*, 1900. Butte *Mining Journal*, October 19, November 16, 1887, January 10, 1888; Polk, *City Directory*, 1889. Donald James, *Butte's Memory Book* (1975; reprint, Caldwell, Idaho: Caxton, 1980), 288–89. Polk's *City Directories* list the BMU's officers. See also the Butte *Bystander*, June 7, 1896. Anaconda Copper Mining Co., General Office Subject file no. 522, ACM Papers, Montana Historical Society Archives, Helena; Bureau of the Census, *12th Census, 1900, Population* (Washington, D.C., 1901), 798. There are repeated references in the "Minute Books" of the Irish association to the mines letting out on Irish holidays. See, e.g., RELA, "Minute Books," June 13, 1889, June 16, 1898, August 3, 1899; AOH, "Minute Books," July 7, 1886, March 14, 1889, March 3, 1898, July 10, 1901, IrC.

22. Missoula *Gazette* in Butte *Semi Weekly Miner*, September 26, 1888. On Clark's preference for Cornishmen see Glasscock, *War*, 74; Butte *Mining Journal*, November 2, 1887; WPA, *Copper Camp*, 210; Malone, *Battle*, 66; Foor, "Senatorial," 34. For the Parrot story, see Hand, "Folklore," 178.

has gone . . . when the men who hail from the west of England will vote one ticket" because "some idiot" tells them that Catholicism was "in direct opposition to the religious trainings of his youth." That was less a prophesy than a devout hope. [23]

It was a hope shared by all Democrats. If the Irish could be held to the Democratic party and the Cornish converted to it, the party's dominance would be assured. Clark's reputed lineal descent from Robert Emmet is a case in point. The party's reminder that the Republican presidential candidate, Benjamin Harrison, had once accused the Irish of being "good only to shovel dirt and grade railroads" was another. Clark personally concentrated his energies on converting the Cornish, perhaps assuming that the Irish vote needed little tending. The columns of his paper, the Butte *Miner*, were filled with stories on the "men from the land of tin and fog." One of them listed the accomplishments of more than two hundred Cornishmen; another asked: "our 1200 Cornish Friends . . . what has the Republican party ever given you? . . . who knifed [you] in 1886?" Some Irish Democrats may have thought this harmless campaign talk. But those with memories of the bitter rivalries between the Irish and the Cornish, whether in the mines of Ireland or Colorado, can only have wondered what was implied by these overtures to English Protestant Republicans. [24]

Clark may have given them an answer in the campaign. On the 29th of September, in Missoula, Clark delivered the first speech in his bid for the office of territorial delegate. Most of it was taken up with a defense of tariff reform. He also made reference to statehood for Montana and, interestingly, the importance of new timber cutting policies. It was, in other words, the kind of speech expected of a Democratic candidate—except for one remarkable lapse. During his defense of lower import duties he referred to the statements of certain critics of tariff reform including those "made in the *Irish World* by a prominent deserter from the federal army in the civil war." The alleged deserter was Patrick Ford, a venerated leader of the Irish-American nationalist movement, especially among working-class Irish. Clark's reckless charge against him was false and easily shown

23. Butte *Mining Journal*, June 16, 1888, November 2, 1887, January 25, 1888, November 12, 1887. See also, for examples of Penrose's courtship of the Irish, September 17, 1887, March 17, 21, September 5, 1888.

24. Butte *Semi Weekly Miner*, August 25, 29, September 22, 1888. The other references are from September 11, 22, October 10, 1888. There is no history of the Irish copper mines in West Cork, but Daphne du Maurier's novel, *Hungry Hill* (1943; reprint, Cambridge: Robert Bentley, 1971) is based on the historical record and contains much useful information on the Irish/Cornish conflicts. For Irish/Cornish feuds in Colorado, see Lingenfelter, *Hardrock*, 103–5.

to be such. The Helena *Independent*, a strong Clark supporter, made the matter worse by writing that "Pat Ford . . . was using his power and influence in deceiving his countrymen," and that this was a "thousand times worse than his desertion." This was five weeks before the election. Toole called this reference to Ford "a silly mistake." It was a good deal more than that. [25]

Neither Clark nor his newspaper, the Butte *Miner*, ever retracted or apologized for the statement. Lee Mantle, editor of the *Republican Butte Intermountain*, thought he knew why. "For fear of offending Mr. Clark," he wrote, the *Miner* "dare not deny the story; and for fear of offending the Irish-American voters of Montana, it dare not affirm it." The issue, however, would not go away, in part because Mantle and the *Intermountain* would not let it. The paper gave full coverage to Ford's heated denial of the charge of desertion, then pointed out that another "sour and virulent Orangeman," the New York journalist E. L. Godkin, had called Ford a "dynamiter and deserter . . . and a cowardly cow." Linking Clark to Godkin was like linking him to Cromwell. [26]

Penrose was in no position to retract the story, so he dissembled. Clark's "sympathies," he wrote, "have ever been enlisted in [the Irish] struggle for independence." He was "too intelligent to insult the Celt"; the Republicans were "trying to poison the minds of the Irish people against" Clark, and Carter was "trading on his nationality." Besides, "Pat Ford cuts no figure in the Montana campaign . . . [he] has no . . . claim to represent the Irish vote of the U.S." As for Daly, the boss Irishman, "he will in every legitimate way, exercise his influence in behalf of Mr. Clark. Mr. Daly is not an intimidator nor a bulldozer. . . . He has no possible personal interest in the coming contest." [27]

Penrose may not have known better. There was no public Irish response. Daly said nothing, although it was about this time that rumors of his disaffection for Clark began. The Irish associations also made no reply, though the RELA heard a speaker tell its members in September of a national revival of nativism; two years later the Emmets received instructions from their parent organization, the

25. Butte *Semi Weekly Miner*, October 3, 1888. For Ford's standing among Irish-American workers, see Foner, "Class, Ethnicity, and Radicalism." Ford's Massachusetts' regiment also answered the charge of desertion. See the Butte *Semi Weekly Intermountain*, October 10, 1888. The Helena *Independent*'s remarks were reprinted in the Butte *Semi Weekly Intermountain*, October 7, 1888. Toole, "Marcus Daly," 98. The APA later argued that 72 percent of all Irish-American Catholics in the Union Army deserted. *The Examiner*, October 5, November 2, 1895.

26. Butte *Semi Weekly Intermountain*, October 10, 14, 1888. See also October 7, 17, 21, 28, 31, November 4, 1888.

27. Butte *Mining Journal*, October 17, 28, 31, November 4, 1888.

Clan-na-Gael, on how to "keep down the nativist element by electing
. . . men . . . favorable to us." But, with the exception of one man
who wrote that all Irishmen should vote against Clark because "he
is a Know Nothing," there was no public Irish response. This may
have been because, as Democrats, they were without an effective
forum in which to protest; perhaps they had already determined to
avenge Ford and understood that an Irish protest would only serve
to warn Clark. More likely, however, there was no organized Irish protest because they were waiting, individually not collectively, for Clark
to retract the story or apologize for it. [28]

He did neither. In fact, his insensitivity to the issue, or that of his
advisors, seems almost calculated. For example, on the 19th of
October, less than three weeks before the election, the Democrats
held a much-publicized barbecue in Anaconda, Montana. On the
18th, a virulently anti-Catholic organization known as the Patriotic
Order, Sons of America had a formal ball in that same city. Clark
hoped that the "good Democrats" in the Patriotic Order would attend
both functions. This was bad enough, but then a "son of Erin" pointed
out that the 19th, the day of the barbecue, was a Friday, hardly the
day for Irish Catholics to be eating "roasted bullock and fatted calf." [29]

The *Intermountain* began almost visibly to celebrate. The Democratic effort to convert the Cornish was failing and it was beginning
to appear that Clark's candidacy could cost it the Irish vote. The
Friday barbecue, it noted with tongue firmly in cheek, had to have
been a "studied attempt to curtail expenses." Then, more somberly,
it noted that "dietary regulations are sacredly observed by a large portion of our most intelligent citizens." The Ford incident was a source
of even greater pleasure. "We submit," said the *Intermountain*, "that
the Irish-Americans of this country who read Patrick Ford's paper
will not be slow to resent Mr. Clark's aspersion upon his loyalty." It
is tempting to believe that the *Intermountain* knew that Marcus Daly
was among those readers. "Verily," the paper continued, "it begins
to look as though the Patrick Ford issue will side track Mr. Clark."
Verily indeed. [30]

The Irish case against Clark could probably have rested on his
background, his hiring practices, and his remarkable insensitivity.
But there was another related issue. Both Toole and Malone point
out that the stockmen of eastern Montana were strongly protectionist
and that Carter's strength in that region came from his support for

---

28. Ibid., October 31, 1888; Butte *Semi Weekly Miner*, October 31, 1888; RELA,
"Minute Books," September 13, 1888, April 3, 1890, IrC.

29. Butte *Semi Weekly Miner*, October 17, 20, 24, 1888; Butte *Semi Weekly Intermountain*, October 21, 1888.

30. Butte *Semi Weekly Intermountain*, October 7, 21, 1888.

high protective duties. The Republicans also attempted, with mixed results, to convince the working class that protectionism kept production and wages high. One element of that working class, however, needed no convincing. For Irish nationalists, whether in the United States or in Ireland, free trade was one of the props supporting England's imperial domination of Ireland. Ireland's freedom required, among other things, a weakened England or an England at war. High protective tariffs, particularly for the United States and Germany, strengthened England's trade rivals and might produce that war. Moreover, the independent Ireland that would emerge from the conflict would have to claim the small nation's right to protect its industries. The principle of protectionism thus became a litmus test of Irish nationalism, and Patrick Ford, among others, made it a featured part of the "Irish question." [31]

Mantle's Butte *Intermountain* turned the Irish/tariff issue into a kind of partisan incantation. Protectionist editorials reprinted from the *Irish World* appeared in almost every issue; joining them were Mantle-inspired articles playing more directly to a Butte audience. Clark's attack on Ford, as Mantle pointed out repeatedly, was not a gratuitous ethnic insult; Ford, according to Clark, was a protectionist as well as a deserter. Other stories extended the argument. In a "open letter to the Irish Americans of Montana," published before Clark's attack on Ford, the *Intermountain* reminded the Irish that "free trade ruined the industries and disrupted the homes of Ireland." The result was "wholesale immigration." To Irishmen, whose list of England's sins against them began with their own exile, this had to have been a powerful argument. So must have Mantle's story in which a "British peer" was quoted favoring Cleveland, the Democrats and free trade because protectionism allowed American workers, many of them Irish, to afford "carpets and pianos." [32]

The point repeatedly made was that Cleveland and, by direct political association, Clark were pro-British. In addition to the substance of this argument there is considerable significance in the mere fact that it was made. The remarks of British peers were not the ordinary stuff of American territorial elections—unless, of course, those elections turned on ethnic issues. This one was beginning to appear

31. Toole, "Marcus Daly," 64, 98; Malone, *Battle*, 86; Thomas N. Brown, *Irish-American Nationalism, 1870–1890* (Philadelphia and New York: Lippincott, 1966), 142. *Irish World and American Industrial Liberator*, September–November 1888, passim.

32. Butte *Semi Weekly Intermountain*, October 7, 17, 31, 1888. The "open letter" was in the edition of September 26, 1888. On the "exile mentality" of Irish immigrants see Kerby A. Miller, *Emigrants and Exiles: Ireland and the Irish Exodus to North America* (New York: Oxford University Press, 1985). The "carpets and pianos" story was from Butte *Semi Weekly Intermountain*, October 7, 1888.

that it might, and Mantle was relentless in his efforts to link Clark with England. Three weeks before the election he quoted from nine British newspapers, including the London *Times* and the London *Economist*. Each insisted that Britain would be "the chief beneficiary" of American tariff reform; each embraced Cleveland and the Democratic party. Then, late in the campaign, Mantle was handed another issue. The English ambassador to the United States, the wonderfully named Sir Lionel Sackville-West, wrote that Cleveland was his and England's preferred candidate. Mantle wasted little time pointing out that Sir Lionel would probably like Clark, too. [33]

As noted, Irish Catholic support for the Democrats was always conditional; Irish Catholic Butte made that clear when it gave Carter his 1,500 vote majority. Penrose understood precisely what happened. It was in a "real estate and insurance office on West Broadway" that the decision to "inject religion into the campaign" was made. The only such office on West Broadway was co-owned by Lee Mantle. Obviously, Mantle made a wise decision, though it might have been argued that Clark had forced the issue with his attack on Ford. "The religious principles of both candidates . . . ," Penrose went on, "cut some figure in the contest," adding that Clark's invitation to the Patriotic Order, Sons of America alone cost him "1,500 votes." So persistent, in fact, were the rumors of religious influence that Father Van de Ven, pastor of St. Patrick's Church, publicly had to deny that he or his church had anything to do with the election. He denied specifically that he was "driving around . . . advising his congregation to vote for Mr. Carter." Those denials notwithstanding, Penrose reported in 1890 that Carter "claims that he owns the Irish vote," evidence enough that the Republican delegate-elect knew exactly the forces that had elected him. [34]

---

33. Butte *Semi Weekly Intermountain*, October 17, 1888. On the Sackville-West affair see Charles S. Campbell, *The Transformation of American Foreign Relations, 1865–1900* (New York: Harper and Row, 1976), 131; H. C. Allen, *Great Britain and the United States* (New York: St. Martin's Press, 1955), 520–21; Charles C. Tansill, *America and the Fight for Irish Freedom, 1866–1922* (New York: Devin-Adair, 1957), 107–11.

34. Butte *Mining Journal*, November 11, 1888, October 30, 1890; Polk, *City Directory, 1889*. Three years later Penrose was shot down and killed on a Butte street. No one was convicted of his murder, but three Irishmen, identified by some as "Molly Maguires," members of a secret and violent Irish society, active in Pennsylvania in the 1860s and 70s, were arrested. The English society, the Sons of St. George, offered a reward for the conviction of Penrose's murderers. This is further evidence of the tensions between the two ethnic communities at this time. Lingenfelter, *Hardrock*, 192–93; Malone, *Battle*, 77, says, without offering any evidence, that those who suspected "a Montana version of the Molly Maguires" were "probably right." Rowland Berthoff, *British Immigrants in Industrial America, 1790–1950* (Cambridge: Harvard University Press, 1953), 189–90.

Penrose was a close and interested observer. But given the history—and historiography—of the Clark-Daly feud, Clark's own assessment of his loss is of greater significance. There is strong evidence that he also understood the nature of the "gigantic conspiracy" that defeated him. The *Miner*, a week after the election, noted that "at least 1,000 Democratic votes" in Silver Bow County were cast for Carter, and not for "any tariff considerations, but solely as a result of potent influences which are well understood and deeply deplored by the best thinking citizens of this county, Democratic or Republican alike." Citizens were identified as "best thinking" precisely because they deplored the insinuation of ethnicity into politics, however routine that insinuation had become. But the *Miner* was not always so vague. Earlier it had labeled the "conspiracy" that defeated Clark as one "that originated in Republican circles to influence religious prejudice against" him. It then asked, and it was a most interesting and instructive question, if the tactics of 1888 were to become a permanent part of Montana politics. Specifically, the *Miner* wanted to know, "*will religious feelings be worked upon and men employed in the mines be commanded to vote so and so or be dismissed?*" It made no references to any other motives.[35]

Thus did Clark explain his defeat. It was a most credible explanation—at least so far as it recognized the significance of the Irish factor. Its credibility is enhanced, moreover, by Clark's and, by inference at least, Penrose's later charges against Daly and the Irish. Among Daly's unpardonable sins was his use of the boycott, a peculiarly Irish tactic and one which aroused the rage of both Clark and Penrose. As Penrose put it, less than three years after the election of 1888, "the boycott is a foreign importation only a little less obnoxious to decent American citizens than nihilism, communism and kindred tenets of foreign cut throats and robbers." On another occasion he referred to the boycott as "the lowest, meanest, most despicable instrument of malice and revenge that was ever imported. . . , an un-American principle." Penrose's specific references are unclear. But, given the close association of boycotting with the Irish—the word is of Irish derivation—it was obvious his courtship of Irish voters was over. He may have been talking about the boycotting of merchants and he did not link the practice to the Irish—only to certain Irishmen, Daly *not* among them.[36]

---

35.   Clark referred to the "gigantic conspiracy" in a private letter. Toole, "Marcus Daly," 58–59. Butte *Semi Weekly Miner*, November 10, 14, 1888.

36.   Butte *Mining Journal*, April 19, May 10, 1891. See also the edition of June 17, 1891. The word came from the action of Irish Land Leaguers against the agent of their English landlord. The agent's name was Captain Charles S. Boycott. See, among many sources. Norman D. Palmer, *The Irish Land League Crisis* (1940; reprint, New York: Octagon, 1978), chap. 10.

The struggle between Anaconda and Helena to be chosen state capital in 1894 constituted another round in the Clark-Daly feud, and when Anaconda lost, Butte and Anaconda's Irish Catholics raised the money for this statue of the Irish hero, Thomas Francis Meagher, dedicated in 1905. (Montana Historical Society Photograph Archives)

Clark, however, was more direct. "The boycott," he said in 1900, "is another great weapon used by Daly and his associates." It was used, moreover, for very specific purposes. In language remarkably similar to that used by the *Miner* in 1888, Clark accused Daly of "boycotting all who don't vote as dictated to. They can not get a job or work." In other words, Daly boycotted working men by refusing to buy the labor of those whose politics he could not control, a tacit acknowledgement, made explicit later by the APA, that Daly hired Irishmen because he wanted to assemble a work force he could control. Then, having boycotted non-Irish labor, Daly and the Irish were in a position to boycott Clark. Here was a conspiracy vaster by far than any described by Toole. [37]

Like all the conspiratorial explanations of the events of 1888, however, Clark's suffers from one obvious defect. It did not ask if the Irish had to be commanded to vote as they did. It did not take into account the possibility that Clark's impolitic remarks about Ford, among other indiscretions, might themselves be interpreted as a form of ethnic or religious prejudice and that the Irish needed no urging or threats from Daly to rebuke Clark for them. It is certainly possible that the Irish, Daly included, boycotted Clark, and boycotting did require a certain discipline. But this is not the same as saying that Daly and his shift bosses choreographed the vote. It is unfortunate that so elementary a point needs to be made. However, the possibility that Montana's Irishmen, including Marcus Daly, simply did not like or trust the Anglophilic Clark and voted accordingly was not considered—at the time or later. In fact, it is plausible that Daly never forgave Clark for the latter's implied insult to the political independence of that community. This is, of course, a frankly speculative argument. Given the flaws in the story of the timber cutting plot, however, and the frank admission that ethnicity and religious feelings were enlisted in this campaign, as they were in the later battles between the two men, it seems clear that the origins of the Clark-Daly feud are to be found not in the rascality of a copper king but in the abiding tensions between the Orange and the Green. [38]

------

37.   *Cong. Record*, May 15, 1900, p. 5535–36; Senate, *Report*, 3:1934, 2068–71.

38.   On the discipline required of boycotting, see Joseph Lee, *The Modernisation of Irish Society, 1848–1918* (Dublin: Gill and Macmillan, 1983), 94. Daly granted one post-election interview to Penrose. In it he denied coercing anyone, denied even he had the power to coerce. The interview appeared in the Butte *Mining Journal*, November 18, 1888. See also Daly's testimony regarding his role in the election of 1888 in Senate *Report*, 3:2232–35. The next round in the feud, the struggle to determine the permanent site of the state capital, also had an ethno-religious dimension. Helena, Clark's choice and the eventual site, was identified by the APA as having been the "Protestant town." *The Examiner* October 31, 1896. Anaconda, Daly's choice, was "the fiefdom" of "Pope Marcus." Ibid., September 3, 1896. Butte's and Anaconda's Irish Catholics responded to Helena's selection by raising money for a statue of the Irish hero Thomas Francis Meagher. The statue was placed on the capital's front lawn where the "APA's . . . must look in his face and salute his glorious memory for all ages." There can be little question that, had Meagher not been mounted, a different part of his anatomy would have been referred to. Daly was honorary chairman of the Thomas Francis Meagher Memorial Association. Butte *Montana Catholic*, July 15, 1899; RELA, "Minute Books," July 3, 10, 1899, and, for the APA reference, October 15, 1903, IrC.

Montana's Political Culture
A Century of Evolution
Michael P. Malone
and Dianne G. Dougherty

"Political culture," for one behavioralist, is "a historical system of wide-spread, fundamental, behavioral, political values . . . classified into subsystems of identity, symbol, rule and belief." You can decide whether this effort by Michael P. Malone, who was Dean of Graduate Studies in Montana State University at the time this essay was written, and Dianne G. Dougherty, who was a graduate student in history at Montana State University, measures up to that lofty definition. Beyond a broad liberal/conservative dichotomy, does the article define and analyze a Montana ideology? It does provide an admirable summary of political and economic developments over a hundred years of history. And it has a thesis: that Montana politics once was a wide-open, no-holds-barred dogfight but matured into a bland, consensual, middle-of-the-road process. "The political spectrum," the authors assert, "seemed to narrow toward convergence upon the center." Are we really that dreary lately? Do Malone and Dougherty properly emphasize the impact of reapportionment, environmentalism, ethnicity, and other more contemporary concerns? This essay, if nothing else, is a sound building block, a point of departure for further investigations.

S tudents of regional history seldom write explicitly about the concept of "political culture." Yet they often seem to work on the tacit assumption that such a thing does exist. For what is political culture?

*Michael P. Malone and Dianne G. Dougherty, "Montana's Political Culture: A Century of Evolution," *Montana The Magazine of Western History*, 31 (Winter 1981), 44–58.

It is, simply, the configuration of ideas, attitudes, biases, and emotional attachments which characterize a political community, whether that community is a city, a state, or a nation. If this general definition is accepted, then it follows that each of the fifty states must exhibit a political culture which is somewhat uniquely its own. In each case, that culture is a product of several long-term factors: geography, history, economics, demography, and social developments. In the following essay, we propose to study the evolution of a changing political culture in Montana over the course of 100 years, from the late territorial period to the present.

Remote, sprawling, and thinly populated, Montana is an interesting case. This enigmatic state is in no real sense a "natural" community at all. Neither its boundaries nor its history and its politics follows the patterns of any particular logic. Rather, like most, if not all its sister states, Montana is the product of a long succession of historic occurrences, many of which have been random and undirected. The "Treasure State" spreads endlessly across three variously defined "regions": the eastern reaches of the Pacific Northwest, the cross-cutting mountain ranges of the "Northern Intermountain" area, and the northwestern expanses of the Great Plains. Western Montana looks westward toward the Columbia basin, toward the cities of Spokane, Portland and Seattle, and southward toward Salt Lake City, while the eastern plains face eastward toward Minneapolis-St. Paul and southward toward Denver. Despite these centrifugal forces, however, the state's disparate parts are also drawn closely together, most strongly by Montana's political boundaries and by its political culture.

How should the study of the complex, multi-faceted political cultures of the individual states be approached? Probably the best known interpretation is that of political scientist Daniel Elazar in his book *American Federalism: A View from the States.* Painting with broad strokes, Elazar identifies three fundamental American cultures, each of them radiating westward from the Atlantic settlements of the colonial and early national periods. Extending westward from Puritan-Yankee New England, the culture that he describes as "moralistic," later enriched by Scandinavian immigration, favors an activist government and welcomes social and political reform. Elazar sees an "individualistic" culture stemming primarily from the Middle Atlantic region. The individualist culture is essentially utilitarian, preferring a minimal government to deliver only basic services. Finally, he finds a "traditionalistic" culture based in the deep South and favoring a planter-style elitist system. In Montana and the Northwest, Elazar judges the Yankee-Scandinavian moralistic culture to

Montana politicians (left to right): Sam C. Ford, T. J. Walsh, Burton K. Wheeler, Judge James Baldwin, Joseph Scanlon (Montana Historical Society Photograph Archives)

be dominant, but he also finds a heavy influx of the individual-istic impulse. [1]

How valid are these sweeping generalities? Although they seem overly facile and simplistic, at least they raise the right questions. So do other regional studies by social scientists like Ira Sharkansky and Raymond Gastil. [2] In the following pages, we choose to avoid such broad-gauged conclusions and to look instead more closely and

1.   Daniel J. Elazar, *American Federalism: A View from the States*, 2nd ed. (New York: Thomas Y. Crowell, 1972), 84–126, quote on p. 89; and Daniel J. Elazar, "Political Culture on the Plains," *Western Historical Quarterly*, 11 (July 1980), 261–83.

2.   Ira Sharkansky, *Regionalism in American Politics* (Indianapolis: Bobbs-Merrill, 1970); Raymond D. Gastil, *Cultural Regions of the United States* (Seattle: University of Washington Press, 1975).

carefully into the fascinating political evolution of this one state. In the past, Montana's political history has been too often oversimplified, too often viewed as a clearcut struggle between corporate titans and heroic but beleaguered reformers. The truth is more subtle, more complex, more deserving of close analysis.

THE NINETEENTH-CENTURY HERITAGE

Like most other western states, Montana experienced a long and unhappy period of political "gestation" as a territory of the federal government, with only limited powers of self-government. Again like most of its neighbors, Montana Territory (1864–1889) evolved from an early unsettled period of what Kenneth Owens describes as "chaotic factionalism" into a more settled commonwealth in which local economic interest found their political identity. At first, the territory's population centered almost wholly upon the remote mining camps of its southwestern corner, and it seemed convulsed by the heated animosities of Civil War and Reconstruction. The Democratic party, carried in especially by Irish miners and immigrants from the border states of the Confederacy, took quick and lasting root as Montana's majority party. Locally elected Democratic legislatures fought angrily with governors, judges, and other territorial administrators appointed by Unionist-Republican governments in Washington. [3]

Gradually, as the passions of Civil War faded, the thinly settled territory began to show signs of political maturity during the long tenure of capable Governor Benjamin F. Potts (1870–1883). The boom of the 1880s and the arrival of railroads brought a burgeoning silver-copper industry to western Montana and a scattering of open-range ranches to the eastern plains. An inevitable development then surfaced as the two dominant economic groups—freewheeling mining barons of the west and cattle barons of the east—took control of territorial government and politics. The mining men usually predominated. They could normally maneuver the large voting majorities of Butte-Anaconda, Missoula, Helena, and Great Falls, majorities which were all the more imposing since they were concentrated in the Democratic party and spoke increasingly with the Gaelic accent of Marcus Daly's Irish miners. By the late 1880s Montanans talked commonly of baronial rule by the "Big Four"—Butte mining kings Marcus Daly and William Clark, and Helena capitalists C. A. Broadwater and

---

3.   Kenneth N. Owens, "Pattern and Structure in Western Territorial Politics," *Western Historical Quarterly*, 1 (October 1970), 373–92; Merrill G. Burlingame, *The Montana Frontier* (Helena: State Publishing Co., 1942), chap. 7; James L. Thane, Jr., "Montana Territory: The Formative Years, 1862–1870" (Ph.D. diss., University of Iowa, 1972).

Samuel T. Hauser. These men clearly dominated politics in the "Treasure State," as Montana styled itself when it became the forty-first star on the flag in 1889. [4]

From the perspective of ninety years, the frenzied decade of the 1890s seems a critical period in the development of Montana and the Mountain West. The Panic of 1893 and the resultant hard depression gripped the region; two powerful and unsettling forces, the Populist party and the notorious Clark-Daly feud, shook the newly formed state government of Montana. The Populist party emerged in 1892 as a farmers' protest party mainly based in the South and Midwest, but in the silver producing states of the Intermountain area, such as Idaho, Nevada, and Montana, it thrived as a miners' protest party. For, in addition to radical calls for reforms to aid distressed farmers, the Populists also demanded currency inflation by means of the free and unlimited coinage of silver dollars. This, of course, promised much to the depressed mining industry of the West.

The Populist-silver crusade took Montana by storm. In 1896 a fusion ticket of Populists, majority Democrats, and Silver Republicans swept the state for William Jennings Bryan and "free silver," and Butte's Marcus Daly was reportedly Bryan's greatest single campaign contributor. The Populist tide ebbed after 1896, but by then it had already worked profound changes. Populism scrambled party lines in the state and left an enduring legacy of party irregularity and anti-corporate, anti-Eastern radicalism on the left. While the Populist party died, Populist ideology and rhetoric lived on in future farmer-labor attacks upon banks, railroads, and corporate "exploitation" in general. Montana liberals like Burton K. Wheeler and Lee Metcalf would echo the neo-Populist outcry against the economic "colonization" of their region for many years into the future. [5]

Even more unsettling than Populism was the epic feud between mining moguls Marcus Daly and W. A. Clark, which raged from the election of 1888 until Daly's death in 1900. The details of this story are familiar enough and are too complex to repeat here, but it must be noted that the feud left deep and lasting scars upon the body politic. First Clark, and then Daly, bought up newspapers and blatantly used

---

4.   The authoritative study of Montana Territory is Clark C. Spence, *Territorial Politics and Government in Montana: 1864–89* (Urbana: University of Illinois Press, 1975); K. Ross Toole, *Montana: An Uncommon Land* (Norman: University of Oklahoma Press, 1959), 173; John W. Hakola, "Samuel T. Hauser and the Economic Development of Montana: A Case Study in Nineteenth-Century Frontier Capitalism" (Ph.D. diss., Indiana University, 1961).

5.   Thomas A. Clinch, *Urban Populism and Free Silver in Montana* (Missoula: University of Montana Press, 1970), 51, on Daly's contributions; Thomas A. Clinch, "The Northern Pacific Railroad and Montana's Mineral Lands," *Pacific Historical Review*, 34 (August 1965), 323–35.

them for his own partisan ends. Both men spent freely to manipulate legislators and other public "servants," and Clark seems clearly
to have bribed certain members of the 1893 Legislature in his quest
for a Senate seat. His wholesale bribery of the 1899 assembly was
attested by the fact that, of the fifteen Republican members of
that August body, eleven voted for Clark the Democrat. The feud
ended in 1900–1901 when, after being forced to resign from the
Senate due to charges of bribery, Clark managed to win reelection,
this time serving out a full six-year term (1901–1907). [6] Needless to
say, Montana's reputation suffered terribly as these antics gained
national attention.

The marathon political-economic struggle to control the great
Butte mining district climaxed and subsided during the years
1899–1906. In 1899 a tough and ruthless group of Standard Oil executives, led by Henry Rogers and William Rockefeller, bought control
of the mighty Anaconda Copper Mining Company and made it the
foundation of their newly created holding company, Amalgamated
Copper. The domineering Rogers and his cohorts aimed to "con-
solidate" ownership of the Butte Hill by buying up the major holdings
there and gathering them into Amalgamated. Control of Butte, they
assumed, would bring control of American copper production, which
would allow them to corner world copper just as they had earlier
cornered oil.

The "Standard Oil Gang" ran into unforeseen problems in their
Butte caper. First off, in the frenzied political campaign of 1900,
Butte's two major independent mine owners, Clark and the brilliant
and brash young F. Augustus Heinze, pilloried the Amalgamated men
as out-of-state robber barons. Following Daly's death in 1900, the
mercenary Clark quickly dropped his antitrust posture and joined
forces with Amalgamated. This left Heinze struggling alone against
the Standard Oil-Amalgamated colossus. He fought on ruthlessly and
ingeniously, portraying himself as Montana's champion against the
"Kerosene Crowd." His friends occupied two of the three judgeships
of Butte's Second Montana Judicial District, and with this weapon
he tied up the trust in endless litigation while his cronies ruled the
government of Silver Bow County.

---

6. K. Ross Toole, "The Genesis of the Clark-Daly Feud," *The Montana Magazine
of History*, 1 (April 1951), 21–33; K. Ross Toole, "When Big Money Came to Butte,"
Pacific Northwest Quarterly, 44 (January 1953), 23–29; C. P. Connolly, *The Devil Learns
to Vote: The Story of Montana* (New York: Covici Friede, 1938); C. B. Glasscock, *The War
of the Copper Kings* (New York: Bobbs-Merrill, 1935); K. Ross Toole, "A History of the
Anaconda Copper Mining Company: A Study in the Relationships Between a State
and Its People and a Corporation, 1880–1950" (Ph.D. diss., University of California
at Los Angeles, 1954); Forrest L. Foor, "The Senatorial Aspirations of William A. Clark"
(Ph.D. diss., University of California at Berkeley, 1941).

Desperately, the lords of Amalgamated fought back with their own lawsuits, their own dirty political tricks, and with a campaign of buying up newspapers across the state to bend a hostile public opinion in their favor. Inevitably, they finally won. With a dramatic shutdown of its mines, mills, smelters, and refineries late in 1903, Amalgamated forced the governor to convene the legislature in special session to pass a company-drafted judge-disqualification law that effectively neutralized Heinze's control of the courts. Heinze and his allies continued the fight for a while, but in 1906 he sold out the majority of his family's Butte holdings to the copper trust for a reported price of $12,000,000. [7]

Heinze's sellout and subsequent departure paved the way for the corporate consolidation of the Butte Hill. In 1910 the Amalgamated grouped all of its once independent Butte companies into one, Anaconda. And in 1915, the now purposeless Amalgamated holding company was dissolved, which meant that the enlarged Anaconda Copper Mining Company was once again an independent corporation. The world's greatest nonferrous metal mining company, mighty Anaconda controlled much more than Butte. In addition to properties beyond Montana, it held mines at Butte; reduction works, smelters and refineries at Anaconda and Great Falls; vast timber acreage and mills in western Montana; and coal properties in Carbon, Cascade, and Gallatin counties. In short, it was a giant and well-integrated corporation, one of America's greatest, which ruled supreme in a remote and thinly populated state. In 1912 Anaconda executives took steps to extend that rule by creating the Montana Power Company through a merger of small scattered plants already in operation. Closely tied to Anaconda at the executive level, Montana Power eventually carried "the Company's" presence far into the hinterlands of west-central Montana. [8]

Thus the "War of the Copper Kings" left behind a heavy political residue. Dominated by Marcus Daly's lieutenants John D. Ryan (until 1933) and Cornelius F. Kelley (until 1955), the Company held sternly to the tough and ruthless practices it had acquired in the battles of its youth. By 1910 roughly 65,000 of Montana's 376,000 people lived in the firm's two "company towns" of Butte and Anaconda. Thousands more depended upon it, either directly or indirectly, for livelihood.

---

7.   Michael P. Malone and Richard B. Roeder, *Montana: A History of Two Centuries* (Seattle: University of Washington Press, 1976), chap. 9; Sarah McNelis, *Copper King at War: The Biography of F. Augustus Heinze* (Missoula: University of Montana Press, 1968).

8.   "Anaconda Copper," *Fortune*, December 1936, 83–94ff.; and "Anaconda II," ibid., January 1937, 71–77ff.; Issaac F. Marcosson, *Anaconda* (New York: Dodd, Mead, 1957), chaps. 5–7; on the formation of Montana Power, see *The Montana Power Company: Reclassification of Electric Plant* (Butte: n.p., 1940), copy in possession of the company at its Butte central office.

Its lobbyists, pet legislators, and allies seemed ubiquitous in the halls of state government at Helena. Perhaps most ominously, its growing network of newspapers soon included all of the major urban dailies of Montana except for the Great Falls *Tribune*. The Company used these papers unflinchingly to pursue its interests. In sum, as University of Montana professor Arthur Fisher wrote in 1922:

> On the one hand, firmly entrenched, stand the ramifying and inter-linked corporate interests centering in the copper industry, now under the leadership of the Anaconda Copper Mining Company. On the other stands the rest of the population which feels it has no stake in the Company's prosperity but suffers from the Company's exploitation of every natural resource and profitable privilege, its avoidance of taxation, and its dominance of the political and educational life of the State. [9]

New Arrivals and New Politics

Even as the Company consolidated its economic and political power during the years after Heinze's defeat, the political profile of Montana was being drastically altered by new demographic and ideological forces. In a peculiar coincidence of historical events, the homesteading frontier and the Progressive movement occurred simultaneously here, and each had a sizable impact upon the political development of the state.

The northwestern Great Plains, covering eastern Montana and the western Dakotas, witnessed the last great land-taking in the United States. During the period 1909–1918, thousands of families followed the siren call of railroad advertising into the vast expanses of east-central Montana, especially into the "Highline" plains lying north of the Milk and Missouri rivers. The homesteaders, or "honyockers," as they were sometimes disparagingly called, came heavily from the upper and central Midwest. Many were first- and second-generation Scandinavian and German immigrants. Their scattered farms and ambitious little towns rapidly broke the monopolistic hold of the stockmen upon eastern Montana and planted there the "moralistic" political culture that Elazar sees extending in a Yankee-Scandinavian amalgam from Wisconsin and Minnesota to the Dakotas and Montana. Largely Lutheran in faith and activist-moralistic in politics, the agrarians immediately began agitating against the mining-based

---

9. Arthur Fisher, "Montana: Land of the Copper Collar," *The Nation*, September 1922, p. 290; Jerre C. Murphy, *The Comical History of Montana* (San Diego: E. L. Scofield, 1912); Richard T. Ruetten, "Anaconda Journalism: The End of an Era," *Journalism Quarterly*, 37 (Winter 1960), 3–12, 104.

status quo. They demanded that the mining interests pay a heavier share of the tax burden, for instance, and voted in a state dry law in 1916. Many of them, especially the Norwegians and Germans, tended toward an advanced liberalism, in some cases toward socialism. Like their political "relatives," the Robert LaFollette Progressives of Wisconsin and the Farmer-Laborites of Minnesota, thousands of North Dakota and Montana farmers joined the radical Nonpartisan League, which advocated an anticorporate program of state-owned banks, grain elevators, and utilities. [10]

These politically active homesteaders had much to do with Montana's Progressive movement. As Richard Roeder has convincingly demonstrated, Montana produced a hearty and rather typically western variety of state progressivism during the years after 1902. Like their counterparts around the country, the Montana progressives aimed, with a good deal of moralistic and highblown rhetoric, to counter corporate political power and malfeasance by fostering direct democracy and direct political action. They succeeded in passing into law an impressive amount of direct democracy and regulatory legislation: the initiative and referendum in 1906, the direct primary in 1912, direct election of U.S. senators in 1911–1913, women's suffrage in 1914, workmen's compensation in 1915, and state-wide prohibition in 1916. [11]

In Montana as elsewhere, the progressives produced an impressive and colorful group of leading personalities. On the Republican side there was the handsome and capable young Missoula lawyer Joseph M. Dixon, who during his long career served as a U.S. congressman (1903–1907), senator (1907–1913), manager of Teddy Roosevelt's national Bull Moose Progressive presidential campaign of 1912, and governor (1921–1925). And Jeannette Rankin, who combined a peculiar blend of pacifism, feminism, radicalism, and practicality, became America's first congresswoman. She served terms in 1917–

---

10. Elazar, *American Federalism*, 104–9; Gastil, *Cultural Regions*, 225–36; on homesteading, see Joseph K. Howard, *Montana: High, Wide, and Handsome* (New Haven: Yale University Press, 1943), 167–209; Malone and Roeder, *Montana*, 178–94; K. Ross Toole, *Twentieth-Century Montana: A State of Extremes* (Norman: University of Oklahoma Press, 1972), 25–98; Mary Wilma M. Hargreaves, *Dry Farming in the Northern Great Plains, 1900–1925* (Cambridge: Harvard University Press, 1957).

11. Roeder's most succinct statement (countering K. Ross Toole's argument in *Montana: An Uncommon Land*, 226, that progressivism amounted to little in Montana) is in "Montana Progressivism: Sound and Fury and One Small Tax Reform," *Montana The Magazine of Western History*, 20 (October 1970), 18–26; see also, Roeder, "Montana in the Early Years of the Progressive Period" (Ph.D. diss., University of Pennsylvania, 1971); and Jules A. Karlin, "Progressive Politics in Montana," in *A History of Montana*, ed. M. G. Burlingame and K. R. Toole, (3 vols., New York: Lewis Historical Publishing Co., 1957) 1:247–80; David Sarasohn, "The Election of 1916: Realigning the Rockies," *Western Historical Quarterly*, 11 (July 1980), 285–305.

1919 and 1941–43, and remarkably cast votes against American entry into both World War I and World War II. The progressive Democrats also had their notables, like Thomas J. Walsh, the taciturn and accomplished Helena attorney who represented Montana in the Senate from 1913 until 1933 and won national fame in unearthing the Teapot Dome scandal. Walsh became the only Montanan ever appointed to a presidential cabinet when Franklin Roosevelt named him attorney general, but he died in 1933 before assuming his duties. Finally, among the outstanding younger progressives there was Democrat Burton K. Wheeler, who served in the Senate from 1923 until 1947 and gained national headlines as an outspoken isolationist and as the leader of the Senate coalition that defeated Roosevelt's "court-packing" bill in 1937. [12]

Montana's progressives did quite well in their efforts to extend public participation in politics, but they fared badly in their attempts to counter corporate power in government. Logically enough, the reformers viewed the bare-knuckled might of Amalgamated-Anaconda as the very epitome of political abuse. In the heated election campaign of 1912, Republican-Progressive Senator Joseph Dixon carried the battle directly to the Company, which responded in kind. Dixon's Progressive party stationery carried the forthright letterhead: "Put the Amalgamated Out of Montana Politics." The senator had made his point, but he lost his seat to Democrat Thomas Walsh. [13]

In the Treasure State, as in the nation at large, the liberal momentum of the Progressive movement halted abruptly with the tidal wave of reaction and xenophobia that accompanied America's entry into World War I. Montana and the other states of the Northwest held large German and Scandinavian populations, and these groups, as well as the anti-British Irish and the anticapitalist radicals of the far

---

12.   On Dixon, see Jules A. Karlin, *Joseph M. Dixon of Montana* (2 vols., Missoula: University of Montana Publications in History, 1974); of the many writings on Rankin, see especially Joan Hoff Wilson, "Jeannette Rankin and American Foreign Policy: The Origins of Her Pacifism," *Montana The Magazine of Western History*, 30 (Winter 1980), 28–41; Joan Hoff Wilson, "Jeannette Rankin and American Foreign Policy: Her Life Work as a Pacifist," *Montana The Magazine of Western History*, 30 (Spring 1980), 38–53; Hannah Josephson, *Jeannette Rankin: First Lady in Congress* (Indianapolis: Bobbs-Merrill, 1974). J. Leonard Bates is the biographer of Thomas J. Walsh, see especially his "Senator Walsh of Montana, 1918–1924: A Liberal Under Pressure" (Ph.D. diss., University of North Carolina, 1952). Similarly, Richard T. Ruetten is preparing a definitive study of Wheeler, see his "Burton K. Wheeler, 1905–1925: An Independent Liberal Under Fire" (M.A. thesis, University of Oregon, 1957), and his "Burton K. Wheeler of Montana: A Progressive Between the Wars" (Ph.D. diss., University of Oregon, 1961). A colorful memoir is Burton K. Wheeler with Paul F. Healy, *Yankee from the West* (Garden City: Doubleday, 1962).

13.   Karlin, *Dixon*, vol. 1, chaps. 8–12; Toole, *Montana: An Uncommon Land*, 214–15.

left, greeted the war effort either with a lack of enthusiasm or with outright criticism. The radicals of the left were numerous and powerful in Montana. A healthy Socialist party thrived in working class cities like Butte, Anaconda, and Livingston; at Butte, the Socialists garnered enough support to elect Lewis Duncan mayor. The leftist-syndicalist Industrial Workers of the World (IWW) grew rapidly by recruiting the lumbermen and miners of western Montana. A radical faction of the Butte Miners' Union, sympathetic to the IWW, battled openly for control of the organization, leading to riots and dynamitings in 1914. Meanwhile, on the eastern Montana plains, the outspokenly radical—and sometimes antiwar—organizers of the Nonpartisan League (NPL) swept in from North Dakota, winning thousands of new members. [14]

By taking an antiwar stand, the radicals of the left placed themselves in a dire position, facing the wrath of superpatriots, many of whom were led by right-wing leaders of the corporate community. IWW organizer Frank Little was lynched at Butte after delivering fiery antiwar speeches there in July of 1917. Butte was gripped by a near class war, and the army and national guardsmen repeatedly occupied the city in order to insure maximum copper output and to stifle dissent. Spokesmen for striking lumbermen and for the Nonpartisan League frequently faced similar repression, sometimes even beatings. An atmosphere of near hysteria gripped the state. Led by a state-sanctioned Montana Council of Defense, flag-waving superpatriots actually crushed any free speech they found offensive. Early in 1918, the legislature enacted a repressive Criminal Syndicalism law, a gun registration law, and the notorious Montana Sedition Act, which actually made it illegal to criticize the government. This latter measure served as a model for the federal Sedition Act of 1918, one of the most severe violations of civil rights in the history of the United States. [15]

---

14. The forthcoming study of Montana's socialists by political scientist Jerry Calvert will place that fascinating group in perspective for the first time. There are no complete studies of the IWW and Nonpartisan League in Montana, but see Melvyn Dubofsky, *We Shall Be All: A History of the Industrial Workers of the World* (Chicago: Quadrangle Books, 1969), 301–93, passim.; Joseph R. Conlin, *Bread and Roses Too* (Westport, Conn.: Greenwood, 1969), 129–30, 141; and Robert L. Morland, *Political Prairie Fire: The Nonpartisan League, 1915-1922* (Minneapolis: University of Minnesota Press, 1955).

15. Arnon Gutfeld discusses these events in a somewhat narrow focus in *Montana's Agony: Years of War and Hysteria, 1917-1921* (Gainesville: University Presses of Florida, 1979), and also in a series of articles which may be found in that volume's bibliography; for a similar viewpoint, see Toole, *Twentieth-Century Montana*, chaps. 6–7; see also, Kurt Wetzel, "The Defeat of Bill Dunne: An Episode in the Montana Red Scare," *Pacific Northwest Quarterly*, 64 (January 1973), 12–20; and Benjamin G. Rader, "The Montana Lumber Strike of 1917," *Pacific Historical Review*, 36 (May 1967), 189–207.

Thus the war ended in an atmosphere of unreality and incredible tension. Hitherto powerful, the far left was shattered, and it would never fully recover its lost strength. Radical politicians like U.S. District Attorney Burton K. Wheeler, who had bravely opposed the terrorizing of antiwar critics, and Congresswoman Jeannette Rankin were temporarily driven from public life. Yet, paradoxical as it seems, progressive and radical fortunes momentarily revived after the war, given new life by the unrest generated by a severe drought and recession. Hard-pressed farmers, in particular, took up the old Nonpartisan League war cry for a tax reform that would force the mining companies to bear their fair share of the property tax burden. The tax revolt dominated the heated gubernatorial race of 1920, which pitted two foes of Anaconda, progressive Republican Joseph Dixon and radical Democrat Burton Wheeler, against one another. A tough, outspoken, and brilliant campaigner, Wheeler mustered a hard-hitting campaign against the Company. But the country was in an anti-radical mood in 1920, and the corporate press vilified Wheeler as a dangerous "Bolshevik." The result, in what probably ranks as the toughest campaign in the state's history, was a sweeping victory for Dixon. [16]

In his single-term administration (1921–1925), Governor Dixon faced myriad perplexing problems. The dominant right wing of his own Republican party distrusted him as an old Bull Moose Progressive; the Company dug in against his program to equalize taxation; and he shouldered the burdens of a severe agricultural depression. Despite some limited successes, Dixon thus failed to win support for his programs in the conservative legislatures of 1921 and 1923. Running for reelection in 1924, he went down to defeat under a barrage of corporate criticism, even as his pet Initiative 28 passed, instituting a higher and more equitable rate of taxation on mines. Some observers, like K. Ross Toole, view Dixon as a heroic figure battling the corporate Goliath. In his defeat, they see the collapse of progressivism in Montana. Dixon was an honest and able public servant, perhaps the state's best chief executive. His defeat did end the old-style Progressive movement in Montana, but it did not end liberalism as such. Temporarily set back, liberalism would burst forth again with the New Deal of the 1930s. [17]

---

16. Ellis Waldron and Paul B. Wilson, *Atlas of Montana Elections: 1889–1976* (Missoula: University of Montana Publications in History, 1978), 76–89; Karlin, *Dixon*, vol. 2, chap. 5; Wheeler, *Yankee*, chap. 8.

17. Karlin, *Dixon*, vol. 2, chaps. 6–11; Toole, *Montana*, 223–27; Toole, *Twentieth-Century Montana*, chaps. 9–10.

A MATURE POLITICAL CULTURE

During the years following Dixon's defeat in 1924, a period of political calm set in across the Treasure State. In part, the calm simply reflected the national mood of Calvin Coolidge–Herbert Hoover conservatism, and in part it resulted from the end of the drought and the momentary return of a measure of prosperity. Democratic Governor John E. "Honest John" Erickson, a conservative favorite of the Company, typified the stand-pat mood of the time, and so did the Republican-dominated legislatures of 1925–1931. Montana's sole liberal manifestation of the time was in Washington, where its prestigious team of Democratic senators, Thomas Walsh and Burton Wheeler, made a sensation with their exposures of wrong-doing in the Harding administration. Both men rose to the front ranks of prominence in the Democratic party. Wheeler ran for the vice presidency in 1924 on the liberal Progressive party ticket with Robert M. LaFollette of Wisconsin. Walsh chaired the national Democratic party conventions of 1924 and 1932 and ran a short-lived race for the presidency in 1928.[18]

The peculiarly schizoid posture of conservatism in the state government and liberalism on the national stage, which first surfaced when Wheeler joined Walsh in the Senate in 1923, is puzzling and has never been fully explained. Liberals have sometimes argued that conservative interest groups work to keep friendly politicians in key state offices while pragmatically relegating dangerous reformers to faraway national offices. Conservatives frequently counter with the argument that an intelligent electorate simply votes its own interests by choosing frugal conservatives to state offices while sending big-spending liberals to "fetch" federal dollars in Washington. Certainly, the fact that senators and congressmen are elected by broader-based constituencies has given liberal candidates for these offices an edge over those liberals who run legislative races in smaller, rural-conservative districts. One must also agree with Clark Spence's judgment that Montana's small, wide-open, and highly personalized political order enables popular politicians like Wheeler and Mike Mansfield to draw

---

18.   Waldron and Wilson, *Atlas*, 97–124; Richard T. Ruetten, "Senator Burton K. Wheeler and Insurgency in the 1920's," in *The American West: A Reorientation*, ed. Gene M. Gressley (Laramie: University of Wyoming Press, 1968), 111–31; Paul A. Carter, "The Other Catholic Candidate: The 1928 Presidential Bid of Thomas J. Walsh," *Pacific Northwest Quarterly*, 55 (January 1964), 1–18.

votes freely from across weakly defined party lines. In any case, Montana's preference for liberal-Democratic senators is indisputable. Since the popular election of U.S. senators began back in 1913, the state has elected only one Republican to that body! [19]

In this and in other ways, Montana had struck its "classic" political profile by the 1920s. The frontier settlement process had truly closed with the collapse of homesteading agriculture after World War I, and the state had by now entered the modern era. On the right side of the political spectrum, Montana conservatives drew strong support, of course, from the Company—Anaconda-Montana Power. And, contrary to the stereotype of Montana as a "one-company" state, they also garnered support from other economic interest groups. Other corporations, like the five major railroads of the state, as well as lesser lumber, coal and oil companies, usually lined up behind Anaconda on major state-wide issues. Often, they were joined by the conservative stockmen, organized mainly in the Montana Stockgrowers Association, and by the closely related large-acreage grain farmers, who were by now gathering under the flag of the Montana Farm Bureau Federation. Frequently overlooked by those who saw Montana as a corporate bailiwick, this alliance between western Montana corporations and eastern Montana ranchers is critically important to understanding the state's political development. The "cowboys" often wielded greater strength than the businessmen, especially in the legislature. Of course, the conservatives also drew ample support from the small middle class, and from the main street business communities of the towns and cities. [20]

The progressives, who by the 1920s were beginning more frequently to call themselves "liberals," also drew middle-class support. The stereotype of Montana as a corporate colony of Anaconda, which was obviously inaccurate in accounting for conservative strength, was even more misleading in its discounting of Treasure State liberalism. The essence of Montana liberalism was an alliance—often more dream than reality—between small farmers and union labor, somewhat similar to the formalized Farmer-Labor movement in Minnesota. During the 1920s, the agrarian reformers moved *en masse* from the

---

19. Thomas Payne, "Montana: Politics Under the Copper Dome," in *Politics in the American West*, ed. Frank H. Jonas (Salt Lake City: University of Utah Press, 1969), 202–30; Clark C. Spence, *Montana: A Bicentennial History* (New York: W. W. Norton, 1978), 165–66.

20. Michael P. Malone, "Montana as a Corporate Bailiwick: An Image in History," in Peter J. Powell and Michael P. Malone, *Montana: Past and Present* (Los Angeles: William Andrews Clark Memorial Library, 1976), 55–76; for an insight into the conservatism of the Montana Stockgrowers Association, see Robert H. Fletcher, *Free Grass to Fences: The Montana Cattle Range Story* (New York: University Publishers, 1960).

dying Nonpartisan League into the less radical, but still outspokenly liberal National Farmers Union. especially along the Highline, the Farmers Union was a potent political force. It frequently aligned with the mine-mill union men who were now organized by the International Union of Mine, Mill and Smelter Workers, and with the numerous locals of the Railroad Brotherhoods scattered along the main lines of the Great Northern and Northern Pacific railroads. The mining unions lay dormant during the twenties under an "open shop" arrangement instituted by the Company back in 1914, but they would soon regain the "closed shop" with New Deal encouragement in the big strikes of 1934. [21]

The Montana political culture that had coalesced by the post-frontier 1920s was a more complex and closely balanced alignment of interests and populations than is usually believed. Despite a continuing Democratic majority, the two parties competed on quite even terms. And despite a sometimes imposing conservative bias in Montana politics, the opposing forces of the political left and right competed on even terms, too. Prior to Dixon's debacle in the early twenties, Montana's Republican party held a stronger progressive wing than did the Bourbon-style Democracy, but this situation began to change as the conservatives now gained clear control of the GOP with Dixon's defeat. It would soon change even further as the New Deal drew the progressive community of Montana overwhelmingly into the Democratic party. These changes, which mirror a national trend, have persisted to this day. Like the other mountain states, Montana seems to accommodate few liberal Republicans. Its Republican party is strongly rightist, and its Democratic party is usually visibly divided into liberal and conservative wings.

DEPRESSION AND POLITICAL TURMOIL

The onset of the Great Depression, accompanied by another terrible drought cycle, ended the political calm of the late 1920s and ushered in an era of political turbulence and change comparable to the 1890s and World War I. By 1931, the depression had devastated every sector of the Montana economy, from the parched eastern plains whose farm commodities were at rock-bottom prices, to the dormant mining and lumber regions of the West. Governor Erickson and the conservative legislators tried simply to meet the problem by

---

21. See Vernon H. Jensen, *Heritage of Conflict: Labor Relations in the Nonferrous Metals Industry up to 1930* (Ithaca: Cornell University, 1950); Vernon H. Jensen, *Nonferrous Metals Industry Unionism: 1932–1954* (Ithaca: Cornell University Press, 1954).

cutting costs and payrolls in an effort to cope with the falling yields of the property tax. In 1931 the legislature adopted a limited income tax to broaden the base, but it steadfastly refused to follow the depression trend of states putting in sales taxes. Like most states, Montana lacked the initiative and the resources to combat what was in reality a *national* calamity. [22]

As the depression steadily deepened, it naturally carried down in its wake the fortunes of President Herbert Hoover and the Republican party. In Montana the election of 1932, which brought Franklin D. Roosevelt and his New Deal to Washington, was a truly epochal event. The election ushered out the conservative Republican legislative majorities and brought in Democrats who would follow the lead of the White House. Montanans played the most conspicuous role in national politics of their entire history as Senator Walsh chaired the 1932 Democratic convention in Chicago, Senator Wheeler brought key supporters like Huey Long of Louisiana onto the Roosevelt bandwagon, and longtime Democratic national committeeman J. Bruce Kremer chaired the powerful convention Rules Committee. Partly as a reward for such service, no doubt, Walsh garnered appointment as attorney-general in FDR's cabinet, although he died before he could assume the post. [23]

The New Deal reform program of 1933–1938, which had an enormous influence on all states, had a giant impact upon Montana. Its spending-regulatory programs brought millions into the state, drastically enhancing the federal role in Montana. It also stimulated state government into a new growth and activism. By 1935, relief agencies like the Public Works Administration and the Works Progress Administration offered some kind of support to nearly one in every four Montanans, and the Agricultural Adjustment Administration was paying up to $10,000,000 annually to Treasure State farmers. Federal agencies like the Civilian Conservation Corps and the Rural Electrification Administration brought in valuable and highly popular new services. Montana boasted one of the New Deal's greatest projects, the giant, earth-filled Fort Peck Dam on the Missouri. Montana ranked second among the forty-eight states in federal spending per capita, a fact largely explained by its small population and broad acreage. [24]

---

22. Michael P. Malone, "The Montana New Dealers," in John Braeman, Robert H. Bremner and David Brody, eds., *The New Deal*, (2 vols., Columbus: Ohio State University Press, 1975), 2:240–42; and Michael P. Malone, "Montana Politics and the New Deal," *Montana The Magazine of Western History*, 21 (Winter 1971), 2–11.

23. Michael P. Malone, "Montana Politics at the Crossroads: 1932–1933," *Pacific Northwest Quarterly*, 69 (January 1978), 20–29; Waldron and Wilson, *Atlas*, 126–31.

24. Leonard Arrington, "The New Deal in the West: A Preliminary Statistical Inquiry," *Pacific Historical Review*, 38 (August 1969), 314–15; James T. Patterson, "The

Inevitably, such far reaching measures had a sizable impact upon politics. The popularity of Roosevelt and of the New Deal, reflected in FDR's four landslide victories in Montana, naturally raised the political fortunes of Treasure State Democrats. In fact, the period 1933–1940 marks the single greatest era of one-party domination in the history of a state that is normally characterized by close inter-party competition. Republicans barely figured in political contests at all. But as always happens, the lopsided Democratic majority soon factionalized and broke up. Senator Burton K. Wheeler, now the state's dominant political figure, broke his earlier friendship with President Roosevelt over FDR's controversial 1937 effort to "pack" the Supreme Court. Indeed, Wheeler actually led the Senate coalition that handed the President his most stinging defeat on this issue. [25]

Wheeler, who broke into Montana politics twenty years earlier as a young radical, was becoming an elderly, anti-statists conservative. His break with the administration sped up the polarization of the Montana Democratic party into a conservative, pro-Wheeler faction and a liberal, New Deal majority led by the steadfast liberal Senator James E. Murray (1935–1961) and the fiery radical Congressman Jerry O'Connell (1937–1939). In the hot campaign of 1938, the Democratic infighting broke into the open. Congressman O'Connell boldly announced that with administration support he planned to challenge Senator Wheeler in 1940, but O'Connell got a lesson in practical politics when Wheeler Democrats joined Republicans and voted for O'Connell's Republican opponent for his House seat in 1938. [26]

The chasm between liberal and conservative Democrats steadily widened. Senators Murray and Wheeler feuded openly, and in 1939–1940 Wheeler again enraged the Roosevelt men by launching a vigorous isolationist attack against the president's pro-Allied foreign policy. Showing a deft political maneuverability, Wheeler faced off his liberal Democratic enemies and won reelection in 1940 by gathering in thousands of votes from his newfound Republican admirers. By the end of the depression decade, the great New Deal Democratic majority vessel had thus run aground on the reefs of factional discord. This allowed the Republicans to regain their share of the turf, most

---

New Deal in the West," ibid., 317–27; James T. Patterson, *The New Deal and the States: Federalism in Transition* (Princeton: Princeton University Press, 1969); Malone, "Montana New Dealers," 246–48; and Malone and Roeder, *Montana*, 229–33.

25. Richard Ruetten, "Burton K. Wheeler and the Montana Connection," *Montana The Magazine of Western History*, 37 (Summer 1977), 2–19; Ruetten, "Wheeler of Montana," chaps. 7–8; James T. Patterson, *Congressional Conservatism and the New Deal* (Lexington: University of Kentucky Press, 1967), chap. 3.

26. Richard T. Ruetten, "Showdown in Montana, 1938: Burton Wheeler's Role in the Defeat of Jerry O'Connell," *Pacific Northwest Quarterly*, 54 (January 1963), 19–29.

notably by electing Sam Ford to the governor's chair in 1940. Nonetheless, the New Deal undeniably cast a long shadow into the Montana future. It heralded a massive, new federal role in the state, began the growth of the modern governmental bureaucracy in Helena, and organized a liberal coalition in the Democratic party which is still there today. [27]

World War II coincided in Montana with a period of confused, labyrinthine politics. Party lines once again disintegrated as angry liberal Democrats fumed at what they called the "Wheeler-Ford-Rankin Axis," an informal marriage of convenience between Wheeler Democrats and moderate Republicans led by Wheeler and his GOP pals Sam C. "Model T" Ford and land developer-politician Wellington Rankin. All three of the principals, Wheeler, Ford, and Rankin, were not inappropriately referred to as "tired radicals"; all three had started out years earlier on the left, and all three now stood to the right of center. While they failed in their effort to place Rankin in Jim Murray's Senate seat in 1942, they succeeded in holding control of state government through the war years. In 1944, Ford won reelection in an angry campaign against liberal Democrat Leif Erickson, who championed the idea of a TVA-style Missouri Valley Authority. The end of this strange interlude of bipartisan politics came in 1946 when the old warhorse Burton Wheeler failed in the Democratic primary, a victim of angry internationalists and union liberals who retaliated against him for his isolationist and conservative leanings. Wheeler's fall ended the most colorful and powerful career in the history of Montana politics and ushered in a new political era. [28]

MONTANA POLITICS RESHAPED

After a decade and a half of political turmoil and change, the postwar period began in Montana as a new era in which long-term social and economic forces, already long at work, were fundamentally recasting the state's political culture. Agriculture, for instance, had ranked as the state's key industry since the early years of the century. But by now, the national trend toward fewer and larger, more

---

27. Waldron and Wilson, *Atlas*, 150–64; Malone, "Montana New Dealers," 252–59; John M. Allswang, *The New Deal and American Politics* (New York: John Wiley and Sons, 1978), 105–7.

28. Waldron and Wilson, *Atlas*, 165–83; Malone and Roeder, *Montana*, 237–40; Joseph Kinsey Howard wrote with flair and partisanship of wartime politics in "The Montana Twins in Trouble," *Harper's*, September 1944, pp. 334–42; "Golden River," ibid., May 1945, pp. 511–23; and the beautifully written "The Decline and Fall of Burton K. Wheeler," ibid., March 1947, pp. 226–36.

heavily mechanized and capitalized units was having a heavy impact upon Montana. From a total of 46,904 farms and ranches in 1925, the Montana total sank to 35,085 in 1950 and 23,324 in 1974. [29] Subsistence farmers left the land, and larger operators gathered up their holdings. This demographic hemorrhage of rural population caused most of the counties of northern and eastern Montana to lose sizable percentages of their people, and this trend fostered a conservative attitude that tended to view change as threatening. Naturally enough, the remaining, highly capitalized farmer-businessmen leaned to the right, while the Farmers Union, that traditional bastion of liberalism, saw much of its support base crumbling away.

Just as the old-progressive "family farmers" were being reduced in numbers by national economic forces, so were their longtime liberal allies of the Butte-Anaconda-Great Falls miners' and smelter-men's unions. By the forties and fifties, the old, labor-intensive deep mines of Butte could barely compete with the mass-production, open pit mines of Arizona and Utah. The Anaconda finally bowed to the inevitable and began open pit mining at Butte. In the years that followed, the Company eventually closed all of its deep mines, terminating thousands of jobs. So the miners' unions lost much of their membership, even as other, less ideological unions like the Teamsters expanded. A similar loss of membership afflicted the declining rail brotherhoods of cities like Livingston and Missoula. What all of this amounted to was a serious erosion of the proletarian base of the Democratic party and Montana progressivism.

The losses of these farmer-labor constituencies, it must be remembered, were gradual and long-term occurrences, which were partly offset by an inflow of middle class liberals to Montana's small but growing cities. Long into the postwar era, therefore, Montana continued to manifest a strong liberal presence, a farmer-labor brand of progressivism that contrasted sharply with such neighboring states as Wyoming or Idaho, whose conservative cultures were less alloyed by strains of liberal tradition. For instance, the *People's Voice*, the outspoken advocate of farmer-labor liberalism, continued publication until 1969. Thus the old Montana pattern of liberalism in Washington and conservatism in Helena persisted on and on, even through the 1970s.

Postwar liberalism in Montana found special embodiment in three liberal Democratic U.S. senators: James Murray, Mike Mansfield, and Lee Metcalf. One of the most devoted of New Deal–Fair Deal liberals,

---

29. U.S. Department of Commerce, Bureau of the Census, *Statistical Abstract of the United States: 1942* (Washington, D.C.: Government Printing Office, 1943), 698; *Statistical Abstract of the United States: 1979* (Washington, D.C.: Government Printing Office, 1979), 689.

Congressman Lee Metcalf (left) with Senator James E. Murray (center) and Senator Mike Mansfield (Montana Historical Society Photograph Archives)

low-keyed old Jim Murray, heir to a Butte mining fortune, closely resembled such "urban" liberals of the time as Robert Wagner of New York in his voting record. He played a significant role in promoting such progressive legislation as the United Nations, national health insurance, a Missouri Valley Authority, and the Employment Act of 1946. Mike Mansfield, the soft-spoken history professor from Missoula, served ten years as a workmanlike congressman (1943–1953) before winning a Senate seat from conservative Republican Zales Ecton in the bruising election campaign of 1952. During his long and distinguished Senate career, Mansfield won respect from both sides of the aisle as a moderate progressive with special expertise in foreign affairs; he served longer as Senate majority leader than any other man in history. Probably no public servant ever won more federal plums for Montana than did Mansfield. Lee Metcalf resembled Murray, more than Mansfield, in his reliance upon the old farmer-labor coalition for support. He was an outspoken liberal who often antagonized the right. During both his congressional (1953–1961) and his senatorial (1961–1978) careers, Metcalf consistently held to his progressive and environmental ideals and commanded a devoted liberal following. [30]

Of course, in time there were changes not only to the left, but also to the right. The most fundamental change was the decline of Anaconda's political role in Montana. This decline can be traced back to the 1920s, when Anaconda expanded by purchasing the country's foremost brass fabricator, American Brass, and then bought up the great Guggenheim mines in Chile. Gradually, as the firm came to rely overwhelmingly upon its Latin American mines, its obsession with Montana politics waned. The loosening of its political grip was barely discernible until the fifties, but then changes came rapidly. Following the retirement of Cornelius Kelley, Marcus Daly's aging successor, the Anaconda giant seemed to shrink appreciably. The Company sold its newspapers in 1959 and moved away from its age-old alliance with Montana Power, allegedly because of corporate rivalries and disagreements over the benefits of public power generated at Hungry Horse Dam. By the mid-1960s, Anaconda seemed to differ little in its political tactics from other western resource companies. Its offspring, Montana Power, appeared to be much more politically potent. Atlantic Richfield absorbed the ailing Anaconda in the mid-1970s, and as that decade closed, Montanans worried less about Company political power than about the calamitous repercussions of the closure of the Arco-Anaconda smelter and Great Falls refinery, which the Company announced in September 1980. [31] In short, one hundred years after Marcus Daly's purchase of the Anaconda Mine, his old company seemed to cast but a pale reflection of its once awesome political might.

As Anaconda's power waned, other corporations like the railroads and Montana Power maintained their grip, while new lumber, oil, and coal, and banking companies arrived on the scene. All of this

---

30. There are no definitive biographical treatments of these three individuals, but on Murray see Forrest Davis, "Millionaire Moses," *Saturday Evening Post*, December 8, 1945, pp. 9–10, 103–4, 106, and Joseph K. Howard, "Jim Murray's Chances," *The Nation*, October 9, 1948, pp. 397–99; on Mansfield, Louis Baldwin, *Honorable Politician: Mike Mansfield of Montana* (Missoula: Mountain Press, 1979); and on Metcalf see, Robert Sherrill, "The Invisible Senator," *The Nation*, May 10, 1971, pp. 584–89.

31. Marcosson, *Anaconda*, 136–339; Malone, "Montana as a Corporate Bailiwick," 65–67; "From Riches to Rags," *Forbes Magazine*, January 15, 1972, pp. 24–25; Billings *Gazette*, April 20, 21, 22, 23, 1980; Butte *Montana Standard*, September, 28, 29, 30, 1980.

amounted to a healthy broadening and diversifying of the corporate community in the state. The business interests continued to lobby and politic as always, but the heavy-handed old Gilded Age approach faded into memory. Still frequently allying with the plains ranchers and dry-land farmers, business and industrial interests continued to form the backbone of Treasure State conservatism.

Thus, as the old farmer-labor alliance of the left and the seemingly monolithic Anaconda behemoth of the right both paled with time, the political spectrum seemed to narrow toward convergence upon the center. Montana's small but growing middle classes, centered in the expanding cities of Billings, Great Falls, Missoula, and Helena, came to play an increasingly larger role in politics. And the role they preferred, whether Republicans or Democrats, seemed to be middle-of-the-road, poised between the union-led Democrats to the left and the rural conservatives to the right. The overall tilt in voter preference appeared to be generally rightward, for Montana was drifting along with the general Rocky Mountain region toward a more conservative political culture. Commenting upon this regional edging to the political right, away from the Northeastern-dominated welfare-liberalism of the postwar era, Kevin Phillips states appropriately:

> Liberalism was turning away from the popular economic progressivism with which Mountain states support had been forged — the Norris-Borah-Wheeler era was over and done with — and was shifting into a welfare establishmentarianism lacking in appeal to the old radical Mountain states (where Northeastern causes are suspect whether liberal or conservative). . . . So long as the Democrats remain oriented towards the Northeast, their presidential nominees are not likely to carry the old populist Rocky Mountain states. . . . Sparsely settled though they may be, the Rocky Mountains have become pillars of the new national Republicanism. [32]

Liberal Democrats, it is true, kept their grip upon the Senate seats, and usually upon the western congressional district, which has traditionally been dominated by Butte-Anaconda and Missoula. But conservative Republicans and Democrats normally held sway over state government and over the plains-oriented eastern congressional district. Following the single term of moderate Democratic Governor John Bonner (1949–1953), a long succession of conservatives presided over the government of Montana: Republicans J. Hugo ("the Galloping Swede") Aronson, who genially held office during the Eisenhower years (1953–1961); Donald Nutter (1961–1962), the arch-

---

32. Kevin P. Phillips, *The Emerging Republican Majority* (New Rochelle: Arlington House, 1969), 402, 407.

conservative who perished in a winter plane crash before being able to complete his retrenchment programs; and Tim Babcock (1962–1969); and the veteran conservative Democrat Forrest Anderson (1969–1973). Only with the 1972 election of moderate liberal Democrat Tom Judge did this conservative gubernatorial pattern show any sign of breaking. [33]

This same rightist coloration can be found in the various key agencies of state government, especially those like the Montana Supreme Court and the Public Service Commission that become focal points in struggles between corporations and their adversaries. In a penetrating series of articles in 1972 the Billings *Gazette*, an ex-Company paper, estimated that, during the preceding fifteen-year period, the Supreme Court had ruled in favor of Montana Power-Anaconda-Burlington Northern thirty-two times and against them only twelve. [34] Conservatism also ruled supreme, generally speaking, in the legislature. Rural traditionalists, especially stockmen, often visibly dominated the assembly through seniority and the chairmanship of key committees, even after the court-ordered reapportionment of 1965.

The two houses of the legislature reflect an irregularity in party control that attests to the close partisan competition in the Treasure State. Since the hamstrung first session of 1889–1890, the Republicans have controlled both houses of the legislature sixteen times, the Democrats thirteen times; on sixteen occasions control of the two houses has been divided. Admittedly, the liberals have more than held their own on some legislative issues over the years, for instance in their long standing opposition to the "regressive" sales tax and to "right to work" laws and in their more recent tough stands on the environment. Generally, though, bipartisan conservative coalitions have prevailed on the big issues of restraining taxation, spending, and bureaucratization. This tight-fisted fiscal conservatism is usually popular at election time and it is sometimes justified by pointing to the state's slipping per capita income (ranking approximately thirty-fifth in the nation). But it has also taken its toll in the quality and quantity of state services funded; even on a per capita income

---

33. The best quick guides to general political trends in Montana after World War II are Waldron and Wilson, *Atlas*, 178–288; and the *Western Political Quarterly*, which from 1949 through 1971 carried Western state-by-state election coverages in the spring or summer issues of odd-numbered years; Jules Karlin described the 1948 and 1952 campaigns, Thomas Payne all those through 1968, and Brad Hainesworth the 1970 campaign; Malone and Roeder, *Montana*, chap. 15; J. Hugo Aronson's autobiography, *The Galloping Swede*, coauthored with L. O. Brockmann (Missoula: Mountain Press, 1970) is politically unrevealing.

34. Billings *Gazette*, August 20, 1972.

scale of measurement, Montana ranks thirty-seventh among the states in welfare funding.[35]

MONTANA'S POLITICAL CULTURE

Montana entered the 1970s in an activist mood. In a pivotal special election in November 1971, the voters chose delegates to a constitutional convention that would meet the following year. In the same election, they overwhelmingly rejected a Republican-sponsored 2 percent sales tax, laying to rest that issue for the foreseeable future and leaving Montana among the five remaining states (along with Alaska, Delaware, New Hampshire, and Oregon) that still do not tap this lucrative source of revenue. The voters ratified the new constitution by a razor-thin 50.55 percent margin in the 1972 election, a progressive victory of urban over rural areas. Progressivism surfaced in other ways, too, particularly in the environmental protection laws that the legislature began enacting in 1971. Montana's environmental statutes are today among the toughest in the Union; the current energy crisis is surrounding them—especially the 30 percent coal severance tax—with controversy.[36]

The liberal surge of the early 1970s seems, however, to have brought few enduring changes. In fact, Montana liberals suffered a major setback when Senator Mike Mansfield retired in 1977 and when Senator Lee Metcalf died suddenly in early 1978. The passing of these prestigious and powerful lawmakers, heirs to the earlier Walsh-Wheeler-Murray matchings, cost Montana dearly in federal influence, while raising questions for the future about the state's traditional liberal posture in Washington. Although two Democratic congressmen, John Melcher and Max Baucus, gained election to the Senate seats, many liberals judged Melcher to be well to the right of themselves. As Montana voters revealed in their heavy votes for Ronald Reagan in 1980, and in their election of Republican majorities to both houses of the legislature, they seem to be moving ever closer to the western states mainstream of Republican-conservative preference. The Democratic hammerlock on the state's two Senate seats

---

35. The legislative statistics are drawn from Waldron and Wilson, *Atlas*; the rankings on per capita income and the funding of welfare were graciously supplied to us by John LaFaver, Legislative Fiscal Analyst of Montana. See also, Margaret Scherf, "One Cow, One Vote: A Strenuous Session in the Montana Legislature," *Harper's*, April 1966, pp. 103–9; Payne, "Montana," 222–26; Neal R. Peirce, *The Mountain States of America* (New York: W. W. Norton, 1972), 114–17.

36. Waldron and Wilson, *Atlas*, 255–69; *The World Almanac and Book of Facts: 1980* (New York: Newspaper Enterprise Associates, 1979), 59–60.

may soon be broken. Nonetheless, the persistence of its liberal Democratic tradition still makes Montana more a swaying political weathervane than are its immediate neighbors.

So we must conclude that the political culture which had bloomed in its classical flowering by the 1920s has, during the past half-century, changed markedly. Montana's classic political culture grew naturally, as we have seen, out of its narrowly based economic order. Stockmen and large scale farmers joined the business community, led by Anaconda–Montana Power, on the right in opposition to a coalition of small farmers and unionized workers on the left. The state's small middle class divided between these two poles. Inevitably, the passing years took their toll. The attrition of small farmers and blue-collar workers at one end of the body politic matched the ebbing of nineteenth-century baronial rule by Anaconda at the other. At the same time, the growth in "service" industries, tourism, and especially government employment expanded the middle class population of the cities and towns.

As a result, Montana shed its older, colorful, and combative political culture like a snake molting its skin. The newly evolved culture, although streaked with colorations of heredity, is really more homogenous, more broadly regional and national in tone, with fewer local peculiarities. Even as they enter fully into the national mainstream, though, Montanans show many signs of the lingering influence of their past: in their strong environmental attachment, their gut suspicions of corporations and of a distant federal government, their proud individualism and low regard for party regularity, their lingering fondness of ethnic politics, their impassioned attacks upon and defenses of extractive corporations and tough-minded unions. That is Montana, that *is* the political reflection of its history.

"Pines and mountains," etching by Great Falls artist Branson J. Stevenson (Montana Historical Society, gift of Mr. and Mrs. Donald W. Becklin in memory of Morris C. and Hilda C. Becklin and Prince Albert and Marian B. Mowbray)

PART III

20th Century Montana

The economic crises that struck Montana in the 1920s and 1930s forever altered the nature of the state. The youthfulness and unbridled optimism so apparent during Montana's frontier era disappeared to a considerable degree, victims of the agricultural crash of the early 1920s and the Great Depression of the 1930s. The Montana that emerged from these crises, however, would remain largely dependent upon its natural resources for its economic well-being. More than ever the state's economy would be influenced by policies and decisions formulated outside the state, especially by the federal government. Issues such as water rights, farm subsidies, timber harvests in federal forests, wilderness legislation, interest rates (for home mortgages in particular), and national energy policies all had a major impact on twentieth-century Montana.

While these changes took place, another important feature of late twentieth-century Montana has been the political and economic re-emergence of Native Americans. Despite the tremendous hardships inflicted upon them by vacillating, often counterproductive government policies and attitudes, Montana's Native American tribes have continued to strive to protect their political rights and maintain their rich cultural heritage.

CCC cleanup crew at work in Two Medicine valley in July 1933. (George Grant, photographer, Glacier National Park)

The CCC Experience
in Glacier National Park

Michael J. Ober

Deeply shaken by the immensity of the Great Depression, the American people in November 1932 selected Franklin D. Roosevelt to lead them out of the crisis. Upon entering the White House in early 1933, F.D.R. moved quickly to institute a wide variety of programs designed to get the nation's economy back on its feet while instilling in people a renewed sense of confidence. One of the most publicized programs during the New Deal era was the Civilian Conservation Corps. The CCC hired young men (at $30 per month) to live in outdoor camps, where they engaged in such useful activities as reforestation, firefighting, and flood control. Montana, with its extensive forests and federal land holdings, was a natural location for CCC camps.

Although the CCC was not devoid of problems or critics, it turned out to be one of the most popular New Deal programs. The land, especially western forests, certainly benefited from the increased government attention the CCC provided. Individuals who worked in the camps also benefited from the program. For Montana, the CCC experience was indicative of the state's increasing dependence upon the federal government for economic support—support that would eventually include agricultural subsidies, dam and highway construction, and a variety of other programs. This account of the CCC in

*Michael J. Ober, "The CCC Experience in Glacier National Park," *Montana The Magazine of Western History*, 26 (Summer 1976), 30–39.

Glacier National Park by Michael J. Ober, a longtime seasonal ranger at the Park, is an excellent case study of these various forces at work in Montana.

In the middle of June 1933, a group of young men from New York City stepped off a train at Belton (West Glacier), Montana. They had been riding for many hours, viewing scenes different from any-thing they had ever seen before. All of them were under twenty-five years of age. As soon as the train stopped at the west entrance of Montana's scenic wonder, Glacier National Park, some of the youths gathered around banjos and guitars; here and there a mascot tugged at the end of a rope. One young man optimistically shouldered a set of golf clubs, while another regretted that he had not brought his violin with him. There were, according to contemporary reports, no signs of homesickness, but a great many of bewilderment and interest in these "novel" surroundings.

It was, for these young men, and thousands like them, a novel experience as well. They were the first of 1,278 recruits in the Civilian Conservation Corps to be assigned to Glacier Park. They were, indeed, the vanguard of many more who would follow during the next eight years. Their presence in Glacier Park and the conserva-tion work they performed there is a peculiar and unstudied phenomenon in the history of the park. Taken as a case study, it bears the imprint of a national movement at work on a local level. The hundreds of youths who participated in emergency conservation work in this pristine setting during the years of the Great Depression helped give shape and character to a national preserve which had been in existence a scant two decades and which was still on a low rung of the administrative hierarchy.

The sum of these efforts was expressed early in 1939 by Glacier Park Superintendent Eivind T. Scoyen, under whose administration the CCC camps were most active. Writing to his superior, National Park Service Director Arno B. Cammerer, he said: "There needed to be a proving ground and a show place for those companies, and we provided it. It is of greater note, however, that we had the use of those companies to initiate plans of work that had only been talked about . . . ."

Credit for the idea of putting unemployed youths to work on a multitude of conservation projects belongs with Franklin D. Roose-velt, architect of the New Deal and proponent of the many "alphabet soup agencies" that grew out of his first one hundred days in office. Roosevelt, according to CCC historian John A. Salmond, ". . . brought together two wasted resources, the young and the land in an attempt to save them both." [1]

On March 31, 1933, the President signed a measure passed by Congress providing for emergency conservation work in the nation's forests and parks. To coordinate the activities of the vast armies of CCC enrollees, he appointed Robert Fechner, a prominent labor leader, who, in turn, worked with the departments of Labor, War, Agriculture, and Interior. Labor Department officials selected and registered single men, age 18 to 25, whose families were on the public relief rolls. The young men had to agree to allot $25.00 of their $30.00 monthly cash allowances to their families back home.

Fechner charged the U. S. Army with the enormous burden of training, feeding, equipping, conditioning, housing, and transporting the men. Further along the line of supervision were the departments of Agriculture and Interior which, through their various agencies and bureaus, were responsible for assigning and overseeing specific work projects. [2]

Fechner and army officials divided the nation into quasi-military corps areas for ease of administration. The Missoula District of the Ninth Corps area embraced all of western Montana and both Glacier and Yellowstone National parks. At its center was Fort Missoula, a sleepy relic of the 1877 Nez Perce Indian uprising situated on the edge of Missoula, Montana.

In less than three month's time, Fort Missoula became the training, supply and dispersal point for the entire Missoula District, extending along the ragged western range of the Rockies from Canada to Wyoming, a distance of nearly 400 miles. [3]

To the north, in Glacier Park, Superintendent Scoyen prepared his staff for the arrival of the advance groups of the park's quota and

---

1. The standard work on the history of the CCC is John A. Salmond's *The Civilian Conservation Corps, 1933–1942* (Durham: University of North Carolina Press, 1967). Leslie A. Lacy has authored a more recent treatment, *The Soil Soldiers, The Civilian Conservation Corps in the Great Depression* (Radnor, Pa.: Chilton Book Co., 1975).

2. Labor Department officials set quotas for each county and state based on population and numbers of families on the relief rolls. Each enrollment period was for six months, from May to October and from October to April. At the urging of army advisors, Fechner adopted the standard army unit of 200-man companies for each work camp.

3. The Ninth Corps area included eight western states with a total 1933 strength of 65,000 enrollees. Of this number, approximately half were reassigned to other corps areas during winter enrollment periods. The army, for example, normally transferred companies to southeast states for the winter period where considerable work was done in flood and erosion control and to southwestern states for drought relief work. Total Ninth Corps strength grew to 254,774 before leveling off in 1935 (see *Daily Missoulian*, April 9, 1935 and May 5, 1935).

eagerly resurrected long-range development plans. Never before and never again was so large and steady a stream of labor to flow into Glacier. That the national parks became focal points for indirect stimulation of the economy through the activities of the CCC was no coincidence. Franklin Roosevelt gave executive support to his strong personal conviction that the national parks be identified as "pump-priming agencies."

Fortunately, the national parks were so organized that it was possible, with a minimum of time, to enter actively into the various emergency measures calculated to bring relief to the country. The establishment of CCC camps in Glacier meant that it was now possible to accomplish work which was greatly needed but which had been impossible under normal appropriations. Five-year plans of improvement, detailed schedules of work required of all national park areas early in the decade all aided in the accommodation of Glacier's new reservoir of labor. This explains in part why the Park Service and the Forest Service succeeded in absorbing the thousands of men of the CCC into their improvement programs while escaping many of the endless complexities that plagued other agencies.

What was most significant about the activities of the CCC in Glacier Park, however, was the timing of the first arrivals. Administratively, the park was still young, its staff adequate but widely deployed and lacking in cohesive spirit. It was, to some extent, out of step with other areas of the National Park Service, which flourished during the 1930s, going forth confidently with liberal staff and budget increases and reaping the benefits of ambitious advertising.

In addition to this, the Great Northern Railroad, which had been devoted to the park's development in earlier years through its subsidiary, the Glacier Park Hotel Company, had begun showing signs of disinterest in park operations. As the depression deepened, it became clear to park administrators that they could no longer rely on the railroad as Glacier's chief concessioner for benevolence, labor, and capital. Therefore, the presence of strong young laborers was an event which has not been equaled in numbers, timing, or importance.

Throughout the country, the success of the CCC experiment hinged heavily upon the manner and method of direction given to it by its supervisors. In Glacier Park, all emergency conservation work received the closest scrutiny from engineers and rangers to insure that none of the beauty or natural features would be disturbed. A supervisor, who was also provided for each project, worked with and directed several CCC foremen. Army personnel, meanwhile, had authority for general company supervision and welfare during hours not spent in actual work. Civilian project supervisors within each company divided work parties into sections and sub-sections, each led by technicians and subalterns.

It is worth noting that the relationship between the Park Service and the army was remarkably symbiotic. Frequently heard cries that the army was usurping agency prerogative did not occur in Glacier. The harmony between the ranger staff and the army officers was plainly animated by common purpose.

Nevertheless, order emerged slowly from the chaos that marked that first summer of 1933. Valuable time was consumed erecting camp buildings and installing support facilities. Some progress was made, however, on several items of importance, such as the removal of dead snags from a large area burned in a 1929 forest fire that swept through the Apgar–Lake McDonald area. Through the years, this project occupied the attention of all the companies assigned to camps at Fish Creek, Apgar, McDonald Creek and Belton. Men stationed on the east side of the park embarked on a similar task of removing debris and timber from the flowage area behind Sherburne Dam near Many Glacier. Elsewhere, small work parties, under direction of park rangers, moved into the woods to grade roads, construct trails, and clear auto campsites.

By 1934, army officers and park rangers moved more easily into the established pattern and strenuously rounded out details of work for the new enrollees from several Midwest states. All of the camps were crude but not without basic amenities, frequently isolated but not totally lacking in recreation or diversion. Most isolated of all were the "spike camps" of the summer enrollment period which were located some distance from the main camp when work was more feverish and widespread.

The majority of the eight base camps featured tent houses as living quarters although those camps occupied during the winter enrollment period usually consisted of frame bunk houses, a mess hall, radio room, and library. The arrival and departure of new companies every six months became an accustomed part of park administration as the superintendent and his staff greeted the fresh transfusion of manpower. The next several years witnessed only minor changes in established routine or camp location. [4]

The list of work projects eventually completed by CCC units in Glacier is a long one. The onerous task of removing fire-killed timber from the McDonald Valley continued to occupy companies stationed

---

4.   Through the years there were main camps at Two Medicine, Belton, McDonald Creek, Apgar, Fish Creek, Sun Camp, No Name Creek (Many Glacier), and Sherburne. Numerous spike camps sprang up in the summer, among them: Walton, Anaconda Creek, Bowman Lake, Round Prairie, East Glacier, Logan Pass, Cut Bank, Nyack.

in the area. By 1939 nearly 5,000 acres had been cleared, a saw mill constructed, and thousands of fence posts and telephone poles shipped by rail to the nearby Blackfeet Indian Reservation and to other CCC camps in eastern Montana.

It took several enrollment periods for companies stationed on the park's east side to clear and mark a thirty-mile boundary swath separating park lands from Blackfeet Indian land.

At other locations, CCC youths erected barns and storage sheds, and built sewage and water systems at Sprague Creek, Avalanche Creek, Many Glacier, and St. Mary campgrounds. Rough sections of road received bank sloping and drainage ditches, campfire places were installed in campgrounds, along with lecture circles and hundreds of signs. Fish planting, blister rust control, tree reforestation, landscaping and bridge construction were only a few of the tasks carried out by young men who were, for the most part, alien to any type of outdoor labor. [5]

Probably in no other area did CCC men distinguish themselves more noticeably than in forest fire suppression. Since most enrollees had had little or no fire fighting experience before their assignment in Glacier, this record is even more remarkable. Camp supervisors, using rangers as instructors, organized "flying squads" — well-equipped and mobile twenty-five man crews subject to immediate call during the fire season.

Early in the 1933 season, untested CCC crews established a legacy of responsibility when they battled a 5,000 acre fire that spread across the park's eastern boundary. There, "smoke-begrimed forest workers from the Bronx worked side by side with Indians from the Blackfoot Reservation." [6] The following year, the park suffered a loss of only thirty-one acres to forest fires. But in 1936 the park experienced a fire season of inordinate length and intensity and the eight CCC companies significantly aided in the containment of the Heaven's Peak fire which consumed 7,642 acres.

By 1940 the CCC had contributed nearly 84,000 man-days to forest fire prevention and suppression. This was immensely beneficial to the ranger force which had, in the previous decade, developed little in the way of a formal, organized fire fighting force.

It was during this period, then, largely as a result of the manpower provided by the CCC, that Glacier embarked upon the most ambitious fire-control program in its history. Growing fear of more

---

5. A complete listing can be found in a memorandum to the superintendent from Isabelle F. Story, May 9, 1940, Glacier National Park Archives, West Glacier, Mont. (hereafter GNP Archives).

6. *Daily Missoulian*, July 29, 1933.

disastrous fires like those of 1929 and 1936 gave strength to the argument that the park was sorely in need of trails and roads to remote
areas for quick access. Thus, park officials set about devising a complex and intricate maze of truck routes, man-ways, and fire trails
extending along nearly every valley and ridge line. In all the years
the CCC was involved in Glacier, the construction of the fire trails
received priority on work schedules. [7]

In conjunction with the fire trail construction came installation
of several lookouts at strategic locations and the completion of a
phone system connecting ranger stations, lookouts, patrol cabins, and
road camps. [8]

The year 1938, an especially active season, saw the installation of
Glacier's first trans-mountain telephone line. Enrollees at Hidden
Lake laid twenty-eight tons of underground phone cable for seven
miles over Logan Pass while other companies scaled 500 foot steel
ladders up portions of the Garden Wall to measure the amount of
cable required on the sheer cliffs of the Continental Divide. This
"impossible feat" drew congratulatory comments from Park Service
engineers who toured the site at the end of the season.

President Roosevelt, acting on the popularity of the CCC idea,
ordered the strength of the Corps doubled in 1935, bringing the
national total to 600,000. Nearly all Corps areas received additional
allotments. Glacier, reaching the high mark of CCC activity, operated
eight camps during the summer enrollment period and two during
the winter with a peak enrollment of over 1,500. [9]

Nothing stood still in Glacier Park during the 1930s and the pace
of activity slowed only in the winter months when the army withdrew
most of the companies for assignment to Corps areas with more
favorable weather conditions. The twelfth enrollment period opened
in the summer of 1938 in Glacier with four camps operating
smoothly, sending forth an average of 990 men into the field every
day. In all the camps, especially those near Belton, which were occupied during the winter months, facilities were more abundant than

---

7. The fire trail system in Glacier never attained the full promise of those who
designed it early in the decade. CCC crews, as a rule, received authorization only for
construction work at lower elevations and valley bottoms. Director Cammerer was
also steadfastly opposed to any new motorways or truck trails within park boundaries.
Finally, the general slowdown of all construction activities due to World War II effectively curtailed the plan.

8. CCC crews assisted in building lookouts on Porcupine Ridge, Heaven's Peak,
Reynolds Mountain, and Curly Bear Mountain.

9. Nationally, the enrollment quota soared from 370,000 men to 600,000. Roosevelt
also extended the existence of the CCC another two years to March 1937. See *Daily
Missoulian*, April 29, 1935 and *American Forests*, 43 (August 1937), 401–16.

Many Glacier Camp #4   (George Grant, photographer, Glacier National Park)

six years before. At GNP-1 near McDonald Creek, there were fore-men's quarters, an infirmary, bath houses, a PX, a nearby baseball diamond, a large water tower, and long rows of barracks drawn up around a central compound displaying the ubiquitous flagpole.

Not all, of course, was ceaseless labor. "Liberty parties" to nearby towns and open houses helped vary the work routine. Occasionally, a truck dispatched from Fort Missoula would tour the camps to show movies. Team sports were enormously popular. Each company boasted the best softball squad in the park and there were regularly scheduled meetings to affirm these claims.

Since most enrollees were from states in the Midwest or the East, there was no strong urge to leave camp to visit home or family during off hours. Desertions were rare. The educational features of Glacier's CCC camps, however, were never notably successful. Fechner's plan to appoint an educational advisor to each Corps area and his goal to implement a comprehensive plan of "formal education" came about well enough in some Corps areas, but in far-flung places like Glacier Park, enrollees received only marginal instruction.

Responsibility for educational services was vested in the army supervisors who were already confronted with many tasks alien to army procedure. The selection of educational advisors, when it was done at all, was haphazard and regularly scheduled tours to monitor progress were the exception rather than the rule. There was a shortage of qualified instructors, even among the park's ranger force, and the camps themselves were not conducive to study. They were never meant for permanent occupancy and thus lacked space and facilities for carrying on formal classroom instruction. Nevertheless, the desire to learn was strong. Company 1343 at Belton, for example, listed among its educational offerings classes in shorthand, slide rule, electricity, French, and physical geography. Glacier Park's (East Glacier) company 1240 featured a curriculum of English, French, commercial law, and leadership.

Another, although minor, element which tarnished the fine record of the Corps came as the result of the spoils system so commonly associated with federal agencies. The CCC in Glacier was never entirely free from political maneuverings, especially for jobs at the mid-level or subaltern positions. Other key appointive positions were for camp superintendents, project foremen and technical assistants, all of which enabled the appointee to remain in the park longer than the six-month term for normal recruits. Thus, political appointments became common among the ranks of LEM's or "Local Experienced Men."

Customarily, the Secretary of the Interior made appointments from lists of qualified applicants furnished to him by park superintendents. But the patronage channel could also flow through a member of the Montana congressional delegation to the secretary and then to the park superintendent. It was not unusual, then, for minor power struggles to emerge when Montana congressmen juggled patronage jobs arising from vacancies in the park.

While in Washington, D.C., in 1939, Superintendent Scoyen called on Senator James Murray and Representative Jerry O'Connell who appealed to him to "give them an even break" with Senator Burton K. Wheeler in assigning jobs in Glacier. [10]

Both felt that the park's CCC program was being "run by Senator Wheeler" to the disadvantage of them and their constituents. O'Connell particularly made a strong protest about the way his patronage was being handled by Scoyen, indicating that he had received complaints from men recommended by him who were given "ditch digging" jobs. [11]

---

10. Scoyen to Cammerer, February 16, 1938, microfilm, Glacier National Park Papers, Archives, University of Montana Mansfield Library, Missoula (hereafter GNP Papers, UM).

11. Cammerer from Supt. Scoyen, March 16, 1938, GNP Papers, UM.

Even though the political undertones had a low-keyed role in the workings of the CCC, Montana congressmen dealt regularly with job seekers who felt they were entitled to "something from this old party."[12] One hopeful, attempting to secure a position as senior foreman at GNP-1, wrote to Senator Murray identifying his family as "loyal and faithful members of the Democratic Party" and his father as a "Democratic war horse."[13] Another wrote to Murray in 1936 and explained that Superintendent Scoyen "would be glad to use me if my name appeared on the list" and urged Murray to "put some heat on Washington."[14]

Political staffing procedures used in Glacier to fill supervisory positions created only mild disruptions and actually did much to placate local job seekers and critics who resented the influx of "foreign labor" from the East, for not all who witnessed the arrival of the thousands of non-resident youths to western Montana welcomed them.

As expected, there were cries from the disappointed and the displaced. The appearance of the first companies of enrollees from eastern states brought forth skepticism and distrust. Returning from the confusion and bustle at Fort Missoula in early summer 1933, the editor of the *Daily Missoulian* wrote that more would have been accomplished by enlisting local men from the timbered country adjacent to the camps who had some experience in the work.

"One good timberjack" he wrote, "would accomplish more than a hundred city-bred men" whom, he felt, "aren't attracted by the plan of going into the tall timber and far away from what he thinks of as civilization and earning a dollar a day by the unaccustomed labor of swinging an axe or wielding a pick or shovel." The *Missoulian* continued to press the attack in 1933 saying that the "experiment will be watched with interest."[15] The Kalispell *Daily Inter Lake*, published near Glacier, joined the chorus of protest. Fully a month before the first trainload of New Yorkers entered the Flathead Valley, residents were prejudging the abilities of the "street-slum foreigners" and casting doubt upon the success of the Corps in general. In 1933 the *Inter Lake* editor commented that the big city unemployed "who were used to pavements" would be unsuited to conservation work in the West.[16]

Others adopted even narrower views, stating the CCC recruits would be "mostly babes in the woods who would accomplish little, be sick and disabled half the time."[17]

12. P. S. Jones to Sen. Murray, May 6, 1937, GNP Papers, UM.
13. Thomas McCrane to Sen. Murray, February 18, 1938, GNP Papers, UM.
14. P. S. Jones to James Mahoney, October 25, 1936, GNP Papers, UM.
15. *Daily Missoulian*, May 1, June 3, 1933.
16. Kalispell *Daily Inter Lake*, April 11, May 1, 1933.
17. Whitefish *Pilot*, June 4, 1933.

Unions, too, were disturbed by the influx of cheap labor. A representative of Carpenter's Union Local No. 911 wrote to President Roosevelt protesting the use of CCC labor in Glacier's construction jobs which "should be given to skilled craftsmen on all work that is rightfully theirs." [18]

The hiring of many local residents helped ease the objections to non-resident enrollees. As a former labor leader, Fechner recognized the potential for local discontent while organizing the Corps. "It is clearly impossible," he wrote to the President in April 1933, "to import into forest regions non-residents . . . and have peace there unless local unemployed laborers accustomed to making their living in the woods in that very place are given consideration. . . ."

Wider use of local men, the "LEM's," was a success on two fronts: it silenced critics and placed skilled woodsmen in supervisory positions. After observing the work of a pioneer group of LEM's constructing barracks at GNP-1 before the arrival of eastern recruits, Superintendent Scoyen wrote to Park Service Director Horace Albright that "these local woodsmen are invaluable to the CCC experiment forming, as they do, a nucleus around which the younger, lesser experienced recruits can group. I applaud their inclusion into the Corps and urge that at least twenty-five be assigned to each company." [19]

Finally critics modified their reproach when it was learned that there were substantial economic benefits to be had because of the presence of the camps and the business they generated. Communities around the park swung into line throughout the summers of 1933 and 1934 as purchase orders from the camps flowed into local cash registers.

The CCC began to weaken considerably in 1939. Desertion rates rose, critics multiplied in Congress, morale sagged, administrative friction increased, and, with slight economic recovery, some doubts rose as to the need and purpose of the Corps in a changing atmosphere. With only four active companies in Glacier, the spirit of emergency conservation work suffered from the dullness of routine. The uniformly smooth work pattern was interrupted by an occasional forest fire, but generally there was little excitement and few innovative work details.

This was due more to attrition, however, than a lack of direction by park officials. Superintendent Scoyen had proved to be a tireless proponent of the CCC idea. Not surprisingly, he pushed his superiors and army officials feverishly for expansion of work under the conservation banner. After the Heaven's Peak fire, he won approval

---

18.   Oliver S. Richardson to President Roosevelt, May 11, 1938, GNP Papers, UM.
19.   Scoyen to Horace Albright, May 8, 1933, GNP Archives.

for additional camps near Many Glacier for after-fire cleanup and rehabilitation.

Scoyen was fond of comparing Forest Service expenditures for conservation work to Park Service quotas, and ardently besieged the directors of the Park Service, Horace Albright and Arno B. Cammerer, for equalization. A tireless organizer, he also requested a raise of the "obnoxious limitations" on building construction and often attempted to use CCC crews on normally scheduled park maintenance jobs, such as snow removal on the Going-To-The-Sun Highway, which required trained personnel. In all, he labored admirably to secure as much money and support for the Corps as possible.

Scoyen's successor, Donald G. Libbey, newly arrived from Hot Springs National Park and thrust into Glacier's depression malaise of 1939, was quick to sense the nature of emergency conservation work. His tenure in Glacier, however, spanned the waning years of Corps activity.

From 1939 to 1942, Glacier's companies, like those in other areas, struggled along with weak enrollments. Replacements shipped from other districts and from disbanded companies helped bolster camp quotas, but the decline was palpable. Because of more stable economic conditions nationwide, better employment opportunities were to be found outside the camps. Libbey chose not to agitate as strongly for larger quotas and was not, therefore, able to distinguish himself as notably as did Superintendent Scoyen, who enjoyed several years of relief activity with the CCC under his supervision and who pushed so doggedly for their services.

Despite a strong recruiting campaign begun in the spring of 1941, the Ninth Corps area experienced the loss of its first camps because of reduced enrollments. By the end of the summer, army administrators at Fort Missoula were withdrawing many companies from the field and the demobilization process began. Through the spring of 1942 the Senate completed action on a liquidation bill, and on June 30 of that year, Congress voted the CCC out of existence.

Corps historian John Salmond could well have been describing Glacier's CCC chronicle when he wrote: "Its structure never lost its temporary look and its machinery, though surprisingly efficient, was essentially makeshift, loose and diffuse." And in spite of a survey conducted in 1940 predicting that projects by federal agencies could keep "a CCC of 1500 camps busy for from 30 to 50 years," Salmond correctly stated that "it was frankly experimental; it had no real precedent to follow and no long-term goals to be reached." [20]

Still, the record of the CCC in Glacier during the eight years of their presence there can be counted along with the record of suc-

---

20. Salmond, *The Civilian Conservation Corps*, 221.

cesses registered in other national parks, forests, and monuments. Glacier Park made strong advances in areas of development and improvement of facilities because of the efforts of thousands of CCC workers. There was also a notable rise in the number of visitors to the park in "the terrible decade." [21]

It is most difficult to plumb the depths of the human dividends of the CCC work in Glacier. Superintendent Scoyen, however, gave an accurate appraisal in 1936 when he explained: "It is hardly possible for these young men to spend six months in this or any other park and not depart with a keen sense of the value of reforestation or rehabilitation." [22]

As a participant, one young CCC recruit from Brooklyn put it more poignantly: "We [found] a glorious country peopled with some of the most hospitable people in the world. It took a little time to become accustomed to trees instead of people. The sighing of the wind in the great trees was a sound of mystery and at first terrifying after the roar of the densely populated cities we came from. . . . Coming out here was a great break for me. My muscles are hard as iron and I have gained fifteen pounds in weight. . . . We were given plenty of hard work, which, with regular meals, and rest, as a part of the camp discipline, we became stronger. . . ." [23] So, too, did the safety and beauty of one of America's great wilderness sanctuaries.

---

21.   Far from being a depressed area, Glacier Park experienced favorable tourism rates in the 1930s, chiefly because of the establishment of more and better recreational facilities. There were increases in visitation every year of the decade with the exception of 1932 and 1937.

22.   Scoyen to Joel D. Pomerene, January 20, 1936, GNP Archives.

23.   *Daily Missoulian*, October 18, 1933.

Senator James E. Murray (left) with President Franklin D. Roosevelt, 1942 (Mansfield Library, University of Montana, Missoula)

One River, One Problem

James Murray and the Missouri Valley Authority

Donald E. Spritzer

Dam builders in the West have come under increasing criticism in recent years. They have been labeled despoilers. Powerful books like Donald Worster, *Rivers of Empire* (1986), and Marc Reisner, *Cadillac Desert* (1986), have pilloried both the Corps of Engineers and the Bureau of Reclamation for their unthinking destruction of river basins in the name of powerful economic interests. Could James E. Murray's proposed Missouri Valley Authority have tempered this destruction? Considering the history of its model, the Tennessee Valley Authority, probably not, but this article by Donald Spritzer, reference librarian at the Missoula City-County Library, examines one of the great might-have-beens of Montana history. Next to copper, the state's most priceless natural resource, it has been offered, is water. An elaborate process by which all Montana water rights will be adjudicated already is partially completed, treaties allocating Missouri River water to Indian tribes are under negotiation, and nervously we eye the needs of dry states to the south. But through it all the Pick-Sloan Plan of the 1940s remains operative. This essay

*Donald E. Spritzer, "One River, One Problem: James Murray and the Missouri Valley Authority," in *Montana and the West: Essays in Honor of K. Ross Toole*, ed. Rex C. Myers and Harry W. Fritz (Boulder, Colo.: Pruett Publishing Co., 1984), 122–43.

provides a historical introduction to the ongoing politics of water in Montana.

———————

From its source at the headwaters of the Jefferson River, some 13,000 feet above sea level, the Missouri River when combined with the lower Mississippi flows for more than four thousand miles, making it the world's longest river. Together with its tributaries it drains over five hundred thousand square miles in ten states. Over the years each of those states has jealously guarded its share of the river's water from outsiders, whether they were other states or the federal government.

Twice each year the Missouri rises dangerously—in the spring from mountain snowmelt and again in early summer from heavy rains. In 1943 the river's annual rampage was the worst in more than sixty years. In April it ripped out millions of dollars worth of Army Corps of Engineers' flood control installations and inundated thousands of acres. Most of Omaha went under water; its airport was ruined, and six people lost their lives. Then in mid-May the devastating rains hit and seven million dollars in land and houses were washed away. Three more people died. In June, still another flood struck the middle reaches of the basin in Iowa and northern Kansas, flooding another million acres of farmland. [1]

The 1943 floods and a similar calamity a year later brought the total losses in the basin to over 110 million dollars in less than two years. The disasters led Congress to realize that quick action had to be taken to prevent still more of the basin's wealth from washing to the sea. With two-thirds of his home state lying inside the upper Missouri drainage, it was only natural that Montana's junior senator, James E. Murray, took a deep interest in decisions affecting the region. An avowed New Dealer, Senator Murray began his political career as an influential member of the powerful Irish Democratic organization in his home town of Butte. He did not focus his attention on the plight of the Missouri basin's farmers in eastern Montana until his appointment in 1933 as a state director of President Roosevelt's Public Works Administration. As a PWA administrator, Murray

———————

1. Thomas H. Langevin, "The Missouri Basin: A Study in Multiple-Purpose Water Development" (Ph.D. diss., University of Nebraska, 1951), i, ii; Marian E. Ridgeway, *The Missouri Basin's Pick-Sloan Plan: A Case Study in Congressional Determination* (Urbana: University of Illinois Press, 1955), 3–4; Edward J. Skillin, Jr., "Missouri Valley Authority: America's Greatest Single Peace Project," *The Commonweal*, 42 (August 24, 1945), 446; Joseph Kinsey Howard, "Golden River," *Harper's Magazine*, 190 (May 1945), 511–13.

labored tirelessly to secure federal irrigation and reclamation projects for the drought and depression stricken counties of Montana's plains. His work in this area continued unabated following his election to the U.S. Senate in 1934. [2]

Another problem that the senator determined to solve through federal action was the shortage of hydroelectric power in the upper basin. In 1944 only one-fourth of Montana's farms had electricity; in the Dakotas fewer than one farm in ten enjoyed this luxury. During the early 1940s Murray pushed the Senate to approve huge hydroelectric dams such as the one at Canyon Ferry on the upper Missouri near Helena. [3]

In emphasizing the use of basin water for irrigation and hydropower, Murray reflected the majority interests in the upper basin states. Beginning with the passage of the Reclamation Act of 1902, when the federal government first entered the water development field on a large scale, upper Missouri irrigationists had been squaring off with lower basin interests whose main concerns were flood control and navigation. The sectional rivalry soon took the form of a heated contest between the U.S. Army Corps of Engineers, whose main area of jurisdiction was navigation and flood control, and the U.S. Bureau of Reclamation of the Interior Department, which engaged mostly in irrigation and conservation projects. [4]

Occasionally the two agencies cooperated on multi-purpose ventures such as Montana's massive Fort Peck Dam, but more often they were at loggerheads. So it was to no one's surprise that each agency in the 1940s came up with its own plan on how best to tame the raging Missouri. Following the 1943 floods, Colonel Lewis A. Pick, the army engineer in charge of the corps' Missouri River Division, drew up a thirteen-page document calling for a series of levees along the river's lower portion, together with several dams designed for flood control and navigation.

As expected, the Pick plan aroused a storm of protest in the states of the upper Missouri. It was not long before their own interests were

2. For further information on Murray's early career see Anna Roth, ed., *Current Biography, 1945* (New York: H. W. Wilson Co., 1945), 414; Forrest Davis, "Millionaire Moses," *Saturday Evening Post*, December 8, 1945, p.10; Donald E. Spritzer, "New Dealer From Montana: The Senate Career of James E. Murray," (Ph. D. diss., University of Montana, 1980).

3. "United for Victory," Murray campaign pamphlet, 1942; Small Business Committee press release, July 6, 1944, James E. Murray, Senatorial Papers (hereafter Murray Papers), Archives, University of Montana Mansfield Library, Missoula (hereafter UM); Ridgeway, *Missouri Basin's Pick-Sloan Plan*, 73.

4. Elmo Richardson, *Dams, Parks, and Politics: Resource Development and Preservation in the Truman-Eisenhower Era* (Lexington: University Press of Kentucky, 1963), 9; Langevin, "Missouri Basin," 42.

put forth by W. G. Sloan of the Bureau of Reclamation's regional office in Billings, Montana. Sloan's report called for ninety reservoirs, most of them on the tributaries. The dams would provide irrigation for five million acres and power production for the region. The Pick and Sloan plans differed from each other in nearly every particular. Pick wanted massive dams on the Missouri's main stem in the Dakotas at Garrison and Gavins Point; Sloan felt that these projects were unnecessary. The Pick plan virtually ignored power production while Sloan called for seventeen power plants to generate three billion kilowatt hours of electricity each year. Neither plan mentioned soil conservation or wildlife preservation. [5]

In December Colonel Pick submitted his plan to the House of Representatives. The Corps of Engineers' ideas found favorable ground among congressmen from the lower basin whose districts stood to benefit from the pork-barrel projects embedded in the scheme. They attached the Pick Plan to the 1944 Flood Control bill. When the measure reached the hearings stage the governors of Montana, Wyoming, and North Dakota rushed to Washington in a vain attempt to persuade the House to scrap the corps' program and substitute the Sloan plan. Senator Murray shared the upper basin governors' concern that irrigation would be sacrificed in order to enhance navigation on the lower Missouri. He argued that a plan should be developed to coordinate all of the basin's rival interests and designate the respective areas of jurisdiction of the Corps of Engineers and the Bureau of Reclamation. On May 9, 1944, the House passed the Flood Control bill with the Pick Plan still intact.

In May, at the height of the controversy, the St. Louis *Post-Dispatch* suddenly injected a new element into the fray. In an editorial entitled "One River—One Problem" the newspaper called for creation of a Missouri Valley Authority as the only way to end the "futile struggle between one interest and another" and to develop the valley "to the full measure of its resources." The *Post-Dispatch*, which earlier had endorsed the Pick Plan, now concluded, "with unity we can conquer the one problem which the one big river challenges us to solve." [6]

The idea of a Missouri Valley Authority was not new. During the 1930s Nebraska's Senator George Norris had sponsored legislation similar to the Tennessee Valley Authority bill to create an agency for the Missouri basin. In June 1937 President Roosevelt in a message to Congress proposed dividing the nation into seven

5. Rufus Terral, *The Missouri Valley: Land of Drouth, Flood, and Promise* (New Haven: Yale University Press, 1947), 188–203; Howard, "Golden River," 513–15.

6. Murray to W. F. Flinn, Miles City, February 14, 1944, Murray press release February 16, 1944, Murray Papers; "One River—One Problem," St. Louis *Post-Dispatch*, May 15, 1944, clipping in Murray Papers.

watershed regions in order to coordinate multi-purpose resource development.

The *Post-Dispatch* editorial converted James E. Murray to the Missouri Valley Authority idea. After reading *Democracy on the March* by TVA chairman David E. Lilienthal, the senator asked the TVA chief for advice "as to the essentials of such legislation." Lilienthal gladly assisted Murray and his staff in drafting the first Missouri Valley Authority bill, which the senator introduced on August 18. The measure followed the established TVA pattern. It called for an independent government agency headed by a board of three presidentially appointed directors. This group was to have jurisdiction over the dams and other federal projects within the region. The MVA headquarters would be located somewhere within the basin. The bill designated a citizen's advisory committee of local residents to act as a curb on the board. Still, the directors would hold sweeping powers to make contracts and to acquire the property necessary for MVA projects.[7]

Calling the task of basin development "the most important national project since the Louisiana Purchase," Murray presented his bill to the Senate. He denounced the conflicting programs of the Bureau of Reclamation and Corps of Engineers, and concluded: "So long as we hack the river to pieces and parcel it out to this agency and that agency, to this interest and that interest, stalemate, inaction, and a declining economy will be our reward." He anticipated one of the strongest arguments against the MVA when he promised that the proposed authority would use "to the fullest extent possible" the help and advice of the people, organizations, and governing bodies of the region.[8]

Murray's bill received an immediate boost in September, when President Roosevelt sent a message to Congress endorsing the establishment of a Missouri Valley Authority. Murray's aides together with Benton Stong of the National Farmers Union had drafted the statement at the request of the White House. Yet even with the president's endorsement, the Murray bill did not create a wave of popular support. Shortly after Representative John Cochran of Missouri introduced the companion measure in the House, South Dakota's Francis Case called for its defeat. He pointed out that the bill demanded two more years just to draft plans for the first projects, while both the Army Engineers and the Bureau of Reclamation were prepared to implement their plans at once.[9]

7. Murray to John D. Pope, February 24, 1936, Murray to David E. Lilienthal, Knoxville, Tennessee, June 7, August 15, 1944, Murray Papers; Senate, August 18, 1944, 78th Cong., 2d sess., S. 2089.

8. *Cong. Rec.*, August 18, 1944, 78th Cong., 2d sess., 90:7082–88.

9. Message from the President of the United States, September 21, 1944, 78th Cong., 2d sess., H. Doc. 680; Charles A. Murray interview with the author, Portland, Oregon, May 19, 1978, transcript, UM.

Navigation interests of the lower valley and upper basin irrigationists forgot their differences long enough to denounce the MVA. The Omaha *World-Herald* labeled the proposed authority "a colossus which would be operated completely by the bureaucracy." The Miles City, Montana, *Star* stated flatly that the bill had been written by the same "curly-headed Harvard boys" who ran the TVA. The Anaconda Copper Company's *Montana Standard* felt that the basin could be developed without "placing an irresponsible economic dictatorship" over the people. From Helena, Murray's ally, Leif Erickson, wrote the senator that "the Company" had erected huge billboards extolling "from hell to breakfast" the virtues of private ownership of power. [10]

Countering such vocal opposition, Murray had some influential allies. Editorials in the Bismarck, North Dakota *Tribune*, the St. Louis *Star Times*, the Chicago *Sun*, the Philadelphia *Record*, and *The New Republic* all endorsed the senator's bill. In Montana the liberal journal *The People's Voice* kept up a steady campaign to win residents over to the valley authority. Early in 1945 Joseph Kinsey Howard, Montana's most reputable journalist, wrote a detailed article for *Harper's Magazine* lauding the MVA proposal. [11]

More organized assistance came from the National Farmers Union, led by its dynamic young president, James G. Patton. Over half the Farmers Union membership resided within the Missouri basin, so naturally the organization took interest in any legislation affecting irrigation, flood control, and land use. By 1944 Benton J. Stong was serving as Patton's administrative assistant and editor of the NFU newspaper. As a journalist in Tennessee, Stong had been a leading spokesman for the TVA. As Patton's right-hand man he helped Murray draft the several MVA bills.

The Missouri Valley Authority became the hottest issue in the 1944 gubernatorial campaign in Montana. Leif Erickson, a young populist from the eastern part of the state, opposed one of Senator Burton K. Wheeler's Republican friends, Sam Ford. Ford and Wheeler excoriated the MVA as communistic and a threat to state sovereignty. An avid proponent of the MVA, Erickson attempted to counter their charges. In several statewide broadcasts Murray defended his authority scheme. He condemned the Montana Power Company for its "short-sighted policy" of opposing river valley development. Many

10. Lief Erickson to Murray, January 14, 1945, Murray Papers; Miles City *Star*, September 3, 1944, Omaha *World-Herald*, October 14, 1944, clippings in Murray Papers.

11. Bismarck *Tribune*, September 12, 1944; St. Louis *Star-Times*, October 25, 1944; Chicago *Sun*, November 7, 1944; Philadelphia *Record*, September 23, 1944, clippings in Murray Papers; Helena *The People's Voice* files passim; Howard, "Golden River," 517; "For a Missouri Valley Authority," *The New Republic*, September 4, 1944, pp. 266–68.

interpreted Ford's decisive victory over Erickson as a critical setback for Murray's bill. [12]

Outside Montana the MVA did not do much better. Many congressmen felt that development of the basin could be handled just as efficiently by the pending Rivers and Harbors and Flood Control bills. Yet they realized that the Army Corps of Engineers and the Bureau of Reclamation must integrate their conflicting plans. In mid-October, responding to congressional pressure and the threat of a possible Missouri Valley Authority, two representatives from each agency met in Omaha to resolve their differences. This hasty conference produced the Pick-Sloan Plan, which retained nearly all of the Missouri basin projects contemplated in both the old Pick and Sloan schemes. The six-page document was more a peace treaty than a comprehensive development program. The Bureau of Reclamation received authority over all irrigation and reclamation, most of which was on the tributaries and upper valley; the Corps of Engineers was to control all of the main stem navigation projects. The new plan said nothing about how the water would be proportioned to meet conflicting needs. It called for the "fullest development" of the basin's hydropower potential, but said nothing about how that power should be marketed.

Reactions of MVA proponents ranged from skepticism to hostility. Murray predicted that Pick-Sloan would not mark the end of fighting between the bureau and the corps. Patton labeled the agreement "a shameful loveless shotgun wedding" and concluded that the entire "scandalous performance should arouse the people of the valley . . . to the necessity of a new type of administration where people's needs are given at least minor consideration." [13]

When Congress reconvened after the 1944 elections, the battle lines formed. Murray announced that he would fight any legislation prejudicial to the MVA. John Overton, who had long represented the

---

12. James E. Murray radio addresses, Butte, October 30, November 6, 1944, Great Falls, November 4, 1944, Murray Papers; B. K. Wheeler to William Honey (undated), MC 34, Burton K. Wheeler Papers, 1910–1971, Montana Historical Society Archives, Helena; Michael P. Malone and Richard B. Roeder, *Montana: A History of Two Centuries* (Seattle: University of Washington Press, 1976), 239; Ridgeway, *Missouri Basin's Pick-Sloan Plan*, 241, 278; James G. Patton, taped answers to questions sent by the author, April 10, 1978, transcript, UM.

13. *Missouri River Basin: Report of a Committee of Two Representatives Each from the Corps of Engineers, U.S. Army and Bureau of Reclamation, Supplemented to Sen. Doc. No. 191 and House Doc. No. 475, 78th Cong.*, November 21, 1944, 78th Cong., 2d sess., Doc. 247; New York *Times*, November 9, 1944; National Farmers Union press release, undated, 1944, National Farmers Union Papers, University of Colorado Western History Library, Boulder.

interests of navigationists in water matters, vowed to ram through the omnibus Flood Control bill complete with the Pick-Sloan Plan. The powerful Louisiana Democrat was determined to keep the Missouri Valley Authority bill bottled up in his Senate committee. During floor debate on the Flood Control bill, Murray engaged in heated exchanges with Overton and his ally, Missouri's Senator Bennett Clark. Overton curtly denied the Montanan's charge that backers of the flood control measure had entered into an agreement with the army engineers and the Bureau of Reclamation to block the MVA. Clark then rose and denounced the attempt by MVA supporters to tack their bill onto the flood control measure as an amendment. The Missouri senator accused Murray of closeting himself in his office with representatives of the CIO to draft legislation without the benefit of committee hearings. Murray firmly denied ever having offered a single bill sponsored by the CIO. His usually soft voice carrying to the galleries, the Montanan accused the Missouri senator of casting aspersions on his character.

Facing overwhelming opposition, Murray planned to withdraw his MVA amendment before it reached a vote. Then on November 28, the Senate received a letter from President Roosevelt recommending that the Pick-Sloan Plan be authorized only as the general engineering program "to be developed and administered by a Missouri Valley Authority." The president's message boosted the confidence of MVA supporters, and Murray renewed his attempt to push the bill through as an amendment.

Overton and his Louisiana colleague Allen Ellender then promised the Montanan that if he would withdraw his contemplated amendment, the Missouri Valley Authority would receive committee hearings "at an early date" in the next Congress. Murray expressed justified fear that if Pick-Sloan passed, Congress would feel no need to create a new agency to carry on unified development of the river. Alabama's Lister Hill and Elmer Thomas of Oklahoma assured Murray that such was not the case. Thus mollified, the senator agreed to forego consideration of his amendment. Unknowingly Murray had sacrificed his only opportunity to bring the Missouri Valley Authority to a vote by the full Senate. [14]

On December 1 the Senate passed the massive Flood Control bill without a roll call. The president signed it three weeks later. He emphasized that he was approving the measure only "with the distinct understanding" that it would not jeopardize creation of a Missouri Valley Authority. The new law authorized development of the Mis-

---

14. *Cong. Rec.*, November 28, 30, 1944, 78th Cong., 2d sess., 90:8374–79, 8616–26; Allen Drury, *A Senate Journal, 1943–45* (New York: DaCapo Press, 1972), 298–301.

souri basin by the combined efforts of the Corps of Engineers and Bureau of Reclamation.

Shortly after Congress convened in 1945, Murray reintroduced his MVA bill. The new measure was virtually identical to the 1944 bill. Again the senator denounced the Pick-Sloan scheme as an "incompletely engineered compromise hastily agreed upon." Immediately after its introduction, Murray's bill received a deathblow. The Montana senator requested that the measure be referred to the Agriculture and Forestry Committee which earlier had considered the Tennessee Valley Authority legislation. Instead, Vice-President Truman let South Carolina Senator Josiah Bailey persuade him to send the MVA bill to his Senate Commerce Committee. The conservative southerner was an avowed opponent of valley authorities.

While campaigning for the vice-presidency, Harry Truman had endorsed all of the Roosevelt domestic program including the MVA. So his action on the Murray bill came as a shock. Yet ever since his days as a local official in Kansas City, Truman had been a close ally of the Army Corps of Engineers. To those who criticized his handling of Murray's bill, the vice-president simply replied, "I'm here to send bills introduced in the Senate to the committees where they belong." In responding to one constituent, Truman did not veil his hostility toward the MVA. "The Missouri River cannot be handled in the same manner as the Tennessee, or the Columbia, or the Colorado," he wrote. "It is not a project to be worked out by demagogues or dreamers." [15]

Murray privately admitted that as long as his bill remained in Bailey's committee it would "be licked to a frazzle." The senator decided to attempt a resolution discharging the Commerce Committee from considering the MVA measure. When he presented his resolution, Bailey countered with a motion to allow three separate committees sixty days each to consider the Missouri Valley Authority bill. Murray consented to Bailey's compromise offer since it would at least prevent the powerful southerner from freezing the bill in his Commerce Committee.

Bailey's committee still received the first shot at the MVA measure. John Overton chaired the subcommittee hearings. A longtime crony of Huey Long, the Louisiana senator had recently become president of the Mississippi Valley Association, an organization formed with the declared purpose of blocking the creation of river valley author-

15. *Statutes at Large*, 78th Cong., 2d sess., 1944, Pub. Law no. 534, 58:887–907; *Cong. Rec.*, February 15, 1945, 79th Cong., 1st sess., S.555, 91:1121–26; Harry S. Truman to E. L. Clary, Cleveland, March 30, 1945, Harry S. Truman Vice-Presidential and Senatorial Papers, Harry S. Truman Library, Independence, Missouri (hereafter Truman Library); New York *Times*, October 13, December 2, 1944, February 16, 1945.

ities. Throughout the hearings, Overton allowed opponents every opportunity to label the measure totalitarian and fascist. The adverse report from the Commerce Committee surprised no one. The committee recommended that all provisions affecting navigation and flood control be stricken from the Murray bill in order to preserve the jurisdiction of the Army Corps of Engineers over these areas. [16]

The crippled Murray bill then went to the Senate Irrigation and Reclamation Committee chaired by none other than John Overton. Overton again presided over subcommittee hearings on the measure. He appointed MVA opponents to the other subcommittee positions. In arguing again for his bill, Murray cited a recent Gallup Poll showing that three-fourths of the respondents favored creation of a Missouri Valley Authority. During the two weeks of hearings, the Montanan received support from various local farmers unions, Mayor of Minneapolis Hubert H. Humphrey, and Joseph Kinsey Howard. Murray's aide Dewey Anderson lined up many of the friendly witnesses and briefed them prior to testifying. Leading the opposition were politicians from several basin states including South Dakota Congressman Francis Case, Congressman William Lemke of North Dakota, Colorado's Governor John Vivian, and Governor Sam Ford of Montana. Ford reiterated the views of other hostile witnesses in declaring, "The enactment of S.555 would create a super-government placing in the hands of three men power to dictate and control the social and economic life of the Missouri River Basin. It would be a long step toward state socialism." Again, the adverse committee report came as a foregone conclusion. Senator Overton completed the emasculation of the Murray bill which he had begun in the Commerce Committee. His last report recommended that the jurisdiction of the Bureau of Reclamation over irrigation be maintained.

Stunned by the Overton committee's total condemnation of his bill, Murray objected that the report should not be filed until the minority could submit its views. The Montanan decried the "atmosphere of hostility" which had prevailed throughout the hearings. The Louisiana senator overruled Murray's protests. The MVA bill then went to the Agriculture and Forestry Committee. By then, Murray recognized that the heavy opposition his bill had aroused during the two Overton subcommittee hearings had virtually destroyed its chances of passage in the Seventy-ninth Congress. The senator

---

16. Senate Subcommittee of the Committee on Commerce, *Hearings . . . on S.555, To Establish a Missouri Valley Authority*, April 16–27, 1945, 79th Cong., 1st sess.; *Report on S.555 from the Committee on Commerce*, May 7, 1945, 79th Cong., 1st sess., S. Rept. 246; Murray to Judge Homer T. Bone, San Francisco, February 23, 1945, Murray Papers; Ernest Kirschten, "From TVA to MVA," *The Christian Century*, 62 (May 30, 1945), 649.

persuaded members of the Agriculture Committee to postpone the hearings indefinitely. [17]

As the Murray bill stumbled through the Senate committees, President Truman did little to bolster its chances. Shortly after the new president took office, Murray wrote him a long letter which outlined the provisions of Senate Bill 555 and asked for a public letter of endorsement. Truman refused, but he did include an appeal for valley authorities in both the Missouri and Columbia basins as part of a message to Congress in September. Later, speaking before the National Reclamation Association in Denver, the president again shied away from endorsing the MVA. In January he informed a press conference that he would do everything he could to gain approval of the MVA in 1946. Then three months later he told a similar gathering that the diverse nature of the Missouri River placed it "in a different class from the Tennessee or Columbia River." [18]

While the president vacillated over the MVA, powerful foes were of one voice in condemning the proposal. Foremost among these were the private utilities. The price of electricity to Missouri Basin residents was two to three times the amount paid by dwellers of the Tennessee Valley. Power companies in the region saw no reason to change that situation. The threat posed by the MVA led 167 private utilities from throughout the nation to band together to form the National Association of Electric Companies. The power companies launched an expensive nationwide advertising campaign.

A variety of special interest groups supported the power companies. Upper basin cattlemen and farm bureau officials feared MVA dams would ruin valuable rangeland. Railroads felt that development of river transportation might hurt their business. State and local officials saw the valley authority concept as an infringement of state rights. The Missouri Basin States Committee, formed in 1942 by the governors of the region, played a prominent role in pushing the Pick-Sloan Plan. D. J. Guy of the United States Chamber of Commerce

---

17. Senate Subcommittee of the Committee on Irrigation and Reclamation, *Hearings . . . on S.555, To Establish a Missouri Valley Authority*, September 18–28, 1945, 79th Cong., 1st sess., 1–44, 622–30; *Missouri Valley Authority Act Adverse Report, Committee on Irrigation and Reclamation*, October 18, 1945, 79th Cong., 1st sess. S. Rept. 639; *Cong. Rec.*, October 18, 1945, 79th Cong., 1st sess., 91:9760; Langevin, "Missouri Basin," 91; Ridgeway, *Missouri Basin's Pick-Sloan Plan*, 256.

18. Murray to Truman, April 24, 1945, Presidential Secy. Matthew J. Connelly to Murray, May 2, 1945, Harry S. Truman Presidential Papers (hereafter Truman Presidential Papers), Truman Library; Truman news conferences, January 19, 1945, April 18, 1946, in Harry S. Truman, *Public Papers of the Presidents of the United States: Harry S. Truman, 1945–1953*, (8 vols., Washington, D.C. Government Printing Office, 1961–1966), 2: 34, 210; New York *Times*, November 27, 1945.

reflected the fear of many when he warned that the Missouri Valley Authority would have the power "to do everything but coin money, wage war, and amend the Constitution." A coalition of local reclamation and land and water development associations formed yet another powerful lobby fighting the MVA. Throughout 1945 the so-called water lobby organized letter-writing campaigns and issued anti-MVA pamphlets with such catchy titles as "Totalitarianism on the March" and "Bureaucracy Rides the Rivers." [19]

To counteract these alliances, Murray relied on the assistance of several organizations. Patton's National Farmers Union and the St. Louis *Post-Dispatch* each maintained a steady drumbeat to popularize the MVA idea. Various state labor groups endorsed the Murray bill. Morris L. Cooke helped organize the Friends of the Missouri Valley to mobilize public opinion behind the MVA. In July 1945 valley authority proponents from every Missouri basin state except Wyoming met in Omaha and formed the Regional Committee for the MVA. The group elected unsuccessful Montana gubernatorial candidate Leif Erickson as its president and launched a petition campaign to get congressional approval of Murray's measure.

Murray naturally spoke as frequently as possible in support of his bill. In June 1946 the Montanan introduced a Senate resolution demanding a full investigation of the "strongly financed and unscrupulous lobby maintained by the private power interests of the country." The resolution went to the Military Affairs Committee where it was promptly pigeonholed.

Murray did not fare well in Montana politics either. The 1945 Montana state legislature, at Governor Sam Ford's bidding, passed a resolution condemning the MVA. R. C. Bricker, a former manager of real estate interests for the Montana Power Company, had introduced the resolution. In June the voters of Montana's eastern congressional district chose a congressman to replace Democrat James O'Connor who had died suddenly. The Missouri Valley Authority became a central issue. Republican candidate Wesley D'Ewart ran on a platform advocating the Pick-Sloan Plan. Murray rushed back to his home state to defend his project and to endorse Democratic candidate Leo Graybill. Heavy rains on election day led to a light voter turnout and helped D'Ewart emerge as eastern Montana's first Republican congressman since 1932.

Things did not improve for Murray and his valley authority in the 1946 general election. In the June senatorial primary MVA spokesman

19. Ernest Kirschten, "MVA: Stalled but not Stopped," *The Nation*, 163 (August 17, 1946), 183–84; Omaha *World-Herald*, April 7, 1945; Washington *Daily News*, July 17, 1945; Langevin, "Missouri Basin," 98–109; Ridgeway, *Missouri Basin's Pick-Sloan Plan*, 12–13, 173, 264–68; Terral, *Missouri Valley*, 179–81, 218–19.

Leif Erickson edged out Burton K. Wheeler in one of the most stunning upsets in Montana history. But, in November Erickson fell victim to the nationwide Republican trend and lost to Zales Ecton. Montana's first popularly elected Republican senator, Ecton served six uneventful years as an unabashed spokesman for the private utility industry. [20]

Despite the disastrous results of the 1946 elections, Murray was determined to reintroduce the MVA in the new Congress. The senator's aide, Dewey Anderson, spent months revising the 1944 bill hoping to satisfy some of its critics. The new measure established an advisory committee consisting of residents of the region and representatives of several federal agencies. The group would serve as a check on the three people of the MVA board of directors which critics had charged would have enjoyed dictatorial powers under the original bill. Over Murray's objections, his bill went to the Senate Public Works Committee chaired by West Virginia Republican Chapman Revercomb. In July Revercomb delivered a detailed indictment of the MVA proposal from the Senate floor. The West Virginian then shelved the Murray bill for the duration of the Eightieth Congress. [21]

Murray had no illusions about getting the Missouri Valley Authority measure through the Senate. "The job this year," he wrote a constituent, "is to continue the educational processes in the Missouri Valley area." Late in the spring of 1947, the Missouri River went on its annual rampage again causing millions of dollars in damage. The floods revived Murray's hopes that the Republican Congress might be goaded to take drastic action.

The Montanan introduced a resolution demanding the Senate investigate the floods and propose remedial action. Murray and Ben Stong met with Truman and urged him to push the valley authority program, but the president only promised to think it over. In a subsequent press conference, reporters pressed Truman on the Missouri Basin issue. "Murray was in here . . . just the other day," he told one questioner, "and I told him to push the [MVA] bill . . . I have always actively supported it." When the reporter replied that most of the Missouri Valley crowd did not feel that he was actively backing the MVA, Truman shot back, "I shall support the comprehensive flood

---

20. *Cong. Rec.*, June 18, 1946, 79th Cong., 2d sess., 92:7046–51, index, 593; Omaha *World-Herald*, July 7, 8, 1945; Leif Erickson, interview with the author, Swan Lake, Montana, August 26, 1976, transcript, UM; Great Falls *Tribune*, May 24, June 1, 6, 1945; Message of Gov. Sam C. Ford to Twenty-ninth Legislative Assembly of the State of Montana, 1945, Murray Papers; Ridgeway, *Missouri Basin's Pick-Sloan Plan*, 180–81, 272–77.

21. Dewey Anderson to Claude B. Ricketts, St. Louis, September 24, 1946, to George Sehlmeyer, Sacramento, August 28, 1946, Murray Papers; S.1156, April 24, 1947, 80th Cong., 1st sess.; *Cong. Rec.*, April 23, July 26, 1947, 80th Cong., 1st sess., 93:3854, 10354.

control program. That is the emergency at the present time, not the Missouri Valley Authority." Truman's remarks prompted Murray to telephone the White House. He told presidential assistant John Steelman that he feared that the president's contemplated flood control program could jeopardize the MVA. Murray warned, "I wouldn't recommend them a God damned dollar now for flood control unless they come in on this bigger program." [22]

Despite Murray's admonition, Truman, in July, asked Congress for four billion dollars to continue the flood control program in the Missouri basin. He threw in a general word of endorsement for valley authorities, but critics realized that the requested funds all would go toward further implementing the Pick-Sloan Plan. Supporters of the MVA felt betrayed. "It is obvious," wrote Murray's executive secretary William Coburn, "that although the President said he is in favor of an MVA, what he is most interested in is navigation and flood control. In *The Nation*, Ernest Kirschten reminded readers that Roosevelt had strongly endorsed the MVA, but his successor had given it "only lip service." [23]

Murray remained convinced that a groundswell of local support could win over both the president and Congress. To generate such pressure the senator and his congressional aides traveled to Montana at their own expense and conducted a series of informal hearings. Governor Ford and Congressman D'Ewart accused Murray of using the sessions as a vehicle to launch his reelection campaign. Nearly everyone attending the five hearings endorsed the Missouri Valley Authority.

While Murray was busy encouraging grass-roots backing for the MVA, the Pick-Sloan Plan moved forward. In January 1948, members of the Missouri Basin Inter-Agency Committee adopted a six-year-program for water resources development. The plan sought to coordinate the activities of all government agencies working in the valley. The Army Corps of Engineers and the Bureau of Reclamation continued to let contracts for dam construction. Even the New York *Times*, which had endorsed the MVA, admitted that Pick-Sloan was "a bustling reality." [24]

---

22. Telephone conversation between James E. Murray and John R. Steelman, July 12, 1947, transcript, Murray Papers; Drew Pearson, "The Washington Merry-Go-Round," Washington *Post*, July 7, 1947; Truman news conference, July 10, 1947, in Truman, *Public Papers*, 3:330; Murray to Phillip Murray, Washington, D.C., April 19, 1947, Murray Papers; Benton Stong interview with Dale Johnson, Washington, D.C., February 15, 1978, transcript, UM.

23. William H. Coburn to Richard Shipman, Helena, August 11, 1947, Murray Papers; Ernest Kirschten, "Hell, High Water, and the MVA," *The Nation*, 165 (August 9, 1947), 139–40.

24. Murray to Benton J. Stong, Denver, September 8, 1947, Murray Papers; *The People's Voice* (Helena), October 3, 1947; Lewistown *Democrat News*, September 30, 1947;

Senator Murray remained unconvinced. In March he informed the Senate that "new and alarming evidence" indicated that upstream farmers would be deprived of irrigation water under the Pick-Sloan Plan. He introduced a resolution calling for immediate review and revision of all irrigation, navigation, and flood control programs planned or underway within the basin. Although his resolution went nowhere, the senator did manage to persuade Truman to declare all of eastern Montana a disaster area after the river went on its annual flooding spree.

The thwarting of the Missouri Valley Authority by the Eightieth Congress provided Murray with an issue during his 1948 reelection campaign. Speaking in Great Falls in October, the senator charged that Republicans in Congress had joined utility lobbyists "in a scheme to destroy the western program of reclamation, flood control and rural electrification." Following his decisive reelection, Murray told Joseph Kinsey Howard, "You can say this definitely. MVA is back on the map." Murray's bill received a further boost in Montana when John Bonner ousted Sam Ford from the governor's seat. Outside the state, fifteen new congressmen and at least two new senators won election after endorsing the MVA. Foremost among these was Minnesota's freshman senator Hubert H. Humphrey. In December, Murray confidently wrote Ben Stong: "We urge that you and the supporters of the MVA throughout the Missouri Basin area prepare for a fight that will have only one outcome—the passage of the MVA this session." [25]

In January Senators Murray, Humphrey, and Guy M. Gillette of Iowa visited Truman in hopes of gaining a firm endorsement. Murray assured the president that his new MVA bill would emphasize local control. He even proposed to change the word "authority" to "administration" because of the negative connotation attached to the former term. On March 2, Murray introduced the revised measure. It called for five men instead of three on the board of directors. The governor of each basin state would be placed on the MVA advisory committee. Of even greater significance, Murray's 1949 bill agreed to use existing agencies and programs in the basin. This was done largely to avoid disruption of the Pick-Sloan projects which by then were well underway. In his first formal Senate address, Hubert Humphrey endorsed Murray's bill as "a symbol of liberalism."

Miles City *Daily Star*, October 4, 1947; Dillon *Daily Tribune*, September 27, 1947; Glasgow *Courier*, October 2, 1947, in Murray Papers; New York *Times*, October 17, 1947, January 22, 23, 1948; Langevin, "Missouri Basin," 92–93.

25.   Telegram, Murray to Truman, June 22, 1948; address, James E. Murray, Great Falls, October 4, 1948; Murray to Benton Stong, December 14, 1948; "MVA Wins in the Missouri Valley," undated memo, Murray Papers; S. J. Res. 197, March 16, 1948, 80th Cong., 2d sess.; Joseph Kinsey Howard, "Make Way for MVA," *The Progressive*, 13 (January 1949), 4–8.

Senator James E. Murray (left) with President Harry S. Truman (center) and Senator Thomas C. Hennings, Missouri, touring the Missouri River flood area in spring 1948. (United Press photo, Montana Historical Society Photograph Archives)

The new MVA measure went to the Senate Public Works Committee. Despite the newly elected Democratic majority, the committee still contained a majority hostile to valley authorities. Five of the eight Democrats on the body were from the South. The bill lay dormant, and by July cosponsor Guy Gillette admitted that there would not be "the slightest chance" for hearings during the 1949 session. "We had hoped that the November 2 mandate would be written into law," Murray lamented to a supporter. "We did not reckon with the reactionary coalition which has blocked not just an MVA, but nearly all truly liberal measures."

The conservative coalition aside, Harry S. Truman deserved much of the blame for the continued frustration among MVA's supporters.

Weeks before introducing the legislation, Murray observed that the bill would not receive a favorable committee report "unless the President really gets behind the measure." In his annual state of the union message, Truman vaguely endorsed authority plans, but did not mention the Missouri basin. Later, when asked at a press conference if his flood control report to Congress would contain an MVA recommendation, the president replied "no." After Truman had urged passage of a Columbia Valley Authority bill, a reporter asked if he planned to make a similar endorsement for the MVA. The president retorted, "Not at the present time." In January, 1950, he was asked whether he felt that Pick-Sloan eventually would envelop the MVA. He answered, "Yes, I am very sure it will." [26]

While friends of the MVA continued to hit roadblocks, opponents moved to kill the authority idea for good. In March 1949, the Missouri Valley Development Association announced that it would work for legislation within each basin state to prohibit river authorities from developing natural resources. A year later the National Rivers and Harbors Congress passed a resolution condemning the concept of regional authorities. In a *New Republic* article, "The Rivers and Harbors Lobby," Ben Stong exposed the powerful alliances which he and Murray had been fighting. The article revealed the many close ties between the NRHC and contractors, power companies, big landowners, and the U.S. Army Corps of Engineers.

Early in 1940 the Rivers and Harbors Congress suffered a setback when the Commission on Organization of the Executive Branch of Government, chaired by former president Herbert Hoover, released its final report. The Hoover Commission called the compromise between the corps and bureau in the Missouri basin a mere "division of projects" which could prove "more costly to the public than disagreement." "Successful regulation of the Missouri and its tributaries," the report concluded, "can only be managed on a basin-wide scale." Heartened by such powerful ammunition from an unexpected source, Murray had large sections of the report read into the *Congressional Record*. But the startling conclusions of the Hoover Commission persuaded neither Congress nor the president to scrap the five-year-old Pick-Sloan program. [27]

---

26. S.1160, March 2, 1949, 81st Cong., 1st sess.; *Cong. Rec.*, March 2, 1949, 81st Cong., 1st sess., 95:1705–25; New York *Times*, January 6, 15, July 9, 1949; Truman press conferences, January 8, April 14, 1949, January 5, 1950, in Truman, *Public Papers*, vols. 5, 6, 7; Murray to Jerome G. Locke, Helena, February 7, May 2, 1949, Murray Papers.

27. Benton J. Stong, "The Rivers and Harbors Lobby," *The New Republic*, 126 (October 10, 1949), 13–15; Edward S. Skillin, "Missouri Valley Task Force," *The Commonweal*, 50 (May 20, 1949), 145–46; *Cong. Rec.*, March 30, 1949, 81st Cong., 1st sess., 95:2403; Ridgeway, *Missouri Basin's Pick-Sloan Plan*, 293.

Undaunted, Murray saw the annual spring floods in 1951 as an "opportune" time to reintroduce his bill. Again it went to the hostile Public Works Committee, and Murray realized that it stood little chance. Truman's attitude continued to disappoint the Montana senator. Not only did the president ignore the wish of liberals to create valley authorities, but with the outbreak of the war in Korea he came out against the start of any new large reclamation projects. In August 1951 Murray and four other western Democratic senators sent the president a strong warning. "Slashing of reclamation on whatever theory," they concluded, "spells political disaster in the West."

The death and destruction caused by the flooding Missouri River during the early 1950s was so serious that Truman realized, war or no war, something would have to be done. By the end of 1952, the Army Corps of Engineers and Bureau of Reclamation had spent more than a billion and a quarter dollars on huge dams, canals, and levees. yet the cresting waters were higher than ever. After nearly eight years of effort, the agencies had brought only twelve thousand new acres of land under irrigation, even though Pick-Sloan had promised to irrigate five million acres. Irrigation advocates still feuded with downstream navigationists, and battles between public power and private power interests continued unabated.

In January 1952 Truman, by executive order, created a Missouri Basin Survey Commission. He directed the body to study the basin's land and water resources and to draft a plan for their coordinated development. Murray lauded Truman's decision. Several months earlier he had co-sponsored a Senate resolution calling for just such a commission. Truman appointed the Montana senator one of the new body's congressional members. [28]

In April the president gave valley authority advocates further hope that he might be changing his attitude. During the spring floods he invited Murray and pro-MVA senator Tom Hennings of Missouri to join him in an aerial inspection of the damage. But by then, Truman had already announced that he would not seek reelection. Republican presidential candidate Dwight Eisenhower was calling for a Missouri River flood control program that would give "as much authority as possible" to the individual states.

By the time the Missouri River Survey Commission released its report, Eisenhower was in the White House. After holding seventeen

---

28. "Memorandum for the President by Western Democratic Senators," August 29, 1951, Murray press release, January 4, 1952, Murray Papers; Statement of President Truman announcing creation of Missouri Basin Survey Commission, January 3, 1952, Truman Presidential Papers; S.1883, July 23, 1951, 82nd Cong., 1st sess.; S. J. Res. 93, August 20, 1952; *Cong. Rec.*, July 23, 1951, 82nd Cong., 1st sess., 97:8654–59; Jean Begeman, "Misery on the Missouri," *The New Republic*, April 28, 1952, pp.13–14.

public hearings, the commission recommended a plan that would treat the entire basin as a single unit. The report fell far short of recommending a Missouri Valley Authority, however. Instead it called for the creation of a Missouri Basin Commission of five members to supervise the activities of existing federal agencies in the region, and give them "unified and coherent direction." Murray was disappointed that the Survey Commission had not endorsed the MVA, but he urged the establishment of the suggested five-member body as "a long step forward toward a unified plan and administration." Eisenhower neither endorsed nor condemned the report's proposals. During each Congress of the Republican administration, Tom Hennings introduced bills embodying most of the Survey Commission's recommendations. Each time they went to the Senate Public Works Committee where they died.

James E. Murray remained in the Senate until the end of 1960. During his final years in office he chaired the powerful Senate Interior Committee. Yet, faced with a hostile president, the Montanan did not bother to reintroduce his Missouri Valley Authority Bill during the Eisenhower years. Instead, he consoled himself with the limited gains that had been made while congressional conservatives were forestalling the total victory, for which he had so diligently labored. "If we step back and take a historical view," he rationalized in 1954, "it is clearly evident . . . how we have all come to look upon these problems—flood control, irrigation, domestic water supply, electrical production, economic stimulation, and a dozen other problems—as common problems in regional development programs." While the MVA had forced a "shotgun wedding" of feuding parties in the Missouri valley, he added, in other basins the government agencies had entered "wedded bliss" more or less voluntarily. [29]

29. Murray to Truman, April 21, 1952, Truman Presidential Papers; Missouri Basin Survey Commission, "Missouri, Land and Water," February 20, 1953, Murray press release, February 20, 1953, Murray Papers; *Cong. Rec.*, July 17, 1954, 83rd Cong., 2d sess., 100:10774; New York *Times*, May 8, 1952, February 8, 1957.

Minerva Allen, 1990 (Courtesy of Minerva Allen)

Minerva Allen
Educator, Linguist, Poet

Minerva Allen
as interviewed by John Terreo

Too frequently in the textbooks of the American West, it appears as though the history of Native Americans somehow comes to an end with the close of the nineteenth century. Aside from a brief mention, if that, of the 1934 Wheeler-Howard Act (the Indian Reorganization Act), there is almost no discussion in most of these texts of twentieth-century Native American history. And this despite the fact that in many western states, including Montana, Native Americans represent a significant portion of the population. The following essay, drawn from an extensive interview of Indian educator and poet Minerva Allen conducted by Montana Historical Society Oral Historian John Terreo in 1989, is a step toward filling in the history of Montana's twentieth-century Native Americans.

Minerva Allen was born in a one-room log house on the Fort Belknap Indian Reservation in 1936. Her father was French and Chippewa, her mother Assiniboine/Gros Ventre; she was called "white woman" because she was blond and light-skinned. But she was raised by her grandparents in traditional Native American fashion, and she spoke two Indian languages before beginning to learn English at age five. Her career bridges two times, and two cultures. Readers should note her emphasis on the impact of World War II — a neglected subject in Montana historiography. "Everything was changed," she says. "The war changed everything." Note too the changing relationship between Native American traditions and the larger white society, how

*Minerva Allen as interviewed by John Terreo, "Minerva Allen: Educator, Linguist, Poet," *Montana The Magazine of Western History*, 41 (Winter 1991), 58–68.

the Bureau of Indian Affairs took Indian children from their parents and sent them to far-off boarding schools, and how Native American parents sometimes resist the teaching of Indian languages. Minerva Allen clearly benefited from public education, but just as clearly she still has a foot in each camp. Not exactly "historical," this selection nevertheless offers a Native American woman's perspective and raises issues that still fuel spirited public debate in Montana and the nation.

———

TERREO: Minerva, why not start at the beginning? What of your parents, where were you born, your childhood . . . ?

ALLEN: I was born in 1936 at home in a log house on April 24, and they had four feet of snow. They couldn't take my mother to the hospital so they had two grandmas, two old ladies that came from Lodge Pole, one was A Lady Goes Flying and the other one was Prisoner Wing and they were the midwives. My grandmother Lucille told me that I took a good thirty-eight hours to be born. They took me out and held me up to the sun, and they asked the sun to keep me so that I would live and have children and grow up. In those days they thought of women as people to just have children and they didn't do anything else. Then when the doctor came he just looked at us and we were fine. The Assiniboine tradition is that the firstborn child of the whole family is raised by their grandparents. So I was raised by my grandparents in the traditional way. I dressed traditionally, except the only thing, I was blond and light, you know, so then it was really an ordeal for me to be raised as a traditional person because everybody called me "white woman" because in that time Indians never really married white people.

There were few automobiles. The house I lived in was a one-room log house. On one side was the kitchen area and the other side was the sleeping area. As kids we usually slept four in a bed. I slept with my aunts in one bed and my grandfolks had their bed. That was during the winter months. During the summer months everybody slept outside in tents and tepees because the house seemed to get full of bugs. Different things came in at that time because of no water or sprays. We had to haul our water in barrels. We would hook the team up and we'd go get three or four barrels of water. We had to go after water twice a week. When we bathed we all bathed in the tub. Usually the cleanest bathed first and the dirtiest last. Everything was shared. If it was summertime we never bathed in the tub. We always went to the river. I spoke two [Indian] languages [Gros Ventre and Assiniboine]. I spoke the Gros Ventre language because my grandfather's

Henry Chopwood, the grandfather who encouraged Minerva Allen's education, stands next to Coming Day (also known as Returning Hunter) in Lodge Pole circa 1930. About eighty years old when the picture was taken, Coming Day had fought in the Indian wars. (Courtesy of Minerva Allen)

people were from Hays. At that time the mission was here and all the Gros Ventre people lived around the mission. All the Assiniboine people lived over at Lodge Pole. My grandfather was half Gros Ventre, so I came with him when we came over here. In those days we traveled mostly by wagon and team. When we went we camped—took the tent, and everything. When we went to somebody's house we just put our tent and our stove and stuff up and camped just like campers. We would stay there for like three, four days so my grandpa could visit with relatives. So, for me to understand what they were talking about I spoke the Gros Ventre language, too.

My grandfather always believed in education. He sent his kids off to school, to the boarding schools they had. They had boarding schools for Indians all over the United States, some to Carlisle, to Chemawa, Flandreu, way down in Chilocco, Oklahoma, and all these different places where they sent Indians to be educated. See, that was the great era of sending Indians away to teach them English—to become citizens. So they were willing to send the Indian kids away, sometimes for twelve months, sometimes for four years, sometimes for nine months at the minimum. My grandfather always had his children—younger children that weren't married—sent away, like to Chemwa, Oregon, so they could go to school and become high school graduates. He always believed in education but he never spoke hardly any English. I had to speak to him in Indian. When I was five years old he sent me to day school. They didn't start children until they were six years old [but] he asked the teacher if I could stay with her and learn English. That was really an ordeal for me because I really couldn't speak to the teacher. We did a lot of sign language and body language. She taught me English by singing. She taught me to play the piano. She'd sing a song and then I'd sing it. That was how I learned to speak English—by singing.

My grandfather was an Indian policeman for twenty-five years before he died. So he was really an advocate of education and he always told me that I was different. He always told me, "In your time it is going to be different. You are going to have to have education if you are gonna survive because everything is gonna change." My grandfather was a great philosopher.

TERREO: The teacher you started learning English from, was she white?

ALLEN: She was white. She must have been Italian, Polish, or German. I don't exactly know what her nationality was. She did have a little accent and she had a daughter and they taught school from first grade to the eighth at Lodge Pole. I became a tutor after I learned English. All the kids my age and older . . . they were [in the first grade] because they did not know English.

TERREO: You were six years old and you were a tutor in English?

ALLEN: I was the tutor in English since I learned it a lot better than the others. I would sit with them and say, "me," "spot," or "run." I would sit with them. I would know when they had to go to the bathroom. This school as I remember had a room with a little kitchen. It was the first time I ever saw dolls, beds, and dishes, and everything my size. I can remember setting the table and saying "dish" in Indian and saying it in English to the white kids. We did hands-on types of things in the playroom, and that's how I tutored a lot of the kids because they would poke me and they'd say, "What's this in Indian?" "Naydockoo." I'd just tell them "dish." So I worked a lot like that. By the time I was in the seventh grade—there were boys in that grade twenty and twenty-five years old learning that language. They weren't married or anything but just so far back in learning. When I graduated eighth grade I was twelve, and my grandfolks sent me to Flandreau, South Dakota, where I was a freshman. This was the beginning of the late 1940s or so. Then, everything was changed. The war changed everything. My aunts were wearing high heels and nylon stockings after the war. The traditional clothes started to go out and English started to come in really strong. The assimilation and the change-over—the transition in those days after the war was tremendous.

TERREO: So you were very self-sufficient then in comparison to what came later and right now. Are you saying that during and after the Second World War, people became less self-sufficient?

ALLEN: I don't know how you'd explain that. How they became like, to me, I thought they became bums. That's a really hard term there, [but] they became more dependent on the federal government—the Bureau of Indian Affairs for commodities, or rations. They became more dependent on the BIA to help them, and the BIA seemed to like [it].

TERREO: This moving away from self-sufficiency, if the parents are not being required to be so self-sufficient is it communicated to the next generation?

ALLEN: They lost a lot during this transition. There are surveys now saying that the kids or Indian adult students who kept their traditional values tend not to go into drugs and alcohol. And the kids that don't have an identity, the kids that have not been raised in the traditional way or have not been involved with parents who are really responsible, they tend to lose their identity.

TERREO: It seems they had to choose between traditional values and those manifested by the prosperity of the modern white society. Many Indians it seems felt the traditional ways were no longer needed.

ALLEN: Yes. They liked the better and faster transportation. A lot of them tended to just stay in town and drink, and some became hookers and that which was never done before and which was frowned upon by the elders.

TERREO: You were saying that you were sent to South Dakota for high school. What was that like for you?

ALLEN: It was really hard. A year before I was sent away, my grandfather died. When he died he called me to his death bed. He said,
"I want you to promise me that you will become educated and that
you will be the first one to go ahead and do this for all of the family."
You know, he put a lot on my shoulders, and I told him I would. I
promised him I would do this. That was always behind in my mind.

He died that year. Then my grandmother and I and my two aunts
were left. They [the government] didn't start my grandmother's pension right away. My grandmother was illiterate. She couldn't speak
English. She was learning. She was young-minded. I started to teach
her English. I said, "Grandma, you gotta do this in order to order
stuff at the store. You gotta do this."

When we left there we were almost destitute. We left the home
place, which is still there. We moved to Lodge Pole, which was a bigger settlement than the one we were at then. I remember we were
living in a one-room house that had a dirt floor. We rented, and I
don't know why we moved from our own house, which had a wooden
floor. I never could get that out of my mind. My grandma said it was
because it was closer to people, and since we were women it would
be better. We would get more help than if we stayed out there on
the homestead, which was five miles from there.

We got so hungry that at one time we had a man come and kill
one of our teams so we could eat one of the horses. My grandma
had not gotten any help at all. So then finally when we moved to
Lodge Pole she got welfare for me because I was a minor and the
other girls were eighteen or older. So she got welfare for me, and
I remember she was getting thirty-five dollars a month for me, and
that is what we lived on. Later when her son got killed in the war—
about a year after we moved to Lodge Pole she got his pension
monthly. Then we were better off, and we could move to a better
house with wooden floor and beds and everything.

I always had in the back of my mind that I was going to finish
school regardless because I had promised my grandpa, and this was
what I was going to do. I finished high school when I was seventeen.
When I left there I wanted to join the Air Force really bad. There
was no money to send me to college. I wanted to go to college, and
I thought if I went into the Air Force I'd be able to pay my way through
college. But I was only seventeen. I went to Sioux Falls, South Dakota,
where I got my physical and I enlisted and everything. They said no.
I would have to have my folks sign something allowing me to go. By
then my mother and dad had divorced. I was seven when that happened. In those days marriage between people that weren't of the
same race didn't work good. Dad just couldn't hack it anymore, I guess.
I don't know what it was, but they got a divorce. I begged and begged

for somebody to give me a signature so I could go. I didn't care who it was—just give me the right to go, but nobody did. My grandma said, "No, the Korean War is on. You are not going." So, I came home and went to work.

I was seventeen years old and had no place to go. I went and stayed with my aunts. I stayed with one aunt who had a crippled husband and four children. I had to sleep with the four children and that wasn't a very good situation. I stayed with her about a month or so and then I went to the other aunt who had a lot of children. The houses were small, and there was no way you could have privacy. I lived out of a suitcase. I tried to get into Haskell Junior College in Kansas City. They said I couldn't go because the school was filled up. In the meantime, my uncle got a loan for two thousand dollars for me to go to Northern Montana State College in Havre.

So I went one quarter, and this was the winter quarter my mother died. She froze to death in Hogeland. She was working out there as a cook for a rancher. She had gone to Chinook to buy some stuff. She was going back to work and it got about forty or fifty below. When she was going back that evening the snow—there was snow on the ground. She couldn't make this one hill. She probably had slick tires on her car, I don't know. She slid back on a culvert. Her car high-centered so then she walked. The ranch was eight miles away and she walked seven miles and laid down and died, I guess, just in view of the ranch. It was so stormy and cold that nobody even noticed until the next day. The rancher rode his horse and saw something black out there and it was her. She had frozen to death.

I had to come back from college because I had a sister and two brothers. In those days they sent you away to Minneapolis to foster homes or Baltimore, Maryland, or some place, especially if nobody wanted you. I decided to go home and that is when I met my husband. I knew him all my life, and he said if we got married we could take care of my sister and brothers. So I got married. I raised my brothers and sister and sent them all to school, and then I had my own children.

TERREO: How large a family did you have?

ALLEN: I had eight. I raised fourteen children in my life. I picked up three or four abandoned children and raised them until they were eighteen years old. I have maybe six or seven college graduates out of my family. I took the philosophy of my grandpa that I was going to make sure everybody got educated.

TERREO: You've mentioned your husband a few times. Did you have a traditional wedding ceremony?

ALLEN: Yes. My husband had to bring some horses to my uncle to ask for me. When I was eight years old, I was given to a boy [to] be my husband and to be married after we graduated—after I got of age, I guess. We knew each other. We were good friends, and then when I got seventeen or eighteen, and he got nineteen, twenty, his parents expected us to get married. He fell in love with another girl. So, I told him, "Well, I don't know." We were really good friends and if he didn't fall in love—I don't know, we probably would have had to get married in order to save face. I told him to go ahead and I would tell his folks. I would tell mine, and I would say that I want to go on and get educated and this was a good way of getting out of it. I told my uncle and my aunt that I wanted to get educated, I don't want to be married. I don't want it to hold me down. And so when I told his folks they talked together about it. They thought, well that would be about it, and then he had to marry the girl that he fell in love with [and] "got in trouble." So that was the end of that. So I was really glad. I felt free then, you know. I've always had that in the back of my mind.

So that's the traditional way, but then when I met my husband, he had to bring the horses to my uncle and tell him that he wanted to marry me. So then we went ahead and set a time that we were going to get married and exchange gifts.

We had the regular [wedding]—it was a big, big thing—really big. Had a big dance, and then they had in those days a big rodeo. We had to ride out in the arena and then our friends gave us all our gifts. We accumulated a couple horses and then they went to our— his house. They had redone the whole house. Threw out everything old, put everything new in it. That's the way you do when you get married long ago. The tepee—they fixed your tepee and they fixed everything up new. Like I had new dishes, new bed and [bedding], and new blankets. And all the old grandmas got together; they did all that for us, and so all we had to do was just move in. So that's the way they have a traditional wedding. And later we got married by the priest, because they said it wasn't legal.

TERREO: Did you eventually return to college?

ALLEN: I did after my baby got into Head Start. I told my husband I was going back to college. He said "OK, I'll help you as much as I can." They had said there was money for Indians to be educated. But they said you had to be head of the household. I wasn't head of the household—my husband was. There was no way I could go to college. I said well I'm going anyway. The BIA has never financed me to go to college. So when I decided to become a parent I got involved in everything. I became a community leader. I just thought, "I'm gonna take all this opportunity while I am married, but I'm going to college even so." I started writing to places. The Montana Indian Scholarship out of Denver paid for my Head Start training, and then I took a two-year college course.

I went two years, and then they would let you teach school. That was the way teachers were at one time. I got two years of college and became a teacher. I taught one year at Lodge Pole in 1968. In 1970, I became a Head Start director because it was opening up, and it was more money, and I thought I could save money and finish my college education. So, through Head Start and through the United Scholarship—Northern [Montana State College] gave me a scholarship—through scholarships I became educated.

I went and got my [bachelor's degree] at Central Michigan University in Mount Pleasant, Michigan. I went on and got my master's degree at Northern and then I went to Weber [State College]. I sent two daughters to Weber. I went down there [to Ogden, Utah] and went to school with them. I got an endorsement [for studying] in early childhood because at that time, I was working in early childhood. Since then I have been to various other colleges getting endorsements. I really worked to become educated.

I did a lot of work with the Montana Legal Services for awhile before I went to college. I worked with lawyers. I've always wanted to be a woman activist. But like my husband said one time, "You've always hauled your own water and chopped your own wood and did all your own work." A lot of people want to do their own thing, and I've always been able to do it—to do what I wanted to do.

TERREO: What of your time as director of the Head Start Program?

ALLEN: I was director here at Fort Belknap, and I had three centers. I had one here at Hays and one at Lodge Pole and Windham. It is a federally funded program, and every year you have to write [grant] proposals. You hire teachers and teacher's aides to work with about fifteen kids in each classroom. I had two classrooms at Fort Belknap, two at Hays, and one at Lodge Pole. We worked with over a hundred children.

TERREO: What was the general attitude of the community when it first began?

ALLEN: It was something different, and they were very suspicious of it. They wondered what the federal government was bringing us again to eventually phase out. They were afraid of it. I have always been one of those people who trust. I had to go to the homes and recruit people, recruit children, talk to parents, tell them the best positive parts about it. I told them, "You have to pay for the baby-sitting services." They said, "Well we don't have any money." I said, "Yes but you can pay for them with volunteer hours with being involved with your children's education, and you gotta come to the classroom. Bring something that you can do so that you will be involved in what your child is doing."

We worked like that, and we had regular parent meetings— monthly parent meetings. We brought in first aid, how to fix your car if you are a woman. We brought in extension agents. We worked all that into where the parents could learn about it. That was the main emphasis on Head Start—train parents and also work with their children. It was the country we went by—how to do things for frost-bite, car accidents, drunks, and stuff like that. That's what we worked on—training parents.

I went to Washington, D.C., and got money for training programs. I educated eight teachers here that are my age and still are teaching someplace. I received funds—I brought in college courses. I fought husbands. I did everything to get these kids, these people educated so they could be self-sufficient.

That's what I did for about the eight years that I worked with Head Start. After that, I resigned in January or March, I don't remember, 1978, I think. I resigned because in April, I remember, I had to have a kidney operation. It was giving me heck since 1975 and I just [had] hung in there. So, I had the operation and the doctor told me I would probably be tied up for six months. I did the operation in April, and by August I was all right. The school was looking for a community education director here at the Hays/Lodge Pole schools. The super-intendent came to see me and asked me to apply. So that's what I did. I applied there, and I started working here at the school, and I've been working here ever since.

TERREO: The Foster Grandparent Program . . . what exactly is that?

ALLEN: Oh, that started back when I was in Head Start. The Foster Grandparent Program doesn't have to be parents, it has to be anybody that is sixty years [old] or older. It's a volunteer program, which is funded by the federal government. When I started the bilingual pro-gram here in 1980, I needed some aides. The kids needed foster grandparents, who spoke the language and who could work well with the kids. Because like now, you know, these kids speak almost all English. I brought them in to help teach the language and to help the kids, because, when you speak another language—I don't know

Lodge Pole third-grade students performed at the Fort Belknap Education Conference in 1981, when Minerva Allen was honored as the Fort Belknap Educator of the Year. (Courtesy of the *Harlem News*)

if you do—but when you speak another language besides English, they always say the other language like French, German, and Indian is backwards. But it's the English language that's backwards, you know. So what you have to do is translate it in your head before you could say it in English. A lot of Indian kids will hesitate when they speak because they have to translate. It makes them speak different, or something, and not the real perfect English. Like in Alaska they call it bush English.

In 1980, we were working with the language, both languages. In 1984 Congress passed a new law and said that we cannot teach restitution of the native languages. So in 1984, we changed it to transitional bilingual programs. We could use the language to teach the children if needed, but otherwise we had to teach English proficiency. So that's what we are doing now in our bilingual programs.

TERREO: What kind of opposition to the bilingual program did you run into and on what levels?

ALLEN: On all levels. Many [parents] said, they don't want our kids to have bilingual. Because they said they don't want their kids to learn their language, they don't want their kids to go backwards. They finally got them where they are speaking English. "Why should we have them speak Indian?" A lot of parents had made it out as a kind of a communist act. They said "you [bring] the language back and then want to control us with the language." And yet it wasn't. I had to fight the superintendents, had to fight the principals. The principals said the same thing, because they didn't understand what bilingual meant. And the teachers were the worst because they felt you were infringing on their territory, that you were going to put people in there [their classrooms] who will watch them teach and criticize, and that you were taking their time and their space.

TERREO: From perhaps a historical perspective, do you feel that you really can't obliterate someone's heritage, history, or culture?

ALLEN: Yes. And see, they finally realized that. That's why bilingual now is different from 1980. We have more people involved in bilingual because they want to know, they want to use it to help their children and also to help themselves. They ask us for materials, or ask us for all these books that I've helped to publish, and worked on and translated. I get people from everywhere—all kinds of Native Americans, trying to use it for a guideline—a format to do their own culture and language and history and stuff.

TERREO: So there is a more positive outlook being bicultural.

ALLEN: There is! At first the kids wouldn't respond too much. They found out from their parents and from their grandparents and everybody else that it is OK to tell the teachers what you know. So they just came out—kids that you think didn't know their language came up and started talking their language. It was like you open a curtain and all of a sudden all things stopped and they just started blossoming out, saying, "Oh, I know that. I know! This is what my grandfather told me. Come and tell us all kinds of stories relating to history."

TERREO: It seems to me that the Native American language is more descriptive than English.

ALLEN: Yes, it is. You write a sentence in a Native American language that long [Allen indicates about twelve inches] and it might be this short in English [indicates about three inches]. But you have to describe all things. Like cars, they never had cars. They had to invent words for those terms. Like car, in their native language, is "it goes by itself." That's a car. "Goes by itself." If a truck, it is "goes by itself and carries." They didn't add on to the language.

TERREO: How do you feel about the 1984 law in which Congress has mandated English proficiency?

ALLEN: You hear of the English-only law that's been passed. It is mostly, I think, to get back at the Hispanics. They claim that by 1990, 20 percent of the population in the United States is going to be speaking Spanish. Congress feels that [by] having one language, one group can't dominate the United States. That's what they think. But they don't realize that the Hispanics, the Asian people, the Vietnamese, the Moslems, are learning English faster because they want to be assimilated. Whereas the Indians don't want to be assimilated, you know. They don't have to be. They are here. They were here first. They don't have to be and don't want to be assimilated. But the others want to. That is the difference.

TERREO: Do you feel that certain factions have favored the one-language-only law not necessarily from prejudice but from the view that one primary language is needed to better facilitate communication between the various elements of United States society?

ALLEN: Yes. Bilingual has always been a bad term to people who do not understand it. So they use it as a derogatory term and don't realize that it means the ability to speak two languages rather than wanting to be different. But they treat you different. I'm always afraid to use bilingual. When I talk to people nobody understands it, even some of the teachers here. I have to explain bilingual completely to them continuously every year. I'm glad the older teachers here have been involved in bilingual as have the principals and can explain it well. And you always have to get your administrators into it or you are just fighting a blank wall.

TERREO: What of the series of [bilingual] readers you have published for the classroom?

ALLEN: With one of the bilingual programs, I decided to do some readers so the kids could take the readers home and work with the parents. That is how that came about. So, I told the kids if they brought traditional stories and everyday type stories we would write them both in English and the native language on their grade level. So we did that on the first-grade level. And now we're doing them on first-grade to third-grade level. We're doing them now on fourth- to six-grade level. I wrote the stories that they told me, and then I translated them in both the Gros Ventre and the Assiniboine languages. That was another way of reinforcing our bilingual program.

TERREO: Aren't you also a poet? How did you get interested in poetry?

ALLEN: I was raised alone, so, I've always had this—I don't know what it is—I think it is I've always been curious. I've always listened to a lot of stories that my grandfolks told me, their friends, their neighbors, and I've always sat there. I was a quiet child. So I always sat and listened. As I went into grade school or high school, I started writing down things, keeping like a diary. I still do it. Later, VISTA workers came to Fort Belknap. I got to know them real well. One was an English major, and his wife was an artist. One day they happened to see some things I wrote. He said, "WOW!" He said, "You are pretty good at this. You should just start writing more." So I said OK. And that's how I got started.

TERREO: Is poetry a tradition in the Native American languages?

ALLEN: Yes, poetry goes along with songs. They sing the songs at pow-wows, the honor songs, the victory songs. In the modern day now, it's the "Forty-Nine Songs," or the "Round Dance Songs," the "Love Songs," the "Owl Dance Songs," all have short poetry in them. And it tells a story. My grandma told me a lot of stories which I wrote into poetry. She told me stories—Indian stories—when she would be putting me to sleep. We have a person I wrote a lot of stories about. His name is Inktomi. He was—is—the trickiest of the tribe. He was always doing things that had an antidote—a disciplinary type of an action. And so you read it to your grandkids. I still read it to my grandkids. It tells them why you should not do this. Like fairy tales but in Indian version. And I guess other tribes have the coyote man, or spider man, or different things like that. Tales like legends and myths to the tribes. So, we have one and we call him Inktomi. I use that, like some of the stories that the kids brought me were about their trickiest, which told antidotes of why you don't do this or do that because this will happen to you. Why the sun, or why the chinook wind blows, where they came from, little things like that.

TERREO: Have you found that the attitude towards women has changed?

ALLEN: Yes, I have. And it took a long time—even for my husband. It took a long time for him to realize that women can do things just like men or can be responsible and can do other things besides raising children and working at home. Long ago you couldn't even be passed twenty you were considered, I guess, [un]able to get married. You know you had to get married young. If you didn't get married after you were twenty-one, there was something [the] matter with you. Nowadays, it [has] changed. The Indian people believed that you should get married and have children and keep the tribe going. And now its not like that. You can marry anybody you want to. You don't have to just marry whoever they want you to marry. And so that's why, you know, there never were too many mixed marriages. And since the 1980s that's changed. Since the eighties, there's been a lot of mixed marriages, which is acceptable. Before, they weren't. That was one reason my dad and mother couldn't be together because they weren't accepted by either side.

TERREO: Do you find that with students in the classroom now there is more projecting of themselves into future occupations because there's a greater variety of things that they [women] can do now than before?

ALLEN: Yes. In my day, all we could think about was being nurses or teachers. That was acceptable. Now you can do most anything and be accepted. Yet there is still a lot of discrimination on women. Like me, for instance. I might be educated and everything, but I'm still Indian. I'm still a minority, and I'm still a woman. And its really hard for me to be on the level of men. They won't accept me. I still have the problem. Especially in Native American society because Native American men are number one.

In a way I still do that myself. I've kind of had inbred into me as an innate type of thing that my husband is number one in my family and then, my sons are, and they get served first, they get everything first. They don't do anything hardly. They gotta have all the clean clothes, they gotta have it laid out, they gotta be tended to when they come in. They are the masters of the house, that's the Assiniboine tradition. And I still do that. And I've taught my daughters to be like that and my sons' wives are like that. That is the way I was raised—that I did everything for the males in my family and my grandmas did that for me and my mom did that for her and it's just the traditional thing. So my girls, I've trained them to do that, but, it does make a good marriage. My brothers and sisters have never had any divorces. But it's a two-way street. The woman is held—without the woman you won't have the man. We were always held high as a woman, but in your place.

TERREO: In your past experiences as an educator have you had many difficulties with teenage pregnancy?

ALLEN: You never had any [teenage] pregnancies when I was growing up. You never had any kids out of wedlock. You were shunned out of the tribe if you did. You had to leave the country. And then all of a sudden after World War II—just like [that], it's acceptable. [Then] all of a sudden it just quit again. You know. It just quit. We started working with parents [and] with the public health people. I just wrote letters galore and did everything trying to curb it and work with the teachers. So these last two years its been pretty good. We haven't had any problems with it. The school is the center of the community. And without the school there wouldn't hardly be anything here.

TERREO: Would you say there are fewer distractions, say in comparison to a large urban area?

ALLEN: Yes, thank goodness. Because our greatest problem here is alcohol and then that isn't that bad, but its pretty bad with the kids. Drugs and other things haven't reached us yet. It's mostly because of the isolation, I suppose. And then no money. Our kids don't have that much money; our parents don't have that much money, and the money is used for more important things than to buy things that are not necessary. So that helps a lot. That's their life: just teeny bits of money. So they don't have enough money to buy drugs. So we are lucky.

One Cow, One Vote
A Strenuous Session in the Montana Legislature
Margaret Scherf

The French have a saying—the more things change, the more they stay the same. Interpreting this evocative memoir depends on your angle of vision. On the one hand, much has changed. Reapportionment is an accomplished fact, the "territorial integrity" conflict disappeared in 1971, the legislature now meets for ninety days, and Tracy's is gone. Yet public education, property taxes, workers' compensation, the universities, and the state's institutions remain controversial. Money—how to raise it and how to spend it—is the always-encompassing issue, and, as of this writing, Francis Bardanouve is still the legislature's Chairman of Appropriations. In 1965, when the last unreconstructed legislature met, the Democrats controlled Margaret Scherf's House by 56 to 38; in 1991 the margin was 61 to 39. The legislature's record is never as bad as the public and the press perceive it, but legislators are still crooks, fools, and party-goers. One would never know that a world of difference separates 1965 from the 1990s. Yet one important continuity persists. The legislature remains our cockpit of representative government, our indispensable arena of democracy.

O n the last day of the 1965 session in the Capitol in Helena, as we legislators took our hacking coughs and our masses of bills and correspondence to our cars, we said goodbye with "Never again!"

---

*Margaret Scherf, "One Cow, One Vote, A Strenuous Session in the Montana Legislature," *Harper's Magazine*, 232 (April 1966), 103–9.

A Montana House member accused the Senate of believing in "one cow, one vote" during a testy debate over reapportionment, which would shift legislative seats from rural districts with more cows than people to urban areas. L. A. Huffman photographed this roundup in eastern Montana between 1910 and 1915. (Montana Historical Society Photograph Archives)

But now, come spring, the old firehorses are beginning to prick up their ears. Not long ago I met a couple of them cheerfully planning this summer's campaign. Even the chairman of Fish and Game, who developed a distinguished ulcer, is willing to go through it all again. And those members of either house who saw themselves written off by reapportionment were deeply hurt and full of gloom.

What attracts men to the legislature? The pay is $1,200 for a sixty-day biennial session, with duties that continue during the off years. Since the legislature meets during January and February, a member has to fight from fifty to five hundred miles of icy roads to get home to tend to his own affairs. One lawyer estimated it cost him more than $5,000 to serve in two sessions. Winter in Helena is bright, beautiful, and often 30 degrees below zero. The Capitol is heated to a toasty 90, so every lawmaker has at least one revolting cold.

It isn't the charm of Helena that lures them. The Helena *Journal* of 1891 described the capital as "the richest city on earth per capita," and "the magnificent banking houses that line Main Street" as "superb specimens of the architects' and builders' skill," but today the center of Helena—Last Chance Gulch—is moribund. Gone is the splendor of the old Broadwater Hotel with its pink marble and gold-inlaid bathtubs. The town's iron fences and red-brick turrets and towers, built by the mining and banking millionaires of the 1880s, are quaint and amusing for an afternoon, but gradually the dismal decay of most of these old mansions, including the building once occupied by our Governors, becomes depressing.

So it is not the pay nor the luxury of life in the capital that brings men back session after session, and adds new recruits in each election. There are, of course, personal ambitions, special axes to grind, and always there is party loyalty. The Republicans come to Helena to fight the Democrats. The Democrats come to fight the Republicans and "the companies." The ultraconservatives come to fight the federal government on the last available battleground. But I believe there is something more than these usual incentives. We seem to have an old-fashioned faith in the importance of state government.

Montana, which became a state in 1889, is no more Wild West now than New Rochelle or Dayton. It is churchy. We have a goodly number of alcoholics and a high divorce rate, but it's the solid Lutherans, Methodists, Catholics, Presbyterians, believing in the simple virtues, in progress, in individual effort, who set the tone. Our largest cities— Billings and Great Falls—are well under 100,000, and most of us live in small towns or on farms and ranches. The legislature reflects this earnest, middle-class respectability.

This respectability has been growing since I first observed a session a decade or more ago. At that time there was a casual air about the House—feet on desks, spittoons, big hats, open newspapers, and the gavel grasped by a "company man." As a writer I was keenly interested, but had no thought of putting my own neck on the block.

LISTENER, PROBER, CROOK, FOOL

In 1964, the Democrats needed four candidates for the House in my county, and they had only three. Would I run? "You won't have to do a thing," the county chairman promised. "Just file."

I was skeptical, but I filed. Our county is roughly sixty miles wide and seventy-five long, runs north to Canada and east to the top of the Rockies. Early one summer morning I put my dog and a sandwich into the old red Plymouth and set out to see the voters. I stopped in front of a farm gate bearing a large sign: BEWARE OF VICIOUS DOG. As I debated the wisdom of getting out, a large springer came trotting down the road, his red tongue flapping and his brown tail wagging. He escorted me to the door. Campaigning, once I overcame my initial fright, was rather like that. People were nearly always friendly, wanted to talk. They told me their country school was over-crowded, or their boys couldn't find work in the winter, or property taxes were too high. There was a good deal more poverty than I had suspected. I began to see the candidate, as I later saw the legislator, as a listener, a prober.

National candidates appear at large meetings, dinners, rallies. They make TV appearances, talk strategy with party leaders, shake many hands, but they haven't time to listen for an hour or two to a logger injured in the woods who is unable to collect from the Industrial Accident Board. It is the legislative candidate alone who can be button-holed and complained to, scolded, instructed. He is on the voter's level.

We had to be screened by the Taxpayer's Association, the Timber Haulers, Wildlife, REA, MEA, the Sawmill Worker's Union, the Carpenter's Union, and half-a-dozen PTAs. We passed out cards in the supermarkets, went to dozens of teas and coffees, ate our way through mammoth church and grange dinners, shook hands and ate midnight lunches in country bars and taverns. Three days before the November election, the chairman called me at eight in the morning. "Be over at the high school at eleven," he said. "English class, room 12. You can discuss Medicare, Kerr-Mills, public power, and federal aid to education. You'll have about twenty minutes." That same afternoon, a party member said reproachfully, "You should be working, you know. Get out and ring doorbells."

I came through with a triumphant twelve-vote landslide. My opponent called for a recount and we both spent the next three weeks in a chilly old potato warehouse, watching every ballot as the County Commissioners tallied. I held on to ten points of the margin, and was the first woman to represent our county in the legislature in fifty years, and the only mystery writer who ever served. As my weight went down and my color approached that of a boiled cauliflower, I kept asking myself why I had left a comfortable typewriter to get into this fight. And yet at the lowest point in the session I wouldn't have gone home, even if it had been possible. Because I did not feel that this was a meaningless fight, that the endless, exhausting caucuses and committee meetings and debates were about nothing. They were about the things that mattered, and the divisions reflected fundamental differences in philosophy.

The job could be made less of an ordeal for the legislator by length-ening the session and chopping out some of the accumulated under-brush. It is impossible to take care of the business of the state in sixty days every two years.[1] There is no time to study and reorganize

---

1. See Senator Joseph D. Tydings' article, "The Last Chance for the States," in *Harper's Magazine*, 232 (March 1966), 71–79; state legislators meet only once every two years.

our obsolete boards and bureaus, so that each session merely adds its own bandages. The constitution forces the legislature to waste its time on minute details: Is the fox a predatory animal? How much shall a city fireman be paid?

Another frustrating factor is the constant ridicule from the press. We spent many weary hours on heavy issues, but the reporters glee- fully seized on one bill intended to force the owners of pets to furnish shelter, called it the Cat House Bill, and tried to make its sponsors look like idiots. The presentation took perhaps fifteen minutes in each house, but readers back home were led to believe we were spen- ding most of our time on trivia. There was little press enthusiasm for the long hot battles over air pollution, education, minimum wage, investment of state funds, mental health, reapportionment, and how to raise the money.

Newsmen are of course cramped by their editors' caution. They didn't report that on the minimum-wage bill certain dubious characters were consulted, made demands which enraged the labor members, and helped to scuttle the bill. Leaks from caucuses on this topic would have made lively reading but were ignored. This timid editorial thinking didn't begin in recent years when our small papers were sold to the chains. The so-called independent hometown paper was never really that — it would have starved to death in the old days without subsidies from the railroads and other corporations. Nor is the amused condescension of the press a matter of one-party domi- nation. Montana has only one Democratic paper — the Great Falls *Tribune* — but it isn't the Democratic sessions alone that suffer. The legislature is treated habitually as a gathering of crooks and fools. But we were too busy with the battle to worry about the snipers in our midst.

Before the session began, it looked as if reapportionment would be the big job. Actually, it played a minor role in the House, where it was accomplished, and only in the Senate, where it finally expired, did it consume much time.

Reapportionment in Montana, as elsewhere, was far more lethal to the Senate than to the House. The House committee went rapidly through hearings on a device called the "weighted vote" and disposed of this last hope of the condemned small counties, then turned to population maps for other plans. There were halfhearted efforts to roll back the Supreme Court decision — two resolutions regarding Constitutional Amendments — but a majority conceded that Petro- leum County with 894 people didn't deserve the same representa- tion in the Senate as Yellowstone with 79,016.

We were well along with our work in the House before we met with the Senate committee. They sat with stony faces and folded arms

while we displayed our merchandise. We pleaded that if the legislature, rather than the court, did the job we would have something
to say about how it was done. No response. At last one the of the
senators said, "If I have to have my throat cut, I'm not going to hold
the knife."

"What you senators really believe in is one cow, one vote," a House
member accused.

The maneuvers that followed in the Senate, drowning and resusci-
tating the same bill over and over again, meant nothing. The members
in cowboy boots, representing the beef, wheat, and oil counties with
small populations, had made up their minds before they came to
Helena that the first order of business was to kill reapportionment.
It took them fifty-five of the sixty days to do the job. They told us
frankly they would not act on congressional redistricting either, so
we did not attempt that.

In July the U.S. District Court handed down a temporary reapportionment plan for the legislature and the congressional districts
which seems to have aroused no great resentment. Although some
astute and valuable members will lose their seats, there will also be
a welcome pruning of dead wood. Theoretically, the Democrats
should benefit from the new plan, but some of the strongest opposition to the change came from Democrats in the Senate.

Lobbyists with Angora Mittens

Money was the legislature's basic problem. Montana is a huge state
(147,000 square miles), immensely rich in timber, oil, waterpower,
beef, wheat, minerals; and yet our average personal income is below
the nation's. Stocks in our big enterprises—St. Regis paper, Anaconda
copper and aluminum, Montana Power, the oil fields—are largely
held outside the state. We have areas of great prosperity, like Cut
Bank, where garage doors open by electric eye and houses are
designed with a bathroom for every boy, but these are balanced by
pockets like Martin City, a leftover from the construction of a
mammoth federal dam, where many families must accept welfare as
a way of life.

For decades it has been accepted Democratic party doctrine that
"the companies"—the Anaconda Copper Mining Company and the
Montana Power Company—are to blame for our lagging economy
and our failure to attract industry and population. We still ship our
wheat, timber, beef, and minerals to other states for processing. Probably the two companies prefer the status quo, and undoubtedly they
aid substantially those candidates who will be kind when it comes
to regulation and taxation. They have, in the past, had their fingers

in many pies, including higher education. But what could the companies do if the voters were not so easily divided?

The wheat and cattle men have a deep distrust of Butte and labor;
Butte has no love for agriculture and its problems; the urban population resents the grip of farmers, stockmen, and oil men on state and
local government. These divisions are handy tools for the company
lobbyists. Add to this the fact that news coverage is shallow and
meager; we are better informed on affairs in Paris and Sacramento
than we are on the business and politics of our own state.

Anaconda and Montana Power—though they use different lobby-
ing methods—seem to cooperate to achieve the same objectives: to
keep things as they are and to allow the Democrats a governor or
a legislature, but never both at the same time. A shrewd lobbyist knows
that threats and bullying are not nearly so effective as a few well-
planted seeds of fear. To frighten a legislator, a lobbyist need only
tell him a certain bill will hurt his county—where the votes lie. The
easy ways to kill a bill are to spread the fear that it will (1) hurt the
farmer, (2) ruin business on Main Street, (3) throw men out of work,
or (4) raise local property taxes. When Anaconda was threatened by
a net-proceeds tax, word went around that this bill would close every
small mine in the state.

At present Anaconda has such a skillful and agreeable lobbyist
in Glen Carney that a legislator is ashamed of his suspicion that the
old dragon is still there, wearing angora mittens. There are signs that
officials of Montana Power would like to dispel its public image of
the wicked fairy with a wand in every stew—they recently took on
a smooth and pleasant young lobbyist who had been working for
Great Northern.

The big two are not the only powerful lobbies. The railroads,
Northern Pacific and Great Northern, are Madison Avenue in their
approach. Their decorous young men take a legislator to lunch,
attempt to arouse sympathy for their cause by earnestly describing
the legal tedium that follows a meeting between a steer and a loco-
motive. One drink, a little chicken à la king, and back to the mine.
Dull stuff compared with the days when hundred-dollar bills were
tossed over transoms in the Placer Hotel.

Pacific Power and Light flooded us with uniform wires and letters
on the REA "territorial integrity" bill. The Timber Haulers are well
organized and alert to such threats as higher taxes on diesel fuel,
truck weights, truck licenses. When the air-pollution bill came up
we felt tremendous pressure from lumber, pulp, sugar-beet, and
paper-mill interests.

Montana, with more fresh air per person than almost any other
state, has pockets of contamination as aggravating as that in Los
Angeles. Missoula's air contains five tons of measurable contamina-

tion per day per square mile, according to Elmer Flynn, author of the bill, and every twenty-four hours the average person inhales as much Benzo-a-pyrene (a cyclic hydrocarbon found in cigarette and wood smoke) as he would in smoking fifty-six cigarettes. The day the legislative committee visited Missoula to inhale some of this controversial air, the industry guilty of pollution had been shut down and the sky was an innocent bright blue.

When the Party Gets Rough

After a long, hard fight, not on party lines, the air-pollution-control bill went through both houses, and was flushed down the drain by Governor Tim Babcock's veto. The nurses' collective bargaining bill, vocational education, and sixteen other bills met the same fate. The governor's attitude toward the legislature was one of continuous pain and surprise. He seemed affronted by our very presence in Helena, and scolded us almost daily for doing nothing—and for passing so much ruinous legislation. It is one of the strange contradictions of Montana politics that the state sends Mike Mansfield to the U.S. Senate, yet elects a governor who could not bring himself to proclaim UN Day, and was, until the chances looked bad, a proud supporter of Goldwater.

The fight over the minimum-wage law was the bitterest political battle of the session. Montana has no general minimum-wage law, and a modest proposal to start with one dollar raised howls of pain from small restaurant and grocery owners, some of them members of the assembly. The wage picture is chaotic. The scale for plumbers is $4.75 an hour, while a mechanic may get as little as $1.50 from a farm-implement dealer. Retail clerks in the variety stores average 80 cents an hour; unskilled workers in hospitals get 75 cents. Farmhands, unorganized and often itinerant, were until recently among our poorest-paid workers, but the elimination of the Mexican braceros has improved this area.

Everyone agreed that a minimum-wage law was a fine thing, in principle, but everyone seemed to have a friend whose business would be ruined by it. The lawyer for the Yellowstone Park Company pleaded that a dollar an hour would be disastrous, and anyway the college students had so much fun making beds and waiting on tables and seeing the park from the hotel windows that they shouldn't expect an exorbitant reward in cash. This company and Glacier Park Inc. have guaranteed monopolies largely because the National Park Service doesn't want to bother with more than one concessionaire in each park. Students work an eight-hour day, receive about $100 a month, and pay room and board out of that.

Many a legislative debate found safe harbor in watering holes such as Tracy's on Helena's Last Chance Gulch. (Courtesy of Tom Mulvaney)

While the minimum-wage bill was being dragged in and out of committee, debated on the floor, fought over in caucuses and bars, Mel Engels, the Republican State Chairman, rode it daily in his radio talks, calling it the baby-sitters' bill and making a mountain lion out of what appeared to be a pretty tame house cat. When the bill reached the Senate so many exceptions had been tacked on that it was scarcely even a gesture. The last straw, for the chairman of the Senate Labor Committee, was the exemption of employers in towns of under 2,500 population. He moved to table the bill.

WHERE DO WE GET THE MONEY?

The governor's budget included $17 million for a building program for the institutions and the university system. There was little doubt that even more was needed. The geology and physics buildings at the University of Montana (Missoula), housing over $1.5 million in equipment and collections, were declared unsafe more than twenty years ago. The prison, built in 1869, has never had any major improvements. The correctional school for boys and the home for the mentally deficient are overcrowded and outmoded. Everybody wanted help. The question was how much help we could give, and where we would get the money.

The battle over money for the institutions centered around Francis Bardanouve, husky rancher from Blaine County, and chairman of Appropriations. He takes a passionate interest in our neglected custodial centers. He appeared one afternoon at the state hospital, said he would like to look around. When he didn't come back to say goodbye, the administration was puzzled. Next morning they discovered he had set up camp in a vacant room and had no immediate plans for leaving. He stayed a week, studying the hospital, the prison, and the other nearby institutions.

Usually gentle and forbearing—Bardanouve can't vote to put an animal on the predatory list—he was not so gentle when he faced the minority after their plea for a suddenly generous building and repair program. "The institutions have been living on jackrabbits for decades," he declared, "but it's only when a Democratic majority can take the blame for increased taxes that we got these crocodile tears from the Republicans over their sorry state." Right here a split developed in the Democratic majority. Haunted by past experience, a block of Democrats opposed any increase in taxes, no matter how worthy the cause, but finally members willing to run the risk of defeat in the next election prevailed.

Experienced members deplored these caucus fights, but as a freshman I found them exciting, revealing, useful. In anger there is frankness. Of course the divisions were an embarrassment to the leadership. The Democrats were much harder to hold in line than the Republicans; they had a plethora of generals. During one caucus an aggressive member commanded, "Watch me on the floor." The leader asked with a rueful smile, "What about me?"

It is important for a new member to size up quickly these jockeying prima donnas, decide who can be trusted on taxation, education, conservation, etc. No one is equipped to judge more than six hundred bills in sixty days, and if you don't want to make an ass of yourself you'd better locate the experienced and reliable minds. You must learn to discount charm—and also the lack of it.

In spite of all our difficulties, a quantity of progressive legislation went through both houses. A mental-health center was allocated $1,300,000. Kerr-Mills had no opposition. Vocational education was to be expanded. Driver education carried its own revenue provision—a tax on traffic fines and 5 percent of drivers' license fees—but nearly everything else required a slice of the budget, and one of the largest slices was increased state aid to schools.

There was general agreement we would have to raise more money. The question was, how?

The Republicans, led by the governor, wanted a $5 tax on every individual income tax return, even if the return called for a refund, plus the use of an existing cigarette tax to finance the building program. The cigarette tax had been imposed to pay for veterans' bonuses, and the Democrats argued that it was illegal to divert it to a new use without the permission of the voters. Eventually both houses agreed to a modest increase in the individual income tax, and earmarked 5 percent of the income tax and corporation license tax revenues to a long-range building program.

The debate on money raising was bitter and hard to endure because it came at the end of the session. We were by that time working seven days a week, taking an hour off for dinner, and coming back in the evening.

"Why doesn't somebody say how much we need, so we'll know what tax increases have to be put through?" I asked an old-timer. For answer I got a tolerant smile, and at the last I understood that these pragmatic approximations are inevitable because no one knows until the closing days what the session will vote for, either in taxes or appropriations. To the committees in charge it must be like preparing dinner for an unknown number of guests from an unstipulated quantity of roast.

Tempers flared occasionally, attention lagged sometimes, especially in the late afternoon, and the assembly had moods, like a person. There were moments when almost anything would go through, and moments when nothing would. Late one afternoon a bill to make possible the investment of state funds in common stocks went over to final reading without debate, had to be hastily hauled back later.

Each of us had his own private anguish. The afternoon I climbed the stairs to a gloomy committee room on the balcony to defend my billboard-regulation bill I found forty outdoor admen from all over the state. It was not David meeting Goliath; it was the lamb chop meeting the wolf.

I noticed, as the weeks went by, how much I had to learn, particularly as a member of the State Administration Committee. We studied the fees and duties of architects, the regulation of well drillers, new concepts in mental health, Montana's ailing exhibit at the World's Fair. I discovered for myself the massive bureaucracy of the highway department, almost a fourth branch of government, so well nourished as to be largely independent of public opinion. This fat in a lean state budget is laid on by our assumption that all gasoline taxes must go to the highway department. Montanans never complain about the cost of roads. We love distance, the moving landscape seen from a fast heavy car. We still drive four hundred miles just to have lunch;

our fishing and hunting enthusiasts, as well as the ranchers, want good roads. Now and then a brave but foolish legislator starts an investigation of the highway department, usually the payments for right-of-way, begins with headlines, subsides into the back pages like a damp firecracker.

It Was Not All Grim Toil

Although there was scarcely a night when I didn't go to sleep thinking about a bill, and wake up to think about it again, there were entertainments and sideshows. Each big lobby gave us a dutiful dinner, but the Helena people, old hands at this business, gave us the sort of soothing evenings we needed, like the one at Henry Loble's amusing old Victorian house. We were always fed roast beef, as if they feared our blood count was down. At Henry's, amidst the flowers and soft lights, as at every other, we talked about bills.

Some of the entertainment required more patience than a committee hearing. I think we all hated the sound of the human voice after the first week, and one or two parties included speeches. Then there was the ordeal of the governor's ball. Shy wives worried over what to wear, but experience showed that the best costume would have been a coating of Havoline 20 to facilitate passage through the crowd. We had our orders—senators to the north and representatives to the south end of the ballroom, for the Grand March. A baffled milling about took up the time before the governor and his lady arrived. The music began. The men believed that to a march, one marched. The ladies preferred to walk. The effect was lumpy.

Along with the other entertainment should be included a maneuver of the governor's. He had, during the final days, become so disenchanted with us, so anxious to have us gone, that he must have decided to pretend we were no longer there. He sent his veto of a minor bill to the secretary of state rather than to the speaker. Rage and threats from the Democrats, hasty telephoning by the Republicans, and just before midnight the bill was exhumed from the secretary's office and rushed to the House.

Gusts of humor helped us through some heavy days in the chamber. After he had explained a bill, Francis Bardanouve told us, "Now, if you're not confused you haven't been listening."

Vivid figures walked on and off stage. Our chief clerk, holding a long cigar and wearing vestments of hunting red or Good Humor white, leaned on the podium and let us know what he thought of our votes when he intoned the count. The speaker displayed a passionate and inexplicable interest in daylight saving time for Butte.

Two ex-governors were busy in the corridors—John Bonner and J. Hugo Aronson, the affable Swede who came to Montana as a boy on a freight train and prospered in the oil fields around Cut Bank. Aronson told me with a twinkle, "Old Governors don't just fade away, they become lobbyists."

There were a few sideshows put on by alcoholic or amorous members, but the legislature is much less a holiday from marriage than it was in the old days when a few earnest souls carried on the business while the rest drank and roared in the lobby and the hospitality rooms. Now the wives come along, bring their knitting, sit on the leather lounges on either side of the House and listen to their husbands' speeches, take them to task later for what they said or didn't say. It is a domestic, carefully watched scene. There are always schoolchildren and voters from home in the gallery. This tends to make the sessions a good deal more businesslike.

Is It·Moribund?

As soon as I began to campaign I saw the legislator as a sort of meat grinder or Univac, into which are fed the demands and complaints of the citizens, and out of which is supposed to come something useful in the form of law. The legislator is a mediator, a listener, an adjuster. He discovers sores, needs, inequities he had no idea existed. Who is to act on these frictions if not the legislature? Shall we dump all the business of fifty states in the lap of Congress, ask the Senate to decide, while it is debating foreign policy, whether Fish and Game or the Highway Department shall supervise Montana parks?

There has been some harsh talk about state legislatures, some students of the system stating flatly that they are "dead and ripe for burying." [2] This blanket condemnation, it seems to me, is unrealistic. The things these gentlemen find wrong with the state legislature are the things that are exasperating in the democratic process wherever we study it—the snail's pace, the trial and error, the wrong decisions made because their proponents have the gift of persuasion, the occasional corruption. These flaws are the inevitable lice on the hide of democracy. Shall we butcher the beast to get rid of the lice?

If we throw out the state legislature, we lose more than its lawmaking function. As national legislation is on the whole more progressive than state legislation, so I believe state legislation is more progressive than local thinking. It is largely because of the crusty viewpoint of

---

2. *Newsweek*, April 19, 1965.

some of our city fathers that we have burdened the legislature with such matters as city salaries and pensions, air pollution, safety in swimming pools. Further, during the session a legislator learns where his state stands in the national picture—is it above or below the national average in income, education, institutional methods, economic growth? He must indicate, by his vote, what he believes should be done about the shortcomings. A live legislative session helps a state to reconcile its thinking and its aims with national thinking and national aims.

The assembly serves to reveal to the state its pockets of eccentric opinion. In this session there were ultraconservatives who professed a fierce allegiance to states' rights, but given the power they would have made state government impossible because they were never *for* anything. They voted No except on small favors for their own counties. They were full of fears, especially of federal aid, which they saw as the cheese in the trap of federal control. Less timorous members argued that we are entitled to all the federal aid that's going because we educate most of our young people for export to other states.

I should not like to see any state legislature disappear, but in Montana where the sparse population is divided by miles of mountains, this is a forum, a battleground, a town meeting we must have. Its creaking machinery, its tedious debate, its insane rush at the end, may impede but do not cancel its primary function, which is to voice and deal with the stresses and the needs of the people of Montana. In our state, the legislature is very much alive.

The Origins of
Twenty-first-Century
Montana

Harry W. Fritz

The present, someone once said, is the point where the future pauses
and becomes the past. For historians, this means that the contemporary era, and even the future, are no less important, no less "graphically historical," than the distant past. The purpose of history, after
all, is to explain who we are, how we got that way, and where we are
going. No one can accurately predict the future, but predictions are
always based on history.

All this is to justify the following article, which holds that contemporary Montana, the period since 1965, is just as important, as
transformational, as the more heralded and more intensively inves-
tigated periods of Montana's more remote past. Indeed, since most
people live in the here and now, not the there and then, the present
and the future are more significant in their lives. In the period since
1965, and continuing today, Montanans have been buffeted by economic and political upheavels incompletely understood as they happened. Today, as always, the state is poised at the present, between
past and future. A sense of history, even contemporary history, will
help chart an achievable future.

History is the study of the past, but not for the past's own sake.
Historians are not antiquarians. Only if we utilize the past to
comprehend the present and engage the future is its study worth-

*Harry W. Fritz, "The Origins of Twenty-first-Century Montana," *Montana The
Magazine of Western History*, 42 (Winter 1992), 77–81.

The September 18, 1982, demolition of the smokestack in Great Falls marked the failure of the Anaconda Minerals Division of Atlantic Richfield, which had closed the copper smelter in 1980. (Steve Velaski, photographer, courtesy of the Great Falls Tribune)

while. As always, Montana is at a crossroads, poised between past and future. But today's roads are perhaps more crossed than usual, and they point in new directions. Here is one historian's view of where we have been, and where we may be going.

Between 1965 and 1980, Montana pursued a triple revolution: political, economic, and ideological. Politically, the revolution began with legislative reapportionment and culminated in the new state constitution of 1972. The census of 1960 revealed that for the first time in its history Montana was an urban state. More than half of its people lived in cities and towns. Montana's cities aren't very large by national standards, and an awful lot of empty land lies between them, but the statistics do not lie: about 52 percent of all Montanans are urban residents.

Yet Montana's political system had been designed in 1889 for a rural polity. The "little federal" system of representation gave each county one senator and at least one representative in the state legislature. With the expansion over time of the number of counties from thirteen to fifty-six a once-equitable system got completely out of whack. Montana was one of the most malapportioned states in the union. At a time when half of the state's people lived in just seven urban counties, a minority controlled seven-eights (87.5 percent) of the state senate. Senators representing just 16 percent of the people constituted a legislative majority. Apportionment rested on the time-honored formula of "one cow, one vote."

Montana's political revolution began with federally mandated legislative reapportionment. In *Baker v. Carr* (1962) and *Reynolds v. Sims* (1964) the United States Supreme Court held that state assemblies must represent people, not trees or acres. Under threat of district court action Governor Tim Babcock agreed: "the theory of 'one person, one vote' simply does not fit Montana," he informed the 1965 Legislature. But the "rotten-borough" representatives refused to apportion themselves out of their jobs, so the court, citing "invidious discrimination" against the more populous counties, did it for them. Each county could retain one senator only if the senate itself were enlarged to 754 members! Judicial apportionment was more moderate, but for the first time since 1889 political power fell into line with residence. The revolution shifted political strength from farms to towns, from the wide-open spaces to the widely scattered cities, from cows to people.

Reapportionment occurred again in 1971 and 1974 as part of ongoing constitutional reform. As in thirty-three other states, the process triggered revision of fundamental law; Montana went the whole way and adopted a brand new constitution in 1972. The new document capped a period of intensive review begun by the reapportioned 1967

Legislature. A 1970 referendum, "For Calling A Constitutional Convention," passed with 65 percent of the vote. One hundred delegates, elected in November 1971, convened in Helena in early 1972. Their handiwork was ratified by a razor-thin popular margin in June.

The Montana Constitution of 1972 was an environmentally conscious monument to a modern, urban, self-confident state emerging from the long shadow of the Anaconda Company. Although only twelve counties supported ratification, they contained 55 percent of the total population and eight of the ten largest cities. City voters liked the provisions for single-member legislative districts, the liberalized procedures for direct legislation, the open-meeting requirements, and the protection given environmentalism. Symbolically as well as substantively, the state's new constitution defined modern Montana.

As much as anything, concern for what the constitution called "a clean and healthful environment" set the new Montana apart from the old. Springing from both national concerns and local threats, environmentalism scored major legislative victories in the 1970s. Montanans sought not so much to clean up pockets of pollution as to prevent future degradation. The state's greatest resources, it appeared, were clean air and water, unspoiled forests, and wide-open spaces. Farsightedly, the state slapped a 30 percent severance tax on the contract price of strip-mined coal and used the proceeds to promote economic growth and development over the long haul.

Montana also experienced fundamental economic transformations after 1965. Every one of its basic primary industries was radically altered. In the West the timber industry found itself constrained by recessions, high interest rates, and environmental restrictions. Retrenchment ended the diversification that had added pulp, plywood, and formaldehyde factories to the wood products repertoire. Both the cutting rate on public lands and the work force edged downward. In Butte, the once mighty Anaconda Company ceased to exist. Beset by foreign troubles, the loss of its market, and a declining price for copper, Anaconda sold out to the Atlantic Richfield Corporation in 1976. By 1983 ARCO had shut down all its mining and smelting operations in Montana.

On the plains of eastern Montana, however, business was booming. Farmers set all-time records for the yield per acre and the price per bushel of wheat. OPEC—the Organization of Petroleum Exporting Countries—sent the price of gas and oil skyrocketing and spurred the search for these suddenly elusive resources. New uses for coal, particularly in electrical generating plants, expanded Montana's production by a whopping 8,927 percent between 1967 and 1979. The 1970s was Montana's decade of coal, measured by production, taxes, and the size of the Coal Tax Trust Fund established in 1976.

In the mid-1970s the three great revolutions of modern Montana coalesced. A spirited and progressive legislature, confronting both the promise and the threat of coal mining, set down basic environmental conditions for further development. Steady economic progress is encouraged; environmental quality is protected. All Montanans share this vision of sound public policy. Even the Montana Mining Association, given to shrill denunciations of "no-growth obstructionists," applauds a middle ground that will allow economic growth while protecting the environment.

The years from 1965 to 1980 were both pivotal and prosperous for Montana. Not since the 1880s, when railroads, copper, cattle, and statehood propelled Montana, had changes of such magnitude occurred. The future paid well. Per capita income, steadily falling with respect to national levels since World War II, reached a nadir in 1969 and rebounded to a respectable 96 percent of the national average—highest in twenty-four years—in 1973. Three years earlier in 1970, unemployment bottomed out at 4.3 percent, lowest since 1957, and the fifteen-year average was 5.3 percent. Severance taxes, based on the value not the quantity of resource production, returned unexpected riches to the state. The triple revolution, it seemed—political, economic, and ideological—was good for business.

The world caved in, however, in the decade of the 1980s. A sudden and steep depression simultaneously attacked all aspects of Montana society. Every component of the Montana economy suffered. The state lost 13,000 primary jobs. Per capita income dipped to 79 percent of the national average—an all-time low. Unemployment rose to 8.8 percent in 1983—a record high. The population spurt of the 1970s, during which Montana grew at a rate higher than the national average for the first time in six decades, slowed during the early 1980s, stopped, then abruptly retrograded, costing the state a congressman after the 1990 census reapportionment. Tax revenues shriveled; state and local governments faced permanent shortfalls; and funding of essential public services, including education, fell far below standards.

Consider the components of the crisis: In 1980 the Anaconda Minerals Division of Atlantic Richfield shut down its copper smelters in Anaconda and Great Falls, eliminating more than a thousand Montana jobs. Less than three years later, precisely a century after Marcus Daly transformed Anaconda, ARCO pulled the plug on the Berkeley Pit in Butte. The nerve center of the Montana economy slowly filled with toxic wastewater. What was the Treasure State without copper?

Montana's timber industry, extremely susceptible to national economics, was felled by the recession of 1982–1983. Since then markets are down, milling capacity is up, and structural changes, primarily the shift to small-diameter logs, have all cost jobs and lowered wages. As the United States Forest Service reduces the allowable cut on public lands, and as private companies log timber at twice the growth rate, the future availability of an adequate supply of sawlogs is in serious doubt. "The wood products industry," opines the *Missoulian*, "is in the midst of industrial Darwinism, a life-and-death struggle where only the fittest will survive." [1]

The 1980s was no time to be a farmer. Montana graingrowers lost their export market after the 1980 embargo and they have not regained it. A searing mid-decade drought, the worst since the 1930s, reduced agricultural income to negative numbers. A national debt and credit crisis forced hundreds of marginal operators off the land. Commodity prices remain low. Ranchers watch disbelievingly as per capita consumption of red meat declines annually. Pigeons were better off than farmers in the 1980s because they could still place a small deposit on a piece of machinery.

When oil sold for $40 a barrel, Montana's energy industry boomed and its coffers overflowed. Now oil is less than $20 a barrel. When coal production increased from 364,509 tons to 32,538,792 tons per year between 1967 and 1979, the future seemed limitless. Since then, coal production has averaged barely 30 million tons per year. Montana is a victim of the international energy glut. Saudi Arabian oil is far cheaper, and the market for Montana coal is limited by distance and railroad rates.

The Great 1980s Depression exposed the fatal flaw in the modern Montana economy: a dangerous fault line running across the economic spectrum. Technological improvements in every one of the state's bedrock industries have simultaneously enhanced productivity and profits and reduced jobs and income. Montana Resources in Butte is hauling as much copper ore as Anaconda/ARCO once did, but with one-fifth the labor force. The wood products industry is down nearly two thousand jobs with more to go. General Mills in Great Falls increased its productivity by 28 percent—and cut its work force by 33 percent. A record year for coal production in 1988 was achieved with one-half the number of miners employed just seven years earlier. The list goes on, in every one of the basic, primary, extractive industries that have hitherto sustained Montana. But this traditional economic base will no longer suffice. Even a modest recovery will not translate into prosperity because industry does more with less.

The number one public concern in Montana, especially in election years, is jobs—or the lack of jobs. Each year hundreds of Montana

---

1. *Missoulian*, April 23, 1989.

high school and college graduates leave the state in search of employment. Job creation is the goal of every measure intended to spur
economic growth and development. But there are no easy answers.
Structural changes in international manufacturing and trade place
Montana at a permanent disadvantage. Montana's inability to generate
employment opportunities commensurate with its population is
inherent in an economy based on the extraction of natural resources.
With this depressing bottom line, Montana faces an uncertain future.

Montana in the 1980s proved unable to address this situation forth-
rightly. The state's politics were bitterly partisan, extremely com-
petitive, and legislatively truncated. Montana has not enjoyed a
period of one-party supremacy since the exceptional era of Democratic dominance in the mid-1970s. That unusual eruption was fueled
by urbanization, reapportionment, the Constitution of 1972, and
political fallout from a sales tax debate and the Watergate scandal.
Unusual economic prosperity and a rising environmental tide also
contributed to Democratic fortunes. But the political revolution of
contemporary Montana is history; now it's politics as usual. No governor has enjoyed a partisan majority in both houses of the legislature
since Tom Judge in 1975. Across six legislative sessions, 1979 to 1989,
the voters returned 450 Democrats to Helena—and 450 Republicans.
Throughout the 1980s one United States congressman was Democratic, one Republican; after 1988, the Senate, too, was divided. No
closer, more evenly balanced political system existed in America.

Less well understood are the costs of this political stasis: stalemate,
inaction, and the postponement of critical decisions. Persistent incre-
mentalism produces disaffection and resentment and encourages
irresponsible direct democracy. Already Montana has barely weath-
ered a potentially devastating property tax revolt; its educational institutions are badly underfunded; and laissez-faire economics leads
unerringly to corporate domination. The unfinished agenda demands assertive leadership, constructive persuasion, and a healthy
supply of political courage.

The new Montana of the 1990s will in some ways resemble the
old, and already there are signs of a modest recovery in traditional
industries. Two years after ARCO threw in the towel, Dennis Washington's Montana Resources began mining copper in Butte's East Pit.
A number of gold mines employing the cyanide heap-leaching
process, enormously profitable but environmentally devastating, dot
the state. Montana *grows* 1.3 billion board feet of wood annually; that
fact assures a permanent timber industry. Farmers experiment with
new and profitable crops, such as mint in the Flathead; they continue to roll the dice for the double winners of ample rainfall and
high commodity prices. Sooner or later a new energy crunch will

help; meanwhile, Montana's low-sulphur coal remains cost-effective in midwestern markets. So far, the old order survives. But the new Montana cannot be restructured along traditional lines. A resource/extraction economy is no longer dependable. What should Montana do?

Montana must create its own manufacturing base and encourage a "value-added" marketing economy. There are sound historical reasons why the state has not pursued a manufacturing option, and they are linked to its corporate past. When in 1923 Anaconda Copper purchased the American Brass and Foundry Corporation, with its plants located in Connecticut and New Jersey, the future was clear: there was no need to build such plants here. Corporate investment in Montana had benefits, but this was not one of them.

Economists tell us that two ingredients create a dynamic economy: the ability, first, to make things, and then second, to sell them. Montana does little of either. Its raw materials are extracted and peddled without much intermediate processing. Eighty percent of the timber cut, for example, is simply sawed into dimension lumber and studs and sold out of state.

A jump-started manufacturing economy requires applied research, technology transfers, market and feasibility studies, business plans, and capital formation. The ideas are out there in a host of economic analyses, state development policies, and remanufacturing studies. They must be appropriated and applied systematically in Montana. They can be. Already the wave of the future is here in the form of the Science and Technology Alliance established by the 1985 Legislature—the single most creative, productive, and portentous act of public policy in the decade. The alliance supports businesses using new or "high" technologies with loans and subsidies. It has created "Centers of Excellence" at units of the university, which conduct research into new uses for wood, metal, and agricultural products.

Montana must enlarge and enhance its nascent travel and recreation industry, for in this regard it is the most underdeveloped state in the nation. For too long the state has relied on the federal government to promote tourism by pitching the national parks and the Custer battlefield. A sales tax on motel rooms enacted in 1987 helps to promote Montana, but that is not enough. A modern travel economy is geared to development. It requires investment and a good telecommunications network. The list of destination points which might be touted—from Absarokee to Zortman—is endless.

Montana must also encourage what is already its top-ranked industry as measured by total income—the "transfer industry" of pensions, retirements, rents and royalties, and Social Security payments—all new money coming into the state and spent here by residents. The transfer industry compels a new look at the old cracked whip eco-

A hiker looks north into the Rocky Mountain Front Range in the Bob Marshall Wilderness, a premier example of the pristine Montana environment conservationists hope to preserve. (Courtesy of Bob Cooney)

nomic interpretation of Joseph Kinsey Howard and K. Ross Toole. It also suggests ways of expanding the economy, primarily via tax policies and environmental preservation.

In the final analysis "a clean and healthful environment" is Montana's greatest asset. Already people are moving here for non-traditional, non-economic reasons. They are attracted particularly to the counties of western Montana, not especially noted of late for their dynamic, expanding, labor-intensive economies. Who are they? Without much hard data to go by, suppositions include retirees, small-business people, students, granolas. Surprisingly, for the first time in the modern era, the fastest growing cohort consists of young adults, aged 20 to 39. Why are they coming? For scenery, recreation, education, residential privacy, safety, and cultural amenities—qualities in short supply in much of America but readily available in Montana.

As always, the future beckons Montana, but it will not be the same as the past. More and more Americans are finding it possible to separate their residence from their workplace. Computer technology will allow twenty-first century Montanans to be employed by a big-city firm while living here. "There are really no geographic restrictions," says one recent refugee from Tacoma, Washington. "With a FAX and modem, you can be anywhere." [2] Montana is poised to overcome its greatest historical economic disadvantages—long distances, high transportation rates, and the social costs of space. For if "you can be anywhere," why not be here?

---

2. Ibid., September 29, 1991.

Richard Mulligan portrays Custer in Little Big Man *(Cinema Center Films, 1970).* (Courtesy of Paul Andrew Hutton)

EPILOGUE
Of Bullets, Blunders, and Custer Bluffs

Brian W. Dippie

In the following essay, academic historian Brian W. Dippie, professor of history in the University of Victoria, British Columbia, examines the important role that history buffs — or amateur historians — play in defining the study of history. History buffs, generally known for their single-mindedness and passion for their subject, are found in nearly all areas of American history — from colonial history to Civil War history to the history of sports. But few fields have attracted more history buffs over the years than that of the American West. The sense of adventure inherent in western history, often conjuring images of fur trappers, miners, cowboys, and pitched military battles on the Great Plains, has been a natural draw for amateur and professional historian alike.

We often assume that important topics or issues in history are self-evident. Yet, what a society, or a group of authors, chooses to focus on as history often tells us more about contemporary society than it does about the past itself. By examining the past in a selective fashion, a society may use historical events and figures to reinforce certain cultural values. For many people, for example, western history seems to epitomize wide-open spaces, rugged individualism, mobility (both personal and economic), and, above all else, courage.

What accounts then for the enduring fascination of the battle in southeastern Montana in June 1876 known as Custer's Last Stand?

*Brian W. Dippie, "Of Bullets, Blunders, and Custer Buffs," *Montana The Magazine of Western History*, 41 (Winter 1991), 76–80.

In early 1991, debate exploded over a proposed Indian memorial on the battlefield, over changing the name from Custer Battlefield National Monument to Little Bighorn Battlefield National Monument, and over whether Custer's bones or those of an imposter rest beneath his tombstone at West Point in New York. The tabloid newspaper, the *Sun*, claimed that George Armstrong Custer survived the Last Stand and died in Canada in 1906! All this as if the fight had occurred in the previous year instead of more than a century ago. Dippie suggests that because we will never know exactly what happened on the bluffs above the Little Bighorn River south of modern-day Hardin, we will be forever trying to figure it out.

Moreover, Dippie's essay shows that how we choose to define historical significance may help to explain why it is that the Battle of the Little Bighorn has attracted such extraordinary attention over the years, while an equally tragic event occurring in Montana—the 1870 Baker Massacre that took 173 innocent lives—has been all but forgotten.

A buff, according to the *American Heritage Dictionary*, is "one who is enthusiastic and knowledgeable about a given subject." A Civil War buff, for example, or a Custer buff. Custer buff—it seems the perfect partnership. How else to explain that preternatural hold Custer has had on certain people since he went down in a blaze of glory—and controversy—nearly 115 years ago?

Of course the public knows of Custer's Last Stand in that same vague, mildly curious way it knows of other legendary episodes in the nation's past. Most people can still see the battle in their minds, thanks to old barroom prints and Errol Flynn movies, and they may entertain an opinion (usually negative) on Custer himself. The Custer buff is something else again. From the details of what happened to the countless speculations about why, he (and most are he's) simply cannot get enough.

Assigning responsibility for the outcome of the Battle of the Little Bighorn is a critical buff task, central to the Great Custer Debate. The Indians cannot be the reason for Custer's defeat, a premise reflecting the biases of 1876 (Indians were thought to be backward savages who could be brushed aside at whim) and the fact that most Custer buffs are military historians, far more comfortable working with white sources than with Indian testimony. Custer's Last Stand is a white preoccupation, and a white man must be held accountable. But who? *Who was to blame* for Custer's Last Stand?

Interpretations generally indict one of four men: Custer (rash, impetuous, vainglorious, he disobeyed orders, attacked prematurely, split his command in the face of an unknown enemy, and doomed it to death); Major Marcus Reno and/or Captain Frederick Benteen (through Reno's cowardice and Benteen's malice, they failed to carry out Custer's orders and deserted him on the field of battle, precipitating tragedy); the expedition commander, General Alfred Terry (inexperienced in Indian-fighting and knowing neither the size nor exact location of the enemy, he devised a coordinated strategy impossible of execution and then, when disaster followed, defended himself by scapegoating the dead).

Custer buffs traditionally divide into pro- and anti-Custer factions. Recently, perhaps because Custer's popular reputation has been so negative, most have been his ardent champions. For the buff, partisanship is not something to be avoided; it is to be worn as a badge of honor and proudly proclaimed. This implies a selective use of evidence, but then objectivity has no place in a war. We know who won in 1876; what concerns the buff is who wins in 1991.

The obsessive, internalized nature of buff history and its almost perverse disregard for larger historical significance repel most academics, who approach the latest Custer book as though it were tainted, sniffing suspiciously before proceeding to slash and burn. (The buffs get their revenge whenever academics stray onto their turf. Those who condemn them for knowing a great deal about very little, they love to note, seem to know very little about a great deal.)

Anyway, buffs do not write for academics, they write for one another, and are published by specialist presses, or themselves. It is an honorable tradition. The best-known Custer writers of an earlier generation—E. A. Brininstool, William A. Graham, Fred Dustin, Charles Kuhlman—were self-published at least some of the time. Even Robert M. Utley, who cut his teeth on Custer, first broke into print with a pamphlet bearing the no-nonsense title *Custer's Last Stand* "Copyright 1949 by the Author." *That* should give heart to the many self-published Custer buffs who hold Utley in highest esteem. A prince of Custer buffs, the late John M. Carroll, included a *Robert M. Utley Bibliographic Checklist* among his scores of publications; like many of the rest, it was published by J. M. Carroll & Company. Private publication makes sense. Occasionally a title takes off—James Willert's *Little Big Horn Diary* (1977) comes to mind—but most buff books are printed in editions of a few hundred copies for an audience targeted through groups like the Little Big Horn Associates and the Custer Battlefield Historical and Museum Association.

Buff literature is not intended for the general reader either, any more than a popular history like Larry Underwood's *The Custer Fight and Other Tales of the Old West* is intended for the buff. Underwood's book tells an old story without adding anything new. It does, however, serve as an introduction to issues and personalities that intrigue the buff in mini-essays on the likes of Custer, Reno, and Lonesome Charley Reynolds, which open on the day of battle, then pull back for the overview. Apparently not trusting his material to sustain enough interest, Underwood peppers his prose with exclamation marks—cavalry! Indians! blood and gore!

Nevertheless, his book is entertaining, and just may persuade a casual reader to delve deeper, perhaps into Richard Upton's compilation, *The Custer Adventure*. First published in 1975 and now reissued, it narrates the Custer portion of the 1876 Sioux Expedition through the accounts of actual participants. In the give-and-take of diverse voices, recollecting and ordering experience is the essence of the Great Debate. Passersby should be forewarned: beyond *The Custer Adventure* lies Graham's classic *The Custer Myth: A Source Book of Custeriana* (1953), and beyond it, addiction.

The hardcore Custer buff is a junkie. Thus, that incessant activity, that poring over maps and retracing marches and pacing the ground and digging beneath it, that snooping into the careers and habits of every officer who served in the Seventh Cavalry, that fascination with the horses they rode and the dogs they loved and with their families, of course, and the graves scattered across the land marking their final resting places, and with the enlisted personnel who served that day, their backgrounds, their aliases, the color of their eyes, and the particulars of their equipment, and all the rest of Custeriana.

This obsession with minutiae, the despair of academic historians, is the definition of buffdom. Maybe the next new fact will be the key that unlocks the mystery of Custer's Last Stand. The enormous premium placed on novelty helps explain why Utley's much-praised Custer biography *Cavalier in Buckskin* (1988), a History Book Club and Book of the Month Club selection, did not win the Little Big Horn Associates' literary award for 1988. Utley offered a masterful synthesis; the book that won, however, was Roger Darling's *Custer's Seventh Cavalry Comes to Dakota*, which offered "significant and extensive new information about Custer and the Seventh Cavalry." One cannot argue with the "new"—no one else has written a monograph on the Seventh's 1873 transfer to Dakota Territory—but "significant"?

Darling's first Custer book, *Benteen's Scout-to-the-Left—the Route from the Divide to the Morass (June 25, 1876)* (1987), was also narrowly focused. But with maps and photographs pinpointing Benteen's route, it contributed directly to the core debate over responsibility: What was Benteen doing while Reno was getting whipped in the valley and Custer was riding to disaster? *Custer's Seventh Cavalry Comes to Dakota* is another matter. It retraces a march on which, from any objective historical standpoint, nothing of significance happened.

*Indians draw their bows against Custer and the Seventh Cavalry troopers in a scene
from ABC's mini-series* Son of the Morning Star *(1991).* (Capital Cities/ABC, Inc.)

There were procedural disputes, to be sure, and personality clashes
and inclement weather. But *nothing happened.* Darling could play social
historian and make the transfer a case study in military routine;
instead, digging in unworked soil, he is content to turn up new facts
by the shovelful about individuals who would reassemble three years
later to fight a legendary battle. That is his contribution, and the
award from the Little Big Horn Associates suggests it is a worthy one,
proving that significance, like beauty, is in the eye of the beholder.

Besides assigning responsibility, the Custer buff wants to piece
together a satisfactory version of what happened on the Little Big
Horn. Because the battlefield remains relatively unchanged, it is the
starting point for all serious inquiry. Alas, Richard G. Hardorff
contends in *The Custer Battle Casualties: Burials, Exhumations, and
Reinterments* that the physical evidence is tainted. The tombstones supposedly marking where each man fell were too often randomly
placed, the skeletal remains too frequently moved about, to constitute
reliable evidence about troop dispositions and thus the sequence of
events that led to calamitous defeat.

A research essay posing as a book, *The Custer Battle Casualties*, is unburdened with speculations on responsibility, but goes beyond previous studies in systematically examining the disturbances of the soldiers' remains and the terrain itself on Custer Hill. Hardorff concludes that Custer's present marker designates the spot where he was first buried, not where he was found. That spot disappeared long ago when the hill was graded and the granite monument erected in 1881. Since positioning the key actors is everything in scripting plausible scenarios of what happened, this will interest Custer buffs. So will Hardorff's meticulous appendixes ("Anthology on the Dead"), compiling what is known about the fates and burials of individual officers, enlisted men, and civilians.

In *Custer, Cases & Cartridges: The Weibert Collection Analyzed*, Don Weibert does what Hardorff chooses not to do: he offers an interpretation of the fighting at the Little Big Horn based on the physical evidence that has excited the most interest of late, the cartridge cases that denote Indian and trooper positions during the battle. Weibert is not concerned with historical personalities. But he does speculate about the motives of those who have ignored or discredited the findings of his father, Henry Weibert, and dismissed him as a mere relic-hunter.

It is a classic buff set-up; the dedicated amateur versus the closed-shop professional establishment (historians, archaeologists, battlefield personnel), and was first elaborated in Henry Weibert's feisty, opinionated 1985 buff bestseller, *Sixty-six Years in Custer's Shadow*. Weibert, a local rancher who has pursued his investigations around the battlefield with a metal detector and determination since 1967, found evidence of a neglected Indian position (Weibert Ridge, his son calls it) that casts doubt on the official version of events.

Custer is commonly said to have reached the Little Big Horn River at Medicine Tail Coulee ford before retreating through a series of defensive maneuvers ending on Custer Hill. Weibert argued that Custer was actually on the offensive when he passed Medicine Tail Coulee a full mile from the river on a direct route to Custer Hill. From there he attempted an attack on the northern-most Indian village, advancing parallel to Deep Ravine before he was turned back, disaster following. Weibert concluded that Custer was fatally wounded in this action, and his body transported to the Last Stand position on Custer Hill.

Theories like this always intrigue the Custer buff, and Weibert in *Sixty-six Years* claimed to have the archaeological evidence to support them, including some distinctive casings he had found and assumed to be Custer's own ("the Custer Brass"). The major report from the archaeological surveys sanctioned by the Custer Battlefield in 1984 and 1985, *Archaeological Perspectives on the Battle of the Little Bighorn*

(1989), gave short shrift to Weibert's views but opened the way for a full presentation of his data.

Custer, Cases & Cartridges is the result. A large, oversized volume, it describes, illustrates, analyzes, and catalogs the hundreds of relics in the Weibert Collection. The interpretation section is still feisty, and there is a good deal of dueling with the "official" archaeologists. But the overall tone is conciliatory, and Don Weibert has backed off his father's more extreme positions on Medicine Tail Coulee, the Deep Ravine advance, the positive identification of the Custer Brass, and the worth of Indian testimony. This may disappoint buffs who relished Henry Weibert's Custer-like stance in *Sixty-six Years* as he defied the whole tribe of professional experts. Still, there is not a serious buff alive who will be able to resist *Custer, Cases & Cartridges*. It is essential grist for the mill.

Roger Darling's latest book gets "new" into the title— *A Sad and Terrible Blunder: General Terry and Custer at the Little Big Horn: New Discoveries*—but its data is encased in verbiage, and it does not have the evident appeal of Weibert's book. Most Custer buffs side with someone; Darling is a stern schoolmaster handing out critical reports on everybody's performance. Too, he dismisses the buff fascination with what happened at Custer's Last Stand as insignificant, all the elements ensuring defeat having been set into motion earlier by the command decisions that he prefers to analyze. His goal is to place the 1876 campaign in its strategic context by focusing on General Terry's role as coordinator and field commander. The series of maps correlating the marches and campsites, day by day, of the Montana Column under Terry and Colonel John Gibbon and the Dakota Column under Custer should delight every buff. But Darling also wants to write a biography of Terry, an unnecessary distraction.

Distracting also is Darling's theory concerning Custer's promise to support Reno. Custer's order directing Reno to charge the Indian village with the promise that he (Reno) would be supported by the whole outfit referred, according to Darling, not to the vast village on the Little Bighorn, but to a small party retreating in front of the calvary, "the fleeing lone tepee village band." Darling concludes from this that Custer had no justification in turning north to sup-port Reno's charge since he could not know there was a village in that direction.

Thus, theory feeds on theory, defying the logic of a campaign pre-dicated on the assumption that a sizable concentration of Indians would be located and must be contained. *A Sad and Terrible Blunder* is strongest when it sticks to the Montana Column's muddled advance to the Little Bighorn on June 24–25. Like previous students Darling blames faulty geographical knowledge and inadequate maps. And he adds a new wrinkle—an unwillingness to heed the intelligence provided by Indian scouts that made the "sad and terrible blunder" Terry's own.

W. Kent King goes further, much further, in *Massacre: The Custer Cover-Up*. General Terry, he argues, actually possessed excellent maps giving precise geographical information, a fact purposely suppressed as part of a top-level cover-up designed to shift responsibility for the disaster from Terry onto his dead subordinate. It is conspiracy theory time—and King has the tone just right. "A great many mouths must be kept shut for any such a cover-up to work." Some "must be silenced." There are "powerful forces" at work. Who? The FBI? The CIA? The President? Oops, wrong conspiracy, though this one, too, indicts a president for orchestrating a plot to set Custer up for failure. It goes as follows. President Ulysses Grant knew that Custer (a Democrat) could link him personally to the corruption in the War Department even then under investigation. As long as Custer was in the army there were constraints upon him; but in 1876 he had about decided to resign his commission and accept a lucrative offer to go on the public lecture circuit. Free to speak his mind, he would undoubtedly expose Grant before the world. And so the plot was set in motion. Custer on this, his last campaign, must be silenced through disgrace—or death. Terry's role was to issue contradictory written and verbal orders, putting Custer in a no-win situation that would ensure his court martial whatever he did. With his credibility destroyed, he could pose no threat to Grant.

But things went terribly wrong on the Little Big Horn and Custer's entire command perished, creating the potential for explosive recriminations. A cover-up was mandatory if high command was to escape criminal charges once the diabolical plot to embarrass Custer was exposed. The maps actually used by the military in 1876, geographically correct and reliable, proved the impossibility of Custer's orders and the fact that Terry's delays in getting to the Little Bighorn were not accidental at all. Terry had "deliberately shatter[ed]" his own battle plan in order to carry out the "premeditated destruction of another man's career."

All else follows. The maps went missing, replaced with bogus ones, and the lie was entrenched in history that geographical ignorance was a key factor in Custer's defeat. The Reno Court of Inquiry, convened in 1879, was a whitewash—perhaps half the testimony actually given disappeared from the official transcript. Thus were the careers of subordinates who had failed Custer at the Little Bighorn spared in the interests of higher-ups who had everything to lose if the truth inadvertently leaked out in the hearings.

Top-drawer coverups. Calculated scenarios of "disobedience and disgrace." Missing documents, only now surfacing through the sleuthing of a persistent few unwilling to accept history's version of events. Gaps in the record, inconsistencies, convenient memory lapses, stonewalling, silence. King dishes it all out with the breathless prose, insinuations, rhetorical questions, and heavy-handed ironies characteristic of conspiracy theories. When facts don't fit, discard them; when they nearly fit, pound on them until they do; and when they fit naturally, praise them for their daring honesty and repeat them as often as possible.

King's *Massacre* abides by this formula. It may not be for everybody, but it represents a contribution to the Great Debate more fun than most. Who can resist the image of swords crashing through reputations, of stones "deliberately aimed to distort the pool of history," of midnight plottings and creeping tendrils in the forest of facts that, skipped over by so-called authorities rushing to confirm what everybody knows, trip up the conscientious researcher, leading him into "a quagmire of confusion," then slowly, inexorably, to the monstrous truth at the root of the Custer mystery?

Buffs? Academic historians, especially in a field as sensitive of its professional stature as western history is, too often regard them as buffoons impeding serious historical inquiry. Better to see them as buffers between academic high seriousness and public indifference. They are in history for the love of it; the same amateur enthusiasm that keeps the Great Custer Debate going keeps history's torch alight.

Consider the love/hate relationship between the Custer buffs and the Custer Battlefield. An intense, unreasonable partisanship has led some buffs to make vitriolic personal attacks on battlefield staff over matters of interpretation and perceived bias. But an intense devotion to the subject also leads buffs to volunteer for archaeological digs and seasonal posts. Buffs spearhead the drive for funds to acquire additional land that will preserve the integrity of the battlefield site for future generations, serve on committees, attend conferences, present papers, lobby congressmen, and care. They can be peevish, mulish, and tiresomely obsessive. They can also be generous, receptive, and wonderfully informed, models of that enthusiasm and knowledge that define the buff everywhere. Let us salute them.

Books considered in this review essay include: Larry D. Underwood, *The Custer Fight and Other Tales of the Old West* (Lincoln, Nebraska: Media Publishing, 1989); Richard Upton, compiler, *The Custer Adventure: As Told by Its Participants* (El Segundo, Calif.: Upton and Sons, 1990); Roger Darling, *Custer's Seventh Cavalry Comes to Dakota: New Discoveries Reveal Custer's Tribulations Enroute to the Yellowstone Expedition* (Vienna, Va.: Potomac-Western Press, 1988); Richard G. Hardorff, *The Custer Battle*

Casualties: Burials, Exhumations, and Reinterments (El Segundo, Calif.: Upton and Sons, 1989); Don Weibert, *Custer, Cases & Cartridges: The Weibert Collection Analyzed* (Billings, Montana: Don Weibert, 1989); Roger Darling, *A Sad and Terrible Blunder: Generals Terry and Custer at the Little Big Horn: New Discoveries* (Vienna, Va.: Potomac-Western Press, 1990); W. Kent King, *Massacre: The Custer Cover-Up: The Original Maps of Custer's Battlefield* (El Segundo, Calif.: Upton & Sons, 1989).

About the Authors

MINERVA ALLEN is a school administrator at Hayes, Montana. She has written several books that translate Indian history and folklore into English, and she has published two books of her own poetry, including *Spirits at Rest* (1981).

COLIN G. CALLOWAY has taught in England, New England, and Wyoming. Before moving to the University of Wyoming in 1987, he was editor/assistant director of the D'Arcy McNickle Center for the History of the American Indian at the Newberry Library in Chicago. Although he has written several articles on northern plains Indian history, he tends to concentrate on eastern tribes. His books include *Crown and Calumet: British-Indian Relations, 1783–1815* (1987); *The Western Abenakis of Vermont, 1600–1800: War, Migration, and the Survival of an Indian People* (1990); and *Dawnland Encounters: Indians and Europeans in Northern New England* (editor, 1991). He is working on a book about American Indians during the American Revolution.

THOMAS A. CLINCH did his undergraduate work at Carroll College in Helena, Montana, and received his Ph.D. in history from the University of Oregon. Prior to his death in 1971, he taught in the Department of History at Carroll College for seventeen years. His most influential publication was *Urban Populism and Free Silver in Montana: A Narrative of Ideology in Political Action* (1970).

BRIAN W. DIPPIE is professor of history in the University of Victoria, Victoria, British Columbia, and an editorial board member of *Montana The Magazine of Western History*. He is author of numerous books and articles on western history, including *Custer's Last Stand: Anatomy of an American Myth* (1976), *The Vanishing American; White Attitudes and U. S. Indian Policy* (reprint 1991), and *Catlin and His Contemporaries: The Politics of Patronage* (1990).

DAVID M. EMMONS is professor of history in the University of Montana, Missoula, and specializes in the history of American immigrant workers. He is author of the prize-winning *Butte Irish: Class and Ethnicity in an American Mining Town, 1875–1925* (1989).

DIANNE G. DOUGHERTY did her graduate work in history in Montana State University, Bozeman, before completing her law degree in Gonzaga University in Spokane, Washington, where she is currently a deputy prosecuting attorney.

HARRY W. FRITZ is professor of history in the University of Montana, Missoula. He is editor, with Rex C. Myers, of *Montana and the West; Essays in Honor of K. Ross Toole* (1984) and has served in the Montana Legislature from 1985 to 1992.

WILLIAM KITTREDGE is professor of English in the University of Montana, Missoula. His book of fiction, *We Are Not In This Together* (1984), won the Montana Governor's Award for Literature in 1985. He also is author of *Owning It All* (1987) and co-edited with Annick Smith *The Last Best Place: A Montana Anthology*, published by the Montana Historical Society Press in 1988. His memoir, *Hole in the Sky*, will be published in 1992.

MICHAEL P. MALONE taught history in Montana State University, Bozeman, for many years and currently serves as the university's president. He is author of several books and articles on Montana history, including *Montana: A History of Two Centuries* (revised with coauthors Richard B. Roeder and William L. Lang in 1991), and *The Battle for Butte: Mining and Politics on the Northern Frontier, 1864–1906* (1981).

LAURIE K. MERCIER is a doctoral student in history in the University of Oregon, Eugene. In 1991 she received *Montana The Magazine of Western History's* Merril G. Burlingame–K. Ross Toole Award for the best student essay. She is former oral historian for the Montana Historical Society, where she conducted oral history projects on Montanans at work, small towns, metals manufacturing, women as community builders, and Helena businesses.

MICHAEL J. OBER holds masters degrees in history and library science and is on the faculty of Flathead Valley Community College in Kalispell, Montana. His deep interest in the history of Glacier National Park began in 1967, when he initiated his "career" as a seasonal ranger. He is researching two commercially oriented homesteaders who settled the head of Lake McDonald in Glacier National Park.

PAULA PETRIK is associate professor of history and associate dean in the College of Arts and Humanities in the University of Maine, Orono. She is author of many articles on Montana history and of the book, *No Step Backward: Women and Family on the Rocky Mountain Mining Frontier, Helena, Montana 1865–1900*, published by the Montana Historical Society Press in 1987.

JAMES P. RONDA is the Barnard Professor of Western American History in the University of Tulsa, Oklahoma, and a member of the editorial board of *Montana The Magazine of Western History*. He is the author of *Lewis and Clark Among the Indians* (1984) and *Astoria and Empire* (1991). He is writing a biography of William Clark, to be published by the University of Oklahoma Press.

MARGARET SCHERF of Kalispell, Montana, served in the House of Representatives during the 1965 session of the Montana Legislature. She was a published mystery writer who set many of her books in the Flathead Valley. She died in an automobile accident in 1979.

DONALD E. SPRITZER is reference librarian at the Missoula City-County Library, Missoula, Montana. He received his doctoral degree in twentieth-century United States history from the Unversity of Montana, Missoula, in 1980. "One River, One Problem: James Murray and the Missouri Valley Authority" is part of his doctoral dissertation. He is author of *Senator. James E. Murray and the Limits of Post War Liberalism* (1985) and *Waters of Wealth, The Story of the Kootenai River and Libby Dam* (1979).

ROBERT R. SWARTOUT, JR., is associate professor and chair of the Department of History at Carroll College in Helena, Montana. A specialist in both western history and American–East Asian relations, he has published four other books and numerous articles. Swartout spent the 1986–1987 academic year as a Fullbright Senior Lecturer in Korea University, Seoul. He conducted research on the Chinese in Montana as the 1983 James H. Bradley Research Fellow at the Montana Historical Society.

JOHN TERREO is archivist and oral historian at the Montana Historical Society, Helena, where his oral history projects include the New Deal, Native American educators, and medicine in Montana. He also conducted interviews with members of the 103rd Public Affairs Detachment of the National Guard before their departure for Operation Desert Storm and on their return home. Currently he is interviewing twentieth-century Montana military veterans.

DAVE WALTER is Montana historian at the Montana Historical Society. He has published many articles on Montana history and compiled *Christmastime in Montana* (1990). He is a member of the Montana Committee for the Humanities.

Bibliographical Essay

This bibliographical essay is not meant to be exhaustive. Rather, we have attempted to include major secondary works that will enable students of Montana history to build upon information contained in *The Montana Heritage*.

By far the best single volume covering the entire breadth of Montana history is Michael P. Malone, Richard B. Roeder, and William L. Lang, *Montana: A History of Two Centuries*, revised ed. (Seattle: University of Washington Press, 1991). In addition to representing the most recent scholarship in the field, this volume also contains a detailed bibliographical essay that all students are encouraged to examine. Two older studies that have had a major influence on Montana historiography are Joseph Kinsey Howard, *Montana: High, Wide, and Handsome* (New Haven, Conn.: Yale University Press, 1943), and K. Ross Toole, *Montana: An Uncommon Land* (Norman: University of Oklahoma Press, 1959). Clark C. Spence's *Montana: A History* (New York: W. W. Norton, 1978) is also well worth reading.

Supplementary readings containing valuable individual essays include Michael P. Malone and Richard B. Roeder, eds., *The Montana Past: An Anthology* (Missoula: University of Montana, 1969); Robert R. Swartout, Jr., ed., *Montana Vistas: Selected Historical Essays* (Landam, Md.: University Press of America, 1982); and Rex C. Myers and Harry W. Fritz, eds., *Montana and the West: Essays in Honor of K. Ross Toole* (Boulder, Colo.: Pruett Publishing Company, 1984). An important collection of primary materials is *Not in Precious Metals Alone: A Manuscript History of Montana* (Helena: Montana Historical Society Press, 1976). Three books that eloquently capture much of the spirit of Montana, and thus effectively compliment William Kittredge's essay, are Ivan Doig, *This House of Sky: Landscapes of a Western Mind* (New York: Harcourt Brace Jovanovich, 1978); William Kittredge and Annick Smith, eds., *The Last Best Place: A Montana Anthology* (Helena: Montana Historical Society Press, 1988); and Mary Clearman Blew, *All But the Waltz: Essays on a Montana Family* (New York: Viking, 1991).

For sources concerning the background to the Lewis and Clark expedition, and the age of exploration in general, consult the bibliographic essay at the end of James Ronda's article in *The Montana*

Heritage. The best general account of the expedition itself is David Lavender, *The Way to the Western Sea: Lewis and Clark Across the Continent* (New York: HarperCollins, 1988). An especially valuable study is James P. Ronda, *Lewis and Clark Among the Indians* (Lincoln: University of Nebraska Press, 1984).

Important representative studies of Native Americans in Montana include John Fahey, *The Flathead Indians* (Norman: University of Oklahoma Press, 1974); John C. Ewers, *The Blackfeet: Raiders on the Northwestern Plains* (Norman: University of Oklahoma, 1958); Thomas R. Wessel, *A History of the Rocky Boy's Indian Reservation* (Bozeman: Montana State University, 1974); Edward E. Barry, *The Fort Belknap Indian Reservation: The First One Hundred Years, 1855–1955* (Bozeman: Montana State University, 1974); Robert H. Lowie, *The Crow Indians* (New York: Farrar and Rinehart, 1935); Rodney Frey, *The World of the Crow Indians: As Driftwood Lodges* (Norman: University of Oklahoma Press, 1987); and John Stands in Timber and Margot Liberty, *Cheyenne Memories* (New Haven, Conn.: Yale University Press, 1967).

There are no book-length studies to date that focus exclusively on the Chinese experience in Montana, but valuable studies with a more national focus include Jack Chen, *The Chinese of America* (San Francisco: Harper & Row, 1981); Shih-shan Henry Tsai, *The Chinese Experience In America* (Bloomington and Indianapolis: Indiana University Press, 1986); and Roger Daniels, *Asian America: Chinese and Japanese in the United States since 1850* (Seattle: University of Washington Press, 1988). The most important single account dealing with nineteenth-century American-Chinese relations is Michael H. Hunt, *The Making of a Special Relationship: The United States and China to 1914* (New York: Columbia University Press, 1983). One of the best case studies on the Chinese experience in America is Sucheng Chan's *This Bittersweet Soil: The Chinese in California Agriculture, 1860–1910* (Berkeley and Los Angeles: University of California Press, 1986).

During the past two decades, a significant amount of new research has been done on the history of women in the American West. Examples of this new research include Julie Roy Jeffrey, *Frontier Women: The Trans-Mississippi West, 1840–1880* (New York: Hill and Wang, 1979); Sandra L. Myres, *Westering Women and the Frontier Experience, 1800–1915* (Albuquerque: University of New Mexico Press, 1982); Glenda Riley, *Women and Indians on the Frontier, 1825–1915* (Albuquerque: University of New Mexico Press, 1984). The most important new study on the history of women in Montana is Paula Petrik, *No Step Backward: Women and Family on the Rocky Mountain Mining Frontier, Helena, Montana, 1865–1900* (Helena: Montana Historical Society Press, 1987). A moving, first-person account of the role of women in the homestead era is Elinore Pruitt Stewart, *Letters of a Woman Homesteader* (Boston: Houghton Mifflin Company, 1914; paperback ed., 1982).

The dramatic events of the late nineteenth and early twentieth centuries that led to the rise of industrialization in Montana have captured the attention of numerous historians in recent years. For the rise of Populism in Montana, see Thomas A. Clinch, *Urban Populism and Free Silver in Montana: A Narrative of Ideology in Political Action* (Missoula: University of Montana Press, 1970). The latest and most thorough study of Coxey's Army is Carlos A. Schwantes, *Coxey's Army: An American Odyssey* (Lincoln: University of Nebraska Press, 1985). Three extremely important studies focus on the place of Butte in Montana's history: Michael P. Malone, *The Battle For Butte: Mining and Politics on the Northern Frontier, 1864–1906* (Seattle: University of Washington Press, 1981); Jerry W. Calvert, *The Gibraltar: Socialism and Labor in Butte, Montana, 1895–1920* (Helena: Montana Historical Society Press, 1988); and David M. Emmons, *The Butte Irish: Class and Ethnicity in an American Mining Town, 1875–1925* (Urbana: University of Illinois Press, 1990). The most valuable study of the IWW remains Melvyn Dubofsky, *We Shall Be All: A History of the Industrial Workers of the World* (Chicago: Quadrangle, 1969).

The explosive history of Montana's political culture, in addition to the general works cited in this essay, begins with Clark C. Spence, *Territorial Politics and Government in Montana, 1864–1889* (Urbana: University of Illinois Press, 1975); flares in Michael P. Malone, *The Battle for Butte*, cited above; and continues in Arnon Gutfeld, *Montana's Agony: Years of War and Hysteria, 1917–1921* (Gainesville: University Presses of Florida, 1979). The latter should be augmented by David Kennedy, *Over Here: The First World War and American Society* (New York: Oxford University Press, 1980), which helps to place Montana's World War I experiences within the national context.

During the 1930s and 1940s, Montana's economic well-being was influenced increasingly by the policies and decisions of the federal government. Although no detailed study has yet been done on the New Deal and Montana, a good introduction to this period at the national level is Gerald D. Nash, *The Crucial Era: The Great Depression and World War II, 1929–1945*, 2nd ed. (New York: St. Martin's Press, 1992). The best account of the CCC is still John Salmond, *The Civilian Conservation Corps, 1933–1942* (Durham, N. Car.: Duke University Press, 1967). Two critical views of the federal government's management of water resources are Donald Worster, *Rivers of Empire* (New York: Pantheon Books, 1986); and Marc Reisner, *Cadillac Desert: The American West and Its Disappearing Water* (New York: Viking, 1986). To understand the interplay between economic and political issues, see also Donald E. Spritzer, *Senator James E. Murray and the Limits of Post-War Liberalism* (New York: Garland, 1985); Alonzo L. Hamby, *Beyond the New Deal: Harry S. Truman and American Liberalism* (New York: Columbia University Press, 1973); and Marian Ridgeway, *The Missouri*

Basin's Pick-Sloan Plan: A Case Study in Congressional Determination (Urbana: University of Illinois Press, 1955).

Much more scholarly work is needed on twentieth-century Native American history in Montana, but a starting point in this field is William E. Farr, *The Reservation Blackfeet, 1882-1945: A Photographic History of Cultural Survival* (Seattle: University of Washington Press, 1984); Frank B. Linderman, *Pretty-Shield: Medicine Woman of the Crows* (1932; reprint, Lincoln: University of Nebraska Press, 1974); and Gretchen M. Bataille and Kathleen M. Sands, *American Indian Women: Telling Their Lives* (Lincoln: University of Nebraska Press, 1984). A remarkable film that all Montanans should see is *Contrary Warriors* (1985), a documentary based on the life of Robert Yellowtail and the history of the Crow tribe. Produced by Rattlesnake Productions, the film is available through the Montana Committee for the Humanities in Missoula. Another noteworthy film is the three-part video, *Place of Falling Water* (1991), by Roy Bigcrane and Thompson Smith, produced by Salish Kootenay College and Native Voices Public Television Workshop. The documentary, which covers the historical precedents and events surrounding construction and management of Kerr Dam by Montana Power Company on the Flathead Indian Reservation, is available through Native Voices at Montana State University in Bozeman.

An indispensable source for understanding contemporary political history in Montana is Ellis Waldron and Paul B. Wilson, *Atlas of Montana Elections, 1889-1976* (Missoula: University of Montana, 1978), which provides a running commentary on most political issues. The best attempt to survey clearly the events of the second half of the twentieth century is found in the final chapters of Michael P. Malone, Richard B. Roeder, and William L. Lang, *Montana: A History of Two Centuries*, cited above. To understand how environmentalism has developed as an issue in contemporary America, a valuable study is Samuel P. Hays, *Beauty, Health, & Permanence: Environmental Politics in the United States, 1955-1985* (New York: Cambridge University Press, 1987). Three Montana books that capture the sense of urgency and anger surrounding the conflict between economics and the environment are K. Ross Toole, *The Rape of the Great Plains: Northwest America, Cattle, and Coal* (Boston: Little, Brown, 1976); Michael Parfit, *Last Stand at Rosebud Creek: Coal, Power, and People* (New York: Dutton, 1980); and Richard Manning, *Last Stand: Logging, Journalism, and the Case for Humility* (Salt Lake City: Gibbs Smith, 1991).

Brian Dippie's essay in *The Montana Heritage* demonstrates the ways in which historical events and issues are often used to reinforce contemporary social and cultural values. With nearly eight hundred books written on the Battle of the Little Bighorn and George Armstrong Custer, it is easy to be overwhelmed by the available literature on the subject. Perhaps the best place to begin is with Brian Dippie's own *Custer's Last Stand: The Anatomy of an American Myth* (Missoula: University of Montana, 1976). The writings of Robert M. Utley are especially worthwhile, including *Custer and the Great Controversy: The Origin and Development of a Legend* (Los Angeles: Westernlore Press, 1962); and the more recent *Cavalier in Buckskin: George Armstrong Custer and the Western Military Frontier* (Norman: University of Oklahoma Press, 1988). The most judicious account of the battle remains Edgar I. Stewart, *Custer's Luck* (Norman: University of Oklahoma Press, 1955). Four other valuable books are John S. Gray, *Centennial Campaign: The Sioux War of 1876* (Norman: University of Oklahoma Press, 1988); John S. Gray, *Custer's Last Campaign* (Lincoln: University of Nebraska Press, 1991); and Paul L. Hedren, ed., *The Great Sioux War, 1876–77* (Helena: Montana Historical Society Press, 1991); and Paul Andrew Hutton, *The Custer Reader* (Lincoln: University of Nebraska Press, 1992). The latest best-seller is Evan S. Connell, *Son of the Morning Star: Custer and the Little Bighorn* (San Francisco: North Point Press, 1984).

Finally, anyone seriously interested in the field of Montana history should peruse the back issues of *Montana The Magazine of Western History,* undoubtedly the most important single resource for understanding the history of the state.

Index